Inferno by Committee

_423_

Titles by Tom Ribe

Los Alamos, New Mexico, An Area Guide for Visitors and
Residents (Otowi Crossing Press, 1997)

Inferno by Committee

A Natural and Human History of the Cerro Grande (Los Alamos) Fire; America's Worst Prescribed Fire Disaster.

TOM RIBE MS

FOREWORD BY DR. TIM INGALSBEE

Order this book online at www.trafford.com
or email orders@trafford.com

Most Trafford titles are also available at major online book retailers.

Printed in Victoria, BC, Canada.

ISBN: 978-1-4269-2987-8

*Our mission is to efficiently provide the world's finest, most comprehensive book publishing
service, enabling every author to experience success. To find out how to publish your book, your
way, and have it available worldwide, visit us online at www.trafford.com*

Trafford rev. 5/04/2010

 www.trafford.com

North America & international
toll-free: 1 888 232 4444 (USA & Canada)
phone: 250 383 6864 ♦ fax: 812 355 4082

Dedication

For my father, Dr. Fred L. Ribe who taught me so well about the value of genuine education and curiosity and supported that education. His love of the western outdoors and for New Mexico in particular led to my own love of the same, and his hikes with me into the western Mountains in the 1960s and 1970s changed my life in ways I can never fully express. Most of all, he taught me the supreme value of generosity.

And for the people of Los Alamos who lost property and the beautiful forest behind their town to the fire.

Preface

The Cerro Grande Fire was one of the most misunderstood yet important events in New Mexico and Western United States history. It was important in New Mexico because it was the culmination of many human affects on the environment spread out over centuries. Many of those affects are largely hidden from all but trained eyes. The fire was a study of cumulative unintended consequences.

The Cerro Grande Fire had large affect on the Western United States, as the lessons learned from it changed federal fire policy permanently. The story told here boils down to the hard lessons learned and the new practices enacted on every prescribed fire and even most wild fires in America ever since.

I wrote this book after reading and listening to media and investigative accounts of the fire which were at times poorly informed. I felt the public and the land managers deserved to have a more complete story of the fire told so the they would be able to better understand this region's beautiful environment and its environmental history and so that we all could get beyond the blame and recriminations that dominated popular accounts of the fire in 2000.

If any theme dominated my study of the Cerro Grande Fire, it was the complexity of environmental history and the complexity of wildfire and fire management. Fire truly is a fascinating event that is driven by multiple environmental factors that play into each other in ways that even career professionals never fully understand. The natural world is sensitive and delicate and our exploitations have long lasting consequences.

Prescribing fire on the landscape involves risk. Sometimes, as with the Cerro Grande Fire, the risk taken results in disaster. For land managers, there really is no option but to prescribe fire and take risk, to restore fire to a landscape where fire is native and necessary for the survival of the biological systems. Cerro Grande showed us both the consequences of taking a risk with fire and more dramatically, the consequences of avoiding that risk.

I hope readers will appreciate this paradox and the difficulty it poses to those who manage our public heritage in the federal land management agencies.

I have worked hard to put aside any biases I might have while writing this book. I have worked as a part-time fire fighter since 1980, and most of that work has been on prescribed fire crews at Yosemite National Park and Bandelier National Monument. However, I was not involved with Bandelier's fire program in 2000 and had not been for a few years prior. Thus I had considerable distance from the program and the people involved in Cerro Grande, many of whom I did not know. Given this history I tried to be fair to all involved and, as the pages will reveal, found plenty of fault to go around, even within the National Park Service.

This book is presented in two parts. Part one is the story of the Cerro Grande Fire from its historical roots onward. This part will be of interest to all readers. Part two is a more in-depth look at the management of the fire and will appeal to people in the wildland fire profession as well as to readers wanting a more detailed analysis of events.

Tom Ribe
December 2009

Acknowledgements

To approach my standards for accuracy and depth of research, writing this book took far longer than I had planned at first. While I wanted to have it out a year after the fire, it turns out the book is out a decade after the fire. I take solace in the fact that many books about events have been written years or decades after the event and the master of fire history, Norman Maclean, published his seminal <u>Young Men and Fire</u> forty years after the Mann Gulch Fire.

Even so, my immersion in the fire world and research took me away from my family and other projects at key times. I thank my wonderful spouse Monique Schoustra above all others for her patience, unending support and faith in me and this project.

Key people helped me understand the topic and get it right. I thank first John Lissoway for mentoring me in fire management and his helping me understand the history of fire at Bandelier. I also thank Dr. Craig Allen, for his support of all my research projects and for his commitment to the genuine health of the Jemez Mountains over his career.

I thank many people who were involved with Cerro Grande for their candid conversations in my search for the truth. In particular Chief Doug Tucker of the Los Alamos Fire Department, Charisse Sydoriak of Sequoia and Kings Canyon National Parks, Bill Armstrong of the U.S. Forest Service, Al King of the National Interagency Fire Center, Chuck Maxwell of the National Weather Service and Roy Weaver. Many others contributed perspectives and stories as well.

For logistical support with research and in obtaining documents I thank Richard Mietz, Flo Six of the National Park Service Omaha office, Michael Gonzales, NPS librarian. For editing help I thank Sarah Rabkin, University of California, Santa Cruz and Monique Schoustra. Final edit by Joe Maes. Thank you Bruce Bannerman for your help with graphics.

I thank the General Accounting Office for the use of their graphics from their report on the Cerro Grande Fire. Also, thanks to the US Geological Survey for allowing me to use the regional fire year graphic. All photos by Tom Ribe except where noted otherwise.

Finally, for inspiration I thank the late Dr. Ken Norris, and Mally Kemp Ribe, and the alive and thriving Sam Bush.

Tom Ribe
Santa Fe, New Mexico
March, 2010

Table of Contents

Foreword

by Timothy Ingalsbee PhD

A decade has passed since the Cerro Grande Fire that ignited the "millennial fire season" of 2000 and ushered into America's psyche the current epoch of "megafires." Tragic as it was for razing hundreds of homes and thousands of acres of public forest—and ruining what had been one of the vanguard prescribed fire programs in the country--our memory of the Cerro Grande Fire disaster has largely been shrouded both by the haze of time and the smoke from so many other wildfire disasters that followed it. Inferno by Committee does us all a great service by rescuing this tragic event from the ash heap of history where at best it would have been forgotten, but at worst, the wrong lessons would have been extracted, leading to repeated similar disasters.

If journalism is the "first draft of history," Ribe's book embarks on a wholesale rewrite, providing a clear-eyed, comprehensive analysis of the Cerro Grande Fire that corrects many of the myths and misrepresentations that have tainted our memory of that event. The wildfire ignited a media frenzy and political firestorm of recriminations against the Bandelier fire crew and the National Park Service's prescribed fire program, but Ribe exposes the fallacious statements made by government employees from rival agencies that fueled the media's erroneous accounts and government's flawed investigations. His rigorous research of long-suppressed government reports, personal interviews with key players, and his insightful analysis of the historical, cultural, and ecological context in which the fateful events unfolded makes the book an important historical contribution and a compelling read.

In many respects, Ribe's book answers a call for justice: on the one hand he vindicates the actions and reveals the true heroism of National Park Service employees who were unfairly vilified and whose reputations remain sullied by false charges made by the press and politicians, and on the other hand, he exposes the terrible incompetence and cowardice of some individuals and agencies whose actions and inactions had hitherto escaped the scrutiny of the press or wrath of politicians. The Cerro Grande Fire was indeed a tragic inferno by "committee," but most of the blame for the disaster has been shouldered by a few individual scapegoats, until now.

The Big Lie perpetrated a decade ago was that a few Bandelier employees were woefully incompetent if not criminally negligent in performance of their duties, and the National Park Service was a reckless if not rogue agency willing to put communities at risk and waste valuable natural resources in order to push its pro-fire environmental philosophy. Yes, mistakes were made by Bandelier employees and the NPS, but exculpatory evidence was ignored, and the mistakes made by many others were overlooked, ignored, or swept under the rug in the reactive rush to judgment. To this day, it is still mind-boggling how the honorable Secretary Bruce Babbitt who had been the most passionate promoter of prescribed burning ordered Bandelier and the Park Service fire program to stand silent in the face of outrageous false accusations, assume total responsibility for the disaster, and essentially fall on their swords. Their sacrifice was apparently made for the sake of preserving the Federal Wildland Fire Policy and to deflect criticism from the Clinton Administration during the fateful election year of 2000, but this tactic fed into the general rightwing attack on government regulation, and its legacy endures in the public's lingering fear of prescribed burning. Ribe's book now provides us with the whole story of the Cerro Grande Fire disaster, including its many inconvenient truths.

After the Bandelier's prescribed fire program was suspended and a few Park Service employees' careers were ended, few actionable reforms were extracted by the disaster because many critical lessons failed to be learned and still loom as potential sources of future wildfire disasters. Ribe's book thus provokes a number of haunting questions asking "what if" other mistakes had been properly identified at that time—what might have been our responses to avoid future similar mistakes?

The Cerro Grande prescribed fire operation was caught short-handed almost from the outset, first by an unfit crew that had to be sent home early for their own safety, and then by the incompetence of the Forest Service's fire dispatch office who delayed the Park Service's request for extra firefighters to help keep the prescribed fire within its planned boundaries. Telling the Bandelier fire manager who called for help in the middle of the night to call back in the morning when others would be awake should have been a national scandal, but the added injury to this insult was compelling the Park Service to officially declare the prescribed burn a wildfire emergency in order to receive the requested firefighters and aircraft. This conversion of the prescribed fire to a wildfire forced a gestalt shift in the entire approach to the blaze, turning what had been an ecological restoration project into a combat operation.

The lack of boots on the ground throughout the entire event was a major causal factor behind the disaster, but what if those mistakes that prevented full staffing of the controlled burn had been exposed at the time? Would the response have been to check that every firefighter is guaranteed to be fit for duty before staffing any fire? Would agencies have worked to ensure that all employees staffing a fire dispatch center are fully trained in the policies and procedures for quickly responding to calls for help? Throughout Ribe's book lurks the uneasy issue of a long-running interagency rivalry between the National Park Service/Bandelier National Monument, and the Forest Service/Santa Fe National Forest that raises the question: was it simply a blunder by a few individuals or was it "bad blood" between agencies that caused those fateful delays in delivering contingency firefighters?

After the prescribed fire was declared a wildfire, suppression actions departed from the burn plan, including the ignition of a backfire in the worst possible location on the mountain. It was the backfire, not the 30 acre prescribed fire "slopover," that served as the actual ignition source for the inferno that spread across 42,400 acres of forest in New Mexico, and destroyed 235 homes in Los

Alamos. This critical fact about the backfire appeared in the last sentence on the last page of the 134 page May 18th investigation report, appearing almost as an after-thought, or worse, a crude attempt to bury the truth.

Instead of appearing on the last page, what if that mistake had been placed prominently in the investigation report's executive summary and properly highlighted by the media at the time? Would that have initiated a wider critical examination of the effect that suppression backfires and burnouts play in spreading high-severity wildfire? This failure to identify the precise ignition source of the conflagration that hit Los Alamos is part of the reason why so many people have zero tolerance for the rare prescribed fire that accidentally escapes control, but accept without question the routine use of suppression backfires that are inherently uncontrolled and intentionally destructive, essentially "destroying a forest in order to save it." This vicious double-standard between the risks and effects of prescribed fires versus backfires continues in large part because we failed to learn the right lessons during a teachable moment on the Cerro Grande Fire.

When the controlled burn was first ignited on top of Cerro Grande it was during cold, damp, windless weather, conditions that made it difficult to light the burn in places. But then the weather unpredictably changed for the worse in the days that followed, culminating in a windstorm that had not been forecast by the National Weather Service. It was the extreme winds that quickly whipped the fire totally out of control, as it is the case in most large-scale wildfires—they are driven by high winds, and the ignition source or fuel load of large blazes are almost irrelevant in comparison to the role of weather conditions. What if that unforeseen windstorm had been properly identified as a major factor in the rapid spread of the wildfire to Los Alamos, would people have written off the disaster as an unfortunate "act of God?" Would that have prevented some of the "hot air" from some politicians who opportunistically used the tragedy to push their own anti-prescribed fire/pro-commercial logging agenda? Would government agencies have responded with investments in staff and technology needed to improve fire weather forecasting?

These are just a few of the "what ifs" that come to mind from

Ribe's thorough expose' of the many mistakes, accidents, and flukes of nature or history that fed into that "inferno by committee." If the Nation's response to the Cerro Grande Fire had been something different than the character assassination of a few well-intentioned individuals or an indictment against the National Park Service's philosophy of science-based fire ecology restoration and its prescribed fire program, then we might be in a very different place ten years later instead of our current predicament with annual megafires consuming lives, homes, habitats, and tax dollars with no end or alternative in sight.

While there were several missed opportunities for learning, perhaps the most important lesson to be learned from Cerro Grande came from the post-fire analysis performed by Jack Cohen, a Forest Service fire scientist who carefully reconstructed how the wildfire spread through Los Alamos neighborhoods. He determined that it was not a "tsunami of flame" roaring through tree tops that ignited the homes, but rather, falling embers or creeping flames burning on pine needle-covered rooftops and lawns. Homes that were ignited by the tiniest ember or flame would spread flames to other nearby homes in a kind of domino-effect, thus transforming what had been a wildland fire into an urban conflagration. Cohen's vivid Los Alamos photos of charred home foundations lying beneath green tree canopies gave momentary pause to those who were crudely claiming that "big trees cause big fires." Although Cohen's analysis of the Los Alamos Fire was not able to prevent the incoming Bush Administration's white-hot zeal to use wildfire hysteria to increase commercial logging on public lands, his ideas on reducing the flammability of the "home ignition zone" have since become a major force behind the FireWise Program and Fire Safe Councils across the country.

There were other positive outcomes and progressive reforms salvaged from the Cerro Grande disaster. The National Fire Plan was launched, investing millions of tax dollars into fire and fuels management programs. While there was very little actual fire planning done with that money, and too much money was spent on purchasing fleets of new fire engines that sat idle during wet wildfire seasons, or funding so-called "fuels reduction projects" that were really commercial timber sales that sometimes increased the fire hazards on logged sites, the National

Fire Plan did get the American people to begin thinking about taking proactive steps to manage fuel hazards and fire risks. The 1995 Federal Wildland Fire Policy was also reviewed, updated, and even improved in the wake of the Cerro Grande Fire disaster. Miraculously, that progressive policy document was mostly ignored by the incoming Bush Administration. This enabled the Obama Administration to further expand the scope of the policy and increase opportunities to manage fires for their social and ecological benefits rather than simply "fighting" them in an endless and ultimately unwinnable "war" on wildfire. As Ribe points out, the Federal Fire Policy basically represents an affirmation of the National Park Service and Bandelier National Monument's philosophy of ecological fire restoration.

There are some who argue that the decade of the "double zeros" ought best be forgotten, but the wildfire that ushered in the new Millennium and the current epoch of megafires must be remembered. Tom Ribe's book is so important today not because we have forgotten so much about Cerro Grande, but because so many of the memories we retain are tainted by flawed or false information. His book helps us get beyond the false tales and failed lessons to understand the whole story behind the tragic Cerro Grande Fire. Ribe's dramatic retelling goes far beyond a journalistic account of that event, though. He combines rich natural history and his own intimate sense of place and with a critical analysis of the ecological, social, political, and cultural factors that aligned with human actors to create the "committee" structure for that tragic disaster. Even though we know the ultimate outcome of events, Ribe's book is thrilling and suspenseful as he offers dramatic play-by-play description of actions on the ground, and produces some shocking revelations from his analysis of long-suppressed government documents.

No promises can be made that by "re-remembering" Cerro Grande with new facts to replace old falsehoods will we be able to avoid repeating similar wildfire disasters. But Cerro Grande stands apart from other more recent wildfire disasters that followed it because of its tragic irony: a prescribed fire lit with the best of intentions to restore the ecosystem and protect the local community turned into its terrible opposite, and came terrifyingly close to triggering a nuclear release. By remembering Cerro

Grande and reminding ourselves of that radioactive near-miss, perhaps a concerted effort to secure all nuclear power facilities, waste sites, and weapons bunkers from the potential threat of wildfires will be initiated.

By setting the record straight, Ribe creates an opportunity for us to learn the right lessons from America's worst prescribed fire disaster. Doing so compels us to advance, not retreat, in our use of fire in land management. Indeed, the thousands of successful prescribed fires conducted uneventfully across the country by government agencies, nonprofit organizations, and private landowners since the Cerro Grande Fire give testimony that we can triumph over tragedy, and move forward in relearning how to work safely and live sustainably with fire on the landscape.

Tim Ingalsbee is Executive Director of Firefighters United for Safety, Ethics and Ecology and Co-Director of the Association for Fire Ecology. He also teaches sociology at Lane Community College in Eugene, Oregon.

Introduction

On May 5, 2000, I stood near the Bandelier National Monument fire lookout in northern New Mexico watching a forest fire spill off a peak and into some of the most fuel choked wild lands in the American west. What began as a prescribed fire, known as the Cerro Grande prescribed burn, was at that moment changing to the Cerro Grande wildfire, a fire that would have profound impact not only on nearby Los Alamos (the "Atomic City") but also on the national fire fighting world.

Standing three miles from the flame front, I could pick out particular groves of trees, particular shelves of land I knew well as the fire swarmed into these places. My memory raced across more than 40 years of walking and camping in that landscape for it is the landscape of my childhood, the geography of my first steps away from home.

Within what seemed like a very short time, the fire had bolted to the edge of the last canyon south of Los Alamos. Standing astonished with another Los Alamos native, Bruce Bannerman, we both shared a sense of shock and inevitability. We had always known a fire would occur here as we had watched drifts of pine debris accumulate under ever thicker stands of small trees that hid the trunks and stumps of bigger ones in the forests surrounding Los Alamos. We had always placed the inevitability safely in an ever receding future. Now the fire *was* burning and we could see it gain ferocity as it bit into the staggering fuel loads that cloaked the mountains like so much fur on an animal.

The Cerro Grande Fire burns north of Cerro Grande, in Valle and Pajarito Canyons on May 7, 2000. Photo by Bruce Bannerman

Our feelings changed as the fire grew alarmingly. We could feel the obvious threat to the town we both were raised in, but had long since left. We could see the landscape changing irretrievably and violently. Further, I knew some of the people who were involved with the prescribed burn for the National Park Service. I had worked with them on other prescribed burns over the last 20 years. Bruce and I knew the prescribed fire program at Bandelier and elsewhere was the right course of action for forests, wildlife and communities, ironically to help prevent disasters like the one that was unfolding before us. Yet here something was going wrong, terribly wrong, and as the minutes rolled by we shared a sense of fascination and horror with a gathering group of National Park Service staffers who had slowly joined us on the catwalk of that old Civilian Conservation Corps fire lookout tower[1].

Later that night we were in Los Alamos helping an octogenarian friend, a veteran of the Manhattan Project, gather his belongings as the New Mexico State Police drove through his neighborhood in thickening smoke ordering evacuation over megaphones. Air tankers flew close overhead and the pall cast down on the town like a tornado infested thunderstorm.

Our sense of inevitability may not have been shared by many other Los Alamos residents. For them, the fear and immediacy blended with anger as they loaded their cars from their homes.

By midnight we were sitting on crackling dry pine needles in choked woods on the edge of Los Alamos Canyon a mile above town, watching Paul Gleason and his National Park Service fire crew heroically stop the flame front from jumping into the 400 foot deep Los Alamos Canyon; all that separated Los Alamos from a very active wildfire. That crew, racing up and down the "Camp May Road" was in a forbidden zone, a place now closed to the public, a place of danger and awesome responsibility. We watched, pleased that the fire seemed to be calming, drawing back on itself and sparing the town with its 50 year-old houses built among dry pine trees.

Little did we know what was to follow over the next two weeks.

Six days later we stood on the saddle of Santa Fe Baldy, a peak directly opposite Los Alamos east across the Rio Grande Valley. The swath of reddish smoke that drifted over us from the Cerro Grande Fire trailed off to the northeast across the Pecos Wilderness and on to the eastern plains of New Mexico. It was there that a new wave of disbelief swept us. For days we'd been watching the fire play in the national forest lands between Bandelier National Monument and Los Alamos, but now, we could see clearly that the fire was *in* Los Alamos. The smoke took on a sickening hue and no longer was our concern for landscapes changed, wildlife killed and displaced. Now we were seeing a disaster of human proportions. Looking with high powered binoculars, we could see that fire was spreading broadly into the town. History was being made, human misery was compounding with each new pulse of smoke into the plume that drifted across the valley.

We had no idea of the struggle the Los Alamos Fire Department with the help of community fire services from throughout New Mexico was experiencing as it scrambled to deal with numerous house fires in multiple neighborhoods. The dramas taking place were beyond the imagination even of those participating in them. As the fire drafted down the sides of Quemazon Peak, it erased brittle fifty-year old wooden quadraplexes with punishing efficiency[2]. Each of these old buildings was a fire trap in itself, burning together they became an essence of hell.

For Los Alamos, the fire was an ironic event. The birthplace of the first nuclear weapons, Los Alamos had a direct role in the incineration of Nagasaki and Hiroshima, Japan in 1945, where, in the context of war, Los Alamos scientists had developed the atomic bombs that the US military had used to burn those cities to the ground. In the years since, most of America's nuclear arsenal had been developed at Los Alamos National Laboratory, a high security compound set in serenely peaceful surroundings. Now those surroundings were attacking the community and the once-peaceful mountains bore down on the town with a heat that no technology could stop. The town of the ultimate high technology was helpless before wildfire, the most primal and ancient of all forces.

Everyone who was in or near Los Alamos in May 2000 has a story about the Cerro Grande Fire. Many of these stories have been told, but what hasn't been told well is the story of why the fire really happened, its historical and ecological roots and the fire management on Cerro Grande (mountain) that spawned disaster. The fire was a complex event and the media and many members of the public looked at it within a narrow timeframe, when the fire was an inevitable culmination of many decisions made by numerous people over more than a century.

Understanding the natural and human history of this fire can lead us to a better understanding of the natural world, and help land managers improve wild-land fire management in the future and help the public comprehend its own role in providing for the safety of our properties and our communities.

Much of this story is not unique to Los Alamos or the Jemez Mountains. It is the story increasingly being told, year by year, across the West, as climate change intensifies wildfire and lengthens fire seasons. While the scale of disaster to personal property in Los Alamos during the Cerro Grande fire was unprecedented in recent decades, the scale of this fire and its causes were not. In fact the year 2000 turned out to be the most active fire year throughout the intermountain west until 2002 and then 2006 exceeded acres burned in 2000. Yet 2000 was a big year for fire with 90,821 fires reported on all federal and state agency lands and 886 fires on National Park Service lands alone [3].

Repeatedly after the Cerro Grande disaster, people were asking why anyone would light a fire intentionally in wildlands and why they would do such a thing in the windy spring season? Was the National Park Service crazy? This is a natural and honest question, yet the answer is complicated.

In New Mexico, where land management has been oriented toward traditional multiple uses like logging, grazing and firewood gathering, the National Park Service brings a completely different perspective on restoring lands and protecting the few small areas that agency manages here for the public. Over 20 years the Park Service at Bandelier had many successful prescribed fires with only one minor control problem before Cerro Grande. Overall, since the National Park Service began its prescribed fire program in 1968 less than two percent of its prescribed fires have had control problems nationally and the agency has conducted thousands of prescribed burns[4].

Prescribed fire is a the intentional setting of fire to a wild land area when carefully measured conditions such as fuel moisture, relative humidity, wind and other factors that affect fire behavior are right to allow the land manager to achieve specific goals. Since fire is a natural part of forest ecosystems, it can be applied to a place in whatever intensity the land manager desires to improve the ecological condition of the forest for plants and wildlife.

Native people understood this and applied fire to the landscape intentionally in many parts of the Americas, though apparently not in New Mexico, before Europeans arrived. In the 1930s early National Park Service scientists began to understand and apply fire to landscapes in the southern Sierra Nevada with great success and the practice spread nationwide and is now used by all federal land management agencies.

The Cerro Grande prescribed fire was one of hundreds of prescribed fires set in the West in recent times. The particulars of why it went bad are instructive both from a fire management perspective and for those simply wanting to understand the natural world and our difficult relationship to it.

Cerro Grande was a tragic teaching moment, and the reasons for the escape are complex. Following the fire, virtually the entire wildland fire community focused on the event to try to understand what had happened and to make certain that such an escape would never happen again.

In wildland fire, there are major events that stand out in the history of the West and the profession of fire management. There are the fatal fires such as South Canyon, Mann Gulch, and Dude where fire fighters lost their lives. There are the fires where plenty of private property was destroyed such as the huge fires of 1910 where entire towns were leveled in Idaho and Montana. Cerro Grande stands as the single worst fire disaster started by a prescribed fire and as such, and because of the property losses resulting, it will go down in history with the great fire disasters of all time.

To an experienced eye, big forest fires all follow a similar pattern. Beginning as a thin gray wisp of smoke they quickly gather their power and build momentum. The first flames may be at the base of some old snag. They test the wind and the dead sticks and leaves to see if conditions are right to become a truly big fire, a huge adventure of running through the woods, leaping into the trees, scouring the landscape with ferocity and beauty, defying the people who would fight them. Dry leaves, sticks and logs welcome the first embers and flames from the source and the fire spreads fast, encouraged by wind, low humidity, abundant fuels. A gray and white roiling plume rising to the upper atmosphere means the same thing to all experienced fire watchers; this is going to be a big fire, a project fire. Experience also tells that beyond a certain point, large fires are beyond human control. We manage them on their margins and wait for the weather to change or for the fire to run out of fuel.

Across the West, big forest fires are replacing moderate fires that for centuries burned through grasslands and forests. Each forest fire has its own roots, feeding on the geography, forest type and landscapes most often changed by human activities. People have been manipulating landscapes in most of the western US for more than a century and a half. Livestock grazing, logging, fire suppression and hunting have all changed forests in ways that favor big unruly fires.

In the western United States, human history is strongly influenced by the particular geographic qualities of each region. In some places people have used the land intensely while in others the shear scale of the wilderness has stymied all but the most ambitious people. In most parts of the West, European influence began in earnest in the 1830s, intensified in the 1880s, and increased almost exponentially from there. Native influence on landscapes goes back much farther but is much more benign than the industrial influences of present times.

Forest fires, more than any other natural event respond to the conditions on the land where they burn. Many subtle changes made by people (and nature herself) over decades will mean a forest is either highly flammable or fosters moderate, non destructive fire. Extensive research done since the 1970s shows that fire is a normal weather event[5] in most western forests but human activities have changed forests and rangelands so that contemporary wildfires burn strikingly differently from the fires of old[6].

The Cerro Grande wildfire of 2000 was high among the recent catastrophic wildfires that blazed into the American popular and political consciousness. Though other fires had burned in previous decades, in some cases making national news with tragic loss of life, Cerro Grande was the first fire since 1910 that had burned hundreds of homes. Started by government foresters, however well intentioned, and thus turned public attention to federal fire management as a potentially fallible and culpable act. That attention has grown in the years since Cerro Grande.

For decades, wildland fire management has been an esoteric science, practiced by the sorts of people who live out of the public eye, in the woods, in land management agencies with customs and tools that are obscure and remote from most people's experience. It is a craft with less in common with urban fire fighting than many people understand.

Cerro Grande provides an ideal study in all that is right and wrong with wildfire management, land management and the demands the public puts on land managers and our public lands. By understanding the Cerro Grande Fire we can understand important aspects of virtually any other large western forest fire, and we see how fire is related closely to the broader health of forests and grasslands and the way people relate to local landscapes. Though the details will differ, the historical roots of Cerro Grande will in many ways resemble those of any other fire outside the Pacific Northwest rain belt.

[1] Hal K. Rothman <u>On Rims and Ridges</u>, (University of Nebraska Press, 1992) pg. 193

[2] Quemazon is a Spanish word derived from quemado, "to burn."

[3] Tom Zimmerman, "The Unprecedented 2000 Fire Season" <u>Natural Resource Year in Review</u>, (published on www.nature.nps.gov).

[4] <u>Study of the Implementation of the Federal Wildland Fire Policy Phase I Report, Perspectives on Cerro Grande</u>. (National Academy of Public Administration, December 2000). pg. viii.

[5] Natural fire is often a product of lightning and fire responds absolutely to the particulars of the weather present while it is burning. Weather can start a fire and weather will govern the fire's behavior and ultimately its demise.

[6] Stephen Pyne, "The Fire of Life" in <u>The Wildfire Reader</u>, (Island Press, 2006), pg 17.

Part One

Chapter 1

Land of Fire

In early May 2000, a group of forest managers and fire fighters began a prescribed fire project in Bandelier National Monument that would turn into a disaster and a nightmare for thousands of people. The project was relatively routine, one of 59 such burns that had been done in Bandelier by the National Park Service since 1980. For complex reasons, the project would spin out of control over the next five days. Given the proximity of Los Alamos, New Mexico the fire would have consequences for the residents of the town and the national energy laboratory there.

Cerro Grande was one of a series of super fires that plagued the Southwest in the early 2000s. Climate change, wind and drought are huge factors in the explosion of these large fires, as is the history of human meddling on the landscapes of the Southwest. People have inadvertently changed the Southwest from a land where fire was common and nurturing to the land, to a place where fire has become a menace and a danger both to people and to large areas of forest and their resident wildlife.

The region of the Cerro Grande burn provides a good vantage point from which to look back and see the unraveling of the natural world that culminated in the catastrophic wildfire of May 2000.

The stage on which the Cerro Grande disaster took place is the Rocky Mountain's southern end in northern New Mexico. The imposing Sangre de Cristo Mountains and the Jemez Mountains to their west are the last ranges of the Rockies, which form a spine of the continent from northern New Mexico all the way to Alaska.

Less than twenty miles west of Santa Fe, across the Rio Grande, a field of now quiet volcanoes rises to 11,400 feet forming the Jemez Mountains. Among the Jemez Mountain's many round, forest and grass cloaked peaks stands a single peak called Cerro Grande. Its grassy top faces the broad volcanic plateau of canyons and mesas where Bandelier National Monument includes almost 34,000 acres across four forest types. Just north of Bandelier lies Los Alamos National Laboratory, a federal nuclear research facility spread over thousands of pine covered acres, with its supporting town of 18,000.

North and west of Cerro Grande the Jemez Mountains circle around three collapsed volcanoes, or calderas, forming mountains densely forested with fir, pine, spruce, and aspen above the vast grasslands on the floors of the calderas. These "mixed conifer forests" support rich grass and wildflowers except on the dense north or west facing slopes where old forests of fir and spruce cut off much of the light to the forest floor.

At the foot of the Jemez Mountains on two sides, large plateaus of eroded volcanic ash stretch away from the now-quiet volcanoes. Composed of a soft rock called tuff, these plateaus support forests of ponderosa pine, juniper and pinon before the cliffs at their ends fall away to the valleys below. On the east side, the Pajarito (little bird) Plateau is deeply cut by canyons with steep cliffs, many of them pocked with the ancient cliff homes of the Puebloan tribes that lived there for more than a thousand years. The Cerro Grande fire burned far out onto the Pajarito Plateau.

The valley between the Jemez and Sangre de Cristo Mountains is a messy mix of pinon pine, juniper, grass, and scattered houses and towns. Deeply cut by dry gullies or "arroyos" that course toward the Rio Grande (Big River).

The forests of these northern New Mexico mountains vary only in minor ways from the forests (at similar elevations) of northern Arizona, southern Colorado, and Utah. In the Southwest, Ponderosa pine dominates the middle elevation forests that band mountains between the lower scrubby pinon and juniper woodlands and the wetter mixed conifer forests above. The montane and alpine zones above the mixed conifer are wet forests, watered by the increased rain and snowfall characteristic of high elevations. This ponderosa pine forest type is highly flammable and depends on regular fire for its health. The Cerro Grande fire fed most voraciously in this band of ponderosa pine north of Bandelier National Monument.

Wildfire is a weather event, natural, normal and beneficial in an otherwise sound forest or grassland. A healthy ecosystem is one with a full compliment of native plants and animals that evolved together and where natural processes are unimpaired by human intervention. Vigorous forests endure strong weather influences such as floods and fire because the diversity of plants and animals make those forests resilient.

When Fire was Free

Approximately eight thousand years ago, a group of people camped in Pajarito Canyon near present day Los Alamos. They made a fire on a rocky shelf above a stream that comes down from the rim of the Jemez Volcano. We don't know what these people looked like or where they came from, but their camp was deep in a forest different from the one that presently grows where geologists unearthed their old hearth[1].

About two thousand years before these campers made their campfires in Pajarito Canyon, a shift had begun which radically changed the vegetation and wildlife in what is now New Mexico. During the most recent ice age (roughly 12,000 years ago), valleys (such as the northern Rio Grande Valley) from northern Mexico all the way to north of where Santa Fe stands today were covered with deep pine forests, and the middle elevations (7,000 to 8,500 feet) were forested in mixed conifer. The Jemez and Sangre de Cristo Mountains were cloaked in alpine forest and alpine grassland. These forests were home to saber toothed tigers, short-faced bears, giant ground sloths, mastodons and many other now-extinct animals, as well as other animals that survive yet today[2].

These ancient conditions are important to today's vegetation since many of the species we have today are relics of the forests that persisted in the colder, wetter times of the ecologically recent Pleistocene.

As the climate dried over the last 12,000 years, plant communities shifted up in elevation. The pine forests left the low valleys (~6,000 feet or 1828 meters) for the middle elevations (~7,000 to 8,000 feet or 2,133 to 2,590 m) and were replaced there by large dry grasslands. In turn, mixed conifer forests shifted higher (to 9000 feet o r 2,743 m and above) from middle elevations while the pinon and ponderosa pine moved to the middle elevation. Alpine forests moved to the 11,000-foot (3353 m) and higher zone. Today treeline in northern New Mexico lies about 12,000 feet (3657 m). Treeline was around 8,000 feet (2,438 m) 12,000 years ago.

The overall coolness and wetness of the early Pleistocene had lasting effects on today's southwestern landscape. Remnant deeper soils built up under wetter forests than exist today coated the rocky mesas throughout the region. Likewise much of the canyon forming erosion in rock-dominated landscapes such as the Pajarito Plateau and southern Utah may have occurred during the relatively wet times of the Pleistocene and it's likely that much of the deep groundwater under parts of the Southwest and Texas accumulated during this earlier period.

Our ancient campers in Pajarito Canyon would have been camped in a forest that was transitioning in these ways. They also would have been witness to some part of a massive extinction of animal life that still baffles scientists. For thousands of years animals like mammoths and saber-toothed tigers, cheetahs, dire wolves, ground sloths and short-faced bears had dominated North America. Camels, miniature horses, muskoxen, llamas and countless other animals died off in an extinction that eliminated 35 species of mammals and many species of birds and left the landscape open to population by a modern mix of birds and mammals, including humans[3].

People sparsely inhabited the Southwest and the Pajarito Plateau in the time of the people who left their hearth near Pajarito Creek. For the next seven thousand years humans left few artifacts behind in the Southwest as the climate dried. Not until the early ancestors of today's Pueblo Indians began to build settlements of pit houses around 1,400 years ago do we find increasing

evidence of humans in the upper Rio Grande Valley and its surrounding region.

The post Pleistocene wilderness world settled into centuries
where the animals that somehow survived extinction (the exact
cause of which is still generally a mystery to scientists) populated
the mountains and valleys. In a real sense, this pristine, human-
less or nearly human-less ecology offers us a baseline against
which to measure changes that present-day and ancestral humans have made to life and the land itself in the southern Rocky
Mountains since the time of the Paleo hunters we envision on the
plateau.

Since we don't know what became of the ancient hunters and
their descendents of 10,000 years ago, archaeologists assume that
the Pueblo people who next left artifacts on the landscape in the
500 AD period were new settlers to the Southwest and that the
earliest people who left artifacts here may have moved north
with the retreating glaciers. It is possible that the people were
very early Puebloans (it's possible that late archaic people farmed
maize in the southern Jemez Mountains). Perhaps migrating up
from what is now Mexico, the Pueblo people started out as hunters and gatherers in the American southwest in what was a broad
wilderness world, sparsely inhabited by humans for millions of
square miles.

This wild and sparsely inhabited world would have lasted
to today had humans not exerted waves of increasingly intense
change on the landscape and its life. Many elements of the natural world were strongly influenced by early native cultures, but
especially by later European settlers.

European settlers were the first to write about the natural
world and their accounts, along with the record of pack rat mid-
dens, bog sediments and other natural artifacts, which are all
we have to reconstruct the past before large human populations
began to drastically change native plant and animal life. Using
scientific studies and early accounts, we can piece together an
environment that existed fifteen hundred years ago, before there
were substantial human populations in the Southwest.

People moving through the Rio Grande Valley around a thousand years ago would have found a vastly different place than
the one we experience today. Plenty of water in several strong

perennial streams ran down from the sides of the old Jemez volcanoes whose mountains like Cerro Grande had changed from the alpine icy world of the ice age to the softer, warmer mixed conifer forests similar to those cloaking these highlands today.

Early hunters would have been wary, as the forests of the Jemez Mountains were deeply wild, populated by wolves, grizzly bears, wolverine, mink, martin and mountain lions in considerable numbers. The diversity of birds, plants, and small mammals was beyond anything modern people can imagine and the relationships between all these plants and animals formed a complex web of dependence, the product of each species evolving among the others.

The largest streams running down from the Jemez Mountains (and virtually all other Rocky Mountain ranges) a thousand years ago were rich with thousands of beaver whose woody dams created ponds and wetlands where many plants, animals, birds and fish could thrive. Beaver ponds were common from the subalpine to the Rio Grande cottonwoods. Beaver dams slowed stream runoff, which allowed tremendous amounts of water to soak into the ground in many places. The water infiltrating the ground fed numerous springs and streams at lower elevations and kept the water tables high so streams and wetlands were abundant. Beaver ponds supported fish, amphibians like salamanders and frogs, and many insects, microbes and plants. Abandoned ponds filled with nutrient-rich silt and in time gave way to a succession of plants and trees including willows and nitrogen-fixing alder, that provided excellent food for beaver building new dams elsewhere.

Not only are beaver key for abundant ground and surface water supplies; their dams also help shift stream courses to a meander instead of running straight and fast. This stream dynamic helped keep alive wide riparian forest and marsh areas, vastly improving wildlife and plant habitat for many species and building soils while slowing and filtering runoff. In the time before beaver trapping and livestock grazing, the beaver was critical to creating and protecting riparian areas in the Southwest, the most productive and important habitat for wildlife in the region.

Plenty of these beaver streams would have reached the Rio Grande much of the year. In turn the Rio Grande usually ran clear, from its headwaters in the beaver rich southern Colorado Rockies through the wetlands and riparian forests that lined it all the way to the Gulf of Mexico.

Along the Rio Grande, a rich forest of Rio Grande cottonwood and other willows grew, nurtured by floods that washed around their bases as the spring runoff or summer rainstorms swelled the river. Grizzly bears lived along the Rio Grande, feeding on river otter, beaver, various small mammals, trout and huge sturgeon that lived in the wild waters. The bosque forests were filled with birds and wildlife, coming to drink or to feed on the plant life that depended on nutrient rich waters that frequently overflowed the riverbanks.

All around the riverside cottonwood forest (the bosque) a wide expanse of dryland grass grew across the Rio Grande Valley. Dotted with juniper and pinon pine, these rich grasslands supported herds of pronghorn antelope, elk, mule deer and some bison who wandered in from the larger herds on the Great Plains east of the Sangre de Cristo Mountains. Grizzly, wolves and coyotes wandered the valley grassland preying on mice, prairie dogs, ground squirrels, and other small mammals and the weak among the larger animals. Great flocks of birds flew over the river and the grasslands; Sandhill Cranes, many species of geese, ducks, heron, and pelicans. Many species of hawks, osprey, eagles and falcons preyed on the small mammals and fish in the rivers and streams. Snakes and other reptiles were abundant in the flower-strewn grasslands and wetlands up and down the Rio Grande Valley.

In the summer, moist air from the Gulf of Mexico flows up over the Southwest. Warm air rising off the land cools as it rises, condensing moisture from the upper atmosphere into huge thunderheads that spike the land below with lightning. The Jemez Mountains have more lightning strikes than most areas in North America. These lightning strikes start fires and have started fires for millenniums. In the Jemez Mountains, 160,000 lightning strikes were detected between 1985 and 1994, a frequency that probably has occurred for centuries. Seventy percent of the 5000 fires mapped in the Jemez since 1909 were started by lightning and Bandelier National Monument alone averages 11 lightning fires per year[4].

In the wilderness world before 1800, a lightning strike would hit an old pine tree in the middle-elevation mountains, smolder in the dead wood for a few hours then start to flame. The dry wood gradually dropped coals onto the grasses below. Fire would spread and soon the knee-high grass would be burning away from the tree, killing most of the pine and fir seedlings that managed to sprout in the grass bed among towering pines and firs. The big trees would hardly be singed by the passing fire, which would spread far from the lightning struck snag, burning low and cool over large areas until it hit the wet high country or a barrier such as a cliff, or was doused by a rainstorm. Such fires often spread from the pine forests into the low grasslands and mesas, killing many invasive juniper trees, reinvigorating the grasses and moving far out into the valley.

Before large human populations came to the Rio Grande Valley, wildfire smoke was common from spring through fall. Almost every acre of land below 10,500 feet (3200 m) burned with a low-to-the-ground fire every five to twenty years. These fires were essential to the health of the forests, grasslands and all the associated animals that depended on them. In the higher, mixed conifer forests, widespread fires were slightly less frequent because these forests tend to be wetter much of the year. Even so, mixed conifer forests sometimes burned hot enough to burn out patches of trees, opening the land for new aspen groves and grass.

Not only did small fires occur in a given patch of the Southwest uplands frequently, regional fire years roughly every eighty-five years occurred (and in altered form occur today) in which fire may be widespread over tens of thousands of acres (in separate patches) across the Southwest due to lightening, drought, wind and past buildup of fuels. These regional fire years can be detected by looking at fire scars on tree rings from trees that survived fires. This is one of the main methods for reconstructing fire history in woodlands since fire will often scar some trees each time it burns around their bases and the succession of fire scars can be used to pinpoint the year and even the season that the fire passed through a given stand of trees.

In regional fire years, fire scars appear on trees over a wide area, even affecting trees in Utah, Arizona, Colorado and New

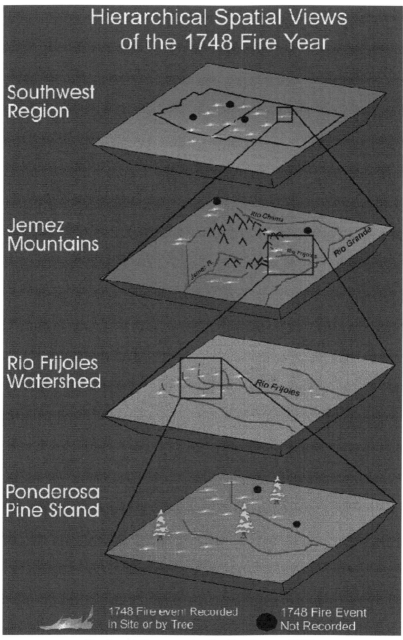

Regional fire year in the Southwest 1748.
Graphic courtesy of US Geologic Survey.

Mexico in the same year. Today regional fire years continue with many major forest fires occurring in the same year. Two thousand, the year of the Cerro Grande Fire was such a year[5].

Adolph Bandelier, for whom Bandelier National Monument is named, experienced part of a regional fire year while camped at San Ildefonso Pueblo in the spring of 1879. In his 1880 essay "Po-Se," Adolph Bandelier describes a severe drought with dry winds, creeks drying back to their headwaters and the Rio Grande flowing "like a brook." He wrote: "by May, the forests of the lower mesas and the sides of the mountains had caught fire. The fires appeared in the distance as a pillar of cloud and by night a pillar of smoke[6]." (Forest fires often create intense columns of smoke that accumulate moisture in the upper atmosphere, creating cumulus clouds. These clouds can in turn produce lightning and intense, dangerous downdrafts.)

It's not clear that the Pueblo people made a regular practice of intentionally starting wildfire as many other native groups did elsewhere in North America and if they did, such fire use was masked by the frequent lightning fire starts that led to wildfires[7]. Natives in places like California often lit fires to improve wildlife habitat, increase accessibility of the countryside and perhaps, just for fun. Mr. Bandelier's time spent among the pre-1880 Pueblos gave him the impression that Pueblo people did not have a positive impression of wildfire but natural fire was so common that there may have been little need to encourage it. The people Bandelier spoke to said that the Navajo, who first migrated into the Southwest in the 1300 or 1400s, were wont to start forest fires.

In prehistoric times, fire's most important role was as a population control for pines, juniper, sage and pinon trees which struggled to grow among grasses. Native grasses have dense roots that make if difficult for tree seedlings to germinate. In the Rio Grande Valley and elsewhere in New Mexico, juniper was lightly scattered across the landscape because the grass both prevented tree germination and carried rapid, relatively cool fire that killed many small trees and even larger junipers. Juniper is often killed even by light burning. Pinon pine is slightly more fire resistant but it too is easily killed by fire. Even older pinon and juniper trees can be killed when fire burns their bases with great intensity.

Thus the valley and the higher ponderosa pine forests had frequent fires that kept the forest floor and valley grasses healthy and kept the forests open and park-like. The early people living in northern New Mexico in the year 1300 would have watched fires spread from the mountains, into the valleys or from the valley to the mountains over long time periods. These fires could have covered tens of thousands of acres or just a few hundred, but would have been dominantly grass fires, controlled only by rain and snow and the nuances of geography.

Yet many places would not support grass, such as the thin-soiled ends of mesas or areas where juniper and pinon forests shaded out or so changed the soil chemistry beneath them that only minimal grass would grow. The cliff faces that line much of the plateau country surrounding the west, south and east sides of the Jemez Mountains could have been a barrier to fire spread, keeping plateau and valley fires separate in many cases except where canyon floors acted as fire corridors between plateau and valley.

In the Southwest's arid climate, grasslands were not as lush as those of the Great Plains; rather perennial grasses adapted to varying elevations had evolved with animal life, geography and frequent droughts. These were short-grass-prairies, populated with grasses like blue and side oats gramma, false buffalo, needle and thread, and galleta that grew on the plateau and in the valleys. Rocky places with thin or no soil would have supported sparse grass while thick soil in the forests or open valleys supported richer stands.

Montane grasslands, such as those that cover much of the peak of Cerro Grande, spread bunchgrass across the sides of many peaks in the Southwest, surrounded by aspen and fir forests, which only burned in the driest years and with very low intensity. Frequent fires here too kept trees from invading these high open meadows, which today are one of the most endangered habitat types in the Southwest.

Productive grasslands formed the foundation of a diverse ecosystem that combined with associated wetlands like marshes and stream corridors supported millions of birds and mammals. Open grasslands provide excellent habitat for predatory birds like hawks and falcons that preyed on the millions of mice, moles, voles, prairie dogs, rabbits and other rodents. Small mammals also provided the main food source for wolves and coyote. Grasslands extended into the under-story of ponderosa pine forests as well.

Thousands of white tailed and black-tailed prairie dogs built long burrows among the Southwest grasslands. These vegetarian rodents were key to the hydrology and ecology of grasslands. Browsing the grass surrounding their villages, the prairie dogs created an area of fresh grass shoots where they could see predators such as snakes and ferrets. The "lawns" that surround the prairie dog colonies also supported birds such as plover and burrowing owls that nested in abandoned prairie dog towns. Fire burning across prairies would bypass prairie dog villages where dry grass was absent and the green shoots that remained around the villages were key grazing grounds for elk, buffalo, and pronghorn as they waited for the flush of new grass that would follow fast-moving fires.

Prairie dog burrows served as plumbing that allowed the short, intense rainstorms of summer to soak into the root zone and the shallow water tables that were abundant and close to the surface because of the many beaver ponds across the landscape. These water tables fed streams and rivers. Prairie dogs fertilized and turned over the soil, helping it provide for insects, worms and fungi critical to the base of the regional ecology.

Today, it is nearly impossible to imagine the rich southern Rocky Mountain world before large human populations came into it. Nobody alive today witnessed that landscape and few stories remain from it. Moreover the diverse, long-evolved wilderness deteriorated into the simple, heavily damaged landscape of today gradually, over generations and few people understood or even noticed the changes we brought to this once plentiful landscape.

By 1860 the stage began to be set for Cerro Grande and other Southwest fire disasters of our time.

[1] Vierra, Bradley J. et al., Ancient Foragers of the High Desert County in The Peopling of Bandelier edited by Robert P. Powers, (School of American Research Press 2005) pg. 23.

[2] A good description of the Pleistocene forest conditions in the Southwest can be found in Aton and McPherson, River Flowing from the Sunrise, An Environmental History of the Lower San Juan (Utah State University Press 2000) pg. 15.

[3] Pielou E.C. After the Ice Age, (University of Chicago Press 1991) page 251.

[4] Allen, Craig, Ecological Patterns and Environmental Change in the Bandelier National Monument Landscape, June 2002. Pg. 61.

[5] ibid pg. 62

[6] New Mexico Historical Review Vol 1, 1926 pg. 339.

[7] Allen Craig D., "Lots of Lightning and Plenty of People," An Ecological History of Fire in the Upland Southwest in "Fire, Native Peoples and the Natural Landscape" Edited by Thomas R. Vale, (Island Press 2002) pg. 145.

Chapter 2

People Change the Landscape

On May 11, 2000, when Los Alamos homes began to burn in the Cerro Grande fire, the media and politicians looked for someone to blame for what was fast becoming one of the most expensive wildfire disasters in American history. Splashed across the national news, the fire was drawing negative attention to the National Park Service and its long-standing program of prescribed burning. Park rangers worked to explain this counterintuitive, somewhat obscure method of restoring damaged wildlands to a skeptical press while images of burning houses and lines of shocked Los Alamos evacuees filled television screens.

The National Park Service endured intense criticism for their role in the fire as politicians and various agency personnel sought to deflect blame from themselves while the press played on public suspicion of government and widespread ignorance of forest fire management. Since this was a fire started on federal land by government employees, fear of lawsuits gripped politicians as home after home in Los Alamos was rendered smoking ash among foundations and scrap metal.

The year 2000 was an election year and the Clinton administration and its point-man in the disaster, Interior Secretary Bruce Babbitt, sought to control damage to their generally conservation oriented administration (and its hoped for successor Vice

President Al Gore). The administration had been actively promoting fuel reduction on federal land to prevent disasters like Cerro Grande[1].

In the case of the Cerro Grande Fire, some responsibility lies with those who lit the prescribed fire on Cerro Grande the night of May 4. Yet the Cerro Grande story has two important dimensions; one involving fire crews, judgements made and a wind blown prescribed fire, and another deeper dimension involving human and natural history that combined to make this wildfire disaster inevitable. Setting the stage for the rapid events of May 4 through 13 requires some understanding of the centuries leading up to that fateful week. The Cerro Grande Fire was a product of its environment and the things people had done to that environment for more than a hundred years.

Only recently has science come to a good understanding of ecology and how forests function with their wildlife, plants, watersheds and people. For the decades until the 1980s, people used the landscape of the Southwest and the broader west with optimism that the land could absorb their actions and that economic uses of this dry land would be benign. We know now that the earliest European exploiters of the Southwest landscape were the first members of a multi generational committee of people who created the conditions for the Cerro Grande blaze.

Pushing the Land Past its Limits

The Cerro Grande blaze, and most other recent "super-fires" erupt in landscapes greatly changed by human activities over the last four centuries. From the time that the Pueblo Indian population grew in northern New Mexico and when the Spanish first settled here, to the time when federal agencies took over management of much of the Southwest, critical and profound changes were inadvertently made to range and forest land, changing it from a place of frequent natural, non destructive wildfires, to a place where one of the hottest blazes in regional history wiped out trees that were centuries old.

In the general area burned by the Cerro Grande Fire, there are many prehistoric Pueblo settlements, dotting all but the highest areas of the Jemez Mountains. The Pajarito Plateau, as well as the western Jemez were particularly heavily populated as exhibited by the many clusters of cave dwellings and abandoned villages on mesas and canyons. At least six large villages existed on the Pajarito Plateau at the peak of Pueblo civilization in or near present-day Bandelier National Monument. Even so, whatever damages the Puebloans did to the Jemez Mountain environment; it had little long-term effect and probably had little effect on how the Cerro Grande fire evolved.

By the time the Spanish first arrived in northern New Mexico in 1540, most of the Pueblo people had abandoned the Pajarito Plateau and had joined others already living in large villages near the Rio Grande. Drought struck again in 1500 and the people gradually left their dry farm fields, low streams, scarce game and cleared firewood stands.

Human affects largely shifted from the plateaus and mountains to the Rio Grande and other river valleys of the Southwest around 1500. The first Spanish explorers of the Rio Grande Valley reported finding extensive Pueblo farms clustered along the Rio Grande near where Sandia, Santa Ana and Isleta Pueblos lie today. In the northern Rio Grande and Chama Valleys, Pueblo farms likely were clustered along the river from White Rock Canyon to present-day Abiquiu. As Pueblo population shifted to the Rio Grande Valley, so did demand for firewood. The Rio Grande Valley in those times was largely grassland with scattered pinon, juniper and cottonwood around springs or on north facing slopes.

By 1839, explorer Joshua Gregg found little left of the Rio Grande cottonwood forests in northern New Mexico and reported that the Pueblo people were again ranging far into the mountains for firewood. This pattern had occurred at Chaco Canyon in the 1300s, when firewood supplies close to the great villages were depleted; likely one of the major factors that led to the abandonment of the Chaco Wash. Photos of San Ildefonso Pueblo taken in the late 1800s show virtually no cottonwood forests along the Rio Grande. The heavy cutting of cottonwood for firewood must have greatly reduced the "bosque" causing loss of beaver, fish and birds and alteration of ground and surface water flows over large areas.

The damage early Pueblo people exacted on the Southwest was relatively short-lived compared to what followed when the Spanish and other Europeans arrived. The Pueblos deforested large areas in the pinon/juniper zone, yet the tree cover on those areas was likely sparse to begin with. Most important, the Pueblos had little effect on grass cover or on the natural fire cycles. If anything their deforestation of pinon and juniper could have enhanced the all-important grasses, while keeping the critical cleansing ground fires common.

When the Spanish brought livestock into New Mexico in 1540, we can truly mark the beginning of the ecological decline that would lead directly to the Cerro Grande Fire more than 400 years later.

Livestock such as cows, sheep, and goats were unknown in North America until brought to this continent by the Spanish and English in the 1500s and 1600s. Carried aboard Spanish galleons, livestock was a basic mobile food source for settlers and travelers. Responsible for dramatically overgrazing and denuding much of southern Europe from Greece to Portugal by the time the Spanish set sail for Mexico, livestock landing with the Spanish in the Gulf of Mexico would alter the North American ecology dramatically from the time of the first hoof print on the beach sand.

The Coronado expedition in 1540 traveled into what is now Arizona and New Mexico from Old Mexico with 5,000 sheep. When Onate set out on a similar course to colonize and claim the northern Rio Grande Valley for Spain in 1598, he brought with him 7000 head of livestock including horses, cows and 3,000 sheep. Setting these out to graze in the fields near San Juan Pueblo, the impact of these animals caused immediate tension with the Pueblo people.

By 1700, some Pueblo people had acquired livestock. Excavation of an old village ruin near Cochiti Pueblo exposed the remains of 61 cows, 8 horses, 58 sheep and goats and 2 pigs, left from the 1700 to 1750 period. The Pueblo people however, never adopted live-stock husbandry into their lifestyle to the extent the Spanish did.

Spanish settlers spread out among lands granted them by the King of Spain throughout the Rio Grande Valley in the early 1700s. Bringing cows and sheep with them, they established com-munal villages along streams in the high tributary valleys of the region. Yet their movements and freedom were severely restricted by the Comanche, Plains Indians who, having captured horses from various Europeans, raided far into the mountainous New Spain, effectively containing the colonial spread of Spanish settlers and their livestock.

The Pajarito Plateau and the eastern Jemez Mountains were only lightly grazed before 1860 because the Apache and Navajo presence there. Pedro Sanchez who attempted to support 12 children and servants on the thin soils of the plateau claimed a Spanish land grant, extending from Frijoles Canyon to Guaje Canyon and a considerable distance east and west in 1742. Sanchez was the first of a succession of Spanish homesteaders who tried to live on the Pajarito Plateau, but the harsh landscape did not lend itself well to homesteading. Few perennial streams cross the rocky country since most of the Jemez Mountain drainages flow west, leaving only a few spring fed streams on the Pajarito Plateau. The glassy water of these streams run down forested canyons, making flood irrigation of the neighboring mesa tops difficult. The thin soil, dry climate and short growing season also made life difficult for the Spanish as it had for the early Pueblo people before.

In 1851 Ramon Vigil bought the land grant and he too grazed small herds of sheep and cows on the plateau. He allowed other friends and family members to graze the plateau as well. These herders tended to put animals on the grass before it had time to grow and seed in the spring and the scarcity of water meant that areas near streams bore the brunt of grazing pressure as livestock gathered near the lush streamside vegetation. Even so, livestock numbers were relatively small and the Spanish homesteaders did little to disrupt the natural fire cycle, which renewed the grasses, and kept the forests open and generally carpeted with grass.

Before 1840, the Southwest environment benefited from being far from the mainstream American industrial economy. The rural Pueblo and Spanish cultures depended more on barter and direct subsistence than they did participation in the cash economy. Such a local economy encouraged people to scale their activities to the capability of the environment to sustain them. People were poor, but their isolation kept expectations in check and a strong community helped the whole group through hard times. As aggressive capitalism moved into the Southwest in the middle 1800s, both the environment and local cultural integrity declined.

By 1870 northern New Mexico became a center of sheep production in the West as outside ranching interests and wealthy local families took advantage of the lack of regulation, abundant grass and willing workers in the Spanish villages. Sheep ranching had expanded beyond subsistence herding by families or villages and by 1850, 377,000 sheep were in New Mexico. By 1870 the number had risen to 619,000. By 1890 estimates of sheep and cows in New Mexico ran as high as 5 million[2]. Families such as the Perea, Otero, Martinez and Armijos became owners of large flocks while less wealthy herders hired on as "partidos" cared for portions of the large flocks, and could add a few sheep of their own as contractors. Under Mexican law, the whole region was free range so unregulated grazing spread. Though the U.S. had claimed New Mexico and Arizona as territories in 1847, in the void of land use laws promulgated by Americans for these new territories, Mexican law remained the default.

New Mexico was not the only land area under intense livestock pressure. Over the lands west of the one-hundredth meridian, there were 4.1 million cattle and 4.8 million sheep grazing the public domain by 1870. Then by 1900 those numbers had climbed to 19.6 million cattle and 25.1 million sheep, all on land that is generally considered arid and delicate[3].

With no land use regulations at hand and no sense that anyone owned the lands beyond village commons, herders partitioned the range according to who was most assertive in patrolling their portion of the range. Territorial disputes were often worked out violently. Meanwhile, the land was grazed to the bone as ranchers sought to maximize their profit at the expense of the natural capital of the land. The ignorance of conservation that had prevailed in southern Europe for centuries took root in New Mexico as well, and the grass capital of the region was nearly destroyed by unregulated grazing.

The sheep industry also benefited the Navajo and Apache who lived west and north of the Rio Grande. Both these closely related tribes took sheep from the open range and directly from Hispano villages, building up huge flocks of their own. By 1850 the Navajo had a half million sheep. Thus the tradition of sheep herding was born among the Navajo who learned to dye and weave wool into exquisite rugs and blankets and centered their diet on mutton. The dry portion of the Colorado Plateau inhabited by the Navajo was ill suited to heavy sheep grazing and the vegetation declined under grazing pressure.

The Navajo tendency toward staging deadly raids against Hispano and Pueblo villages throughout New Mexico in the 1700s and 1800s became a major concern of the American government after the United States annexed California, Arizona and New Mexico in the War with Mexico in 1846. Livestock thefts in those Navajo raids provoked the US to send various negotiating and military expeditions into Navajo country from the end of the War with Mexico beyond the time of the American Civil War.

In 1862 Kit Carson and others in the US military were sent to control the Navajos. These efforts among the Navajo and Apache freed the last mountain areas of northern and central New Mexico for shepherds, areas such as the San Mateo, Sangre de Cristo and Jemez Mountains[4]. Sheep producers were able to move out of the overgrazed valleys and spread sheep over the remote mountains even above tree line. This movement of livestock into the mountains spread the damage into these somewhat pristine areas and began the destruction of grasses that were the prime vectors of low-intensity ground fires essential for the health of the forests.

New Mexico sheep were sold widely throughout the region. Sheep drives to Mexico were common with tens of thousands of sheep being herded together. The miners involved in the gold rush in California needed meat, and New Mexico sheep walked the hundreds of miles to the gold fields in the Sierra Nevada, driven in flocks of 25,000. Other drives to Kansas, Wyoming, Montana, Texas, Nebraska and Arizona were also common.

The sheep drives in essence exported New Mexico native grasses as mutton. As the sheep population rose, the health of New Mexico range declined. With no analogous native grazing animal, the grasses were not adapted for such intensive consumption as sheep often tear grass out by the roots. Hardest hit at first were the Rio Puerco and Rio Grande River valleys where grasses gave way to bare soil under the teeth of thousands of sheep. Rain-washed the soil away leaving deep gullies creasing the land that caused water tables to drop, soil to dry out, and streamside forests to die. The rivers and streams began to carry heavy loads of silt, destroying fish habitat and clogging irrigation works downstream.

The once thick grasses in the pine and mixed conifer forests in the highlands were reduced to stubble by the sheep. With no regulation, shepherds raced each other to the grass, and often kept grazing it until only dirt showed where grass had been. Competition among shepherds for grass led to violence and lawlessness on the open range.

Valle Canyon, two canyons north of Frijoles Canyon was used as a stock drive between the Rio Grande Valley and the Valle Grande to the west. The vast calderas in the center of the Jemez Mountains were attractive to herdsmen as the calderas were a vast meadowland and had multiple streams and wetlands. The Wheeler Expedition had found 12,000 sheep, cows and goats grazing on the Valle Grande in 1873. (Today range scientists believe the carrying capacity of the Valles Caldera to be around 5000 animals depending on precipitation.) It is still a mystery what the condition of the Valles and their streams were before livestock grazing began there.

In huge grasslands of the Valle Grande, Valle Toledo and Valle San Antonia in the high Jemez Mountains, sheep were released with no regard for the health of the grasslands or the delicate mountain streams. Under Frank Bond, an aggressive businessman who played and important role in the development of Espanola as a regional economic center, the Valle Grande was grazed by as many as 30,000 sheep beginning in 1918. Those sheep were driven over the Valle Canyon driveway and wintered on the Pajarito Plateau, intensely grazing the mesas and ponderosa forests. This environmental insult was at the core of the ecological decline that culminated in the Cerro Grande fire.

In 1877 Stephen McElroy and Daniel Sawyer surveyed the Pajarito Plateau and reported a "fine growth of large pine timber and grass being of good quality and plentiful." This was to be the last report of good grass conditions on the Pajarito Plateau. 1877 was the last year that natural renewing ground fires occurred on the Pajarito Plateau and over most of the Southwest. Soon, changes would come to the region, which plunged the area into irreversible environmental decline that would lead directly to the Cerro Grande fire 120 years later.

Throughout the West, the whistle of the steam locomotive across once remote expanses signaled an important line in history. With the arrival of the railroads to much of the West in 1880, isolated areas with local economies were linked to the larger world. Industrial transportation became possible and relatively luxurious train coaches and freight cars capable of carrying large and heavy loads replaced the slow wagon traffic on rutted dirt roads.

For northern New Mexico, the coming of the railroads would have profound affects on the natural environment.

By 1880, Rio Arriba County had 150,000 sheep, Santa Fe County had 31,000, Taos County had 214,000 and San Miguel County 390,000 most brought in by rail. Spanish-American weavers in places like Chimayo and Los Ojos brought in new sheep breeds for wool production. By the time the railroads came to New Mexico in 1880, sheep production was a major industry with towns like Espanola growing up around sheep merchandising. The wool products from weavers in Chimayo became important tourist curios in shops along the Santa Fe Railroad, increasing demand for local wool.

Two railroad companies competed for access to the northern Rio Grande Valley, the Atchison Topeka and Santa Fe and the Denver and Rio Grande Western Railroad. In northern New Mexico, the Chile Line spur, built by a subcontractor to the Denver and Rio Grande Western, threaded its way down from Antonito Colorado in the south end of the San Luis Valley to Santa Fe, reaching the Rio Grande at Embudo, passing through the Espanola Valley, then down White Rock Canyon before turning east to Santa Fe over Buckman Wash. In Santa Fe, this narrow gauge line ended next to the end of a full-gauge spur of the competing Santa Fe Railroad on Guadalupe Street.

The DRGW was an active company, with networks of rails serving most of Colorado's bustling mining districts in the San Juan Mountains as well as its agricultural and urban centers from the Front Range to the Navajo country at Farmington. Yet the Chile Line, from Antonito, Colorado to Santa Fe proved to be a busy section of track, with thousands of sheep loaded onto two-leveled cars, logs from busy timbering operations in the Chama Valley, and passengers and freight for Santa Fe. Espanola itself was born as a merchant center next to the new tracks, though other villages had long existed nearby.

For the Pajarito Plateau and Jemez Mountains, the railroad would bring real environmental trouble. As the lands near what is today Bandelier National Monument changed hands from traditional users to outsiders, the railroads would make it possible for the land to be exploited and degraded by industrial uses.

By 1875, the Ramon Vigil Land Grant (a tract that ran from Frijoles Canyon on the South to Guaje Canyon on the North) was sold to a succession of outsiders beginning with a Catholic Priest named Thomas Hayes. Unlike many of the other Spanish and Mexican land grants in New Mexico, the Vigil grant was sold willingly when Ramon Vigil reached retirement age. However, three members of the Vigil family refused to sell their portions, so only eight eleventh's of the grant was sold. Father Hayes then sold the land to Winfield Smith, a Wisconsin attorney and Edward Sheldon, an Ohio industrialist[5]. These men sought to make money from their purchase by leasing it to others. (Later, the terms of this sale were subject to a protracted court battle between the Vigil heirs and the purchasers.)

Frijoles Canyon in what is today Bandelier National Monument was grazed by the Pino family from La Cienega near Santa Fe who penned their sheep among the prehistoric cavetes and grew some crops in the canyon. Before public ownership sheep grazed the mesas of Bandelier heavily. Commercial sheep and cattle grazing continued in Bandelier under Forest Service management until the national monument was turned over to the National Park Service in 1932. National Park Service rangers found 15 corrals, watering tanks and drift fences near the heart of the national monument when they took control of the land.

Cattle raising on the grasslands of the Midwest and south was a major industry beginning as early as 1860, with large cattle owners seeking to maximize their fortunes in much the same way the sheep men in New Mexico had been doing for fifty years. With no regulation, vast areas of Texas were grazed to dust. In 1883 the Texas legislature passed bills regulating grazing on private lands to protect the land from permanent damage. Long the source of overland cattle drives to the northern plains, Texas cattle ranchers sought new land for grazing as grass disappeared on the home range in Texas.

The DRG&W railroad opened up access to new grasslands to Texas cattle ranchers. One rancher in particular, W.C. Bishop noticed the Pajarito Plateau, leased access to it and brought 3,000 cows to the Pajarito Plateau by rail in 1883. The Hispano herders who had used the plateau for decades said they had never seen so many cows and with time many withdrew their meager herds, not wanting conflict with Bishop's cowboys. Others got jobs with Bishop but tension between the Hispanos and Bishop escalated. Weather intervened to cool frictions before violence flared.

The winter of 1886-87 struck, harsh and cold with deep snow and high wind. Most of Bishop's herd died. Though he tried to revive his herd after the harsh winter, with grasses declining dramatically from damage his cows had already inflicted, Bishop abandoned the plateau in 1888. The damage his cattle enterprise caused to native grasses, soils and forests of the eastern Jemez Mountains snapped the ecological integrity of the region, beginning a downward spiral of environmental conditions that would lead directly to the Cerro Grande Fire 112 years later.

It is difficult to overestimate the damage Bishop's cattle caused to the eastern Jemez region. Range scientists estimate that Bishop released more than ten times as many cattle as the grasses could sustain.

Overgrazed, the Pajarito Plateau and eastern Jemez Mountains struggled to recover. The perennial native grasses that were common to the area were pushed beyond the point where they could recover. Such grasses as blue gramma store food energy in their roots, but depend on their leaves to recharge the whole plant through photosynthesis. If grass is grazed hard in the spring before it can grow new green shoots, the roots begin to wither and starve and the plant dies. In an ungrazed setting, native perennial grasses carried frequent ground fires which would stimulate and fertilize the grass plants, the black ash quickly being replaced by new green shoots.

Higher up, (above 7300 feet) in the stately ponderosa pine and fir forests, overgrazing had an equally devastating effect.

Grass below the big trees had prevented most tree seeds from germinating, while carrying cool ground fires and helping rain to infiltrate the rich volcanic soils. When the grasses were gone, fire no longer carried across the forest floor every five to fifteen years as it had for the last 2,000 years. The last spreading surface fire on the Pajarito Plateau took place in 1883. Pine needles began to accumulate in drifts, shielding the soil from all but the most significant rains. Tree seeds raining down from the canopy found no competition from grass and took root. Soon the forest floor was crowded with young tree seedlings.

The large parent trees of the millions of seedlings had caught the eye of an Oregon lumberman named Harry Buckman in 1898. Mr. Buckman had been living in Tres Piedras just up the Chile Line rails on the Taos Plateau. Seeing the big stands of ponderosa pine, Douglas and white fir in the uplands of the Pajarito Plateau and the Jemez foothills, Buckman set about exploiting the trees, many of which were between 200 and 400 years old.

Buckman built a small town in White Rock Canyon at the point where the Chile Line left the banks of the Rio Grande and headed southeast toward Santa Fe up a large alluvial wash. He erected a few buildings, a low bridge over the river and built a dirt road up the steep side of Pajarito Canyon, immediately north of where the White Rock Overlook stands today. Buckman's loggers then spread over the plateau building sawmills near Water Canyon ("S Site" at Los Alamos National Laboratory, where the first three atomic bombs were assembled was built near the sawdust piles from the old Buckman mill) and in middle Pajarito Canyon.

Buckman turned his attention to about 2000 acres of big trees on the Pajarito, cutting them indiscriminately and with little regard for the environment or property boundaries. His economically marginal timber operation drove him to cut smaller trees, gouging thin soils as he skidded logs down steep slopes. The big trees that had stood for centuries on much of the land were removed, replaced by tall stumps that can still be seen today in some places. By taking these trees, Buckman ended a legacy of trees adapted to that specific area over thousands of years, trees that had survived a variety of pressures and which had taken root in wetter times. By cutting the older, stronger trees, he removed the most robust tree genetics and the trees best adapted to resist fire and disease as well as the last trees that would live in a balanced, natural environment, free from human interference.

By 1903, Buckman was done and he left the Plateau for the Pacific Northwest. He left behind a land now doubly affected by industrial exploitation. By cutting down many of the large trees, the loggers removed shade that had inhibited the growth of the millions of pine and fir seedlings that now grew where the grass had been. The seedlings bolted upward in the new flood of sunlight and the once open and park-like forests were replaced with often nearly impenetrable thickets of young trees. The early 1900s saw a pulse of small tree growth across northern New Mexico as climate and open ground supported unprecedented increases in tree populations.

Meanwhile, west of the Valles Caldera loggers were cutting big trees from the Jemez and Guadalupe River valleys, with the help of temporary rail lines they built far into the mountains from the town of Bernalillo[6]. The late 1800s and early 1900s would prove to be a time of intense logging throughout the Jemez Mountains.

By the turn of the twentieth century, the Pajarito Plateau and the Jemez Mountains were in serious environmental decline due to grazing and logging excesses. The once grass-covered valleys and plateau lands were barren and cut by rapidly forming gullies that carried topsoil away. The loss of grasses in the highlands meant trees were growing in thickets as sheet erosion washed away soils there as well. The once verdant landscape where cool wildfires and large populations of grass dependent animals flourished, was in shock. The over exploitation by unregulated livestock and logging interests had mined the wealth of the land, ruining its productivity for the long term by destroying the soil and the grasses, the heart of the land's potential.

With similar problems afflicting much of the western United States, the federal government turned its attention to controlling this unfettered exploitation of natural resources. For the Pajarito Plateau and Jemez Mountains, the arrival of federal land managers would prove a mixed blessing as agency managers took over a rapidly declining ecosystem.

---

[1] The Clinton administration promoted thinning small diameter trees and ladder fuels near communities at risk though their efforts in this area were underfunded relative to the vast backlog of overgrown forests on federal lands.

[2] Craig Martin, Valle Grande, A History of the Baca Location No. 1, (All Season's Publishing 2003), pg 56

[3] April Reese "The Big Buyout" High Country News April 4, 2005.

[4] See generally Hampton Sides, Blood and Thunder (Doubleday 2006) regarding livestock theft, and Navajo and Apache dominance of New Mexico mountain ranges and American military actions to protect live-stock producers.

[5] Hal Rothman On Rims and Ridges (University of Nebraska Press) pg. 25.

[6] Vernon Glover, Jemez Mountains Railroads, Santa Fe National Forest (New Mexico. Historical Society 1990).

Chapter 3

How Forest Fires Work

To understand the Cerro Grande Fire, one must look into the world of those people who set prescribed fires and who fight fires that get of out control. How do people control a forest fire? How do they know a fire won't get too hot or big when they set a prescribed fire? How do they predict what a fire will do? How do they plan a prescribed fire?

Fire needs three elements to burn: heat, fuel, and oxygen. Fire fighters think of these three elements as the "fire triangle." We put fires out by depriving a forest fire of one of these elements. Putting water, dirt or fire retardant (a mix of water, certain chemicals and clay delivered from airplanes) on a fire deprives it of both heat and oxygen. The weather can also defeat a fire by cooling or wetting it. Fire fighters take fuel away from fires by pulling organic matter away from an advancing fire and depriving it of fuel. This is the main method of wildland fire fighting. Fighting fires in structures (buildings) involves cooling and wetting fuels since they can't be removed.

In nature, lightning most often provides the heat source to ignite a fire though spontaneous combustion or volcanic activity also occur on rare occasions. People also ignite fires accidentally or on purpose. Human ignitions are frequent and common.

Fire is the chemical reaction called combustion that involves heat breaking the bonds of organic molecules, which results in a rapid release of energy visible as flames or the glow of coals. The heat of fire excites oxygen molecules that collide with carbon atoms in the wood (cellulose) and the oxygen bonds with those carbon atoms and forms carbon dioxide and water, which are released as smoke.

One can extinguish a fire or slow it by adding moisture to a fuel bed. When water is spread on a fire it does two things to defeat the fire. First, it diverts energy out of the combustion process. The heat that was exciting oxygen atoms and combusting the organics of the wood is now lost to the cool water. This reduces the amount of energy in the combustion process and slows it down. Second, water sprayed on a burning material smothers the fire by blocking oxygen from reaching the combusting materials. Fire retardant has clay that sticks to fuels and soapy qualities that spread the moisture out on the fuels. This prolongs the smothering quality of the moisture in the retardant.

Wildland fire behaves the way it does on the land due to the condition and configuration of fuels such as grass, pine litter, sticks and logs, and living trees and brush. Fire behavior is also influenced by topography as fire runs faster up hill than down hill, burns more calmly (in the absence of wind) on flat land than slopes, and can be fed extra air by canyons and draws that it encounters in the so-called "chimney effect." Air movement is concentrated and channeled by canyons or valleys much as air is drawn up the chimney of a fireplace.

Topography also influences where and how flammable vegetation grows. North facing slopes have more moisture and shadow due to their orientation away from the dominant position of the sun and thus can be cooler and less flammable while south facing slopes are warmer and drier and can support more flammable vegetation in most forested areas. Fire fighters are conscious of topography as one of their primary safety concerns[1].

The condition of the fuels (moisture and configuration), the condition of the air (weather) and the amount of heat a fire makes all determine how a fire will behave. By understanding the weather, fuels and heat behavior of a fire, managers can manipulate a fire to extinguish or herd it to manage vegetation, or they can determine that fire spread is beyond their ability to control.

In the Cerro Grande blaze, the fire suppression efforts beginning on May 7 were an effort to manipulate the fire. After May 10 the fire fighters knew that the fire was beyond human ability to control and they were forced to stand back and let it run its course, working to control the fire only on its margins.

Weather

Everyone involved with wildfire pays attention to weather in terms of how hot or cold a day is, whether it's precipitating or sunny and how much moisture the air is holding, and above all, how windy it is and whether the wind speed or direction is likely to change. Fire managers watch the weather on a detailed level because fire behavior responds to the smallest changes in weather.

Meteorologists, scientists who specifically study processes taking place in the atmosphere and their interaction with the surface of the earth, are part of the team of people working on any large wildland fire. Prescribed fires such as the November 2007 prescribed fire in upper Frijoles Canyon at Bandelier, or big fire suppression efforts have an onsite staff meteorologist who specializes in watching and predicting the details of weather changes in the exact locale of the fire. By tracking large weather events and using comprehensive knowledge, these fire weather specialists can make accurate predictions of weather conditions in small areas. These are key to fire control and fire managers of all types pay close attention to the frequent updates these fire weather specialists provide as each fire day continues.

Rain or snow can put out fires entirely if there is enough moisture or at least slow them down and increase smoke output. Fire managers also watch relative humidity very closely hour by hour. Relative humidity is the amount of moisture the air is holding expressed as a percentage of what the maximum moisture the air at that temperature and pressure is capable of holding (saturation). Fuels, such as dead logs, sticks, leaves and pine needles absorb moisture from the air and become less flammable as they do so, burning more slowly because the fire must first expend energy evaporating the moisture before the fuel will ignite. Higher temperatures often mean lower relative humidity and heat increases evaporation of moisture from fuels. Lower temperatures can often mean increased relative humidity. Thus relative humidity has a strong affect on how fast a fire might spread.

Wind is an important and dangerous element of weather for fire managers and fire fighters. When wind hits a fire it increases the amount of oxygen the fire has to burn and increases the intensity of the ignition process.

Fire managers also watch the regional weather forecast closely and get detailed forecasts from the National Weather Service (called "fire weather forecasts" and "spot weather forecasts" for particular locations). These are particularly important when a meteorologist is not working on the fire staff.

For example high pressure over a region where a fire is active often means dry conditions and perhaps calm winds. A front can mean trouble for fire managers, especially cold fronts that are low-pressure ridges that pass over an area as they move across the region. A strong front can bring rain and snow but in the mountains of the West, summer fronts often bring only scattered clouds and wind. Wind can shift directions with a front's passage, forcing fire fighters to change strategy rapidly and face serious safety issues. The Cerro Grande Fire was fanned out of control by a cold front that pushed strong winds that usually blow high in the atmosphere down to the surface creating unusually fierce winds that made for extreme fire behavior. Wind was the center of the Cerro Grande disaster and the quality of wind forecasts and the probability of local winds exceeding forecast wind speeds was a topic of great interest to fire investigators.

On the positive side, fronts can bring higher relative humidity that calms fire as long as the winds are not extreme. Big wet fronts in the West usually occur in the early spring, fall and winter with enough moisture to put big fires out in the Intermountain West. In the Southwest, spring fronts bring lightning but not much moisture. Research has shown that most large fires before 1900 started with spring lighting and that many historic fires happened in the spring[2].

Every day as the sun travels across the sky, it dries out fuels in the forest by increasing evaporation and reducing relative humidity. The warmest part of the day, between roughly ten in the morning and four in the afternoon is known to fire managers as the "burn period" because fire will be most active during those hours. Conversely fire burns with lower intensity at night because the heat of the sun is absent and relative humidity usually (though not always) increases at night. For these reasons fire fighters are most cautious during the day and use the night when the fire is calmer to burn fuels away from an advancing front when such "back fires" are less likely to get too hot.

Fuels

Anyone who has built a campfire or a fire in a fireplace knows the basics about fire fuels. Fine fuels like sticks, needles and leaves burn quickly and easily especially when they have flammable oils in their tissues like pine needles do. Larger pieces of wood burn more slowly because they have less surface area exposed to the heat relative to their mass and they need heat from finer fuels to preheat them before they can burn.

Wildland fire fighters look at fuels to understand how hot a fire might get and how quickly it will spread upward and laterally on the landscape. They have established a system of fuel classifications that take into account such things as the density and types of fuels, how they are arranged, aspect and slope, all factors that allow them to understand how quickly a fire might spread in the fuels available to it.

Fire managers constantly monitor the fuel moisture. Fuels are classified by their ability to absorb and hold moisture and the time it takes for the fuel to reach equilibrium with the moisture (relative humidity) in the surrounding atmosphere. In other words, how quickly can a piece of grass, stick, limb or log dry out. Fuels are measured to calculate the weight of moisture relative to the dry weight of the material. Thus, small fuels less than a quarter inch (needles, small twigs, grass) are classified as one hour fuels since it takes them an hour or less to reach the same moisture level as the surrounding atmosphere, whereas the largest fuels like logs lying on the forest floor are classified as "thousand hour fuels" because it takes a thousand hours (41 days) for those fuels to reach equilibrium.[3] Fire managers also take into account the moisture content of living fuels like standing trees, brush and growing grass. During droughts, living plants can dry out to the point where they ignite quickly. This measurement is known as "live fuel moisture."

All of this is important because the dryness of the fuels tells us how long dry conditions have existed and thus how flammable fuels in a fire area are. One can predict fire-spread rates partly by taking fuel moisture levels into account. This information tells fire managers whether a prescribed fire can be set safely as the fuel moistures will determine how hot and fast the fire will burn.

Once a fire is burning in a landscape, the fire will dry out fuels with its radiant heat. If large fuels are wet, even radiant heat will take a great deal of time to dry them and the rate of spread of the fire will be slower.

The rate that fire will spread through dead ground fuels like those just mentioned varies according to weather conditions. If fine fuels are moist from recent rain or high relative humidity, fire will spread slowly. If wind picks up, fuels will dry because wind increases evaporation rates. Fire managers or fire fighters rarely welcome strong wind.

Fuels on the landscape affect fire spread according to how they are arranged in relation to other fuels and according to what the topography or shape of the land is around the fuels. Accumulations of dead fuel under small living trees can start the small trees on fire and that fire can then carry into the canopy of the larger trees. This "ladder" effect is of key concern to fire managers and thickets of small trees that would have been killed by frequent ground fire in the past are a major cause of large crown fires such as Cerro Grande.

Once a fire gets in the tops of trees it is known as a "crown" fire. Fire carries from tree top to tree top with a certain amount of wind behind it. Without wind trees may "torch" (burn clear to their tops) individually or in groups but the fire rarely spreads tree to tree through a large area without a driving wind. Vast areas of forest near Los Alamos burned in crown fire driven by extreme winds on May 10, 2000.

Fire runs faster up hill because flames, like plants, orient toward the vertical axis of gravity. Thus the flame leans uphill (unless there is a strong down-slope wind) and is closer to the up hill ground than it is to the downhill ground surface. It preheats the fuels up slope as it burns. Heavy fuels on slopes mean fast fire spread up hill. Canyons or draws on slopes channel (or chimney) wind and focus the convection of a fire. Some of the worst fire disasters have occurred when fire fighters were killed when caught in canyons or draws when flames "chimneyed" up those draws, for example in the South Canyon and Mann Gulch fires. The initial strategy to contain the Cerro Grande fire up on Cerro Grande mountain was dictated by fear of chimney affect in the large draw that incises Cerro Grande's south face.

Finally, the direction or aspect that a slope faces has a large influence on the types of fuels and the likely moisture levels in fuels.

Managing Fire

Since fire is a native and necessary force for controlling plant and tree populations, recycling nutrients, and reducing accumulated dead fuels, land management agencies light fires under carefully monitored conditions in order to burn forests or grasslands when the fire will behave in a controllable way. By burning a patch of forest when fire managers know it will burn calmly, managers can deprive a future wildfire burning under dry or windy conditions of fuel, making the future wildfire easier to control and less destructive to trees and wildlife.

Prescribed fire is a science. All the factors that affect how wildland fires burn are taken into account and fire is manipulated on the landscape to alter the fuels and thus the whole ecology of the landscape being treated. While fire suppression involves understanding the topography, weather, and fuels on an emergency basis, prescribed fire involves purposely applying fire to a landscape when the conditions are right to achieve the goals of the fire manager; usually reducing loading of fuel on the landscape and improving the habitat of plants and animals. If the goal of a manager is to kill excessive trees that have grown thick because people have been keeping fire out of a forest for too long, they may choose to burn the area when conditions are drier to achieve a hotter fire that will kill more of the excess trees.

Prescribed fires are usually started with a drip torch, a bottle filled with a mix of diesel and gasoline fuels that pass out of the bottle, over a small torch and then onto the ground as burning fuel. With drip torches crews can set large areas on fire all at once which can be somewhat unnatural relative to how natural fires spread, but it allows the fire to burn efficiently and it allows the agency to minimize the cost of the burn. On large prescribed fires a helicopter may be used to drop little balls of flaming fuel onto the ground to rapidly light fire[4]. This was done in the effort to burn fuels out just after the Cerro Grande Prescribed fire was declared a wild fire.

Today fire managers are sometimes allowing lightning fires to burn in remote areas when conditions are right. Such natural fires are referred to as "fire use" fires that burn in wilderness areas or in remote parts of national parks and forests. Fire use fires are monitored and allowed to burn within limits.

"Wildfire" is a term referring to uncontrolled and unwanted fire, as opposed to the more general "wildland fire" which refers to all types of fire both prescribed and wild. Until the 1970s, almost all fire in western forests was unwanted. Today many lightning caused fires are allowed to burn for the benefit of the land. Fires started by people or lightning fires in extreme conditions or in places where they threaten structures are suppressed.

According to slope and wind, a wildfire will develop a head, which is the front of the advancing fire. Behind that head, like the waves coming off a boat traveling through still water, are the flanks. The flanks spread acutely to the head but with less intensity. When the Cerro Grande Fire burned Los Alamos, its head was in the mountains just west of town and the east flank of the fire burned into the edge of North Community. Yet sometimes fires develop multiple heads according to topography or wind changes. The Cerro Grande Fire had two main heads that started at different times. One burned past Los Alamos as described while a second started near the "Back Gate" and burned separately onto land held by Los Alamos National Laboratory, heading north east rather than north as the main head had done.

Fighting Fire

Fire fighters separate fuels from the fire with fire lines dug down to mineral soil either with hand tools or by using large diesel powered dozers. Another technique involves burning out areas in front of the fire's head so that the head comes across an area already burned, is deprived of fuel and loses its energy. Such backfires must be done within containment lines lest they go wild themselves.

Sometimes fire is lit in strips to create containment lines when it can be put out on one edge. In the case of the Cerro Grande Fire, fires lit to create containment lines for the flames of the pre-scribed fire escaped causing the huge Cerro Grande flame-front that burned toward town. Containment fires can be as dangerous as the fires they are set to contain if not carefully managed and monitored. Back burning can vastly increase the area burned by a wildfire if back burns are set too far from the head of a fire[5].

Fire fighters also use aircraft to cool or smother flame fronts. Helicopters with large buckets of water, hanging from cables underneath, douse flames or helicopters capable of vacuuming water into a bay in their bellies drop that water on flames. These machines can do tight maneuvering and address specific prob-lem areas. However, aircraft are useless in high winds and are grounded when winds exceed 50 miles per hour as they did on May 10, 2000 during the Cerro Grande fire.

Fire fighters also use large aircraft with large tanks inside filled with slurry of clay, water and other chemicals that are dropped on flame fronts from several hundred feet above the fire. These "slurry bombers" or "tankers" are used when fire fight-ers on the ground want to douse a long area of flames or slow a fire's head. They can also be used to coat an area where the fire is expected to cross soon, thus thwarting ignition of fuels. The clay in the slurry smothers the fire while the water cools it yet, once the water evaporates, the fire can again move through an area with more difficulty that has been coated in slurry. Slurry is danger-ous for fire fighters when it crashes through the trees and often has large chunks of undissolved clay that can be lethal to anyone struck by it. Fire fighters vacate an area once they call for a drop then quickly move back in to take advantage of its suppression effects on the fire. Slurry material can also be toxic for fish when it gets into streams.

Fire fighting is organized in the same fashion for all fires regardless of the agency in charge. Even for small fires, a basic structure is normal. Known as the Incident Command System (ICS) the system developed for forest fires has been applied to hurricanes, civil emergencies and other emergencies. An incident commander heads the effort with a team of specialists who join him or her in directing the efforts of the ground workers and any aircraft. On big fires a large organization develops while small fires have smaller teams. All fire crews and equipment are rated according to their skill and abilities from "Type 3" for smaller incidents to "Type 1" for large complex incidents or fires.

In the case of Cerro Grande, when the fire was first declared a wildfire on May fifth, Paul Gleason the National Park Service "burn boss", for the prescribed fire was converted to the "Type 3 Incident Commander" and he directed fire fighting efforts with a team of both Forest Service and Park Service fire fighters for the next day until the "Type One" team arrived to take command of the blaze. Paul Gleason is credited with corralling the fire at Los Alamos Canyon where it stayed for three days until extreme winds blew it across the canyon and into Los Alamos. Ultimately two Type One teams handled the Cerro Grande Wildfire; one camped in a large camp to the west of the town of Espanola and another at Bandelier National Monument. Even so, the fire fighting efforts only affected the behavior of this large wildfire on its margins and the fire finally went out when it ran out of fuel to the north, west and east and when a wet cold front moistened the fuels to allow for some human controls to have some affect.

People have come to an amazing understanding of wildland fire and its behavior. Through long experiences of fighting and observing fires, and through plenty of laboratory and field science, people have come to understand what a fire is likely to do in certain conditions and what they can or cannot do in response to that particular fire. When fires are completely out of control like Cerro Grande was after May 10, the people assigned to fight that fire understand exactly why it is behaving like it is and what they can or cannot do about it. Likewise when a prescribed fire goes well as the vast majority of them do, the burn boss is not surprised by the moderate behavior of the fire.

In cases like Cerro Grande, it's rapidly unexpected changes that push things from control to emergency. Even then, the fire managers are watching the weather and other factors closely and know why a fire escapes and becomes a monster.

[1] When the prescribed fire was first declared a wildfire at Cerro Grande (mountain) the strategy for putting it out was driven by a concern about how the shape of the mountain (topography) would influence the fire and possibly imperil fire fighters on the mountain.

[2] C.D Allen, "Ecological Patterns and Environmental Change in the Bandelier Landscape," in Kohler, T.A. <u>Archaeology of Bandelier National Monument: Village Formation on the Pajarito Plateau, New Mexico</u>. (University of New Mexico Press, 2004) pg. 19-67.

[3] Donald Perry, <u>Wildland Firefighting, Fire Behavior, Tactics and Command</u>, (Fire Publications Inc. 1990) pg. 61.

[4] In the Upper Frijoles Prescribed Burn conducted by Bandelier in November 2007, only the flat perimeters of the fire were ignited by hand with drip torches while the steep canyons were ignited by helicopter with balls of potassium permanganate dropped from above. Though helicopter use is expensive, this technique is safer than putting people in steep areas where fire can make unpredictable runs.

[5] In the case of the Biscuit Fire in the Siskiyou Mountains of southern Oregon in 2002, back burning was the source of substantial amounts of the total burned area of the blaze. See "Collateral Damage, The Environmental Effects of Firefighting, the 2002 Biscuit Fire Suppression Actions and Impacts," (Association for Fire Ecology conference paper 2002) Timothy Ingalsbee pg. 11.

Chapter 4

Federal Agencies on the Pajarito Plateau

Ironically, the National Park Service, which manages Bandelier National Monument, and which started the prescribed fire that became the Cerro Grande Fire, took a significant interest in the fire safety of Los Alamos beginning in the mid 1980s. With budgets and the programs in place, Bandelier worked to reduce the buildups of fire fuel on National Park Service land. Bandelier is an island of land to the south of Los Alamos, one surrounded by US Forest Service and Los Alamos National Laboratory land. The Park Service could work on fire danger in their island but the bulk of the land was outside of its control. Fuel accumulations were heavy across the middle elevations of the Pajarito Plateau beyond the park's boundaries. Thus the National Park Service at Bandelier could only do so much to reduce fire risk to Los Alamos.

Ultimately the ferocity of the Cerro Grande Fire was a result of weather and two highly incompatible fire management philosophies between the National Park Service and the US Forest Service – one agency aggressively interested in restoring fire to its positive, low-intensity role in the landscape and thus reducing fire danger and the other interested mainly in fire suppression with limited budgets for dealing with dangerous accumulations of forest fire fuels that resulted from fire suppression[1].

How was it that the forests around Los Alamos had become a powder keg of thickets and downed fuels? How was it that the Bandelier staff was intentionally lighting fires? Why was the National Park Service with its relatively small patch of land acutely interested in how fire suppression had caused a build up of debris and tree thickets while the US Forest Service with a majority of the land in the area had little interest in this problem?

The formative years of these two public land organizations reveal divergent goals, and misunderstandings of the mechanics of nature beginning in the early twentieth century and continuing through the time of the Cerro Grande fire.

Two Agencies, Two Missions

The US Forest Service and the National Park Service have had an interest in the Pajarito Plateau and Jemez Mountains since the early 1900s. Though the National Park Service and the US Forest Service did not exist as entities until early in the 1900s, federal interests that would ultimately fall into the management of these agencies once they were created were setting land aside. The forest reserve system that encompassed vast areas of mostly western lands beginning in the 1890s later became the national forests under the US Forest Service in 1905. Most of the Jemez Mountains and Pajarito Plateau became part of the Santa Fe National Forest. The National Park Service would come to manage some important lands with archeological resources on the Pajarito Plateau as Bandelier National Monument.

Nationally, the U.S. Forest Service, an agency of the U.S. Department of Agriculture, manages 191 million acres of publicly owned land, subdivided into "national forests." For example, in New Mexico and southern Colorado, the Forest Service manages the Carson, Rio Grande and San Juan National Forests to the north, the Cebola, Lincoln and Gila National Forests to the south. The 1.8 million acre Santa Fe National Forest includes most of the Jemez Mountains and a large portion of the Sangre de Cristo Mountains on the east side of the Rio Grande Valley.

The National Park Service, created in 1916, manages almost 45 million acres across the country and is one of two specialized land management agencies in the Department of Interior. Its mission is to protect natural and cultural resources from human inflicted damage while allowing current and future generations to enjoy those lands. (The other specialized Interior Department agency, the US Fish and Wildlife Service manages national wildlife refuges.)

The National Park Service administers the nearly 35,000 acre Bandelier National Monument south of Los Alamos as well as other scattered national monuments and national parks in the region including Pecos National Historic Park, Great Sand Dunes National Park, Chaco Canyon National Historic Park, and Mesa Verde National Park among others. Nationally the Park Service manages well known parks such as Yellowstone, Glacier, Yosemite and many Civil War battlefields and the National Mall in Washington DC, and millions of acres in Alaska such as Denali National Park, Glacier Bay, Kenai Fjords and the Yukon Charlie National Preserve.

Just as the radically deteriorated environmental conditions on the Pajarito Plateau caused by grazing and fire suppression led directly to the possibility of the Cerro Grande fire storm, how these two agencies responded to and managed the damaged landscape they inherited had everything to do with how the Cerro Grande fire burned, and where. The management history of the lands that burned is critically important, both in terms of why the National Park Service was conducting a prescribed burn at all and why the National Forest land it escaped onto was so explosively flammable.

The US Forest Service on the Pajarito Plateau

The US Forest Service was the first agency to manage parts of rural northern New Mexico, including parts of the Pajarito Plateau. Scarcely 50 years after the United States had captured much of the Southwest in the War with Mexico in 1846, conservation leaders in the federal government saw a need to control land use to protect the public interest.

The federal government had begun to retain lands in the western states as "public lands" starting in 1872 with the setting aside of Yellowstone National Park, the first nonmilitary land holding by the United States government. The idea of permanent federal land ownership was extended to "Forest Reserves" over tens of millions of acres as a solution to range wars and over-exploitation of timber across much of the West.

Previously, in the 1800s, the federal government had been disposing of public domain land to private owners as rapidly as possible but many lands had been ignored or passed over by settlers due to their immensity, low productivity, harsh climate or steepness. The first forest reserves were drawn from such lands but by the end of the nineteenth century, policy makers in Washington recognized the need to address the "tragedy of the commons," the unrestrained abuse of public domain for private gain. They moved aggressively to include most of the forested land of the West in Forest Reserves.

In New Mexico the creation of forest reserves was complicated by Spanish and Mexican land grants left from the time when the region was ruled by those countries. Land Grants established by Spain and Mexico were established under legal systems that were incompatible with American, English-based land law. The Treaty of Guadalupe Hidalgo, which ended the Mexican and American war, guaranteed American recognition of Spanish and Mexican land grants. Efforts to litigate and settle land grant claims in American courts in the middle 1800s resulted in some satisfaction for land grantees, but also subjected many others to fraud and deceit. Overall, the conflict between English law on which American adjudication is based, and the Mexican system created serious problems for the land grant owners. As a result, controversy surrounds many former land grant lands that are now part of the national forests in northern New Mexico and southern Colorado.

The majority of the Pajarito Plateau directly around Los Alamos had been part of the Ramon Vigil Land Grant, within the system of Spanish and Mexican land grants that governed land ownership in New Mexico before 1846. While many land grants in northern New Mexico had villages at their centers such as Cundiyo, Chimayo or Las Trampas, the Ramon Vigil grant had sparse water supplies and poor soils and never supported more than scattered farmsteads before 1880. Many of its Hispano users traveled to it seasonally to graze livestock. Ramon Vigil sold the land grant willingly to Archbishop Lamy's priest in residence at Santa Clara Pueblo, Father Thomas Aquinas Hayes. In turn Hayes sold the grant to a partnership of non-Hispanic industrialists where it remained until it was temporarily withdrawn from private ownership and put into federal ownership under the General Land Office in July 1900[2]. Much of the Ramon Vigil Grant was to become part of that new system of federal "forest reserves" authorized by Congress in 1891.

Specific federal interest in the Pajarito Plateau followed the arrival of archaeologists who recognized the Puebloan ruins across the Plateau as significant and worthy of study and protection. Adolph Bandelier was shown Frijoles Canyon by a friend from Cochiti Pueblo in 1880 and his publicizing the importance of the ruins complex there led other archaeologists to take notice of the area beginning in the 1890s.

In 1905, the Jemez Forest Reserve was established over much of the Jemez Mountains including the Pajarito Plateau, excluding private lands that would become the Los Alamos Ranch School in 1917, and later the core of the Manhattan Project that led to the inception of Los Alamos. The Jemez Forest Reserve was later joined with the Pecos Forest Reserve to form the Santa Fe National Forest spanning the Jemez and southern Sangre de Cristo Mountain ranges[3].

By seating the new Forest Service in the Department of Agriculture, the agency's founder, Gifford Pinchot made clear to Americans that the Service was to be an economic agency, committed to multiple uses of the national forests. The agency's mission was to manage the land under scientific principles to minimize damage to all its elements and to provide for a "sustained yield" of resources such as water, wildlife, wood and forage. This mission would turn out to be controversial and open to interpretation and abuse. By asking the Forest Service to perform scientifically based land management at the same time it was to provide commodities, the agency was opened up to political pressure from various industries. As well, little scientific information was available at the time on the ecology of western forests so the reliance on science was largely hypothetical.

Gifford Pinchot began a culture within the Forest Service that persists today, one that takes a largely utilitarian view of nature, focusing on timber and range as important elements of human economics. Pinchot, and his boss, former rancher

President Theodore Roosevelt felt that the national forests could provide goods to the public while protecting watersheds, recreation and wildlife. They envisioned a system of careful selection of trees for cutting and strongly regulated use of grass by cattle and sheep ranchers on the forests. This idealism launched the Forest Service in a good direction but history complicated the agency's path.

In New Mexico when the first federal forest rangers were sent into the newly designated Forest Reserves in 1903, the mission of those rangers was to bring grazing and timber cutting into compliance with federal regulations designed to stop overgrazing and "high-grading" of forests by loggers such as Harry Buckman who had cut over the Pajarito Plateau in the 1880s (see chapter 2) and the sheep and cattle ranchers who were grazing the desert lands of New Mexico often down to bare dirt. The ranger's job was difficult given the isolated Spanish descendent populations that had accepted American governance reluctantly after the War with Mexico and after more than a century of isolation and self-sufficiency. Many of them were doubly reluctant to accept federal land management given the troubled history of Spanish land grants under American rule. Thus the rangers sent out to places like Coyote or Mora received a mixed, sometimes violent reception from those they were sent to assist and regulate[4].

While the Forest Service was established to stop overgrazing and above all, protect watersheds from damage, grazers and loggers fought back, pushing politicians in Washington to eliminate the agency so they could return to the free-range days of before. The agency found itself trapped between its desire to fulfill its conservation mission and its need to survive its formative years, when hostility toward the federal government was rampant across the West and support for federal land ownership among western politicians was tenuous at best[5]. Pressure on the Forest Service from Washington to accommodate business interests was intense as those in Congress were hearing from ranchers and loggers, and many in Congress were ranchers themselves. Consequently, political pressure prevented significant reduction of livestock numbers in many national forests.

The federal government was eventually forced to respond to

severe degradation of grasslands and forests caused by livestock pressure. Following ineffective efforts at grazing regulation after 1900, Congress stepped in during the Depression, when severe drought exacerbated range degradation, and set up a system to control livestock on the public lands. The Taylor Grazing Act of 1930 asserted a system of federal control of more than 100 million acres of land in the West. Under this act, the previously open range was divided into "allotments" which were leased to ranchers under 10 year renewable permits. A small fee was charged for the privilege of running cows or sheep on the public lands. (This system of allotments now applies to much of the Forest Service's 191 million acres of land and much of the 270 million acres of land managed by the Bureau of Land Management.)

Thus the Forest Service became more accommodating of extractive uses and over time it established a close relationship with the industries it was intended to both get along with and regulate. Congress never defined for the agency exactly how much damage from grazing or logging was too much, nor did it mandate that the agency specifically tie its management plans to the latest scientific understandings of ecological functions. Laws such as the Multiple Use Sustained Yield Act of 1960, one of the primary guiding laws for the Forest Service, did little to clarify the matter for field workers in the agency. Sustaining a yield of grass or trees at some level of use was an abstract idea, which would be proven workable only over long periods of time. Further, maximizing sustained yield was an agricultural approach to specific "commodities" in the wildland setting and it paid little heed to other elements of the environment such as plants, soils and non-game wildlife. Since little was known in the early century about forestry in the arid west or about the impacts of grazing on arid grasslands, sustained yield was a speculative idea and the Forest Service and its constituent industries would not wait for scientific studies to determine ecologically acceptable levels of timber or grass extraction. Also, in marginal tree growing areas such as most of the interior west, tree growth depends on microclimate conditions that can be altered by soil compaction, overstory removal (logging) and reforestation. Trees grow slowly in dry, high altitude areas and replacing old trees can take several human generations, a fact that makes sustained yield logging impossible in most of the West[6]. As well, people had different desired conditions for national forest land depending on where their interests in the land or its uses lay. Within the frontier mentality of manifest destiny, many felt that damaging one area of land mattered little since so many other places existed. Sustained yield turned into an abstraction and a convenient ambiguity for politicians or agency people seeking to deflect criticism of management actions perceived as either too restrictive, or not restrictive enough by members of the public.

After World War II, the Forest Service experienced intense pressure to supply timber to build homes for the thousands of veterans returning home, starting families and needing single-family houses. Though the national forests' contribution to the national timber supply has always been relatively small (around 2% of the total cut on private and public lands), the agency felt compelled to begin a large scale timber cutting and road building operation that would leave the national forests with 342,000 miles of roads by the mid 1990s, most devoted to accessing remote timber stands. These roads were expensive, and the cost of building them far exceeded the revenue the government received for the timber cut. When logging companies built roads on national forest to access timber sales, the government reimbursed them for the cost even though the roads often had no public value beyond logging and caused damage to watersheds, wildlife habitat and led to increased risk of human-caused fires.

In a sense, the Forest Service became an economic development program for the rural west, a conduit for congressional spending aimed at stimulating local economies across the West. The range and timber programs cost the federal treasury far more than they returned but Congress set up the agency's budget so it could retain a portion of revenues from grazing or logging even though those "revenues" were more than cancelled out by actual costs. Thus the agency had an incentive to conduct grass or timber sales to fund its own budget and maintain its political power while the federal treasury experienced a loss from these programs. The Forest Service used its Congressionally mandated budget programs to perpetuate programs within its own bureaucracy even when logging or grazing programs were having relatively minor economic benefits for local economies and when the damage they were causing to the environment was compromising other economic activity such as recreation[7]. Some critics continue to call the federal grazing program a "welfare" program since it cost more to administer than the agency gets in return from fees set by Congress[8].

In the formative years of the Forest Service, around the turn of the century, its founder Gifford Pinchot sparred publicly with the philosophical father of the National Park Service, and the founder of the Sierra Club, John Muir though they also agreed on much and were good friends. At the turn of the century, those wanting to preserve wild nature, like John Muir were somewhat rare as the country busied itself with its westward frontier expansion and the public had the illusion of nearly infinite open space to be used in the West.

Aldo Leopold, a contemporary of Gifford Pinchot, was the early bridge between the forestry world of Pinchot and the preservation ethic advanced by John Muir. Leopold graduated from Pinchot's Yale School of Forestry in 1909 then joined the Forest Service in various places, including the Gila National Forest in southern New Mexico. His view of the land shifted from utilitarian to deeply protective in that time and he came to disagree openly with the exploitation of the national forests by the political descendents of Gifford Pinchot. Leopold, as forest ranger would become far more influential and famous than Pinchot as founder of the Forest Service[9]. By the 1970s, Muir and Leopold's philosophical descendents in various conservation groups had become a major political force in America, clashing with extractive users of public lands while succeeding in passing a series of bedrock environmental protection laws under the pen of a Republican president, Richard Nixon.

For the Forest Service on the Pajarito Plateau all of this mattered a great deal. The land around Los Alamos had been heavily grazed before 1900 and the grasses never recovered. High-grade logging (where most of the largest trees are removed) had occurred in the accessible areas in the 1880s leaving few merchantable trees. Though the land and its forests were reeling from the damage overgrazing had done before the federal government arrived on the Pajarito Plateau, the Forest Service had no program to address the radical changes in forest structure that were occurring. The lands of northern New Mexico in general were in great need of restoration work following the sheep industry yet the agency was not funded to do such work, even if it had recognized the need.

The Forest Service had no grazing program in the mountains around Los Alamos after 1950 largely because so little forage was left from the hoards of sheep that flocked over the area after the 1880s. The rise of Los Alamos after 1943 made livestock management in the area problematic. Further the forests were rapidly getting thicker with millions of young trees growing in over the grassless forest floor. The montane grasslands on the tops of the eastern Jemez peaks offered good grazing opportunity but the lack of water near those made them useless except in the Cerro Grande and upper Valle Canyon area where the owners of the Baca Ranch (now the Valles Caldera National Preserve) had dug water entrapments for cattle.

The slopes of the Sierra de los Valles were mostly too steep to allow road building and thus little logging occurred. A timber sale was carried out near Bandelier in the late 1970s, notably one that targeted the flat area where the 1954 fire had burned north of Water Canyon.[10] This was one of the only areas where timber could be cut without violating rules on road building on steep slopes. Some timber sales occurred north of Los Alamos and thinning happened in limited areas near Bandelier in the early 1990s. These thinning projects involved cutting out most of the smaller trees and leaving a forest of the larger trees. This opens up the forest and encourages the growth of grass. Given its expense, thinning was only done in limited areas. Yet for the most part, the Forest Service focused on its funded multiple use activities elsewhere. Near Los Alamos, the Forest Service became largely an absentee landlord until the late 1990s, except when it came to suppressing fire.

Fire and the Forest Service

From its inception until the 1970s, the US Forest Service was the lead agency in fire policy in the United States, setting the pace for other federal and many state forestry agencies.

Overlaid on the general economic history of the Forest Service was fire, the constant, sometimes destructive element of wilderness that nagged the agriculturalist agency. While federal and private trappers in the Southwest had eliminated wolves and grizzly bears by the 1930s, fire refused to be controlled (like the wiley coyote). The agency's response to forest fire went through a painful evolution, from treating fire as a potential friend, to being the focus of an all-out war, then to being friend and foe alike. On no issue were the contradictions within Forest Service management philosophy more apparent than in its dealings with forest and range fire. On no matter was human misunderstanding of natural forces more apparent than in the effort to eliminate fire from the West.

From 1903 in the Southwest, fire gave the newly hired Forest Service rangers something to do other than control ranchers and their herds or timber cutters. Rangers would patrol their vast districts for fire in the fire season, riding far out into the wilderness to look for smokes (small trails of smoke from new fires) and snuffing out lightning fires with hand tools. In the earliest days of the Forest Service in the Southwest, many forest stands were in a nearly natural condition, only recently having lost their grass understory to the voracious sheep herds that were still present in many areas[11]. In the places the grass had not been eaten by the sheep, such as some of the montane grasslands in the high Jemez. In many places fire was still clearing brush and young trees as it had for thousands of years. Nevertheless, the new rangers were told the pursuit of fire was their number one priority although many had more than 200,000 acres of land to patrol. Henry Graves, Chief of Forests in 1907 commented, "The necessity of preventing losses from forest fires requires no discussion. It is the fundamental obligation of the Forest Service and takes precedence over all other duties and activities.[12]"

As it would turn out, the "discussion" over whether fire ought be suppressed would flare up later, once the lack of discussion had had sufficient effect on the landscape of the Southwest. In the mean time the Southwest Forest Service established the beginning of a firefighting infrastructure that would grow more elaborate and expensive as time went by. In 1910 Regional Forester Arthur Ringland promoted the use of a "fire plan" for all forests which included building lookout towers, stringing telephone lines deep into the back-country, building new fire patrol roads and organizing volunteers from local communities. Then in 1910, five million acres burned in fierce wind driven fires in Idaho, Washington, Montana and Oregon in the first huge fire season since the Forest Service had been established. The Southwest was spared this firestorm year by abundant rain and snowfall over the preceding decade.

The Great Fires of 1910 cemented the Forest Service in unquestioning fire suppression until 1924 when some in the timber industry noted the proliferation of young tree thickets in forests where fire had been excluded and suggested these were vulnerable to disease and conflagration. Others argued for "light burning" to keep forests open and to keep the larger trees healthy, an argument that was largely rejected by the Forest Service establishment. Aldo Leopold, who was by then a ranger on the Gila National Forest in southern New Mexico, at first discarded the suggestion that forests should be subjected to "light burning," but by 1924 the influential forester had changed his mind and joined those favoring controlled burning of the forest floor. Leopold was a person who paid close attention to wild nature and formed his views from his observations rather than from general professional agreements and he had seen plenty of lightning sparked fires burning in the Gila forests. His 1924 article "Grass, Brush, Timber and Fire in Southwest Arizona" in the Journal of Forestry was an articulate argument against fire exclusion, responsible for a reinvigorated debate on fire policy in the Southwest.

That debate slanted toward commercial views of what forests should look like, rather than any tendency to promote forests functioning in a natural or ecologically complete condition. Ranchers favored controlled burning to stimulate grass growth and suppress excessive small tree recruitment in forests. Foresters worried that light burning or wildfire would make ponderosa pine regeneration difficult. While Leopold and others exalted in the vigor of large pines in areas where frequent ground fires occurred, many foresters wanted to cut those pines and get young ones to grow up in their place. Ponderosa pine seeds and sprouts prolifically with or without fire. Fire is needed to kill many seedlings so that the few that survive will thrive. Thus while new seedlings of ponderosa pine may seem to be a good thing, without fire the species will overpopulate to its own detriment as has been demonstrated by fires like La Mesa in Bandelier National Monument where large areas of over-thick ponderosa pine forest were converted to oak brush and grass by the intense fire.

By the 1930s the Depression inspired creation of the Civilian Conservation Corps, a public employment program for young men left unemployed by the failure of the American economy. With his strong interest in conservation, Franklin Roosevelt created the Corps to get work done on public lands across the United States. The CCC set up 15 camps in New Mexico with 3,000 New Mexico crewmembers. Among other projects the CCC built trails, lookout towers, roads and buildings on national forest and national park lands. For example, at Bandelier National Monument the CCC set up a large camp, cleared the existing guest lodge and built the entrance road and the complex of buildings in the park including the whole Headquarters complex, the fire tower and the entrance station. A complex of stone houses, roads, and trails into Carlsbad Caverns National Park was also built along with other projects in New Mexico. The CCC on federal and state lands, from New York to California, even built some hotels.

The CCC also acted as fire crews and they pounced on fires with enthusiasm. The Corps spent 4,235,000 work hours on fighting fire nationally[13]. The idea of "fire crews" essentially began with the CCC. With half the CCC crews in the Southwest under Department of Agriculture, Forest Service control, the CCC cemented both the infrastructure and the idea of organized fire suppression. Nationally the CCC built 3,470 fire lookout towers and 97,000 miles of fire roads. Due to their numbers, the CCC were effective at fire control and a significant drop in acres burned occurred during the 1930s. By the time World War II broke out, fire suppression had taken to the air with smoke jumpers and aircraft. (Many of the surplus military aircraft employed as slurry bombers after World War II remain in service today.)

Before the formation of the CCC, the Forest Service had made fire control and suppression a top priority nationally and its management had agreed that building roads and other fire control infrastructure took precedence over all other agency activities.[14] By 1935, the Forest Service had overruled opinion among some fire policy experts who suggested that fires in remote backcountry be allowed to burn if they were remote from settlements or commercial timber stands. A policy called the 10 a.m. policy was adopted which directed Forest Service workers to have any fire extinguished by ten in the morning the day after the fire was first detected. This policy followed on decades of wilderness fires in the northern Rockies, which defied control, yet burned steep, remote and inaccessible land, as they had for centuries before.

The Forest Service expanded its aggressive fire control programs during the CCC years. With the CCC and other emergency program funding coming from outside the agency, the Forest Service had a large subsidy for its expansive war on fire. When the CCC was disbanded in 1942 the Forest Service had developed an expectation that it could sustain a fire suppression organization that the CCC had staffed for a decade. Congress would have to grapple with the expense of this extensive national program long after the funding for the CCC dried up.

In the 1930s, the Forest Service began to examine its long-standing idea that all fire should be suppressed and excluded from national forest lands. With vast remote areas of backcountry, particularly in the northern Rockies, the service began to question if the cost of putting out fires in remote country was justified by the value of the timber in those areas. Conflicted by its institutional mission to stamp out fire, and evidence the fire was not damaging remote areas where timber cutting might not occur in any case, and that the economics of extinguishing remote fires was difficult to justify for commodities, some in the Forest Service began to question its standing views on fire.

As the 1930s unfolded, the New Deal brought money rushing into Forest Service budgets. Hesitation about the economic wisdom of controlling fire in the backcountry of places like the Bitterroot Mountains or the Gila were swept aside as the Forest Service built the infrastructure, using the Civilian Conservation Corps to control fire across the national forests and on state owned lands as well[15]. Uncontrollable fires such as the Tillamook Fire on the Oregon coast in 1933 again alarmed the country, just as the 1910 fires had. The Forest Service hardened its resolve to fight fire. Fires in the backcountry of Idaho and Montana in 1934 proved unstoppable but the Forest Service expanded its attack on wilderness fires anyway because the money from Washington was abundantly available for fire fighting. Thus ecological and economic arguments against fighting all fires were swept aside as the Forest Service saw firefighting as a good way to increase its budgets.

Through this era a few individuals in the Forest Service argued that fire suppression was allowing dangerous levels of fuel to build up in the forests and that too many trees were sprouting in the absence of fire. Their voices were in the minority and would not affect national policy for decades to come.

The Forest Service in the Southwest was swept up in this continuing effort toward total fire suppression with new roads and fire lookout towers built by the CCC to support the campaign. Yet in New Mexico, the land itself was beginning to suffer from the lack of fire and the loss of grasses. By 1930, a burst of young tree seedlings that would have been mostly killed by fires before human management, were surviving and beginning to grow in thickets across the region's ponderosa pine and mixed conifer forests. Since natural fire occurred on most forested acres every 15 or so years before human interference, up to six of these natural cleansing fires had been missed in most acres of the Southwest forests and the forest around Los Alamos and Bandelier by 1930. The forests continued to accumulate debris and thickets of tree seedlings as a result. Foresters concerned that fire would kill too many young trees seemed not to notice that they now had too many young trees, trees that would grow into dense thickets and become the main fuel for the Cerro Grande firestorm 70 years later.

Harold Weaver, one of the pioneers of prescribed fire and the science of fire ecology had been experimenting with controlled burning on the Colville Reservation in Washington State and was transferred to the Fort Apache Reservation where he began the first prescribed fire program in the Southwest with the Bureau of Indian Affairs.

Then 1961 saw the idea of "hot shot" fire fighters emerge, modeled after military rapid deployment forces. Like helicopter based "helitack" crews and smokejumpers (which came along later), hotshot crews were and are used for initial attack almost exclusively except when no fires are burning and they do other work.[16]

For the Forest Service, a gradual shift in fire policy finally would come in the 1970s; years after the National Park Service recognized the need to allow fire to play an ecological role in wild-lands (see below). It began with pioneering USFS foresters like Robert Mutch on the Selway Bitterroot in Montana who argued for allowing lightning started fires in the remote mountains of Idaho and Montana to burn naturally[17]. He and others argued that the Forest Service couldn't afford to fight remote fires that were unlikely to threaten human structures in most cases anyway. Joined by others, the argument for allowing some natural fires to burn struck a responsive chord in the organization and the idea met with approval at various professional conferences. A nervous transition took place with the habitually fire fighting agency learning to manage fires rather than fight them. Still many in the Service resisted, arguing that one fire escaping the wilderness and burning towns or valuable private timber stands would bring wrath on the Service. Yet with huge areas of remote backcountry, the agency was finally recognizing that fire was inevitable and often ecologically positive.

The Forest Service formally announced its change from "fire control" to "fire management" at the famed Tall Timbers Fire Ecology Conference in 1974[18]. By then the National Park Service had prescribed fire programs at 10 parks including two in the Southwest. For the Forest Service with its emphasis on providing timber for industry and grass for cattle, fire had to be considered in its affect on these commodities rather than purely on the health of the landscape as was the prime focus for the Park Service. Paradoxically, as the Forest Service would find out, excluding fire was far more damaging to timber and forage than allowing low intensity fires to burn under the right conditions.

The cultural revolution of the 1960s and 1970s brought the federal land management agencies into new scrutiny by a public that had succeeded in pressing the Congress to pass a plethora of landmark environmental laws, all of which had direct bearing on the Forest and Park Services. Along with new environmental laws came the "get back to nature" counter cultural movement with thousands of young people studying biology and other field sciences and vying for positions in the federal agencies. The Forest Service was not always receptive to these changes but was bound by the new laws nonetheless.

By the late 1970s, the Forest Service no longer had a monopoly on fire fighting infrastructure that state and federal agencies had long depended on. California's Department of Forestry (now "Cal-Fire"), the Bureau of Land Management, and the National Park Service all had developed crews and tools to fight and prescribe fire on their own. The agencies jointly formed the Boise Interagency Fire Center (BIFC) to allocate resources to project-level fires and to share fire crews with disaster relief efforts such as those following hurricanes, terrorist bombings and floods. Even so, the Forest Service in New Mexico remained the largest fire equipment and personnel source for large fires in New Mexico, something that would later become a major hurdle in addressing problems with the Cerro Grande prescribed fire.

In New Mexico, the Forest Service began allowing some lightning fires to burn and doing some prescribed fires beginning in the middle 1970s, particularly on the Gila National Forest which has long been one of the most progressive organizations in the national forest system for fire management. The Jemez District has done some large prescribed burns in the western Jemez Mountains since the 1980s, near the hamlets of La Cueva and Jemez Springs in land choked with explosively flammable stagnant ponderosa pine thickets where many significant archaeological sites dot the landscape. A sudden windstorm at a 16,000-acre prescribed fire called the Buchanan near Jemez Springs on April 22, 1993, trapped 16 fire fighters. One fire fighter from Jemez Pueblo died.

Agency response to fire fighter fatalities in fires such as the South Canyon fire in Colorado in July 1994 changed firefighting tactics in ways that would directly affect strategy for fighting the Cerro Grande fire and ultimately causes its escape[19].

The Forest Service (and other land management agencies), maintain a "Fire Management Plan" for each national forest. The Santa Fe National Forest updated their fire management plan in the spring of 2000, just before the Cerro Grande Fire erupted. The emphasis of the 2000 fire management plan leans strongly toward fire suppression, though the plan allows for natural (lightning) ignition fires to be managed as "Fire Use" after a set of evaluations are made[20]. Fires that start near human settlements or buildings are suppressed. For this reason, lightning fires that started in the area near Los Alamos always were suppressed and the resulting fuel buildup resulted in the intensity of the blaze that swept into Los Alamos on May 11, 2000.

The Forest Service and Los Alamos

The Cerro Grande Fire left Bandelier National Monument and raged across Santa Fe National Forest land between Bandelier and Los Alamos. There it found extremely heavy fuel loads and thickets of trees on the canyon sides and the mesa tops between the four canyons that cross the area. On May 6 when the fire raced across the tops of Water, Valles and Pajarito Canyons, it exhibited extreme fire behavior, with flame heights exceeding 100 feet at times and spot fires starting in advance of the flame front from a quarter to half a mile.

Such fire behavior and the speed the fire crossed the area was a result of the high winds and dry fuels that caused the fire to leave the prescribed fire unit to start with. Once on national forest land, the fire fed on extreme fuel loads and forests distorted by decades of fire suppression in most areas of the national forest land it crossed. Why had this land been allowed to become so flammable? Given the town-site of Los Alamos and the laboratory nearby, why had fire safety not been a top priority for the Forest Service here? After all, between 1975 and 1996 there were 372 fire starts in the national forest area between Bandelier and Los Alamos, most extinguished by the fire crews from Bandelier National Monument.

The Forest Service sometimes subdivides its land area into areas called Ecosystem Management Areas (EMAs). The 19,000-acre area west of Los Alamos National Laboratory and Los Alamos and north of Bandelier National Monument, up to the crest of the Sierra de los Valles was designated the Valles Ecosystem Management Area in 1998[21]. Fuels had been building to dangerous levels here since the 1920s yet *planning* for fuel reduction only began in earnest in 1998.

As with the rest of the Pajarito Plateau, the Valles EMA had a complex history that would affect the ability of the Forest Service to manage the land with fire in mind. Long a part of the Vigil Land Grant, the area had been homesteaded in the 1800s, and then logged by the Buckman timbering operations of the 1880s. Heavy livestock use in the 1800s had destroyed grass cover, interrupting the frequent cool ground fires that had killed small trees and protected large ones in the past. The Department of

Defense managed the Valles EMA during the 1940s and the area was then transferred to the Forest Service in the 1960s. Both the Department of Defense and the Forest Service suppressed fires in the area.

In 1954, the Water Canyon Fire burned 3,000 acres of the Valles EMA but it was stopped well short of Los Alamos Canyon. Then, in 1985, the Forest Service had its sights on large Douglas fir and ponderosa pine trees in the Valle EMA. Trees were cut in the Valle Timber sale between Los Alamos Canyon and Bandelier boundary to the south. Following the timber sale small trees were thinned on 290 acres and some of the thinned area was burned. The Forest Service and Los Alamos Laboratory cut fuel breaks along highway 501 following the 1977 La Mesa Fire and a thinning project spearheaded by the Forest Service's Bill Armstrong near Pajarito Canyon restored historic tree densities in 1995.

Timber sales, fuel breaks and thinning opened the tree canopy and reduced the thickets of trees in some areas near Los Alamos. Yet the majority of the Valles EMA was steep, unroaded and thick with small trees and dense layers of duff and forest litter. The slopes of the mountains above Los Alamos, the Sierra de los Valles, were particularly vulnerable as no fire or thinning had happened there since before 1940.

Given the extreme fire danger near Los Alamos, the local Forest Service officials were left in a difficult position. Their agency had not taken action on large-scale fuel buildups near Los Alamos in almost 100 years and now the situation was dire. Two Forest Service staffers at the Los Alamos Forest Service office, Robert Remillard and Bill Armstrong understood very well the potential for a catastrophic fire coming from the south given the prevailing winds and the on and off drought conditions. Yet they found their hands tied by budget problems and institutional inertia when they tried to reduce fuels near Los Alamos.

Perhaps the agency was in a sort of denial. Since the birth of the Forest Service the agency had carried out a land management program built on the idea that "multiple use" would take care of forests and insure the health of the forests and nearby communities. They had asserted that logging, road building and livestock grazing were not only benign activities but also corrective and necessary. After a century they were finding out what many on the outside had been telling them from the onset, that forests need attention to their own functions outside of human utility. The ecology of the forests of the West had deteriorated because of the Forest Service's programs and now those out-of-balance forests posed a threat to the very communities the Forest Service felt it was helping to sustain through its economic activities.

Los Alamos, however, was not like other western communities. With its defense and scientific laboratory, it had no use for the logging and grazing economics of the Forest Service and its residents wanted the Forest Service to maintain recreation access to quality wildlands while insuring their safety from fire and flood. Somehow, much of the Forest Service never seemed to register that they had a role to play in America's national security by protecting Los Alamos National Laboratory from forest fire. This rather obvious idea was, in hindsight, outside their institutional thinking and its omission was tragic in the end.

Increasingly communities in the West no longer fit the Pinedale, Wyoming or Westfir, Oregon model of communities where logging on nearby national forests was lifeblood of the town's economics. Like Los Alamos, many communities bring their money in from urban centers and the nineteenth century economics offered by Forest Service multiple uses are irrelevant to these communities (for example virtually all the rural towns within 100 miles of Denver or the communities near any of the national forests in southern California). Logging and grazing in the national forests degrade forests for urban recreationists who live in those towns, though motorized recreation draws a population to the forests who use logging roads and cow trails for their machines.

As mentioned, the Forest Service budget was structured by Congress to encourage logging and grazing. Receipts from these activities could be used for thinning forests but with logging declining nationwide after 1985, funds for land stewardship activities such as thinning or stream restoration, as opposed to logging or grazing, were reduced. Through acts such as the Knutson Vandenberg Act of 1930, Congress allowed the Forest Service to claim funds from timber sales and use them for thinning its lands even though the federal treasury was losing money on the timber sales that supposedly generated the funds[22]. In reality the arcane laws that fund the Forest Service were conduits for taxpayer dollars to industry, and funds for land stewardship were contingent on first subsidizing logging and grazing. Thus the Forest Service could only restore its lands in conjunction with activities that arguably degraded them elsewhere.

Through the 1980s as timber sales declined, especially in the Southwest where commercial quality timber is scarce and the economics of logging were precarious in the best of times even, without the presence of the Forest Service, the Forest Service found itself with less money for thinning out thickets of small trees and brush for fire safety. It found itself without budgets for many land stewardship activities even as the damage done by past grazing, logging and fire suppression was posing a growing danger to towns like Los Alamos.

Before the big fire years of 2000 and 2002, Congress had not yet established a clear funding mechanism for thinning forests to protect communities. Those fires, and Cerro Grande in particular, would revolutionize forest and fire management. After 2000 President Clinton directed federal agencies to develop a new National Fire Plan. That plan would lead to *appropriated* funding for fire protection thinning as well as prescribed fire that is often the most environmentally sound and least costly tool for reducing fuel loads. Before 2000, funding for thinning and prescribed fire to reduce fire danger was difficult for the Forest Service to come by, as Los Alamos area foresters found out.

Ranger Bill Armstrong took it upon himself to try to protect Los Alamos from the inevitable firestorm that he knew would come after the close calls of the La Mesa and Dome fires that nearly burned Los Alamos. He had two approaches in mind for protecting Los Alamos. First, most of the public land between Los Alamos and Bandelier needed to be thinned and controlled burned to reduce fuels so that any fire that came would have reasonable fire behavior. Second, and before the thinning and burning, fuel breaks needed to be cut in close proximity to Los Alamos to slow any flame front and to give fire fighters a buffer to work from in their prescribed burning activities.

The Forest Service succeeded in cutting fuel breaks in 1999, a 91-meter wide swath of greatly thinned forest that wrapped around Los Alamos from Los Alamos Canyon on the south to

Rendija Canyon on the north. Funds for this project came from Los Alamos County because the Forest Service had no money for it. The Forest Service staff did the work. Yet Armstrong knew that this fuel break would not protect Los Alamos from a severe fire. As a professional forester, he was able to develop models of what a fire near Los Alamos could be like based on forest structure and the fuels on the ground, and known weather patterns. He knew the prevailing wind direction and knew that Bandelier National Monument's active prescribed fire program, while reducing fuels in Bandelier, also presented the hazard of a potential fire from the Southwest. He also knew about the many campfire sites used for late night gatherings and the increasing use of off road vehicles in the area south of Los Alamos, both sources of previous large wild fires.

Armstrong had pressed the Forest Service to fund thinning and burning in the forests around Los Alamos beginning around 1985. He had been a tireless advocate, pressing for funds from the Forest Service Regional Office, from the Environmental Protection Agency and from Senator Pete Domenici who had the most power over budgets for projects related to Los Alamos. The Environmental Protection Agency could have provided funds under a surface water quality grant but the Agency declined to fund the thinning while the environmental analysis (under the National Environmental Policy Act) was incomplete. The Forest Service itself gave minimal funds for writing the necessary Environmental Assessment to plan for thinning and prescribed burning, but no money was available for the actual work the document described[23].

The Los Alamos based Forest Service staff knew the area around Los Alamos was a powder keg getting ready to explode. They set about building public and political support for a complex project aimed at reducing fuels and protecting Los Alamos from the inevitable firestorm. Assisted by then Area Ranger Robert Remillard and staff from the Forest Supervisor's office in Santa Fe, Bill Armstrong and others from the agency pressed forward, consulting with environmental groups such as the Pajarito Group of the Sierra Club, people living on the edge of Los Alamos, nearby Pueblos, Los Alamos National Laboratory, and the National Park Service.

Doghair thicket ponderosa pine forest near Los Alamos before the
Cerro Grande Fire.

Upper elevation mixed conifer thicket near Los Alamos before the
Cerro Grande Fire.

The Forest Service staff began writing an Environmental Assessment for the Valles EMA in 1998 with a small team of experts. In it they detailed the fire danger Los Alamos faced from its fuel-loaded surrounding forests. They laid out a series of alternatives for ways the forest fuels could be reduced. They discussed the severe erosion and tree death that would occur if a firestorm occurred.

As part of the National Environmental Policy Act (NEPA) process, the Forest Service formally sought comments on a draft proposal. Comments came in from the Sierra Club strongly supporting efforts to thin the forest and reduce fire danger. Forest Guardians, a regional conservation group in Santa Fe misconstrued the thinning project as a commercial timber sale and sent boilerplate objections to commercial timber sales[24]. In fact the Forest Service did not intend to cut the large trees Forest Guardians sought to protect.

As 1998 progressed the Forest Service particularly sought support from the Department of Energy and the Laboratory at Los Alamos, which had a budget of almost \$2 billion a year. In February, Robert Remillard asked the Department of Energy if they could help fund the Valles fuel reduction project. The local Department of Energy office said they would look into it. Meanwhile the Santa Fe New Mexican newspaper was publishing editorials urging action on the fire danger facing Los Alamos and many in Los Alamos, including the Sierra Club, were offering assistance to the Forest Service in carrying out the Valles thinning and burning plan.

Bandelier fire staff was very interested in the Valles fuel project since they knew any fire leaving the fuel choked upper reaches of Bandelier would spill right into the Forest Service lands near Los Alamos and be in Los Alamos in short order. Both the Park Service and the Espanola District of the Forest Service had been interested in coordinating burning and thinning activities on the north edge of Bandelier in the Water Canyon and American Springs area. Both agencies were aware that the political boundary between the Forest Service and Park Service land did not make sense from a fire control point of view. The Forest Service met with Bandelier's Fire Management Officer Al King in January 1998 to outline the proposed series of controlled burns and thinning projects in the Valles EMA. They again talked about coordinating burns since both agencies knew that a prescribed burn in upper Frijoles Canyon was a top Park Service priority. The Park Service waited patiently through the 1990s for the Forest Service to come up with funding and initiative for controlled burning on their side of the Bandelier boundary in conjunction with burning in Bandelier. The Forest Service never got their prescribed burning funded and the Park Service was forced to carry on alone or continue to wait indefinitely as conditions in Bandelier continued to decline.

In May 2000, the Forest Service came forward with their Valles EMA plan to reduce fire danger in the woods around Los Alamos. The plan called for a combination of thinning small diameter trees that would be either burned or offered to the public for firewood and in other areas burning to reduce fuel loads. The montane grassland meadows would have been burned to stimulate grasses and reduce tree incursions. None of the proposed alternatives involved road building or commercial timber sales.

The Forest Service would have used its completed plan to request funding from Congress for the thinning and burning work they envisioned and would likely have obtained the funding within a half year, according to Bill Armstrong[25]. The decision on the Valles Ecosystem Management Area was due to be released to the public on May 9, 2000. The Cerro Grande Fire was declared a wildfire on May 5, 2000. After the fire, the plan was moot, as a majority of the forest surrounding Los Alamos had been reduced to what would become a grass and brush field.

The National Park Service

Understandably, much of the public was confused at to why a federal agency was intentionally starting a controlled or "prescribed burn" on their land in May 2000. Why would any agency intentionally start a fire? What scientific or philosophical basis would an agency have for purposely starting a forest fire?

The prescribed fire that began the Cerro Grande blaze was part of a national fire management program that had been developing within the National Park Service for more than 30 years.

Bandelier's fire management program is deeply rooted in the broad philosophy of national park management, a philosophy that has set an international standard for land preservation and one that has been controversial because it sometimes conflicts with a utilitarian view of nature common to the American psyche and rooted in the Judeo-Christian religious underpinnings of western civilization.

To understand the National Park Service we can look at the beginning of "public lands" in America. The idea of *public* lands in the United States began with America's first national park - Yellowstone National Park established by Congress in 1872[26], a time when most of the western United States was territorial and when the federal government owned virtually all lands except those that had been claimed by homesteaders, miners or, in the case of the Southwest, claimed by land grant holders or Indian tribes before American conquest.

The undesignated and unclaimed lands of the great west were known as "public domain" lands. In 1872 the federal government was eagerly disposing of the vast western public domain in any way it could to open the West to settlement and tax generating economic activity. For example, the same year Yellowstone National Park was established by an act of Congress, the Mining Act of 1872 passed as well, which allowed (and still allows) miners to claim federal land, if they performed minimal work on a mining claim and pay $2.50 per acre for full ownership of the land. Until 1872, Congress had no intention of owning any land except for purposes of defense and for the national government in Washington. Yet decades of lawless exploitation of public domain lands in the West had given many in Washington pause about releasing obviously beautiful and valuable natural areas to uncontrolled exploitation in the Wild west.

The Yellowstone country with its spectacular geysers and other thermal features, waterfalls, wild animals and miles of wild country attracted the attention of various trappers and survey teams over the decades following 1820. Legend has it that members of the Washburn-Doane expedition, an amateur survey team, camped at the Madison River in September 1870, discussed around a campfire establishing the wonders of Yellowstone as a park in public ownership rather than a place for private exploitation[27].

The idea of a park spread and gained the support of Northern Pacific Railroad executives who were putting tracks across the West (with large financial support from the federal government) to carry freight westward and hopefully tourists to see the region's natural wonders. Thus a decidedly noncommercial view of land use was championed by one of the largest corporations of the time to foster tourism that the railroad executives rightly saw as a moneymaking opportunity. Yellowstone was established as a federal park with little debate in Congress in 1872, to be held permanently by the federal government. For the first time in American history, the national government set aside land to be held and managed, on behalf of the American public, for purposes other than defense.

Once Congress established Yellowstone National Park, the idea of federal land ownership for land management purposes began to be accepted. The Congress and successive presidents agreed that the federal government would own land and despite resistance from many politicians in the West, the idea of federal land management soon expanded beyond the national park idea. By 1891 a land management idea separate from the national park idea gained acceptance and "forest reserves" began to be set aside by 1903. The idea of public lands gained momentum, lands that would be owned by all the people of the United States and managed on their behalf by federal agencies with missions to fit the mandates of Congress or the president.

Following Yellowstone, other national parks were added to the system in the next two decades, including Yosemite, Sequoia, General Grant (now part of Kings Canyon National Park) Crater Lake, Glacier and Mt. Rainier. Yet, the idea of national parks was established long before an agency was dedicated to their care. The army patrolled the parks to keep livestock, poachers, and forest fires out until the National Park Service per se was established in 1916, despite strong opposition from the US Forest Service which saw a National Park Service as a threat to its own domain and argued that it could incorporate the parks into its own land management work with little difficulty[28]. The Forest Service was overruled and a history of discord between these two agencies began.

The National Park Service had strong intellectual backing

in the years before its establishment in 1916. Built on a foundation of reverence toward nature first expressed effectively by John Muir in the 1870s, an intellectual movement in America that valued wild nature, scenery and wildlife was growing opposite the utilitarian, exploitive approach to nature embodied by the pioneer ethic and manifest destiny. Fredrick Law Olmsted Jr. a landscape architect and the designer of New York's Central Park and many facets of the National Mall in Washington D.C., became a proponent of national parks and helped find people to launch the National Park Service including Stephen Mather, the Service's first director.

As the National Park idea took hold in America, it met plenty of opposition from politicians who agreed with those in the Forest Service who held that holding large tracts of land for a "single use" like nature preservation or tourism would prevent tangible economic activity like logging, mining or grazing available on multiple use lands. Thus people advancing the national park idea would assure those in Congress that the land they sought to set aside was "worthless" for any exploitive purpose and could best be used to attract tourists and their spending to whatever region the potential park lands were found in[29].

The National Parks Act of 1916 gave the agency it created, the National Park Service, the mandate to "...conserve the scenery and the natural and historic objects and the wildlife therein and to provide for the enjoyment of the same in such manner and by such means as will leave them unimpaired for the enjoyment of future generations[30]." This inspired, yet sometimes contradictory mandate has guided the work of the National Park Service ever since. The agency has two primary missions: to preserve and protect nature or cultural features and to provide for their enjoyment by present and future generations of the park's owners, the American people.

This two-sided mandate has been at the core of both conflict and intellectual development within the national park movement. Under great pressure from local governments and business owners and their political allies, the National Park Service has had to balance these outside desires to develop parks into commercial-style resorts against a countervailing idea that protected wild nature is the central attraction of the parks.

How nature was to be protected became the focus of an ongoing debate within the National Park Service as the agency moved from treating nature as static scenery to be held in place like a museum diorama, to understanding the workings of nature from a scientific point of view and thus protecting natural *processes*[31]. The scientific management of nature, based on genuine understanding of wildlife biology, botany, and the field of "ecology" which studies the interactions of all the elements of the natural world, grew as both the nation's political consciousness allowed and as these scientific fields grew in importance. Many great scientists in the tradition of Charles Darwin devoted themselves to understanding nature in detail. The application of their science to wildland management rather than tree farming or cattle range management has been centered in part on the national parks.

From the birth of the National Park Service in 1916, until 1963, the agency sought to protect its forests and scenery as a sort of static scenic backdrop for tourism and public education, the economic and political justifications for the existence and expansion of the national park system. In 1963, the son of famed conservation philosopher Aldo Leopold, Starker Leopold issued a report suggesting "biotic associations" within the parks should be maintained, "in the condition that prevailed when the area was first visited by white man." He suggested that the national parks were to protect examples of primitive America, not just scenery arbitrarily judged to be beautiful by shifting public standards[32]. Leopold's idea that the national parks be places where nature be protected and restored to the condition it was in before large scale European intrusion took place was accepted by the leaders of the National Park Service and its public advocates. His advocacy of this idea was not original, but as a Professor of Wildlife Biology at the University of California at Berkeley his presentation of these ideas carried particular credibility, as UC Berkeley was an important center of research and teaching on forestry and wildlife. Implementation of this idea required that park managers understand what nature was like in America when native peoples without modern technology were here and when a full compliment of wildlife and wild forces were functioning. That challenge heralded a new emphasis on scientific management since science is the only intellectual tool available for understanding nature as well as understanding how human activities affect it.

The great American wilderness that existed before 1820 was a vast area of functioning wild landscapes. The National Parks later became mere islands in a rapidly developing human-altered landscape. Promoting natural functions that occurred in the past over huge areas in small islands of land has proved difficult. The Cerro Grande fire was a pure example of what can go wrong and the difficulty of promoting landscape scale natural activity in a small land island.

Since nature has powerful forces at work like landslides, insect attacks on trees, wildlife die-offs, forest fires, drought, etc, Park managers had to learn to work with these natural events that seem unpleasant to many people if nature were to function and the forces that shaped its life forms were to continue. The Park Service thus set out on a course contrary to the prevailing view of nature that existed since the time of European settlement in North America; that nature was to be subdued and shaped to facilitate human safety and human economic activity. The Park Service became an officially sanctioned counterculture for land management. Its management direction was out of step with other federal agencies that were tied to resource extraction interests.

As the decades passed, the Park Service became a natural home for scientific management of large natural areas like Yellowstone, Sequoia or Grand Canyon National Parks. While thousands of academics studied wildlife, geology, botany or ecology in universities, the national parks became places where their understanding could be applied to natural systems even as the National Park Service made those systems available to ever growing numbers of visitors. Even so, the Park Service came to embrace scientific management slowly, with some regions more interested in such management than others.

Eventually the field of "resources management" became a division of the Park Service, along with protection (law enforcement), interpretation (public education) and fire management[33]. Resources management meant dealing with "the resource" which means the natural world in Park Service-speak[34]. Some parks developed a culture of scientific management more than others and some, like Sequoia, Yosemite and Bandelier, with damaged natural environments, developed strong resource management programs complete with researchers on staff. Federal law prohibiting logging or grazing or motor vehicle play on most national parks encouraged a whole new outlook on natural resource management in parks and some resource managers took a deeper interest in restoration than others.

Meanwhile, the US Forest Service was focused on applied science like forestry for management of specific resources within natural systems, such as grass or trees. Applying science to specific elements of natural systems differs markedly from the scientific whole-systems approach of many academics and much of the Park Service.

Predator management became an example of one of the first important departures by the Park Service from conventional wisdom of land management as practiced by the US Forest Service or the Bureau of Land Management (BLM). As the livestock industry moved across the United States in the late nineteenth and early twentieth century, the federal government accommodated it in many ways, such as opening most public lands to ranchers and paying many of the costs of ranching on public land. Also, the federal government destroyed predators like wolves, coyotes, mountain lions and grizzly bears on behalf of the cattle raisers who would graze their cows and sheep on public lands. Those predators were killed by the thousands on national forest lands in the early 1900s, leading to the extinction of grizzly bears and wolves on most national forest lands outside Wyoming, Alaska and Montana by the 1930s. The national parks would have been refuges for these animals except the Park Service had joined other agencies in the hunt, even allowing rangers to sell the pelts of animals killed in the parks. By the 1920s many species were in marked decline on the public lands and predator control programs became controversial in and out of the parks while the biased science that was used to justify predator eradication was called into question[35]. In the 1930s, as predator populations declined to very low levels, the Park Service backed off, pressured by university scientists who wanted the Service to allow predators their place in the parks[36].

Today, grizzly bears and wolves find their best refuge in the United States in northern national parks such as Yellowstone and

Glacier. Most scientists and managers in the National Park Service today have embraced predators as a key element of functioning natural systems and as a result, in the large northern Rocky Mountain parks wolves and grizzly bears are able to move over great distances and sustain themselves on elk and bison prey herds. In other national parks reintroduction of large predators has not been pursued because most parks are too small to contain viable predator populations without the predators ranging outside the parks[37].

However, the Park Service is not an example of purity or excess idealism. All agencies are burdened by limitations. Its activities are often tempered by national or local politics that sometimes force departures from a developing tradition of ecologically based management. For example, since 1996 the National Park Service has assisted the Montana Department of Livestock in its efforts to prevent thousands of wild bison from leaving Yellowstone National Park to travel to their historic winter range on private lands outside the park. Despite scientific research proving that the bison do not spread the disease brucellosis to domestic cattle, the NPS has joined in slaughtering part of the park-based bison herd (which is the last wild bison herd in the United States) to appease ranchers in the area who insist the bison may carry the disease. Clearly a turf battle between the livestock industry and native wildlife, the NPS has found itself on the wrong side of the fight. The NPS has even participated in bison slaughter *within* Yellowstone National Park on behalf of the livestock industry in 2008.

This sort of controversial wildlife management, which caters to outside commercial interests over the interests of park wildlife and the long-term public interest, has a precedent in early national park management of both predators and fire. Yet it is contrary to the developing tradition of wildlife management established since the Leopold Report. In addition, political pressure to allow large-scale public snowmobile use in Yellowstone National Park since 1992 has resulted in damage to Yellowstone wildlife, air and water quality. In these cases the relatively weak political power of the Park Service limits its ability to be a leader and an educator of ethics rather than a capitulator to contrary views of the natural world from outside the boundaries of the parks.

The new emphasis on science, and biology in particular as

the guide for natural resources management in the national parks and monuments signaled a marked parting of ways between the National Park Service and the US Forest Service, from which it had drawn much of its land management expertise in the past. Nowhere would this parting be more evident than in fire management.

The National Park Service on the Pajarito Plateau

The rich prehistory of the Pajarito Plateau brought the area a more interesting and fateful history than many areas of the intermountain west. The Jemez Mountains are the heart of the "Anasazi" (early Pueblo Indian) civilization that spread across the Southwest from roughly 500 to 1500 AD. The Jemez Mountains, including the Pajarito Plateau, have the highest number of archaeological sites of any place in the United States and this attracted people involved in building the national park system in the early century.

Two complexes of archaeological sites exist in the Jemez Mountains. On the west side of the mountain range, the Towa Pueblo Indians had villages on the mesas and in the canyons near present-day Jemez Springs, many of which were inhabited until conflict with the Spanish after 1680 and are among the largest Pueblo ruins in the Southwest. The Towas also built field houses far into the mountains on the west side of the Jemez and left lithic scatters and shrines (some of which are in use today in the high Jemez).

On the south and east sides of the Jemez Mountains the Tewa and Keresan Pueblos left a wide array of villages in ruins from the mesas above Abiquiu across the Pajarito Plateau to the Cochiti Canyon area. These ruins have drawn much more public attention than have the ruins in the western Jemez Mountains perhaps because of their proximity to Santa Fe, a government, art, tourism and intellectual center.

This rich prehistoric heritage of the Pajarito Plateau (eastern Jemez Mountains) had attracted the attention of Edgar Lee Hewett in 1896 as he and others sought to stop the ongoing plunder of

America's prehistoric Puebloan heritage by thieves and museum collectors. Hewett was a national advocate of historic preservation and his particular interest in the Pajarito Plateau was part of his larger interest in protecting ruins in places like Chaco Canyon and Mesa Verde. Hewett, a professional archaeologist and director of Santa Fe's School of American Research (now the School of Advanced Research) had been one of the principal political and substantive architects of the Antiquities Act of 1906, which Congress passed to stop the plunder of archeological and historic resources on federal lands. The act authorized the President to withdraw lands from the public domain for protection as national monuments.

Edgar Lee Hewett came off his successful effort to pass the Antiquities Act[38] and focused on the Pajarito Plateau where he was involved with recording many archaeological sites. He was concerned that increased accessibility and interest in this once remote area could lead to full scale destruction of the many abandoned Pueblo Indian villages. With others, he urged creation of a 153,000-acre "Cliff Cities National Park" to stem vandalism and to establish a large archeology based national park in the Pajarito Plateau's beautiful mesas and canyons. Hewett and others advanced other national park ideas to protect the Pajarito Plateau over the next thirty years[39].

Hewett's efforts ran into local opposition from ranchers and tribes and met with confusion in the General Land Office, which managed national parks and monuments before the birth of the National Park Service in 1916. Efforts to establish a new national park were also complicated by battles between the Department of the Interior and the US Forest Service that managed much of the land Hewett and park advocates had their eyes on.

Repeated efforts over time to establish a large archaeology national park on the plateau floundered, and by 1916, the only option available to those concerned about the looting of ruin sites and the potential for destructive development for the finest of the Pajarito Plateau ruins was exercise of the Antiquities Act to protect a small portion of the plateau, around Frijoles Canyon[40].

President Woodrow Wilson established Bandelier National Monument in 1916 under the US Forest Service that already managed the land as part of the Jemez Forest Reserve. The 22,400-acre national monument remained with the Forest Service as an effort to appease grazers who felt a national park under the Department of Interior would constitute a land grab of "commercial" land that they had considered part of their home ranges. The Forest Service was still establishing itself as a utilitarian conservation agency, allied with logging and grazing interests. Further, Bandelier National Monument was set up under the Forest Service at the recommendation of top Forest Service officials who saw the push to establish a national park in the area as part of a broader, national competition between the Forest Service and the "single use" idea of national parks. The Forest Service sought to prove that the new Park Service would be unnecessary if the Forest Service could manage some lands for tourism while it managed others for commercial use.

The new national monument, named for Adolph Bandelier, the first anthropologist to explore the area seriously in the 1880s, introduced a cultural preservation ethic to the plateau that had been dominated by resource extraction before then. Bandelier National Monument was established six months before the National Park Service itself was established, and though many other national parks already existed, including Mesa Verde National Park (1906), such parks didn't yet have an agency singularly dedicated to their management and protection. For Bandelier National Monument, this meant the Forest Service would have to add a new dimension to its work philosophy and learn to protect cultural sites while helping visitors understand those sites. Even so, the Forest Service continued to allow livestock grazing within Bandelier, a practice that trampled ruins and artifacts and promoted erosion of the fragile soils. In creating Bandelier National Monument President Woodrow Wilson explicitly stated that the purpose of the new national monument was protection of archaeological sites within its boundaries.

President Wilson anticipated conflicts between neighboring land managers and sought to prevent damage to Bandelier from outside land use activities. In the proclamation that created the Monument (Presidential Proclamation 1322 dated February 11, 1916), Wilson wrote "The two reservations (Santa Fe National Forest and Bandelier National Monument) shall both be effective on the land withdraw, but the National Monument hereby established shall be the dominant reservation, and any use of land which interferes with its preservation or protection as a National Monument is hereby forbidden."

Establishing Bandelier as a National Monument under Forest Service control failed to end years of conflict between advocates of a national park in the Pajarito Plateau area and the Forest Service that sought to protect its holdings in the region and keep the Interior Department out. Over the next 34 years, intensive lobbying and studying of the Pajarito Plateau took place with many in the new National Park Service and their allies outside the agency arguing repeatedly for a national park in the area that would encompass most of the Pajarito Plateau and, in some proposals, the Valles Calderas to the west. Ultimately division within the National Park Service over whether the area warranted national park status and continued opposition from the Forest Service, the Los Alamos Ranch School and Santa Clara Pueblo stalled the national park idea repeatedly as it was brought forth in different configurations. Bandelier National Monument, under Forest Service control expanded to include land in Bayo and Los Alamos Canyons where the Otowi and Tsankawi ruins lie (among many others)[41]. (Efforts to get part of the Valles Calderas added to Bandelier failed when a private buyer, Pat Dunnigan, beat the Park Service to the closing table in 1960.)

The conflict over whether Bandelier and other archaeologically rich areas of the Pajarito Plateau would become a national park under National Park Service control culminated in intense negotiations between the Forest Service and the National Park Service in 1925. Support from members of the New Mexico congressional delegation gave the National Park Service an advantage over the persistent argument by the Forest Service that the ruins areas of the Pajarito Plateau should be managed for grazing and logging as well as cultural site protection. After further studies by top National Park Service people, the Forest Service finally offered to turn over Bandelier National Monument to the National Park Service with no other losses of territory to the Santa Fe National Forest. With a rise in tourism to Bandelier and the Forest Service's own admission that they were unprepared for large numbers of visitors, the Forest Service ceded Bandelier National Monument to the National Park Service in February 1932. The Park Service took control of 26,026 acres of Bandelier including 3650 acres surrounding the Tsankawi and Otowi ruins near Los Alamos Canyon immediately east of Los Alamos.

When Los Alamos Scientific Laboratory became permanently established as a neighbor to Bandelier National Monument after 1945, Park Service managers found allies within Los Alamos' administration. After World War Two, Bandelier managers worried that Los Alamos could spread all the way to the north rim of Frijoles Canyon. Land on Frijoles Mesa was owned by the General Land Office at the time, but controlled by the Atomic Energy Commission. The Los Alamos managers agreed to transfer the Frijoles Mesa tract to the National Park Service to buffer the park from Los Alamos. Later a similar agreement led to the transfer of more land west of the Frijoles Canyon ruins that the Atomic Energy Commission controlled. This tract, known as Upper Crossing pushed the park boundary up Frijoles Canyon to the boundary of the Baca Ranch (now Valles Calderas) and allowed the NPS to gain control of much of the Frijoles Creek watershed.

In the 1960s the New Mexico Timber Company was logging the Baca Ranch in the Valles Calderas, removing most of the ranch's mature timber and damaging the Jemez River watershed. As Baca Ranch owner, Pat Dunnigan struggled to buy the timber rights to his ranch from the New Mexico Timber Company, the National Park Service became increasingly concerned about the possibility that the logging would continue into the upper end of the Frijoles Canyon watershed where part of the Baca Ranch came over the ridge and into the area above Bandelier.

In 1973 the National Park Service appraised 3,076 acres of the Frijoles Canyon upper watershed contained in the Baca Ranch and negotiated with owner Pat Dunnigan for its eventual purchase. The purchase happened in January 1977 after legislative approval was granted and Bandelier gained control of the southeast face of Cerro Grande and considerable land in the top end of Frijoles Canyon, the very area where the prescribed fire and fire escape would happen 23 years later[42]. Though this tract had been selectively logged and grazed by livestock for decades, it was in fair condition and it allowed the Park Service to manage some of the Jemez high country. Bandelier then ranged in elevation from

10,200 feet on its western boundary to 5,500 feet at the Rio Grande on the east.

By 1978 Bandelier encompassed 33,000 acres of the Pajarito Plateau. Efforts by sympathetic citizens and some politicians to transfer control of the upper watersheds of the major canyons crossing Bandelier from the US Forest Service to the National Park Service so the agency will have management control of the park's full watersheds have not yet been successful. Those upper watersheds were twice the source of intense conflict between the US Forest Service and the Park Service, conflicts that led to worsening relations between the two agencies locally and a deterioration of cooperation on key matters such as fuels management.

With Bandelier encompassing some of the most dramatic of the volcanic plateau scenery on the Pajarito Plateau, and with wilderness designation of most of its back country, the National Park Service would set out to restore this monument, damaged by livestock grazing and fire suppression. Restoring fire to Bandelier became the key element of that restoration.

Fire in the Parks

The National Park Service had been seeking to differentiate itself from the Forest Service since the Park Service's birth in 1916, in order to defend itself from political charges, advanced by the Forest Service, that the NPS was redundant and the already established Forest Service could better do its work. The Park Service's departure from Forest Service full-suppression fire policy was an inadvertent important step in this process of self-definition[43].

Wildfire provided the largest philosophical challenge to the Park Service from its beginnings to today for two reasons. First, as Cerro Grande demonstrated, fire is dangerous. Second, park managers took time understanding that properly applied fire was beneficial to park vegetation and wildlife. As with predators, the Park Service found itself surrounded by federal and state agencies that felt fire threatened humans and damaged or destroyed the natural resources they wanted such as trees and grass. Fire suppression had begun on federal lands in New Mexico in earnest in 1903 with the early Forest Service. By the time the National Park

Service was born in 1916, full fire suppression on federal lands was the top priority for federal land agencies and the Park Service joined in with fire fighting both to "protect" its own forests and to stop fires from ranging outside the parks to other lands.

Fire was not always to be controlled as the Forest Service had learned with the blazes in Washington, Idaho and Montana in 1910 and as the National Park Service would learn in 1926 when large fires broke out in the fire-dependent lodgepole pine and sub-alpine fir forests of Glacier National Park on the US/Canada border. Especially before aircraft were available for fire fighting, agencies found themselves unable to address every fire start and unable to contain large fires in many cases.

As early as 1925, some dissenters within the National Park Service began to question the policy of putting out forest fires. Superintendent John White of Sequoia National Park noted abundant fire scars on the bases of the huge sequoia trees and suggested that running light fire through forests of giants would clear debris and kill some of the young white fir that were crowding around their bases (The mature giant sequoia is the most fire resistant tree of all with spongy bark inches thick that keeps heat away from the tree's cambium layer.) Far ahead of his time in his understanding of the role of fire in giant sequoia forests, his initiative was quashed by the status quo, but it began to smolder in the consciousness of the Park Service[44].

Around 1925, park managers and federal foresters alike were dealing with forest ecosystems that were still functioning as a whole, fairly well. Fire suppression was well enough established to cause major distortions in forest ecology, yet damage from grazing was not yet evident in forest structure.

Fire suppression had begun partly when foresters outside the parks noticed that ground fires caused by lightning killed many tree seedlings and saplings. Tree mortality was bad in their eyes as they planned to cut the larger trees and assumed the younger ones would be replacements. Further, they had not yet understood that without fire, trees in most western forests tend to over-reproduce. It took more decades for national park managers, who were not harvesting trees at all, to note that fire was a critical element controlling tree populations in the dry inland forests throughout the West. This reality is at the heart of the super-fire crisis in western forests today.

The 1963 Starker Leopold Report shifted Park Service thinking on fire management in a major way and led directly to the sort of management idealism later embodied in the Bandelier fire management program and others across the country. The shift from looking at nature as a backdrop for human activity, to working to protect its dynamic processes was a major and important shift that drew the National Park Service deeper into true scientific management. The agency needed to understand natural processes and assist them in the goal of protecting the parks as pieces of wild America as first experienced by the European explorers of the eighteenth and nineteenth centuries. Starker Leopold's report recommended that the Park Service develop a research program of its own to support its resources management work. This recommendation was also echoed by the prestigious National Academy of Sciences that Interior Secretary Stewart Udall had asked to look at the issue. The National Park Service set up an office of Chief Scientist in response.

By 1958 a full revolution in fire policy was afoot in the national parks. Beginning with Bill Robertson's work in Everglades and moving to the Sierra Nevada with Harold Biswell of UC Berkeley in 1959 and then with Dick Hartesvelt's work in Yosemite in 1962, the National Park Service began serious, though careful experimentation with prescribed fire in Sequoia and Kings Canyon National Parks and Yosemite[45]. This work was risky for the Service as they were burning among giant Sequoia trees in places like Redwood Mountain and Giant Forest at Sequoia, places of unparalleled significance to America's natural heritage where the margin of error was small and public visibility was high.

The National Park Service had a similar resistance to accepting fire as a natural and beneficial part of western forest ecology to that of the Forest Service. While the Forest Service hesitated to allow fire to burn in the national forests for fear it would harm timber and commercial interests, the Park Service feared fire would damage the scenery the public had grown accustomed to and worse, would kill trees or wildlife. It wasn't until 1969 that the first serious work on prescribed fire to reduce the thickets of trees and tons of debris on the floor of the Sequoia forests began in earnest[46].

Meanwhile, research in forest types across the West revealed that many western forests were dependent on fire as a natural part of forest processes. As the Park Service recognized this, it had two options for allowing fire to return to park ecosystems. First, it could allow fires started by lightning to burn their course (fire use), if they started in a place safe for visitors and adjacent landowners and if conditions were right to prevent high intensity fire. Second, the service could set fires intentionally (prescribed fire), when conditions were such that the fire would have predictable and desired results within the forest or other habitat.

Implementation of prescribed fire programs spread through the national parks from that point, taking hold in places like Wind Cave in Wyoming and Carlsbad Caverns National Park in New Mexico.

As the 1960s passed into the 1970s, the nation underwent a revolution in environmental consciousness begun as a subcurrent of larger public rebellion against the Viet Nam war and authoritarian government. Oil spills off Santa Barbara, California, the catching afire of the heavily polluted Chattahoochee River in Ohio and worsening air pollution nation wide sparked a wave of public driven bipartisan action in Congress. President Nixon signed key environmental protection bills into law in 1972 including the Endangered Species Act, the Clean Air Act, the Clean Water Act, the National Environmental Policy Act and a bill creating the Environmental Protection Agency to focus on air and water pollution. As this major shift in public thinking occurred, the Forest Service and its commodity brokering work (logging, grazing, road building and mining) came under greater scrutiny and a new era of intense controversy surrounding that agency began.

The National Park Service's public mission and its mission of protecting natural processes fit well with the new public (though not universal) sensibilities and the Park Service found itself flooded with applicants for jobs in the parks and visitation to the parks increased steadily. As the 1970s passed, the National Park Service advanced its fire management work with increasing emphasis on prescribed fire to replace natural fire that scientists were well aware was native to almost all the western national parks and monuments.

The National Park Service faced its most famous battle with fire and with its effort to get the public to accept fire as a natural element of wild nature in Yellowstone. In the fall of 1988 drought spread over the northern Rockies and a rash of fires began to burn over the region. In Yellowstone a series of lightning strikes set off a complex of fires that would grow together into three large fires during September: the Clover Mist Fire, the Red-Shoshone Fire, and the North Fork Fire. These fires burned almost a third of the park, where lodge pole pine grows in forests that cloak the low mountains like bear fur. Lodge pole pine is a relatively short-lived pine, which, unlike the ponderosa pine of the Southwest, thrives on fires that kill adult trees by burning through their crowns and releasing the seeds contained in the closed (serotinous) cones. Research shows big fires happened roughly every 25 years in the Yellowstone ecosystem as a result of lightning and that the diversity of plants and animals increases three fold following high intensity fire on the Yellowstone Plateau.[47]

Starting in the 1970s, the National Park Service had begun to let some fires burn in Yellowstone to improve forest conditions for grizzly bear, elk, moose and bison. The policy met its greatest test in 1988 with the large fires that made national news by closing the park and forcing the evacuation of many nearby towns (there were other large fires on national forest land just outside Yellowstone at the same time). Some politicians and merchants in the Yellowstone area pointed scathing criticism at the National Park Service for not suppressing the lightning fires immediately. Yet fire suppression was not possible as the Forest Service found when it tried to extinguish fires such as the Huck Fire on its land. The blackened landscape of Yellowstone soon gave way to a lush world of small trees, flowers and thriving wildlife, slowly vindicating the fire policies of the Park Service in the years that followed. Even so, the fire management work of the Park Service would never be the same and the agency developed defensiveness about its progressive fire policy as a result of the Yellowstone blazes.

Through it all, prescribed fire has continued to be used as a successful tool for forest restoration at Yosemite, Glacier and

Sequoia and Kings Canyon National Parks where prescribed burning in the parks began. Prescribed burning is practiced in virtually all the national parks and monuments where science shows fire played a natural role in pre-Columbian America. Further, the work of fire scientists in the National Park Service, joined by others in other agencies has led to widespread prescribing of fire across jurisdictions on federal and state lands.

Through the 1990s the National Park Service gained momentum with its policies to reintroduce fire into the parks and monuments and its fire organization grew in capability. In 1995, in response to the tragedy of the South Canyon Fire in Colorado where 12 fire fighters were killed on national forest land, and other factors, a national review of public land fire strategy set national policy for all the land management agencies and encouraged cooperation between agencies in fire management.

By the turn of the new century, the National Park Service had established a clear philosophy of ecosystem-based natural resource management, so much so that many staunch supporters of multiple-use management in Congress sought to limit the growth of the national park system beyond the roughly 45 million acres it encompassed in 2000. With the rise of the so-called "wise use movement" beginning in the 1980s, new national monuments established in Utah, Colorado and Oregon went to the US Forest Service or the Bureau of Land Management in a departure from the previous tradition of managing national monuments as national parks under the National Park Service.

Bandelier's fire program evolved along with the national program in the parks. Early park managers at Bandelier paid little attention to the deteriorating condition of many of the park's forests that had suffered the twin blows of over grazing and fire suppression. The middle elevations of Bandelier were heavily forested with dog-haired thickets of Ponderosa pine until the La Mesa Fire of 1977 tore through these and converted most to grass-oak scrublands. Most pinon and juniper forests in the park have too little plant growth on the ground to carry fire and fires that start in the middle elevations go out on their own when the grass or Ponderosa pine gives out in the lower elevation areas where topsoil has washed away following the onslaught of sheep grazing in the past.

The pine and mixed conifer forests in Bandelier along with forested canyon bottoms drew the attention of resource managers at Bandelier following the La Mesa fire. John Lissoway, the first resource management specialist hired to create a division of Resource Management at Bandelier in 1980 turned his attention to the obvious need to reintroduce fire at Bandelier in a controlled way so that fire would have less fuel when it started.

John Lissoway, a forester by training and experienced in fire suppression, with a group of veteran Park Service rangers started the first prescribed fire on two acres of a north facing slope near Capulin Canyon in October 1980. It was an experiment that went well as the group backed fire down the slope below ponderosa pine within a circle of hand-dug fire line. Bandelier's fire program thus began in earnest.

At the heart of Bandelier's prescribed fire program lies the understanding that fire needs to return to the park's forests at the same frequency and intensity that it occurred before sheep grazing and fire suppression destroyed the natural fire cycles. Using data gained from examining tree rings and fire scars on a range of trees throughout the Southwest, the Bandelier program seeks to put fire back either through managed fires started by crews or by letting lightning fires burn within boundaries when the conditions are right.

Most of the 59 prescribed fires before Cerro Grande were small, ranging from a fraction of an acre to 350 acres before 1997, when the park staff under Charisse Sydoriak began to ramp up the program with fires ranging from 600 to 1,655 acres. Given all the park's acreage above the pinon and juniper forests of the lower elevations are habitat for fire, two-thirds of the park's 33,000 acres need fire in regular intervals.

Bandelier published its most recent natural Resources Management Plan in 1995 and its first Fire Management Plan in 1987. The Fire Management Plan was updated in 1996 according to nationwide National Park Service policies[48] and the newly emerged National Fire Plan[49] that sought to coordinate fire management in all the federal land management agencies.

The 1996 Bandelier Fire Management Plan reflected the values of the resources management team assembled by Chief of Resources Management Charisse Sydoriak. She had gathered a cohesive and capable team of scientists who implemented a wide-ranging program to restore Bandelier's wildlands and cultural resources. Using the ecological studies of Craig Allen, PhD, who is based at Bandelier as a scientist for the US Geologic Survey, Sydoriak's team addressed fire as a key tool in restoring Bandelier's faltering ecology.

Bandelier, however, is an island in a larger area of public lands and there was danger in the fact that Bandelier's fire program was putting fire on the land more aggressively than surrounding agencies would or could do. The Bandelier fire program had the potential for exacerbating existing, long-standing conflicts with the US Forest Service.

Agencies in Conflict

The early 1900s conflict between the Forest Service and the National Park Service both on the national and local level left a dark cloud in the air between the two agencies on the Pajarito Plateau. Conflict between the Forest Service and the Park Service were not unique to northern New Mexico, as many national parks and monuments had been carved from Forest Service lands and tension between the agencies about wildlife and watershed management had flared throughout the West. In a sense this conflict between the two agencies arose from a sharp cultural division in American society between those who view nature as resource for human economic development and those who believe nature deserves respect, protection and study in concert with use of natural resources for human ventures. At the same time, turf battles between bureaucracies are basic elements of human group behavior as each agency seeks to maximize its reach and its budget.

Following the transfer of Bandelier to the National Park Service in February 1932 incremental additions to Bandelier such as the Frijoles Mesa and Upper Crossing additions became sources of conflict with the Forest Service seeking to gain any lands diverted from use by the laboratory at Los Alamos[50]. The Park Service won many of these land battles until the 1980s when proposed expansions of the western reaches of Bandelier would have involved removal of land from the national forest and transfer to the National Park Service. Given the changing national political climate and political weakening of both the National Park Service and of the broader environmental movement following the 1980 elections, those transfers have never taken place.

On the Pajarito Plateau, Bandelier National Monument has been an island of natural and historic preservation in a hard used land. Two Forest Service districts abut Bandelier, the Jemez to the west and south and the Espanola District on the north. These districts are major divisions of the Santa Fe National Forest and they each have a district ranger and his or her staff that interacts with the National Park Service staff at Bandelier. Historically, relations between the Espanola District and Bandelier have been more congenial than those between the park staff and the Jemez District.

The Espanola District of the Santa Fe National Forest controls the land north of Bandelier and west of Los Alamos. Since the area close to Bandelier to the north is in different watersheds than Bandelier's, the park has expressed little interest in that area since the 1930s when the National Park Service took over Bandelier. The politically drawn northern boundary of the Park makes ecological sense for the most part so little conflict over land management has occurred between the two agencies on that side. Bandelier fire crews provide initial attack service for much of the Forest Service land between Bandelier and northern Los Alamos.

The Jemez District of the Santa Fe National Forest has an entirely different history with Bandelier than does the Espanola District for several reasons. First, Bandelier's western boundary is a politically drawn boundary that cuts across watersheds and divides management of key park watersheds between the two agencies in an arbitrary way. Second, much of the Jemez District to the west of Bandelier includes high, relatively wet country that produces timber suitable for logging and it produces enough forage to interest the livestock industry.

Conservationists and many in the federal government have recognized the importance of managing watersheds as a whole for the health of the land. For decades, public advocates for the National Park Service such as the National Parks and Conservation Association (NPCA) have been trying to persuade Congress to move Bandelier's western boundary to the top of the three major watersheds (to the rim of Cochiti Canyon). So far only Frijoles Canyon has been protected almost completely.[51]

Bandelier's staff has long viewed the landscape in and around the park holistically, understanding that activities near the park's boundaries can affect the waters and wildlife in the park. The legislation establishing Bandelier made the park's interests dominant among local land uses[52]. Likewise park scientists understand how archaeological sites inside the park relate to other archaeological sites outside the park given that the early Pueblo people used the whole landscape for hunting, farming and settlements. Efforts by Bandelier staff over the decades to draw the Forest Service into a shared sense of responsibility for Bandelier on a watershed basis have not always met with success.

The 1977 Sawyer's Mesa timber sale on Forest Service land that extends between Alamo and Frijoles Canyon was a major point of contention. The Forest Service directly on Bandelier's boundary carried out the Sawyer's Mesa timber sale with no consultation between the Jemez District, US Forest Service and the National Park Service[53]. The National Environmental Policy Act (NEPA) requires such consultation. The Sawyer's Mesa timber sale was a logging operation intended to clear timber burned by the La Mesa wild fire. It clear-cut an area, causing silt and debris to flow into the most pristine and wild areas of Frijoles Canyon while creating a scar visible from tourist overlooks in Bandelier.

Bandelier Superintendent John Hunter had objected strongly to the Forest Service's failure to consult with Bandelier staff about the sale and regional Park Service staff to their counterparts in the Forest Service regional offices, echoed his objections.[54] This event strained relations between Bandelier and the Jemez District, which may have felt it had autonomy over its land use decisions. Moreover, the Forest Service failed to demonstrate an understanding of the impacts of logging on adjacent Bandelier and how the law required the Forest Service to assist in protecting Bandelier's natural assets.

The Sawyer's Mesa logging was a test balloon of sorts for other timber sales in the upper watersheds outside Bandelier's western boundary and though it caused friction with Bandelier, the Forest Service seemed unphased by the controversy and Sawyer's Mesa seemed to clear the way for future timber sales. Nationally, the late 1980s were a time of intensive interest in logging by the Forest Service and there was pressure within the agency for local ranger districts to "get the cut out[55]."

In 1989 the Forest Service conducted another timber sale in upper Capulin Canyon, just outside Bandelier's western boundary. The majority of Capulin Canyon lies inside Bandelier, cutting across the south portion of the park. A strong stream flows in the canyon making it valuable to wildlife and wilderness users. Above the park boundary on Forest Service land, Capulin Canyon's headwaters enter an area of springs, meadows and aspen. The Forest Service logged the area in a notorious sale called "Los Utes."

The timber sale turned into a nightmare for both the Park Service and the Forest Service after members of the public discovered that the logging contractor had built logging roads in the stream bed, dragged logs straight down hillsides and had violated provisions of their contract with the Forest Service in ways that were damaging to Forest Service land, Bandelier, and the water quality in Capulin Canyon. The Forest Service had not followed their own guidelines in planning or executing the timber sale, guidelines that had been worked out with the Park Service and the public. The Forest Service had failed to supervise the contractor although the timber sale was happening in an area that had an unusual amount of public interest and interest from the Park Service. By doing long-term damage to the streams and slopes above the stream, the Forest Service appeared to have violated the Forest Service Organic Act that requires the agency to protect watersheds as a top agency priority[56]. The timber sale also violated the Forest Service's own statutory planning process. Worse, despite efforts by the Park Service and interested members of the public, the Los Utes timber sale again proved that cooperative agreements between the two agencies to protect Bandelier waters and wildlife were not followed when logging or other activities took place on the Forest Service side of the Bandelier boundary.

After the Los Utes timber sale, the Forest Service Regional Office in Albuquerque investigated the legal failings of the timber sale and removed Bud Stephenson, then District Ranger on the

Jemez District, from his post. The Forest Supervisor, Maynard Rost also was transferred as a result of the political fallout.

In 1991 the Santa Fe National Forest began a new planning process under the National Environmental Policy Act (NEPA) for the "Dome Diversity Unit" which was a new name for the upper watersheds of the Bandelier Wilderness, outside of the park boundary. Bandelier staff again struggled to participate in the public process and have its concerns addressed. They offered data and suggestions to enhance wildlife habitat, protect archeological sites and reduce motorized use of the upper watersheds. A flurry of staff changes at the Forest Service hindered the process but with the new District Ranger, John Peterson in place, the Bandelier staff suddenly found out in August 1991 that the Forest Service had signed the Environmental Assessment for the Dome Diversity Unit and that Bandelier's comments had been completely ignored.

District Ranger Peterson informed Bandelier staff in an August 1991 meeting that yet another timber sale was being cut on the Bandelier boundary and that the Forest Service commitment to close roads and protect Bandelier and wildlife from off road vehicles, committed to in their own Forest Plan and in the Dome Diversity Unit Environmental Assessment, would not be met.

Here national politics began to affect the Bandelier landscape. With a continuing drive from the Forest Service Washington DC Office, local ranger districts were struggling to "get the cut out" and meet "timber targets" given to them as performance standards. John Peterson and other district rangers scoured their districts for stands of trees to log, at a fiscal loss to the federal treasury, to maintain their good standing within the agency's central planning apparatus. Although no old growth forest remained on the Dome Diversity Unit[57], the Forest Service was "reentering" old timber cuts on the Bandelier boundary in a desperate effort to meet their assigned targets[58].

The 1980s and 1990s had been a decade of intensive logging of national forests across America with plenty of controversy. The northern spotted owl had flown into popular consciousness as the herald of the decimation of the big old forests of the Pacific Northwest and the end of the logging of the last big trees in that region. The timber industry fought to get back in Congress what the courts had taken away under the Endangered Species Act. Senator Mark Hatfield of Oregon attached a "rider" on a must-pass budget bill in 1995 that exempted logging done on trees burned by forest fires from environmental review and the constraints of most environmental law. The so-called "Salvage Rider" which environmentalists would dub the "rider from hell" would play into the history of the land at the base of Cerro Grande[59].

In the spring of 1996 the Dome Fire started from an abandoned campfire on Santa Fe National Forest land near upper Sanchez Canyon immediately west of Bandelier. The fire spread across Forest Road 289 to the east and north, directly toward Los Alamos 15 miles away. It quickly became a project fire as 1996 was a dry year and the national forest land the fire was feeding on was a dry mix of logging slash and small trees which had grown up in the aftermath of repeated logging operations. Within 48 hours, the Bandelier fire crews, joined by fire crews from the Forest Service Jemez and Espanola districts would call for plenty more help as the fire roiled into a black smoke spewing, fast moving monster. Within two days a large (Type Two) fire camp was set up at Graduation Flats, virtually on the Bandelier boundary and fire crews were rolling in from all points in the western United States as air tankers rumbled overhead.

For the many Bandelier staff that were working on the Dome fire (which was a Forest Service project fire) including Charisse Sydoriak and Al King, the Dome Fire was a potential disaster. The fire was poised to leave national forest land and enter upper Frijoles Canyon at the base of Cerro Grande. Bandelier's staff knew this was a "jackpot" of fuels which could create enough heat to propel the fire into the thickets of unmanaged, overgrown, fire suppressed forests that lay between Bandelier and Los Alamos. Everyone was eager to see the fire contained before it got to Frijoles Canyon, yet Frijoles was directly in the path of the fire and as is usually the case with large fires, the efforts of people were doing little to halt the fire's march toward Los Alamos.

Charisse Sydoriak would later recount how the Dome fire arrived at the rim of Frijoles Canyon while a massive air campaign against the fire was unfolding. The incident commanders had called in multiple drops of retardant to "paint" the rim of Frijoles Mesa at Obsidian Ridge to try to stop the fire from burning into the canyon and on to Los Alamos. Just as the fire arrived at the rim, as if some old Pueblo Indian spirits were directing it, the winds changed direction, came up from the north and pushed the fire back into the already burned area. The Dome fire was finished and as is often the case, the weather, not people, had done it in.

The aftermath of the Dome fire was to be a critical time for Bandelier and the health of its watersheds. The upper reaches of Capulin and Alamo Canyons were severely burned. With vegetation that once held soils in place burned away, the potential for scouring floods affecting the canyons, which the National Park Service has a statutory responsibility to protect, became a possibility. For this reason, Bandelier's staff began to take a great interest in the fire rehabilitation effort that the Forest Service was planning.

To make a long story shorter, the Forest Service Jemez District did little to acknowledge the concerns of the Park Service downstream during the fire rehabilitation process despite a flurry of communication from staff and scientists at Bandelier to District Ranger John Peterson. Bandelier's resident scientist, Dr. Craig Allen was concerned that erosion be controlled quickly and he advocated that dead trees be felled across the slopes by the thousands to slow the movement of soils when the rains came. Bandelier staff was also concerned that the aerial grass seeding that would take place after the fire might include exotic (weed) grass seed as it had been after the La Mesa Fire. The Forest Service, beyond the sort of response a member of the public might receive, did not acknowledge their concerns.

Things then deteriorated. While the Dome Fire was still burning, Forest Service District Ranger John Peterson announced at the fire camp that he was going to salvage log the fire area under the accelerated approval regime pressed by Senator Mark Hatfield in the Salvage Rider[60]. No other salvage logging under the eased restrictions of the law had been proposed outside the Pacific Northwest. Perhaps John Peterson was trying to get a feather in his cap with the Forest Service by pushing a controversial timber sale through a highly controversial rider. In any case his proposal came as a blow to Bandelier's staff which felt a complete collapse in trust and understanding with the Jemez District.

Ultimately activists and pressure from Congress defeated the salvage logging of the Dome Fire area but damage was done to Bandelier's relationship with the Forest Service. After years of trying to build a cooperative relationship with the Forest Service on the Dome area, one that would acknowledge the supremacy in law of Bandelier's ecological needs, the salvage logging proposal took both agencies back to square one and gave many in the public a sense of futility in their own involvement with the Forest Service planning process. A great deal of public effort had gone into having the Forest Service designate the Dome area near Bandelier as a cultural resource conservation and recreational use area under the Santa Fe Forest Plan. Yet the Dome Fire had proven the Forest Service saw it as an area for logging and grazing despite outside concerns.

For many the controversy that erupted over the salvage logging proposal eclipsed what could have been a strong education opportunity for the people of Los Alamos and other nearby areas on the need to address fuel loading on public lands near communities. According to many on the scene, the Dome Fire very nearly burned into Los Alamos. Had the Forest Service and Park Service cooperated on pressing the message of fire danger to Los Alamos, perhaps more preparation could have been made by Los Alamos in advance of the inevitable fire to come.

The troubles with the Dome fire recovery effort and the salvage logging proposal fueled a long political effort to have Bandelier's boundary moved from its current position crossing a majority of the park's watersheds to a position at the rim of Cochiti Canyon which would have given the National Park Service control of the whole watersheds of all the park's major streams. Had it not been for the Cerro Grande Fire, this boundary adjustment may well have happened as part of the legislation that designated the Valles Caldera (Baca Ranch) as a public National Preserve in July 2000[61].

The Valles Caldera National Preserve designation did allow for minor additions to Bandelier National Monument from land previously owned by the Baca Ranch; particularly at the base of Cerro Grande near existing Bandelier land. The hoped for adjustment of the whole west boundary was a casualty of the backlash against the National Park Service following the Cerro Grande blaze.

Congress did ask that the Forest Service and the National Park Service jointly prepare a "Report to Congress on Management Alternatives for the Dome Watershed." However, after the Cerro Grande fire the study was completed in obscurity and it had no affect on agency behavior. Since then, the issue has not been revisited.

In private, Forest Service employees would often mention the change in relations that occurred when Charisse Sydoriak replaced Bandelier's Chief of Resources Management John Lissoway in 1993. Mr. Lissoway maintained close camaraderie with his colleagues outside the Park Service, and was well known for gathering Forest Service fire people from throughout the area to help with prescribed burns. John was a native of the redwood country of northern California and never seemed to lose touch with his rural roots. Charisse Sydoriak had a different approach, one reflected in her goal to build scientifically credible programs at Bandelier such as those she had participated in at Yosemite National Park. Charisse is ambitious with good academic credentials and excellent program building and management skills but many complained that her manner was sometimes brusque and her relations with the Forest Service were not always warm according to people in both agencies. In fairness, the relationship with the Jemez District in particular was tense and complicated during Ms. Sydoriak's time at Bandelier, a fact that had very little to do with her.

By the time the Cerro Grande Fire occurred, Charisse had built a resources management organization at Bandelier that was one of the best in the National Park system. It included Fire Management Officer Al King who had responsibility for contacts with Forest Service fire professionals. For whatever reason, the days of sharing crews on an even-trade basis that existed during John Lissoway's tenure ended before Cerro Grande. This lack of cooperation was partly responsible for the short staffing of the Cerro Grande prescribed fire on May 4.

The long and troubled history of public land management on the Pajarito Plateau, punctuated by the arrival of the Manhattan Project and Los Alamos, resulted in agency boundaries that didn't make sense from a landscape level, especially in a fire prone landscape. With the complications of confused mission and decreasing funding at the US Forest Service slowing fuel management to a crawl around Los Alamos prior to 2000, the lack of good cooperation and communication between the National Park Service at Bandelier and the Forest Service led to an explosive fire situation as one agency pursued aggressive fuel reduction through fire reintroduction while the other pressed for funding to safeguard what both agencies knew was a town right in the line of an inevitable firestorm.

[1] Since 2000, much progress has been made in shifting Forest Service management away from reflexive fire suppression through a series of revisions to the 1995 National Fire Plan. Also the Forest Service has, with the help of Congress, increased its budgets for fuel reduction around communities.

[2] Hal K. Rothman <u>On Rims and Ridges</u> (University of Nebraska Press, 1992) pg. 62.

[3] The original boundaries of the Jemez Forest Reserve extended from the Colorado border to the Canada de Cochiti land grant south of present day Bandelier National Monument. The reserve excluded active land grants such as the Tierra Amarilla, Baca, and part of the Ramon Vigil Grant. See <u>Newsletter of the Los Alamos Historical Society</u>, vol. 25, number 2, (June 2006)

[4] Tucker and Fitzpatrick <u>Men Who Matched the Mountains</u>, (US Govt. Printing Office 1972)

[5] William D. Rowley, <u>US Forest Service Grazing and Rangelands, a History</u> (Texas A&M University Press 1985)

[6] A 30-inch diameter Douglas fir cut on Pajarito Mountain in 2005 was born in 1610, the year of Santa Fe's establishment as a Spanish Capitol. This tree was large enough to be useful to a lumber mill. A tree of similar size at low altitude in the Pacific Northwest would be less than half the age.

[7] Randal O'Toole <u>Reforming the Forest Service</u> (Island Press 1988) pg. 138.

[8] Debora L. Donahue <u>The Western Range Revisited – Removing Livestock From Public Lands to Conserve Native Biodiversity</u>, (University of Oklahoma Press, 1999) pg 232.

[9] See Rodrick Nash <u>Wilderness and the American Mind</u>, (Yale University Press 1982) Pg. 129.

[10] The Valle Timber Sale.

[11] Foresters consider the "structure" of a forest to mean the number, sizes and configuration of trees on a given acre of woodland. The structure of southwest forests changed markedly following livestock grazing, fire suppression, and logging of large old trees.

[12] John Herron, <u>Forests under Fire</u>, (University of Arizona Press 2001)

[13] National Association of Civilian Conservation Corps. Alumni, history website.

[14] Stephen J. Pyne, <u>Fire in America, A Cultural History of Wildland and Rural Fire</u>, (University of Washington Press 1982) pg. 273.

[15] Stephen J. Pyne, <u>Fire in America, A Cultural History of Wildland and Rural Fire</u>, (University of Washington Press 1982) pg 275

[16] The Santa Fe National Forest dispatcher was reluctant to send the Santa Fe Hotshots to the Cerro Grande prescribed fire before it was declared a

wildfire because the crew is held for initial attack on new wildfires. Once the fire was declared a "wildfire" the hotshot crews were available without hesitation.

[17] David Carle, <u>Burning Questions, America's Fight with Nature's Fire,</u> (Praeger Press 2002) pg. 176

[18] Supra pg. 180

[19] Twelve fire fighters burned to death on the South Canyon Fire near Glenwood Springs, Colorado when fire moved up a slope from below and overwhelmed them. The same sort of disaster had occurred in the Mann Gulch Fire in Montana in 1949. In response rules no longer allow fire fighters to be placed on slopes or in drainages where fire can move up on them from below. In the first days of fighting the Cerro Grande fire, the upper north branch of Frijoles Canyon that drains from Cerro Grande was considered off-limits to fire fighters due to the potential for this sort of entrapment. A large area surrounding this drainage then became the fire perimeter. Burning out the perimeter of this drainage caused fire to be introduced over a large area and the fire that escaped to Los Alamos was a "black line" fire (as opposed to a "back fire"), not the fire set as a prescribed fire on the top of the mountain. See chapter 5.

[20] New fire starts on the Santa Fe National Forest are evaluated with the same process that National Park Service personnel used in decided if they would begin the Cerro Grande prescribed fire. A Wildland Fire Assessment and a "go/no go" checklist is completed based on fire location, weather conditions, availability of personnel for suppression, and detailed analysis of the fuels in the area and their relative flammability.

[21] The Valles Ecosystem Management Area is not to be confused with the Valles Caldera National Preserve, which is a 89,000-acre area over the crest of the Sierra de los Valles from the Valles EMA.

[22] Randal O'Toole, <u>Reforming the Forest Service</u>, (Island Press 1985) pg. 4.

[23] This information came from numerous interviews with Bill Armstrong between 2000 and 2007.

[24] Letter from Bryan Bird, Forest Guardians to Santa Fe National Forest, dated March 4, 1998. The Forest Service has a long history of using commercial timber sales as tools for other goals like "wildlife habitat restoration." Congress funds timber sales where large trees are removed and sold to industry in the Forest Service budget process. Before 2000 the Forest Service had not done much fire abatement thinning where commercially useless small trees were targeted for removal. With the Forest Service's long history of disguising timber sales as other sorts of projects, Forest Guardians was understandably suspicious of the agency's intent near Los Alamos. Environmental groups use the scoping process during the preparation of an environmental impact statement to ask the Forest Service to consider issues of concern such as those raised by Forest Guardians in the Valles EMA. By asking the agency to look at the economics and affects on specific wildlife, the environmental group is able to appeal the

agency's eventual decision if it fails to consider the matters the group asks about in writing. Such appeals can turn into lawsuits, which are expensive and time consuming for all. Many consider this process an obstruction to management action by the agency, but Forest Guardians was honest in their effort to steer agency study toward issues that could result in better management actions in favor of certain wildlife species or watershed protection.

[25] Personal interview with Bill Armstrong March 9, 2006.

[26] There is some confusion over the first national park. Hot Springs National Reservation in Arkansas was established as the first federal reservation of land in 1832 but did not become a national park until 1921. Yosemite National Park in California was first set aside as federal land in 1864 but ceded to California before returning to federal ownership as a national park in 1906. Yellowstone was the first land carved from public domain as a national park in 1872, thus America's first national park.

[27] Alfred Runte National Parks, The American Experience (Bison Books 1987) pg. 37.

[28] Richard W. Sellars Preserving Nature in the National Parks, a History. (Yale University Press 1997) pg. 37.

[29] Encyclopedia of American Forest and Conservation History (McMillian Publishing 1983) pg. 465.

[30] 16 USCA sec. 1

[31] Richard W. Sellars Preserving Nature in the National Parks, a History. (Yale University Press 1997) pg. 70

[32] Richard W. Sellars Preserving Nature in the National Parks, a History. (Yale University Press 1997) pg 201

[33] Richard W. Sellars Preserving Nature in the National Parks, a History. (Yale University Press 1997) pg. 221.

[34] The fact that land managers in the United States refer to the natural world as the "resource" reflects the Western view of nature as a collection of supplies for human use. Humans in this view are separate from nature. This view has its roots in the Biblical origin myth, where humans were given dominion over the earth and its creatures. Pre Christian European views and those of Indian cultures in North America did not view humans as separate from nature. Arguably, our perceived separation from nature and our sense that nature is a "resource" for our use allows us to abuse ir rather than integrating with it.

[35] Early park managers wanted to protect friendly animals like elk and deer from predators and made arbitrary decisions about tolerable predator numbers to achieve these goals.

[36] Richard W. Sellars Preserving Nature in the National Parks, a History. (Yale University Press 1997). Pg 70

[37] Isle Royale National Park in Michigan has a native gray wolf population. This park is on an island, close to the Canadian border where wolves don't threaten other land users.

[38] 16 U.S.C. 431-433

[39] Hal K. Rothman On Rims and Ridges, (University of Nebraska Press 1992) pg. 142.

[40] Hal K. Rothman On Rims and Ridges, (University of Nebraska Press 1992) pg 133

[41] Much of this land was later transferred to the Atomic Energy Commission that operated Los Alamos Scientific Laboratory.

[42] Bandelier National Monument, an Administrative History Chapter 3. (Published on the internet at www.nps.gov/band/adhi/)

[43] The Park Service remains largely dependent on the Forest Service for fire suppression support to this day due to the enormous Forest Service fire fighting apparatus and the relatively small budgets of the National Park Service and its smaller land base.

[44] Steven J. Pyne Fire in America, (University of Washington Press 1982) pg 111

[45] Jan W. van Wagtendonk Historical Perspective of the National Park Service Fire Program, (USGS Field Station, Yosemite Field Station 2001) Oral presentation.

[46] David Carle Burning Questions, America's Fight with Nature's Fire, (Praeger Press 2002) pg. 140.

[47] Sellers and Despain, Fire Management in Yellowstone National Park. (Tall Timber Fire Ecology Conference Proceedings number 14, 1974) pg. 101

[48] The NPS fire management is guided by a "Director's Order" number 18, known within the service as RM 18 which is updated regularly.

[49] The so-called National Fire Plan was compiled by the secretaries of Agriculture and Interior in 1995 to coordinate and consolidate federal wildfire and prescribed fire policy. The National Fire Plan was revised a the request of President Clinton in 2000 after that year's large fire season.

[50] Hal Rothman Bandelier National Monument, an Administrative History, (Southwest Cultural Resources Center Professional Paper number 14) pg. 18.

[51] The majority of the Frijoles watershed falls within NPS boundaries except for the mesa top above the upper reaches of the canyon to the south. This area is penetrated by a road and was logged by the Forest Service in 1977 over the objection of the National Park Service concerned about erosion and damage to obsidian mines used by the early Puebloans.

[52] 39 Stat. 1764

[53] Memo from Superintendent John Hunter to National Park Service Regional Director John Cook December 14, 1979.

[54] Hal Rothman Bandelier National Monument, an Administrative History, (Southwest Cultural Resources Center Professional Paper no. 14, 1988) pg. 41.

[55] Randal O'Toole, Reforming the Forest Service, (Island Press 1985) pg. 22.

[56] Organic Act of 1897, 16 USC 473-478.

[57] Personal communication with Craig Allen, Jemez Mountains US Biological Survey Office.

[58] Craig Allen of the Jemez Mountains US Geologic Survey Office compiled a chronology of timber sales in the Santa Fe National Forest in the Bandelier headwaters (Bandelier archives) that removed old growth trees from the watersheds. In 1947 a 2 million-board foot logging operation took place on Mesa del Rito above upper Frijoles Canyon. In the late 1960s a huge timber sale took place along the Bandelier boundary that netted 65 million board feet. In 1978 salvage logging took place after the La Mesa fire on 1,250 acres followed by a 1,000 acre cut near Rabbit Hill. The Forest Service plowed 1,000 acres to prepare for tree planting in 1982 without archaeological clearances required by law and destroyed 100 archaeological sites which resulted in a lawsuit against the Forest Service by the state of New Mexico which shut down logging operations in the Santa Fe National Forest for a period of time. The 1983 Sawyer sale cut 2.7 million board feet, the 1985 Alamo timber sale cut 3.8 million board feet, the 1989 Los Utes timber sale cut 4.2 million board feet and the 1993 Dome sale cut 1 million board feet.

[59] A "rider" is a piece of legislation inserted onto another unrelated piece of legislation.

[60] The "salvage rider" was a package of legislative language originating in the Pacific Northwest's timber industry in 1994 and 1995. It was circulated in the House of Representatives by Representative Norm Dicks (D-WA.) and Charlie Taylor (R-NC) and in the Senate by Slade Gorton of Washington. The language relaxed National Environmental Policy Act (NEPA) review of Forest Service and Bureau of Land Management timber sales that targeted dead timber but also focused on 60 timber sales in the Northwest that were held up by Endangered Species Act concerns for the marbled murrelet, a seabird that nests in large old trees near the ocean. Initially the language, later referred to as "Section 318," was attached to an Interior Department Appropriations bill but ultimately was attached to the Oklahoma City bombing relief legislation and allowed for relaxed environmental reviews of salvage timber sales nationwide for a year.

[61] Public Law No. 106-248.

Chapter 5

Lighting the Fire

(Note: Readers may find it helpful to follow events described here in the pages of figures at the end of Chapter 6.)

There are times in all of our lives that stand out in memory, and are cloaked in deep regret over the years that follow. For the twelve people who gathered at the Interagency Fire Cache near Bandelier National Monument on May 4, 2000, the following two weeks would become profoundly life changing. So important were the events that followed for them personally, for the history of Bandelier National Monument and its region and for the whole system of public lands in the United States, that if any one of them could have foreseen the consequences of their coming actions they all would have gone home before ever beginning their project.

The twelve people gathered in a metal sided fire station in a field of scattered trees burned by New Mexico's first superfire, the La Mesa burn of 1978. The building was the new "Interagency Fire Cache" directly near Bandelier National Monument's north boundary. The cache is full of fire fighting supplies and offices for conducting wildfire operations. Yet those who gathered there were not an interagency crew. These twelve people were prescribed fire specialists from the National Park Service.

The cache is built on a peripheral piece of LANL land where sixty years of nuclear research sometimes drove explosives testers to the fringe of the lab's 25 square miles, and therefore to the boundary of a once-remote Bandelier National Monument. In the 1960s, the lab hid an underground nuclear test on the site where the fire cache would someday be, detonating something classified at depth, then virtually abandoning the site and its plutonium contamination deep in the ground, until a sense of urgency about wildfire drove the lab to offer some acres of land for a fire cache to be shared by three agencies[1].

The dull looking new building replaced the old fire cache at Bandelier National Monument that was housed in an old stone garage in the Headquarters Complex in Frijoles Canyon in the heart of this national monument. The Bandelier fire program had outgrown this historic building, used by fire crews since the 1930s. The larger cache fit the expanding fire program conceived by Bandelier's first resource manager John Lissoway in the late 1970s.

Having completed 58 prescribed fires in 20 years, Bandelier's resource managers were finished with the easy areas and were ready to move into the most dangerous and risky terrain, high canyons choked with thickets of big trees and downed logs and branches. Bandelier's controlled burning program was unique on this side of the sprawling Jemez Mountains.

The team gathering in the fire cache was also going to do something else new and risky. Not only were they going to light a prescribed fire on the edge of the park, smack up against some of the most dangerously fire-starved lands on the neighboring Santa Fe National Forest, they were also going to start the fire in spring, the time when research showed many natural fires burned in the high country of the Southwest.

Spring would give the crew many benefits. The same burn had been attempted twice in the fall, but always grass and other fuels were too wet from the summer rains and the lengthening fall shadows to burn hot enough to "achieve objectives" which in this case meant killing enough medium sized trees and trees invading historic meadows to enable the land to function as it did before sheep and cattle depleted its grasses and upset natural fire cycles. Spring was often dry enough to allow fairly hot fires to burn in the high country as they used to. Spring presented great risks. Spring in New Mexico is often windy, very windy, and winds can transform tame fire into a raging inferno.

Mike Powell, the fire boss for this particular burn, and Al King the Fire Management Officer (FMO) for Bandelier went over the objectives of the burn with the assembled crew. Their primary objective, as always, was firefighter and public safety. Objective two was using fire to reduce buildups of standing and dead fuel in the burn unit as well as thickets of young trees. The third objective was to improve the ecology of the highest elevation in Bandelier National Monument, to restore rare Montane grasslands, stimulate new aspen tree growth and open up forests to allow for a wide diversity of plant life, and therefore animal life, to thrive.

These three objectives were key, and park scientists were eager to see the results of the soon to be completed prescribed fire. Bandelier has one of six major montane grasslands in the Jemez Mountains, a rare ecotype where native bunchgrass mixes with wildflowers at the peaks of the eastern Jemez. Once grazed heavily then denied fires by human land managers, the grasslands at nearly 11,000 feet were being invaded by thousands of trees that natural fire would historically have killed before they grew as tall as the grass. Without new fire and other measures, the grasslands would soon be overrun by forest, and the elk, hawks, small mammals, insects and other animals that depend on the grasslands for survival would have to move elsewhere for habitat or die off. All the montane grasslands of the Jemez were in trouble and the National Park Service was the only agency taking an interest in their preservation.

The Bandelier staff had recently experienced the 16,000 acre Dome Fire in 1996, which had started from an abandoned campfire on national forest land to the south and roared across the upper end of Bandelier National Monument before being stopped by saturation bombing with fire retardant along the rim of the gaping 1000 foot deep upper Frijoles Canyon; a strategy that saved Los Alamos from near-certain conflagration. Aware of the danger and aware too that the US Forest Service was doing little to reduce fire danger in the area between Bandelier and Los Alamos, the Park Service was continuing to reduce fuels along its northern edge so that its natural and prescribed fire programs could continue with less worry about fire escaping onto fire starved Forest Service lands to the immediate north.

Bandelier's Unit 8 had been burned in 1995. This area of meadows, fir, pine and aspen lay just east of the current burn unit, on an east-west running shoulder of Cerro Grande. In that case, three engine crews of Forest Service firefighters joined a training crew from Los Alamos National Lab and a crew of National Park Service prescribed fire specialists in guarding the national forest boundary and helping burn the area. The fire had achieved its goals in many areas as thickets of dense fir and spruce trees burned with flames 30 feet high, creating a temporary hell of fire in biologically stagnant areas. Yet elsewhere in the same burn area (unit) the fire had only smoldered, leaving many places fire-prone and virtually unburned.

The Bandelier fire crews had burned almost all the area bordering Los Alamos National Laboratory and national forest to the north, all except Unit 1, the Cerro Grande unit at the top of the park.

Now the Bandelier fire staff, an almost completely new staff to Bandelier, was ready to attempt Cerro Grande again, in a dry year when it was possible they could clear away fuels before any future fire could come out of Frijoles Canyon or out of the Valles Caldera to the west. Doing a spring burn meant risking the unpredictable spring weather.

All winter the staff watched the conditions in the Bandelier high country, using a remote weather station at the base of the prescribed fire unit. Measuring humidity, snowfall, and then in April, the moisture in the sticks, logs, grass and pine debris. To kill many of the trees invading the old grasslands and to remove thickets of middle-aged trees, they would need a hot fire. Getting a fire to burn hot enough to kill standing timber at almost 11,000 feet would be no small feat.

High country is cool and wet with higher precipitation, less solar radiation, and lower temperatures overall. In years of good snowfall, the forests above 8,000 feet may not dry out much before the summer rains come in July and begin to wet them again before fall. May 2000 presented what appeared to Bandelier fire planners to be a perfect opportunity since snowfall had been minimal; yet enough late snow had fallen to keep the area from being tinder dry.

The week before, the same crew had burned Unit 40 down by

the Entrance Road to Bandelier. There they had burned 30 acres of grass, pinon and juniper and ponderosa pine. This much drier area gave the crew no control problems. With this success freshly behind them, the crews moved up to Cerro Grande.

Yet spring burning was making Bandelier's neighbors nervous. It was unprecedented on the Pajarito Plateau. On the Unit 40 burn the week before, Los Alamos National Lab firefighters had seen a tree torching from the highway at about sunset on May 4. Alarmed, they had called Bandelier. Two fire crew members were sent down from the side of Cerro Grande, where they were hefting gear up the mountain, to keep an eye on the hot spot in Unit 40. The Los Alamos Fire Department had little experience with wildland fire, being specialized in structural fire and chemical hazards at a scientific laboratory filled with explosives, unusual alloys, high voltages, and radioactive materials. The laboratory fire crew offered to drive their fire engine overland into the burn area and extinguish the burning tree, something that is forbidden by National Park management standards which protect the land from vehicle traffic, and which would have done little good anyway since the burning tree was well within a burned area and not likely to spread fire. The Park staff recognized that the isolated tree was a routine event in a fire and not one that would cause the fire to heat up or spread.

Given that the torching tree was really a minor spectacle on a dark night and was surrounded by burned area, it posed no threat and everyone left the area, the Bandelier pair returning to the east side of Cerro Grande to resume preparations for the test burn. Yet this meeting between Bandelier fire crewmembers and laboratory firefighters near the torching tree on May 4 left lingering questions that would come up repeatedly following the coming wildfire. Knowing that the Bandelier staff was planning to burn the side of Cerro Grande beginning that night, Gene Darling, the wildland fire specialist for Los Alamos National Laboratory said in passing to Holly Snyder; "I wish you wouldn't light the Cerro Grande burn..." because fuels were extremely dry lower down. This statement would later prove to be a center of dispute as the press reported Mr. Darling was "warning Bandelier not to light the fire."

Fire on the Mountain

Two roads go near Cerro Grande. State Highway 4 sweeps over a pass on the south side of the mountain after curving through the upper end of Frijoles Canyon. The other is an old ranch road, barely two tracks through the grass, that struggles up through meadows and woods and ends at the base of steep grasslands on the east edge of the mountain.

Proposed phases of prescribed Cerro Grande burn

4

On May 4 the Park fire crew staged their fire operation on the highway and were instructed to drive trucks on the abandoned dirt track up the mountain only in an emergency. This is standard practice for burning in a wilderness area, particularly in a national park. The crewmembers hoisted backpack pumps along the east side of the designated "management area" and dropped them off in stages. This way when they started to burn the grass, they would have plenty of water for controlling the flames. This hard work had gone on for much of the afternoon with everyone helping including Paul Gleason, an expert fire specialist from the National Park Service regional office in Denver.

The water hauling was hard work. Twelve Bandelier fire specialists were joined by a fire crew from the Northern Pueblo Agency (NPA), a Bureau of Indian Affairs sponsored fire fighting organization based at San Juan Pueblo (Okay Owinge), a Pueblo Indian reservation north of Los Alamos. Another Northern Pueblo fire crew had helped with the burn the week before down by Bandelier's entrance road. That crew had been strong and able and the crew that was now hauling water up the side of Cerro Grande hopefully would do as well.

In the Southwest, various Indian tribes had organized fire-fighting teams since the 1930s. Some of the Pueblos were particularly well known for having capable fire crews, including Zuni and Jemez Pueblos where long traditions of running made them well suited for grueling work on fire lines[2].

With twelve Bandelier fire fighters and twenty people (a "crew") from the NPA, along with Mike Powell, the Burn Boss and Al King, they felt they had plenty of people to start and control the burn. Twenty of these thirty-two people were to work most of the night then be relieved in the morning while the core Bandelier fire people would work and rest in stages for the duration of the burn.

By six in the evening, the crew assembled near the top of Cerro Grande. Al King, a tobacco chewing[3] veteran fire expert in his late thirties, noticed that some of the Northern Pueblo Agency crew seemed weary from the trudge up the mountain. He noted this as the group gathered to hear Mike Powell give a strategy and safety talk below a dull, cloudless sunset.

The view from the peak was stunning. Spread below them were the upper reaches of Bandelier National Monument with its gaping Frijoles Canyon thickly cloaked in timber. Beyond that the bald mesas burned by the La Mesa and Dome fires reached to the Rio Grande Canyon, the great escarpment that guarded the Santo Domingo Basin and the desert peaks that stood against the dusty sweep of the Great Plains beyond.

Just below the group lay their "unit," the area they planned to burn over the next four or five days. The grassy peak where they stood swept down into a great bowl, bound on either side by timber-covered ridges. The bowl flattened out down near the highway, about 500 feet lower than where they stood. This side of the mountain, facing east and south was a mix of forest types, from high montane grassland where they were, to a blend of ponderosa pine and grass, and pine and fir forests on the ridges. Down in the bowl, relatively wet aspen forest cloaked the top of the Frijoles watershed.

Behind the group, on the backside of the mountain and outside of the National Park Service boundary, Cerro Grande dropped into Water Canyon. The north and west sides of the mountain were densely forested with rarely visited old forests that had not seen fire in more than 100 years. The Park Service/Forest Service boundary crossed through these forests arbitrarily. Five miles and three canyons beyond, Los Alamos sprawled over finger-like mesas.

Following a grueling two hour walk up a mile of slopes carrying backpack pumps with five gallons of water in each (around 40 pounds) through the thick forests and grass, Mike Powell explained to the group that they would burn the area (the unit) in three phases. Beginning with the top grassy ridges and more open forests, then working next into the denser timber and finishing in the dry flats below where they expected the driest and most dangerous conditions. The three phases of the burn would not necessarily be done simultaneously as they might have to wait to burn the bottom when conditions were right for a hot fire to kill many of the overcrowded trees.

To burn the desired area, they planned to contain the interior fire with strips of burn down the edges. This technique, called "black lining" would be the best way to contain a fire in the grasslands. An alternative technique of digging a strip through the grassland down to mineral soil would be time consuming and exhausting and damaging to the bunch grasses that covered Cerro Grande. Thus they would set fire to the grass, let it burn a wide strip then swat out the edges of the fire before burning down into the bowl below.

The area they planned to burn appears vast when you are standing anywhere on Cerro Grande. This was one of the largest prescribed fires ever attempted at Bandelier, one that would involve roughly 1,000 acres in rugged, steep terrain. Standing at the test burn area, the bottom of their unit looked distant. This was a large burn area and having divided it up into three phases helped, but the burn plan was unclear on how the fire would be paused at each phase change.

Knowing that this fire had been attempted twice before, they were counting on the experience of their predecessors as they went. In the 1992 attempt, done in the fall, the fire would not burn in the dense forests. Thus they thought they could count on the grass fire going out once it reached the trees. That happened in 1992, but would it happen in a spring burn in a drier year?

How could the crew predict how the fire would behave? As with all prescribed fires, fuel moisture is measured for weeks before lighting the match. Fire crews either calculate fuel moisture with charts based on weather conditions or use "fuel sticks" or flats of dowel rods suspended close to the forest floor that are weighed against their known dry weight. Doing this repeatedly over time and in different places on the burn unit tells the team how much moisture the woody debris on the site is holding. Sticks (and natural debris) gain moisture both from precipitation and from humidity in the air. Fine fuels like pine needles accumulate and lose moisture rapidly, particularly from humidity.

On Cerro Grande the fuel moisture readings had been calculated periodically, but most recently on April 14 and April 28 when the readings were 25% and 11% respectively. Thus fuel moisture had been dropping since the last snowfall on Cerro Grande in March. The 1.5 inches of moisture that fell over the previous two months was evaporating fast.

A critical element of the crew's "prescription" for the burn was fuel moisture. If moisture fell too low, the fire could be too active and difficult to control. If moisture went too high, the fire would not burn hot enough to kill 30 to 70% of the trees on the site as the team intended to do. Yet it had been a week since a team member had measured fuel moistures on Cerro Grande and when they were last measured, they were drying out.

Regarding the weather, the fire crews contacted the National Weather Service and asked for a "spot weather forecast" which told them what the weather was likely to do in that particular area over the next 12 hours. The forecast they got at noon for Cerro Grande called for temperatures in the low 70s, relative humidity about 15% and winds about five miles per hour. All of these conditions were what they wanted to meet their prescription.

As required with all prescribed fires, the Bandelier team had notified their neighboring agencies, the US Forest Service and Los Alamos National Laboratory, of their intent to burn. Likewise, they had notified the state of New Mexico and obtained an air quality permit. They notified the Santa Fe Zone dispatch office as well, because they knew they might need to call them to send "contingency resources" or additional staff if needed. Through these notifications, no warnings not to do the prescribed fire were received from anyone, contrary to what some of the local press later reported.

Setting Fire

At seven in the evening on May 4, they lit the match, a tiny flicker of flame in the gathering darkness. Nobody knew this tiny flame would become a very big fire indeed. The flame lit two drip torches. As with all prescribed fires, this one would begin with a test burn, a contained experimental burn a few feet across to insure that the fire would achieve its objectives and would behave as predicted.

With most of the crew standing by, the two igniters, those with the drip torches, set about dropping lines of burning fuel into the grass. Their chosen place for the test burn was right below the peak of Cerro Grande, on an east and south facing slope that flattens out into a long nearly flat corridor of grass. This spot was chosen because it represented dry grass with a few trees, and their plan was to burn only this fuel type that night.

Fifty feet north of the test burn area; a dense stand of spruce and fir began a forest that went almost unbroken for 40 miles to the north. This forest rolled into the upper reaches of a series of canyons. West of the test burn, a short slope rose to the peak of Cerro Grande but below the peak thick grassland swept around the hump-like peak joining a long grassy opening that sloped hundreds of feet to a small timbered knoll to south and west. Finally, to the south of the test burn area, the land sloped away into a forest of ponderosa pine with dense grass around their trunks.

Prescribed Burn Area

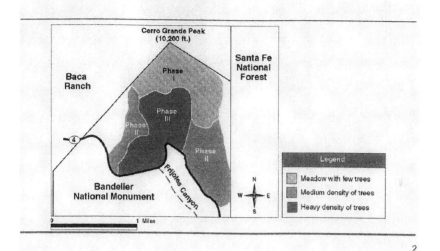

2

If the test burn showed good results, the team planned to begin burning to the east, down the long level grassland bound by dense forest on the north and the open ponderosa pine slopes to the south. In a sense they would be working their way along a corridor of grassland until they got to a point where the ridge turned south and east and began to drop down.

At first the fire was in thin grass but soon moved into deeper grass and began to move downhill. Since it was meeting their objectives, the crew kept going. The test burn blended seamlessly into the larger operation. Almost at once, a tree within the test burn area torched, burning clear to its top in a sudden whoosh. Spruce trees tend to burn this way as they have stiff pitchy branches with bark that invites fire with its broken surface and almost furry twigs. Even so, to have a tree torch from the heat of a grass fire showed how dry the live trees were. More trees would torch this way as the fire crept down into the open ponderosa pine grasslands to the south.

This torching was what the park ecologists were after. They wanted to kill trees in the grassland to restore the meadows. They had been unable to get many trees to do this in their 1992 attempt at the burn.

Yet a torching tree right off the bat could have been a warning to the crew that conditions were perhaps more extreme than their measurements and predictions showed. Live trees torch when they have been subjected to enough heat to cause the sap in their needles to volatize and catch fire. Normally this happens when a tree is preheated for a time, often by other trees burning nearby or by accumulations of woody fuels below the tree. To have a tree torch right out of a relatively cool grass fire showed that the live trees were quite dry and that this would be a feisty fire indeed.

On they went to the east with the Northern Pueblo Crew and 12 National Park Service crew members swatting out the edges of the fire with long fir tree branches and spraying the edges with water from backpack pumps as the fire spread to the east and south. The idea was to create an anchor point for the fire, a cool, burned area from which all fire lines would be attached. So they put out the edges of the burn as they went, making a strip of burned grass about 130 feet wide. This band of burned grass would be the containment line for the burning inside the unit.

Black lining turned out to be exhausting work. The winds picked up, coming from the north and west in gusts, almost right down the corridor of meadow they were working down. At ten that night, the crew gave up on putting out the south, downhill edge of the fire but kept swatting out the north side as they kept lighting. Two fire monitors watched the fire closely, noting its behavior, recording the weather conditions with belt weather kits and conveying the details to Fire Boss Mike Powell. The flame lengths were exactly what they had predicted and wanted. Weather was just as the Weather Service had predicted.

When the team stopped putting out the downhill edge of the black-line, they were deviating from their plan, which was to create a black-line with dead edges as a control line. By letting the fire creep down hill unchecked, they were risking having the fire make uphill runs as it burned unevenly. This was a risky move but one which apparently did not concern the fire command.

In the dark, with the lights of Santa Fe in the distance and Los Alamos spread below, the crew worked in relative peace.

The sweet smell of burning pine and grass filled the air and the flicker of flames in the smoke appeared farther and farther from the place where they met as a group to begin their test burn. As they worked the crew increasingly spread out to follow the fire. (Over the next six months, events would scatter this team across the country.)

Just after ten, with most attention focused on the progression of the fire to the east, Mike Powell noticed that the fire was creeping around the base of the knoll-like peak of the mountain. On its own, it was starting to burn down the sloping western grassland that bordered the vast Valles Calderas[4] whose boundary bisected the western edge of the unit that looked like a great ski slope. Mike was concerned as they had planned to burn that area deliberately later with a rested crew, but now, with a thick forest of spruce and fir on the Baca Ranch, and no permission to burn any of the Baca Ranch property, they would have to get ahead of this fire.

Mike called Al King up to the summit to discuss the situation. They agreed they would have to bring part of the crew over and begin igniting a black line on the west, swatting out the edge so that the fire working its way down the slope below them would stop in the already burned grass. Around 11 at night, they began black lining the west side. This spread the crew thin as they were now working on black lining on two sides of the fire with increasing distance between them. The first domino of disaster was slowly falling.

Just then, the crew working the east side headed by Ed Hyatt radioed Mike and told him the flames over there were getting too long and trees were torching down the slope. They decided to stop igniting the black line and let things calm down.

At this point, a band of blackened grass curved around the top ridge of the fire area with its northern edge cold. It had only entered the trees in one small place and the crew had stopped it before it moved into dense woods. The southern edge of the fire was working its way down into the bowl below and it was moving along more rapidly than they expected. The plan had been to put out the fire on the southern edge, just to establish a black line and then go back later and begin to back the fire down that slope with plenty of people and a secure fire line on the north and east. Since the work of smothering the south edge of the fire line proved to be too exhausting, the fire was moving on its own and the best-laid plans were now obsolete.

Around midnight Al King noticed that the many members of the Eight Northern Pueblo type two crew were flagging and tired. He had observed that many of them seemed out of physical condition as they climbed to the top of the peak at sunset. Later he had noted that some crewmembers lacked experience so he had paired them with more experienced workers so they could learn fire control techniques. At midnight it was clear they were exhausted and though they were in two separate teams, they were sent down to sleep at their trucks[5].

Al later recounted to the Board of Inquiry: "when I'd ask them to do things they wouldn't respond, they would look at each other and look back at me. I would ask again and they'd look at each other. That's when I decided to send them down the hill."

Al and Mike conferred on this problem. Here they had counted on the Pueblo crew making it through the night, albeit at a reduced level of activity, so they could rest many of the National Park Service staff people and have them ready to work fresh when the "burn period" came in late morning and the fire became more active.

The loss of the Pueblo crew would turn out to be a major blow to the prescribed fire and one of the key factors in its escape. Suddenly the bosses found themselves shorthanded and they would have to work tomorrow's crew all night, leaving tomorrow, during the hot dry and perhaps windy part of the day, with too few people or tired crews.

Losing the Northern Pueblo Agency crew opened not a can of worms, but a box of rattlesnakes for the burn planners. Suddenly the burn bosses were confronted with a weakness in their own planning and their hopes of handling this fire with their own team was out the window. They would have to replace the Pueblo crew and soon, and doing so would force them into the larger regional wildland fire organization, a world where Bandelier had not always had good relations over the last decade and where interagency rivalries and bureaucratic confusion often played out.

Fortunately the fire was mostly calm from midnight to three

in the morning. Nine people were on the fire, three on the east line and six on the west line. Overall, the fire was now about 150 acres and it continued to back down the hill into the interior of the burn unit, into the big bowl of timber and grass below. The possibility that the fingers of fire burning to the south could make "head runs" against either the west or east fire lines was a concern to the crew. When a fire gathers into a locally consolidated front, no matter how small, it can pick up steam and move fast, especially up a hill. A head of fire can gather like a snowball, getting bigger and bigger as it goes up hill. As the convection of heat from a head fire grows, it can throw embers skyward and these can drop down into the forest at some distance, starting new "spot" fires.

Mike Powell left the mountain to make phone calls at 1:30 in the morning. He had gone to his truck and driven to the Bandelier fire station where he made calls to try to get more people up to help with the burn early the next morning. His key resource for doing that was Santa Fe Dispatch, the radio center of the Santa Fe National Forest, the same people who had sent him the Northern Pueblo Crew[6].

For the crew on the mountain, the main challenge was to make sure there was a swath of already burned grass across the mountain if the fire should make a run from below. This meant watching the fire on the southern slopes and continuing the ignition of the black line to keep ahead of the downward advance of the fire on the slopes below. This work went on virtually all night on the east, where the winds were now pushing the fire toward their control line, and there were only three people working with the drip torches, backpack pumps and swatters.

At three in the morning, Mike called the US Forest Service dispatch center in Santa Fe. Given that the US Forest Service is the largest wildfire fighting organization in the United States, they take the lead in organizing and maintaining firefighting crews throughout the country. They have thousands of firefighters and they maintain direct organizational ties to the four other major land management agencies; the National Park Service, the Bureau of Land Management, the Bureau of Indian Affairs and the US Fish and Wildlife Service as well as state agencies. All of these agencies have fire crews and fire equipment, and they all help run the zone offices, but the coordination is left to the Forest Service and their national system of dispatchers who call up and send out crews and equipment as needed, mostly for wildfires.

Locally, there are two "zones" where dispatchers standby to assist the agencies. One zone in Albuquerque handles most of the central and southern part of New Mexico and parts of eastern Arizona. The Santa Fe Zone dispatches "resources" to fires in northern New Mexico up to the Colorado border. In fire talk, resources are fire fighters, helicopters, air planes that drop fire retardant (air tankers), engines (fire trucks designed for wildland fire complete with a crew of three) and any other tools and people needed for fighting fire.

These resources are classed according to their ability and sophistication. A "type 2" crew is a crew of able fire fighters with adequate experience. A "type 1" crew is a "hotshot" crew, a very experienced, highly trained and fit crew of firefighters, trained primarily to attack new fires in the "initial attack" process. Likewise wildland fire engines and helicopters are classed as type 1, 2 or 3 depending on their abilities.

Knowing that he needed more resources, Mike called Santa Fe Zone at 3:17 a.m. Joseph Leon, a stand-in Bureau of Land Management employee answered the phone. Mike told Mr. Leon that he needed a type one crew sent up to Cerro Grande for their prescribed fire quickly. Mr. Leon, who was a substitute for the usual night dispatcher did not feel he had the authority to call a crew in the middle of the night. He told Mike Powell to call back at seven in the morning when his boss was back in the office.

Mike Powell put the phone down frustrated. He had understood from previous conversations with the Forest Service dispatch office that he would be able to get more people for the fire within one and a half to four hours from when he called. Now he was looking at least seven hours to get more people on the fire. Powell had not told dispatcher Leon that this was an emergency. It wasn't yet. Powell needed more people for midmorning when the sun would heat up the land and wind was likely to cause the fire to be more active. To tell a dispatcher he had an urgent need for a crew would imply that Powell was having trouble with the fire and that it might not be a prescribed fire anymore but could be a "wildfire." Once a fire is declared a wildfire, the whole game changes. Mike did not have a wildfire on his hands.

Cerro Grande was still a prescribed fire, yet he knew that if he didn't get more help by ten in the morning, he might well have a wildfire on his hands.

Another major domino in the Cerro Grande disaster was now tipping. Since the Forest Service dispatch office in Santa Fe would be key for supplying crews and equipment quickly, the prescribed fire team was now dependent on them to get enough people on the fire the next day. Yet spotty communication between Bandelier and the Forest Service about the prescribed fire, and deeper problems with the way Interior Department agencies such as the National Park Service shared wildfire funding with the Forest Service (in the Department of Agriculture) were about to throw the Cerro Grande prescribed fire into a state of confusion.

Mike monitored his radio to keep track of activity among the crew burning on the mountain up above him. So far things were okay.

After he was told that he would need to call Santa Fe Dispatch back at seven, he went through a list of other fire crew contacts he had which may be more helpful. Of course calling anyone at 3:30 in the morning is problematic but he went through his list hoping to find a fire crew that would be willing to get on the road right away. Mike called the Espanola District of the Santa Fe National Forest and got no answer. He looked through his mobilization guide, a phone book for fire fighters. He called the Zion National Park prescribed fire team hoping they were in the area. No answer. He called Zuni Pueblo fire crews because they have several type 2 fire crews that have worked with the Park Service on prescribed burns before. No answer.

Mike got a call in to the Bandelier engine crew and these three people got ready to come up to Cerro Grande with their type 1 engine. Then he called Al on the radio and told him about his problem with Santa Fe Dispatch. Mike then tried to get a few minutes of sleep.

Meanwhile up on the fire lines, the crew was trying to keep ahead of the fire as it crept down into the unit. This meant they had to fire up their drip torches and get out their swatters from time to time on both the west and east fire lines to make sure the interior fire didn't hook around below them. At that hour, everyone wanted to be relaxing, gearing up for the morning burn period. The continued creep of the fire kept the crews working.

As the fire moved down the slope, flames from three inches to five feet were coming from the fire front as it moved down the hill at about 35 feet per hour. The smoke was making it hard to tell exactly where the flame front was.

Bandelier engine 91 arrived at the prescribed fire command post at four in the morning and drove out into the Valle Grande to the west to see if any errant fire was visible from the west fire line. Al King who was heading up the operation on the west side had plenty to be concerned about there. Thick forests of ponderosa pine with healthy grass and pine needle beds bordered much of the west line. Up higher, where Al was working, dense fir and spruce forests came right up to the meadow's edge. The Baca Ranch, which was still in private hands then had not agreed to allow any of their acreage to be burned by the Bandelier crew, so Al was busy keeping the fire away from the NPS/Baca Ranch boundary as well.

Engine 91 reported that no fire was visible outside of the control lines and they headed back to the base of the eastern fire line and started to hike up. By 4:30 in the morning they relieved Ed Hayatt and took over black lining down the east side. By then, the eastern fire line extended all the way down the long flat north-south trending meadow that dominates the east side of Cerro Grande.

Knowing that the prescribed fire on Cerro Grande may be challenging and planning to perhaps move on to burn the upper end of Frijoles Canyon (unit 9) Paul Gleason had been called down from the National Park Service's Denver Regional Office to help out. Mr. Gleason, a highly respected expert in wildland fire who had been on the NPS regional staff for about a year as a Wildland Fire Specialist, had spent 36 years working for the US Forest Service on all kinds of wildland fires. Recently he had been helping with the Anaconda Fire at Glacier National Park and with prescribed fires at Guadalupe Mountains and Lava Beds National Parks. Paul was also a professor of fire science at Colorado State University and was best known for his development of fire crew safety techniques that had been widely adopted in the fire service.

Paul had been helping haul water up to Cerro Grande and had been keeping an eye on the prescribed fire though he had no official position on the prescribed fire staff per se. In his mid-fifties, Paul had worked on enough fires to know how to deal with most situations. At 6:00 in the morning, Paul called Mike on the radio and told him to get a hot shot fire crew and a helicopter up to the fire as soon as possible.

Once he heard that Mike had been unable to get a fire crew mobilized by Santa Fe Dispatch right away at three in the morning, Paul was worried about holding the fire with such a short staff the next morning. With the early departure of the Northern Pueblo Crew, Paul knew the whole project's staff was "out of rotation" and that they needed to shore up the now tiring Bandelier Fire Use team.

"I was angry when I heard Mike hadn't been able to get a crew when he asked for one," he told investigators later. "This was the first geographic region I had worked in where you call for help and you don't get it."

At the Santa Fe Dispatch office meanwhile, Joseph Leon told John Romero, the head dispatcher about Mike Powell's 3:00 AM call at 7:00 when John came in. "Did they light that thing?" Mr. Romero is said to have exclaimed. Bandelier had called Dispatch at 5:00 the night before to notify them that the burn would go forward. That information had not moved through the dispatch staff very clearly and John Romero never knew until this moment that the prescribed fire had been lit for sure. (Contrary to press accounts at the time, Mr. Romero later testified under oath that he had never warned Bandelier not to light the prescribed fire. He did mention concerns about the "burn plan being unrealistic.")

"I felt we were sending a conflicting message to the public," Romero told the Board of Inquiry later. "On one hand we were fighting a fire north of Los Alamos and banning camp fires and Forest Service prescribed burns, and on the other the Park Service was starting a prescribed fire."

John Romero was now in the center of a cyclone. He knew that if the prescribed fire on Cerro Grande got out of hand it could easily reach Los Alamos in a matter of hours. He had been working over the last few days on the dispatch desk when fire crews had put out a series of arson fires in the woods around

Los Alamos. The largest of these, the Guaje Fire was five miles from Los Alamos to the northwest and it had been a challenge. The arsonist had not been apprehended and the Guaje Fire was still active when the Cerro Grande prescribed fire was lit on the night of May 4.

The Guaje Fire was started near a forest road on May 3. Burning in ponderosa pine forest, the Forest Service had found the fire to be unruly because of dry forest conditions. Even though the fire was only 7 acres, the Forest Service had jumped on the fire with an array of resources including forty people, a helicopter, four engines and a load of fire retardant that was dropped on the fire around suppertime. Bandelier's own engine and crew were on the fire as were the Santa Fe Hot Shots, a type-one initial attack crew.

Back in Santa Fe, John Romero called Mike Powell sometime after seven in the morning on May 5, and asked him if he was having trouble with his burn. Mike responds that it isn't a wildfire, it's a prescribed fire and that he needs a helicopter and a type-one fire crew, a hot shot crew.

"Boy, this is going to be hard to do," John responded. "Let me see what I can do."

John Romero found himself in a bureaucratic tangle. To send crews or other equipment to the prescribed burn, he would need a billing code to charge them to. Given that this was a National Park Service burn he would need a code number that would work with his Forest Service system. If Bandelier had given his office a "standing order" for a certain number of people or tools in advance, with a billing code, he could easily have sent the crew and the helicopter. Yet, according to Mr. Romero, Bandelier had not left a "standing order" for crews. They had not called and said, "Please have three fire crews standing by and one helicopter." If they had, those crews would have been dedicated to the Cerro Grande Prescribed Burn, standing by, even if they were not on the scene. Then Bandelier would have been paying them to be dedicated to the prescribed fire and not available for other burns.

Further, Mike had asked Dispatch for a type-one crew, meaning a hotshot crew. Such crews are paid out of national funds for initial attack, meaning going to control new fires. They were not generally available for prescribed burns until they were declared wildfires.

According to Bandelier's burn plan for the Cerro Grande Prescribed Fire, the Park Service needed only to find out from Dispatch whether crews were available within one to three hours at the time the fire was ignited. They had checked on this at five the night before and such crews were available, in theory.

In the past, with most large prescribed burns at Bandelier, the Park Service had gotten Forest Service fire crews on hand to help out. The Forest Service crews would trade their labor to the park for future labor in return from the Park Service. This friendly exchange of resources had been done as recently as the week before when Bandelier ignited the Unit 40 prescribed fire. In 1993, when Bandelier had conducted a prescribed fire on their north boundary down the ridge from Bandelier, at least 3 Forest Service engines with crews had been on hand, helping hold the fire. Some of these Forest Service people came from as far away as Grants, New Mexico.

For unknown reasons, no Forest Service crews were on hand for the Cerro Grande Prescribed Fire even though the Burn Plan specifically stated that Forest Service representatives would be present, given the fact that the prescribed fire was being ignited right on the National Forest boundary. Mike Powell told investigators later that he did call the Forest Service Espanola District about sending a representative but because everyone was out on the Guaje Fire they were unavailable. Despite the specific note to have a Forest Service representative on the fire, Bandelier's team went ahead without one.

Kevin Joseph, the Fire Management Officer for the Espanola District of the Santa Fe National Forest had told Mike Powell weeks earlier to have him or one of his people present on the Cerro Grande Prescribed Fire because of Kevin's experience with an escaped prescribed burn in Wyoming years before: "When I worked on the Bridger-Teton National Forest in Wyoming, the state of Wyoming did a prescribed burn right up next to the national forest and they didn't tell us anything about it other than we knew they were going to burn sometime and they were burning right up against our boundary. They lost their prescribed fire and it burned onto my district and ran 4,000 acres. I wanted to have our representatives there just so that we could interface with the agency and make sure things were going okay."

John Romero at the Dispatch office found himself in the middle of this mess. Bandelier apparently didn't have adequate staff on the fire, yet for him to solve that problem quickly would require him to treat the Cerro Grande Fire as though it were a wildfire for budget purposes and call up emergency crews as if they were going to a wildfire. Otherwise he would have no way to pay for those crews and he would end up with a paperwork nightmare on his hands. Yet John Romero knew that conditions were dry in the forest and that an escaped prescribed fire on Cerro Grande could be real trouble. He liked the Bandelier people and didn't want problems for anyone.

Just after seven in the morning, John Romero made his move. He called Rich Tingle, the Superintendent of the Santa Fe Hotshots and he called Kevin Joseph, the man in charge of all things fire in the land north of Bandelier. He also called the Sandia Helicopter with its crew of three firefighters from the Cibola National Forest in central New Mexico.

To do this, John Romero charged the cost of sending the Hotshots and the helicopter to the account set up for the Guaje Fire, even though the Forest Service would have to pay for the costs. Though not against any rules, it was a risky move for John Romero as it could raise questions in his own office later. John Romero then called Al King on the radio and encouraged him to declare it a wildfire.

Rich Tingle and his Hotshot Crew were in Santa Fe on their day off. They had been on the Guaje Fire and were tired. John told the Hotshots to get up to Cerro Grande to help the Bandelier team. It's not clear how urgent he made it sound, but he told them to get going. He told Kevin Joseph what was going on up on the mountain and Kevin prepared to drive toward Bandelier. As it turns out, the Santa Fe Hotshots were the only crew available in the area.

The heaviest domino in the Cerro Grande Prescribed Fire tragedy was now falling. With the loss of the Northern Pueblo Crew and with Bandelier's own team near exhaustion, the need for more people on the prescribed fire was urgent. Mike and Al assumed that the urgency of the situation was clear to John

Romero and Rich Tingle and that the Santa Fe Hotshots would show up post haste. It would be five and a half hours until the Hotshots arrived on the fire line. This delay proved disastrous.

Back on the east fire line on Cerro Grande, Jerome and David, the crew from Bandelier's wildland fire engine 91 was taking a break where the meadow elbows to the south with Holly Snyder and Ed Hayatt. They had been working to keep their black line ahead of the interior burn all morning. It was ten in the morning, the time that firefighters recognize as the beginning of the "burn period" since fires get most active in the middle of the day as the sun becomes intense, humidity drops and wind often increases.

Suddenly someone noticed that fire had escaped from their confining black-line and was running in the grass to the north! The four people jumped up and began to work hard at digging a fire line around the escape. The problem was, the fire had run right toward a complex area where a ten foot cliff drops into heavy forest below. They worked as hard as they could, scratching fire line down to mineral soil with their fire tools.

Ed Hayatt called Al King on his radio and told him what was happening.

He said the fire had "slopped over" and was into the woods below the meadow. Ed wanted Al to send more people over to help out from the west line where Al was tending that side of the fire as it burned through beds of pine needles near the little rocky knoll and very dense woods on the Baca Ranch.

At 10:30 a.m. the Sandia helicopter arrived, landed in a flat meadow area and dropped off two firefighters. They joined the four Bandelier firefighters in working on the slop-over, which by now was burning down through an open ponderosa pine studded grassland on the east facing side of the ridge as well as in a steeper mixed conifer forest on the north side of the shoulder of Cerro Grande. (See photos.) With six people on the ground, the helicopter took off to get water to dump on the fire from above.

Fire fighting helicopters can be fitted with a long cable that hangs from a hook on their bellies. The Sandia helicopter flew down to the fire cache where crews hooked a 420 gallon bucket onto a cable. Then it flew off toward a big pond of water that lies in the Valles Toledo, one of the calderas of the Baca Ranch a few miles north and west of Cerro Grande. The pond lies behind an earthen dam across San Antonio Creek and is one of the largest cattle watering ponds in the Jemez Mountains. The helicopter dipped water from this pond two or three times, flying back to the slop-over area, dumping the water according to directions from the Hotshots and returning to the pond for another load.

Just then the Santa Fe Dispatcher called to say that there was no written agreement with the Baca Ranch owner to allow for dipping out of the Valle Largo pond. The helicopter started to work from either Los Alamos Reservoir or Cochiti Reservoir, both of which were farther from the fire and took more flight time.

At least the four Bandelier crew members were now joined by the two "helitack" firefighters. Even so, with wind pushing the fire to the northeast and plentiful grass and forest to burn, the team could not catch the fire. Digging fire line in thick grass or rocky ground is difficult work, normally done by a crew of at least ten people who work together. For six people, progress was too slow given the speed of the spreading fire.

The Bandelier staff had taken as an article of faith that fire would not burn well in the cool north facing woods of Cerro Grande. Just the evening before, Al had tried to get fire to burn with no success on the northeast face in order the strengthen the west fire-line. In 1993 when John Lissoway's team had attempted the second Cerro Grande Prescribed fire, the fire had always gone out once it got in the forest. Yet that was a relatively wet fall day and today was different. The winds had come up and driven what little moisture was left from the last snowfall out of the fuels. Fire was carrying in the forest very well. The burn plan had assumed that fire would burn reluctantly in the woods and staffing had been planned accordingly.

Two more people from the west fire line joined the battle against the slop-over. Now 8 people were digging line, and re-digging line as the fire would creep around below line they had already dug. The crew needed help, help that could have arrived at nine in the morning as hoped by the fire staff, an expectation they had every reason to believe would be fulfilled by their sister agency, the US Forest Service given statements made to them by Santa Fe Dispatch on May 4 about the availability and timeframe for dispatch of "contingency resources."

Given rising confusion and the threat to the whole prescribed fire operation posed by the shortage of people and the fire spreading out of bounds on the middle of the east containment line, the Bandelier staff replaced Mike Powell with Paul Gleason as burn boss at ten in the morning. Mike was exhausted. Paul had been increasingly involved with the prescribed fire and he cancelled plans to return to duties in Denver when it became clear that Bandelier would not be burning the upper reaches of Frijoles Canyon across the highway from Cerro Grande when the Cerro Grande burn was completed; the task he had come down to supervise. That Upper Frijoles burn clearly would not happen after the difficulties encountered with the Cerro Grande burn.

Paul assumed charge of the fire as the slop-over was gaining steam. Fortunately the burn was not giving the Bandelier team trouble elsewhere. Its west line was quiet and fire in the interior of the burn was creeping down with no control problems. Only that one piece of the east line where a run of fire in the grass had escaped over into the north and east facing forests was a problem.

Then at eleven in the morning, the Santa Fe Hotshots arrived at the highway at the base of the burn unit. Under the command of Richard Tingle, a veteran fire fighter, the crew of twenty people began to hike up to the fire. Mr. Tingle split the crew into two groups, one for the west side of the fire and one for the slop-over on the east side. At last Bandelier's exhausted staff would have some help from one of the best fire crews in the West.

Why had the Hotshots taken so long to arrive? According to one crew member, dispatch of the Hotshots takes two hours longer on their days off than on a day when they are on standby. If Richard Tingle got a call at 7:30 in the morning from John Romero at dispatch, the crew would have been ready to leave by 9:30 with more than an hour travel time to the base of the fire area. The Santa Fe Hotshots arrived around eleven in the morning on State Road 4 at the base of the burn unit and took another hour to reach the slopover area.

A Hotshot member (who asked not to be named) was assigned to the west side of the fire, on the saddle below Cerro Grande summit. From there, he and seven others worked to secure the west line to prevent an unlikely fire run off into thick fir forest on the Baca Ranch. This hotshot was then assigned to be a lookout, to watch the fire and insure the safety of others who were working in areas where they couldn't see the burn as well. He watched the fire burn down into the bowl below the peak of Cerro Grande, noting that several fingers of fire were going to join farther down in the bowl. He also noted that some fire was headed north and east, toward the area where the slop-over was already a problem.

This fire running north and east was with the prevailing winds that were around 25 miles per hour at that point. The wind was getting stronger and the fuels drier as the day went by. To complicate matters, the wind varied widely from one part of the mountain to another, depending on the topography of the neighboring mountains and the prevailing seasonal wind. A pass at the base of Cerro Grande forms a notch into the vast Valle Grande to the west and wind often pours through this pass from the southwest. That wind was hitting the south facing slopes and the east ridges, fanning flames in an area that was already dry from its exposure to sun. These winds were the ones that pushed the fire across containment lines on the east side and caused the slop-over.

Yet the shape of the mountains also influenced wind gusts elsewhere on the mountain. The flat area down near the highway tended to have winds from the pass to the west, blowing east along the highway. Meanwhile forest cover kept winds on the lower half of the west line moderate while wind on the top of the burn unit would vary according to larger wind shifts. Overall, the wind was strongest on the upper half of the east fire line along the ridge and on the south facing slopes below the eastern ridge.

On May 4, the night Bandelier ignited the Cerro Grande Prescribed Burn, weather forecast called for high pressure over Northern New Mexico bringing warm temperatures and low relative humidity, especially at night. Forecasters said strong winds in the air well above the mountains could increase wind speeds on the ground, especially on mountain tops. Wind on Cerro Grande could reach ten to twenty miles per hour.

For May fifth, forecasters were predicting increasing winds as the high pressure began to weaken and a weak cold front from the west began to move into northern New Mexico. Winds for Cerro Grande were predicted to be from the west at 25 miles per hour. For fire managers, these are strong enough winds to create concern. Most prescribed fires in forested areas are planned for times with winds below 20 miles per hour. This cold front was the key weather event that would spell disaster for the fire crews. Cold fronts bring high gusty winds and the wind direction can change as the front passes through an area. Thus a fire can completely change direction in a matter of hours, ruining fire control work and endangering fire fighters.

Indeed when the Santa Fe Hotshots arrived at the slop-over they had a challenge catching the fire. With winds to 25 miles per hour spilling over the top of the ridge and creating erratic winds in the woods below, they were scrambling. The Hotshots would dig some line down to mineral soil for many yards, then come back and find the fire had crossed their line and they would begin again farther down. Flames were five to eight feet long, long enough to climb into many of the fir and pine trees. The Hotshots donned full fire protection gear including face masks and confronted fire whorls, tornados of flame that moved through the fire picking up burning debris, sucking it skyward and dropping it at some distance, starting spot fires across the line.

Spot fires were burning down in the woods over the Bandelier/Santa Fe National Forest boundary. Those spot fires grew rapidly. "It was extreme fire behavior," noted one hot shot later. Extreme fire behavior meant conditions on the ground were on a collision course with increasingly dry and forceful winds.

Because the situation was getting out of control fast and with no new crews due immediately, Rich Tingle, Superintendent of the Santa Fe Hotshots called for a slurry bomber to drop fire retardant on the east edge of the slop-over. It was one in the afternoon and Rich called Al King to tell him the fire was moving up into the trees and he was requesting a slurry drop. Rich Tingle called Dwayne Archuleta, a former Bandelier fire management officer who was now working for the Santa Fe National Forest and was in the helicopter above the fire. Dwayne relayed the call for fire retardant, ultimately to the slurry bomber base in Albuquerque that prepared to send a retardant plane to Cerro Grande.

Just after one in the afternoon, virtually all the Bandelier fire team left Cerro Grande exhausted. At that point the fire was left in the hands of the Santa Fe Hotshots, the helitack crew and the Bandelier Engine 91 staff. The Santa Fe Hotshots were already tired when they arrived on Cerro Grande, having done a night shift on the Guaje Fire just two days before.

At this point Charisse Sydoriak, Al King and Paul Gleason had a conference at the fire cache and agreed with Rich Tingle that the call for fire retardant was the end of the prescribed fire. They declared it a wildfire at around one in the afternoon, May 5. For the Park Service team this was a defeat of major proportions since a prescribed fire gone wild is seen in the wildland fire community as a professional failure for the fire managers involved. After all, prescribed fires test fire managers knowledge of landscape, fire behavior, weather and personnel. To have a fire escape is humiliating and prescribed fire managers will avoid declaring a fire wild if possible.

Accepting defeat, the Bandelier staff set about writing their Wildland Fire Situation Analysis, (WFSA) a standard document that sets out plans and priorities for putting out a wildfire. Paul Gleason was appointed "incident commander," essentially continuing in his "burn boss" position, but now as the man in charge of the crews and equipment that would be pouring into the area to put the fire out. Once a fire is declared a wildfire, an account is opened to pay for any crews or equipment that will be needed.

The WFSA was completed at five in the evening as the sun was low on the horizon where a good sized cloud of smoke was rising off Cerro Grande. Charisse, Superintendent Roy Weaver and Paul flew over the fire in the helicopter to see exactly what was happening below. For Roy and Charisse it would be one of their last official acts as the head staff members at Bandelier National Monument.

[1] The fire cache supports the National Park Service, the US Forest Service and Los Alamos National Laboratory. The small plutonium device that was detonated underground there was not immediately below the current fire station, but some distance to the east and at considerable depth. LANL would not have offered the site for public use if it had health threatening levels of radiation at the surface.

[2] The Indian crews tend to be dominantly male though women do serve on them from time to time.

[3] Tobacco chewing is widespread among firefighters.

[4] At the time of the prescribed fire, the Baca Ranch was privately owned. In 2000 the ranch was bought by the federal government and became the Valles Caldera National Preserve.

[5] The Northern Pueblo Crew came from the Eight Northern Pueblo Agency at San Juan (Okay Owingee) Pueblo. They were only expected to work into the second day of the burn before being released.

[6] The Northern Pueblo crew seems to have been a newly hired crew of mostly out of shape and inexperienced fire fighters. This can be attributed to the early season, one of their first assignments in early May. To be certified as a fire fighter and get a "red card" to go on fires, a person has to demonstrate physical fitness and have passed through a classroom and field class. The condition and performance of this crew called into question the validity of the certification procedures they had been passed through.

Chapter 6

Wildfire!

Nineteen hours after the Cerro Grande prescribed fire began, it deteriorated into a wildfire. A sense of apprehension grew among New Mexicans who were watching the smoke from the prescribed fire. The smoke cloud had grown steadily and by ten in the morning on the fifth of May, it had an ominous black tint to it, an indication that pitchy smoke from live trees was joining the white smoke of grass and pine needles. Further, the helicopter that was darting around the plume was soon to be joined by the low rumble of air tankers.

Los Alamos residents had been watching events with trepidation. For those who had been in town since 1978, this fire loomed up in the general area where three other big fires had started, La Mesa in 1978, Lummis in 1998, and the Dome Fire in 1996. All had started as columns of white smoke in the same general direction, all had grown rapidly. La Mesa had nearly roared into town and had burned well into Los Alamos National Laboratory lands.

Up on Cerro Grande on May 5 the dominos in the wildfire disaster were continuing to fall. Rich Tingle had ordered a load of retardant to be dropped on the slop-over on the fire's northeast side at one in the afternoon. The tanker dispatched from Silver City, NM had engine failure in one engine on the way to the fire and had to turn back. This caused a considerable delay at a critical time. A load of retardant well placed on the slop-over could have freed fire fighters to work elsewhere on the fire.

By four that afternoon, the retardant load still had not arrived. With winds still strong, the Santa Fe Hotshots worked away at the slop-over with help from Sandia Helicopter which was ferrying water from either Cochiti Reservoir on the Rio Grande or Los Alamos Reservoir on Los Alamos Creek. By now these firefighters were out of the winds, down slope in mixed conifer and they began to create fire line that would hold. About the time the retardant finally rained down from a deeply droning air tanker, a new crew of hotshots arrived on the slop-over. It was Kirk Smith and his Mormon Lake Hotshots from Flagstaff, Arizona. With their help, the slop-over was contained at about 30 acres in the late evening of the fifth of May; roughly 28 hours after the prescribed fire had begun.

With the slop-over under control, the two crews of hotshots turned their attention to the broader plan to extinguish the Cerro Grande fire. The fire presented a serious dilemma to Al King, Charrise Sydoriak and Paul Gleason who had written the Wildfire Situation Analysis (WFSA). As always, the safety of the public and firefighters was the top concern as they planned how to extinguish the fire. In this case keeping firefighters safe would mean taking some big strategic risks.

As mentioned earlier, fire fighters use two methods for killing large fires. One is to attack a fire "directly" which means you dig fire line, dump retardant or water, or light backfires as close to the existing blaze as you can safely get. The second method is the "indirect" method, which means setting a fire perimeter farther away from the existing blaze and either waiting for the fire to reach your fire lines or "burning out" the area between your new fire line and the edge of the existing fire. In the indirect methods landscape features dictate where fire lines are placed.

On Cerro Grande the shape of the mountain and the condition of the forest foreclosed the direct method in the minds of those planning the campaign. Though it would have seemed sensible to extinguish the blaze by digging fire line close to its lower edge across the big bowl of the mountain it would be perilous to the fire fighters who would be working there. In the lingo of wildland fire, digging a fire line across the bowl would be putting in "under-slung" line that would be prone to trees falling over it and burning debris rolling across it. Since many dead trees were still

Tom Ribe

Aerial View of Direct Option
for Suppression of Fire

17

Aerial View of Indirect Option
for Suppression of Fire

18

standing in the bowl, fire fighters would stand a good chance of being hit by falling snags as those old trees burned through at their bases. Second, as fire professionals had learned at the Mann Gulch and South Canyon Fires, placing firefighters in a draw with the potential for fire to move below them and rush up the hill entrapping them is a potentially lethal risk. So all involved (including experts from the Forest Service and Los Alamos Laboratory) agreed attacking the fire directly was too dangerous.

Thus the indirect approach was chosen. In this case they chose to continue with the fire lines delineated for the prescribed burn, bringing strong containment lines down the west and east ridges flanking the bowl. Because of the heavy grass cover, steepness, and their presence in a national park, the best way to do this would be to continue burning out the lines, making wide strips of blackened area to stop any fire that might burn to the edge from the inside.

Yet an indirect approach was also not without risk. Black-lining meant putting more fire onto the landscape and even though the outer edge of the fire would be put out when a wide swath of burned area surrounded the interior fire, there was always a chance the fire could present more control problems, just as it had already with the slop-over.

With two full Hotshot crews and the Sandia helicopter crew on site, about 45 people, the Cerro Grande fire was now primarily a Forest Service operation though the Incident Commander was Paul Gleason from the National Park Service. Now that the fire had been declared a wildfire, there were no more budget barriers to sending crews and equipment from zone dispatch. The federal checkbook was open and Cerro Grande took its first draws.

Midnight of the 5 of May found Rich Tingle and a portion of his Santa Fe Hotshots working to bring the east fire line down toward the highway. (The rest of the crew was watching the holding-line on the slop-over.) Paul Gleason, Rich Tingle, Kirk Smith and Mike Powell were most concerned about the east line because the winds continued to push the fire against it and thousands of acres of forest thickets lay beyond. If that line broke again, they might not catch it next time. The team worked hard in the dark. By now they were out of the meadow and into a fairly open forest but the slope was steep and they had to make sure the fire didn't make uphill runs against or beyond their fire line.

At two in the morning, the Mormon Lake Hotshots bedded down for some much needed rest. Two engines and their crews arrived on the highway and they patrolled and helped with the firing of the east line. Dawn came calm and still, with many fire-fighters asleep in "coyote camps" along the fire lines.

In a very real sense, the two fire lines were in a race with each other. With the wind blowing across the west line, eastward toward the interior of the burn unit, the commanders worried that the fire could make a run across the unit and slam into the east side where no line existed yet or where inadequate line had been built to hold a head fire. Communication between the two fire lines was spotty and smoke and distance made if difficult to see what was happening on the opposite fire line.

All eyes were on the east line even as Russ Copp and a newly arrived Jemez Pueblo Crew burned down on the west line, digging a line down to mineral soil and then burning out strips into the interior of the burn unit perpendicular to the holding line. This was tiring and tedious work. With smoke and darkness, it was difficult for the burning crew to know what the lines of fire they had started were doing. Were they running across the bowl toward the east line? Were they going out in the relatively wet aspen forests down near the bottom of the bowl? There was no time to find out and little inclination, since nobody wanted to be caught inside the bowl with fire all around them. The danger there was acute.

By sunrise on May 6, tired crews were working the east line down through a messy forest of ponderosa pine and grass. This was the sort of forest that survived ground fires very easily and benefited from them, but with conditions as dry as they were now, the danger of a running grass fire charging into denser forest to the east was very real. This fuel type is volatile and burns very actively and putting a fire line through such fuels was risky and difficult.

By eight in the morning, with some optimism developing among fire fighters that they would soon reach the highway with the east fire line and have the fire surrounded, problems arose. Spot fires were appearing in the woods to the east of the fire line. These fires were anywhere from tiny smoldering places to active fires with flames a few feet high. Each one required attention. Each one drew people off the fire line construction and into the woods. By the evening of the sixth, fifteen to twenty spot fires had been fought off the east fire line. Spot fires indicate dry conditions and strong convection from the fire into a dry, warm atmosphere.

The spot fires were the result of trees torching inside the fire line. As grass and sticks heated trees above them, the trees would suddenly burst into flame, sending flags of fire flapping sparks into the hot black smoke. Those sparks landed across the fire line.

That afternoon, two loads of fire retardant were dropped on the east side of the fire, probably near the slop-over area or on spot fires. At $5000 a load, the fire was beginning to run up a bill.

Meanwhile, on the other side of the fire, in the early morning hours of Sunday, May 7th, Russ Copp and the Jemez Pueblo Crew, with the help of some of the Santa Fe Hotshots brought the west fire line down to the fence at State Road 4. This had been a huge and tiring project and the hope was the fire would mostly go out on the west side, or burn slowly into the interior with no problems.

Then at two in the morning the east fire line made it to State Road 4 at bottom of the north fork of Frijoles Canyon. This was a triumph of sorts for the Mormon Lake and Santa Fe Hotshots since the fire was now surrounded by containment fire line on all sides. The highway would serve as a line on the south side and with patrolling on the east side they could begin to see light at the end of the tunnel.

Everyone knew that the highway would not necessarily make a good fire line, especially where a dogleg cuts back in the bottom of the upper reach of Frijoles Canyon where the east fire line connected to the highway. There was dense timber on both sides of the road and if fire got across the road in the canyon it could make control difficult.

Paul Gleason and Rich Tingle decided with others that it would be best if the burnout continued from the base of the east fire line toward the west along the highway, along the dogleg turn to make sure that any fire running from the west would find a burned area and go out for lack of fuel. Thus a portion of the Santa Fe Hotshot crew continued working to the west along the highway. Fatigue had set in among most of the Hotshots and many went to rest but two members of the crew worked along the road with drip torches igniting the blackline. Rich Tingle, the foreman and one other member were determined to finish burning out along the highway at night so the fire line would be complete when the sun came up and the burn period began.

Rich Tingle and his companions would have made it all the way across the bottom of the burn unit to the west fireline but for two orders to halt from the incident commander who wanted "shift changes" to prevent people from working too long. Those delays turned out to be tragic mistakes, and ones that the two hotshots were aware could cause serious problems.

There were three engines[1] stationed on the highway, patrolling. Yet for whatever reason Russ Copp and his crew were doing few patrols along the highway clear to the west line that was believed to be barely burning and well tended. This oversight was to be another domino in the gathering disaster on Cerro Grande.

The engine crews were busy holding the burn along the hairpin turn on the highway as nobody wanted to see any fire cross the highway into thickets of timber on the south side. Their primary focus was keeping the fire on the north and west sides of the highway and they did an excellent job of doing just that.

As the crew began to burn to the southwest along the hairpin turn, everyone was tense. Here they were in dense forest with a slope of unburned fuels above them. If their firing got out of hand, with the wind pushing fire against their control line, it could send a fire rushing up slope and across the fire line they had just built.

As the morning of the 7th matured into the daily burn period, Kevin Joseph of the Espanola Ranger District drove up to Cerro Grande in his Forest Service truck and watched the burnout operation at the hairpin turn for some time. He got out of his truck around 11:45 and went up to a large dead ponderosa pine that he was worried could start to burn and fall across the highway or scatter embers. He used his McCloud (fire tool) and dug a line around the snag, protecting it from the ground fire nearby. Then he got back in his truck and drove around the hairpin turn and on to the west. Kevin Joseph was about to drive right into a firestorm.

Blowup

Wildfires are often fought by dividing the perimeter of the fire area into divisions and assigning a division supervisor to each one. On a relatively small fire like Cerro Grande, the divisions might be a mile of fire line or less. Each division supervisor is in charge of the crew chiefs who in turn command the line crews and any specialists working on that division. In turn the division supervisors answer to the incident commander who oversees the whole fire.

Within this world, the division supervisors and the crew chiefs have worked their way to their positions over many years and wildfires and qualifying education. Though there is communication between different division supervisors, often they stay out of each other's divisions, not wanting to cause tension by second-guessing one another's work.

Kirk Smith was in charge of the east division that started well up on Cerro Grande and extended to some poorly defined point on the highway. Nobody was exactly sure where the east division ended and the west division started. Kirk Smith was under the impression that his division ended somewhere on the hairpin turn on the highway and Russ Copp, the division supervisor to the west was similarly unclear about the exact boundary of his division to the east. This uncertainty would prove disastrous, as a stretch of fire line along the highway was lost in limbo. Given the focus on the east burn out on the hairpin, everyone there assumed that the flats above and to the west, between the hairpin and the west line, would be overseen by someone else. (Rich Tingle, the foreman of the Santa Fe Hotshots had taken this matter in hand by working to burn out as much of the highway area as he could with part of his crew on Saturday night.)

This uncertainty was understandable. It made sense that most eyes were focused on the east and west lines where fire was being set and where open woods could easily burn. The wind was blowing away from the highway and people were most fearful about the east fire line that had wind blowing across it.

All hell was about to break loose, partly as a result of the ambiguous division boundaries. As it turned out, nobody was watching a key piece of the fire perimeter at all.

Russ Copp had brought the west line burnout down to the

highway at about six in the morning of the seventh. Then the fire was very quiet on the west side. The lack of fire activity on the west side concerned Paul Gleason and others since it meant that large areas of the interior of the burn unit were unburned. Unburned fuels could catch fire as the day warmed up and make runs against the perimeter. Something had to be done to get the interior of the fire burning so the whole "unit" would be blackened and able to cool off without worry of new head fires.

Kirk Smith went over to where the helicopter was able to land near the intersection of State Road 4 and the Dome Road at about ten in the morning on the seventh. He later said, "There was a little piece (of fire) down on the road that was a little active and it was moving down the road a little bit. The fire was just moving down the road without anyone checking it. It was moving on its own. There may have been people watching it but it seemed to me like it was going to be moving down the road unchecked[2]."

At the same time, eleven in the morning, a growing sense that they had turned the corner and were about to conquer the fire was growing among the supervisors, none of whom were on the highway at that critical time. The fire was surrounded by line (including the highway itself), the slop-over was contained, and now they could turn to mopping up the fire and working to cool it down. Roy Weaver, Superintendent of Bandelier National Monument began to write a press release announcing that the fire had been contained and would therefore soon be under control. Meanwhile, Paul Gleason decided, along with others, that it was time to get the interior burned out so they could feel secure about their lines and know the fire was cooling off throughout.

At 11 the Sandia helicopter flew to the Fire Cache and was fitted with a machine used for igniting fires from the air that fire people call "ping pong balls." Ping pong balls are used to set fire to remote areas which are unsafe for fire fighters to enter – such as the interior of the Cerro Grande burn unit. Ping-pong balls are small spheres filled with potassium permanganate that are punctured by a needle that inserts a few drops of ethyl glycol as the helicopter nears its target, creating a tiny fire bomb. The helicopter crew is able to target the balls and regulate how many drop to the forest floor, thus covering a fairly wide area. The balls hit the ground and burn for about ten-seconds, igniting the fuels around them.

In this case, the helicopter moved down the bowl of Cerro Grande from the north, below the west line, making two dry runs then dropping the balls into mixed conifer and aspen forests. Looking down, Kirk Smith who was experienced in this operation noticed that the balls were not igniting the ground well. They would make a black patch several feet across then go out. The aerial ignition operation was not working. Just as Al King had not been able to ignite the mixed conifer forest to help create the west line, the ping-pong machine was failing in the same sort of forest. The east and north facing mixed conifer and aspen forests were too wet to burn.

Just then, someone in the helicopter noticed trees torching down by the highway, near where the Dome Road intersects with State Road 4. This was the same place Kirk Smith had noticed untended fire less than an hour earlier before he got aboard the helicopter. They flew over the torching trees, mature Douglas fir and ponderosa pine growing on flat ground, just in time to see the fire make a crown run, burning hard in tree tops running along the highway to the east and beginning to drop embers into the woods across the highway. This was a worst-case scenario, one that the east line crew had labored to prevent on their division. This fire originated from near the bottom of the west fire line.

Fire had crept virtually unnoticed through grass and down aspen logs in a meadow, making its way to the band of forest next to the highway. There it had found pine needles, dry grass and small trees from which it climbed into the tops of larger trees when increasing wind pushed it from the west. It was as though fire had been sneaking around looking for an escape from its captors and now it was running for the exit.

Unfortunately, the lower end of the west fire line had reached the highway sooner than it should have. Ideally, the black lining that was planned for the north side of State Road 4, from the dog-leg turn to the bottom of the west fire line should have been completed first. Fires are always ignited against the wind so that the wind blows them back on area already burned. When the bottom of the west fire line black line escaped into the dead aspen strewn meadow, it was running with the wind and it had hundreds of yards to go before it would hit blackened ground.

Meanwhile, Kevin Joseph had topped the hill west of the

hairpin turn just in time to see the fire roaring through the trees above him. He saw several spot fires on the south side of the highway and he ran to put them out, laboring alone urgently as the fire roared along to the east. He then noticed at least a dozen more spot fires on the south side of the highway[3]. Calling for three engines and more people, those spot fires were lined and controlled as the two hotshot crews swept down on them. However worse problems were developing to the east.

Kirk Smith, in the helicopter above was cursing himself at that moment for not calling the untended roadside fire to the attention of Russ Copp who he believed was in charge of that division of the fire line. When Kirk saw the trees starting to ignite he knew instantly that this fire had come from the west fire-line.

From the helicopter, Kirk Smith, Mike Powell, and others watched the line of fire roar through the trees toward the hairpin turn. This new head of fire split as it burned east, with one branch searing toward the southeast and to the edge of Frijoles Canyon, and the other blasting toward the hairpin turn. The south branch threw spot fires down into the upper end of Frijoles Canyon below the hairpin. These grew very rapidly, tripling in size within a minute. The fire was blowing up!

Dwayne Archuleta in the Forest Service' daily forest-wide fire reconnaissance flight reported these two spot fires in upper Frijoles Canyon, one hundred yards off the road and burning hot. This was the worst possible scenario for the crews on the scene, since upper Frijoles Canyon was dense with thick timber. If those trees started to crown, they could throw embers into the prevailing wind that was blowing directly toward Los Alamos. These fires in the canyon were not within the fire line. They were south and east of the bottom end of that line.

Fire fighters work hard to keep fire out of the crowns of trees at times like this. They can always chase ground fire, but once the tree crowns get hot enough to explode, they feed heat from one tree to the next until large areas of very hot fire is preheating its way through the treetops, drawing heat upward in ever greater quantities. The heat creates a convection column which vacuums heat and debris upward. Leaves, small sticks, and embers carried aloft in this way rain down elsewhere, lighting new spot fires. These convective fires are the most difficult to control as they burn vertically as well as horizontally, defying ground control efforts. Such firestorms only stop when they run out of fuel.

At noon on Sunday, the Cerro Grande firefighters were doing all they could to prevent these spot fires from moving in a unified head to the north. The crown run along the highway had stopped when it hit the burned area on the highway hairpin turn. Yet time was of the essence. Already Kevin Joseph had clocked winds of 40 miles per hour by the highway.

Given the danger posed by the interior of the burn unit to anyone who might enter it, danger posed by falling trees and the lack of clear escape routes should the fire inside the unit flare up, nobody really knew what was happening inside the area now surrounded by fire lines. One of the Santa Fe Hotshots patrolling the upper end of the west fireline had noticed that the fire was backing down into the bowl from several points above[4]. As that fire backed down, it was headed for a large group of dead trees. The hotshot worried to himself that those fingers of fire backing into the snags could unify in the bottom of the draw, where the wind could chimney the fire into a running head. Yet this never happened according to patterns of burned trees left from that day.

The National Weather Service on which the Bandelier prescribed fire crews relied for all detailed weather forecasts had only predicted winds of up to 25 miles per hour for Sunday afternoon. Yet winds were well beyond that. The National Weather Service representatives later testified to the Cerro Grande Board of Inquiry that they are not able to accurately predict winds in mountain settings, but do their best.

At one in the afternoon on Sunday (May 7), Kathy Allred arrived over Cerro Grande in her Beechcraft Baron 58P lead plane. A veteran forest fire air attack pilot, she had flown many large fires in the West, helping the big air tankers find their targets. Her six-passenger plane buzzed through the smoke plume, as she looked down on the fire below, watching its behavior and trying to predict what it was likely to do next. She would then lead the air tankers to their drop points where they would come down as if they were going to land and drop their ten to twenty-thousand gallon loads of retardant[5] on places where the slurry was likely to slow the advance of the blaze. The drops needed to be targeted carefully. Even more important than the cost, each bomber had about an hour return time between loads, so each one had to be carefully placed at critical growth points in the fire. A missed drop could cost firefighters thousands of acres.

Kathy was leading a force of three air tankers from Albuquerque. From her view of the fire she watched the pivotal moment when the fire blew off of Cerro Grande and began to roar toward Los Alamos[6]. That key event is shrouded in mystery and dispute as investigators and those involved struggled to understand exactly how a fire, nearly in control, could suddenly be so ferociously out of control.

Kathy watched the fire roar through the trees along Highway 4 and she watched the spot fires in upper Frijoles Canyon grow rapidly. She led the tankers into upper Frijoles, helping them begin to surround the spot fires with a complete band of retardant. The topography limited their work as the big planes could only approach the fire from the south or east. Big updrafts and downdrafts at the top of the Cerro Grande ridge made flying north tricky and dropping retardant even trickier.

Kathy Allred was watching the east fire line above the hairpin turn where she could see the wind was heating the fire up as well. Even though the black-line was deep, it was fresh enough that wind could heat up recently burned areas and get fire moving again. With most of the firefighters now working along the hairpin on the highway, the east line was not well tended.

"It looked pretty good, and if the winds hadn't come up, it looked like a good burn," she later told investigators. "We were just taking care of that lower stuff down there." She could see the fire in Frijoles Canyon was fierce enough to burn out the crowns in the stands of pole-sized trees.

Kathy was watching the middle of the east line, half way up Cerro Grande most intently, where she could see active fire inside the black line. The winds were increasing and wind was complicating the retardant drops for the air attack pilots. The winds shifted from the southwest to the south, blowing right up Frijoles Canyon. Retardant is always dropped into the wind, but the winds were making this difficult given the dangerous topography of upper Frijoles Canyon and the wind shift meant they had to change strategy quickly.

Ms. Allred hoped to "paint" a band of retardant on the top

of the ridge to stop the fire from the south. "We initially started laying retardant next to the spot fires, and there were two or three initially. We tried to hit one directly and it didn't slow it down, and so things were going very fast from there on. At the time we said we can't go direct anymore, we're just going to have to flank it because the spots grew and went together very fast." This meant that the fire was blowing out of the spot fire areas across any wetted areas of retardant directly next to the spot fires.

At this key moment, the fire was about to become a major wildfire. Winds rose from the manageable 25 mile per hour winds that had been battering the fire on and off for three days, and increased to 40 to 50 mile per hour, depending on the observer. Whatever the speed, the wind blew the fire apart, sending a line of spot fires running to the north, up through the forest just east of the east fire line. To this day one can easily see the patches of burned out forest left from this skipping-stone of fire running north and away.

Aerial View of May 7 Fire Run

27

Note that this General Accounting Office graphic does not include a second arm of the "fire path" that took fire toward the lower right corner of the photo into Frijoles Canyon. This large spot-fire was likely the source of fire exiting Bandelier National Monument.

The debate continues as to exactly where the fire escaped from on the perimeter of the Cerro Grande prescribed burn unit at that moment. While the point may seem academic, knowing where the fire came from is extremely important for understanding what element of the prescribed fire or the fire suppression efforts led to the disaster that was to follow north of the Cerro Grande ridge[7]. Kathy Allred in her 58P had one of the best views of this key moment as she circled the blaze and led air tankers to their drop points. Her impression was the escaped fire came from the burn unit across the east fireline, and then ran north with the wind shift. Others felt certain that fire spotted from the big spot fires in Frijoles Canyon, a theory supported by the pattern of burned trees.

At one in the afternoon, Paul Gleason, Russ Copp, Mike Powell and Rich Tingle decided the time had come to prepare for the worst and call in a Type One incident management team. These teams are the highest-level forest fire management organizations, meant for handling the most difficult fires. They are dispatched from the Interagency Fire Center in Boise, Idaho. Cerro Grande was being upgraded from a Type Three management structure, put in place when the fire was declared wild around noon on Friday, to a Type One incident. To have the fire jump from a Type Three to a Type One organization showed that the fire fighters understood the threat to Los Alamos.

Meanwhile, for the second time, one of the air tankers had mechanical problems, breaking up the steady delivery of retardant to the blaze as the three planes cycled through from the air tanker base at the Albuquerque airport.

With confusing speed, the fire jumped over Cerro Grande ridge and caught in Water Canyon, the next canyon to the north, and one so choked with fuels and debris that several spot fires there began to grow together rapidly crowning into the trees and sending flags of black smoke into the air. The fire was now firmly on Forest Service land that had not seen fire or fuel reduction over most of the area in the fire's path in almost a century.

As the next few days unfolded with the focus of fire fighting closer to Los Alamos and with minimal personnel on the site of the prescribed fire, no further escapes from the Cerro Grande prescribed fire boundaries occurred. Perhaps if the south containment line of the fire, along State Road 4 had been properly patrolled, the fire would never have escaped from Bandelier National Monument and roared toward Los Alamos. The evidence strongly suggests this is true.

This moment would prove to be a pivotal crushing emotional experience for the Bandelier staff.

Ignited Test Fire for Prescribed Burn

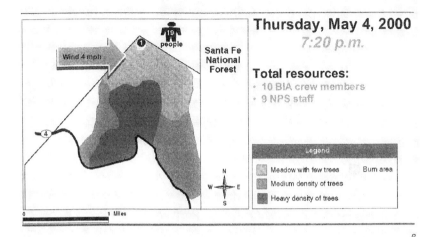

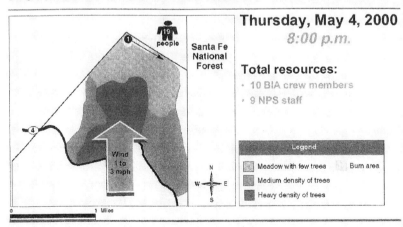

Black Lining Stopped on Northeast Side; Fire Growing Towards Baca Ranch

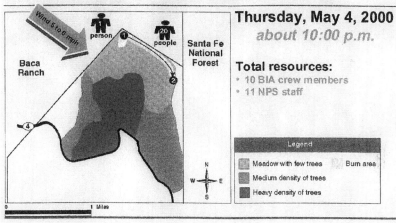

8

Black Lining Started on Northwest Side

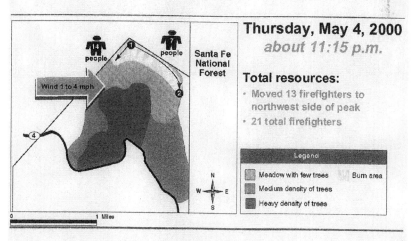

9

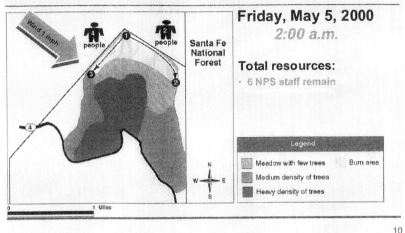

Black Lining Stopped on Northwest Side; Most Crew Released Due to Fatigue

Friday, May 5, 2000

2:00 a.m.

Total resources:
- 6 NPS staff remain

Legend
- Meadow with few trees
- Medium density of trees
- Heavy density of trees
- Burn area

Santa Fe National Forest

10

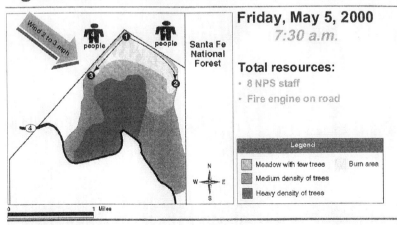

Fire Expands Down Northeast Side; Agreement Reached on More Resources

Friday, May 5, 2000

7:30 a.m.

Total resources:
- 8 NPS staff
- Fire engine on road

Legend
- Meadow with few trees
- Medium density of trees
- Heavy density of trees
- Burn area

Santa Fe National Forest

11

Burn Boss Changes; Slopover Occurs

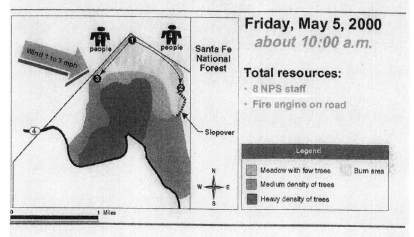

Friday, May 5, 2000
about 10:00 a.m.

Total resources:
- 8 NPS staff
- Fire engine on road

12

Additional Resources Arrive

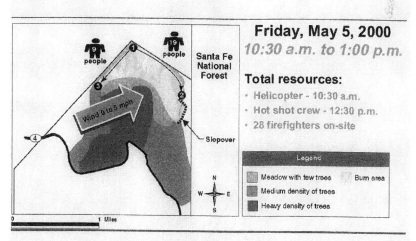

Friday, May 5, 2000
10:30 a.m. to 1:00 p.m.

Total resources:
- Helicopter - 10:30 a.m.
- Hot shot crew - 12:30 p.m.
- 28 firefighters on-site

13

Fire Declared a Wildland Fire

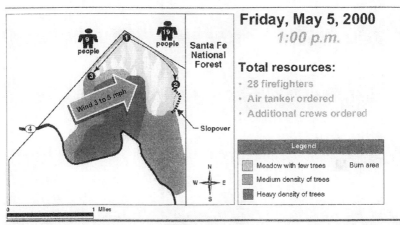

14

Resources Are Added;
Slopover Is Contained

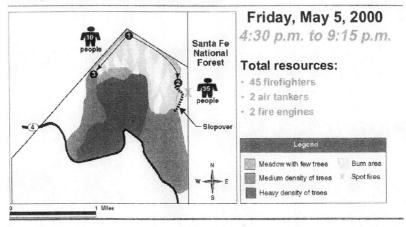

15

Options Discussed to Suppress
Wildland Fire *(indirect option selected)*

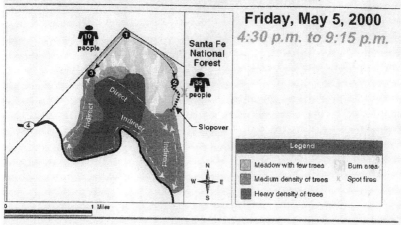

16

Firefighters Begin Blacklining East Side

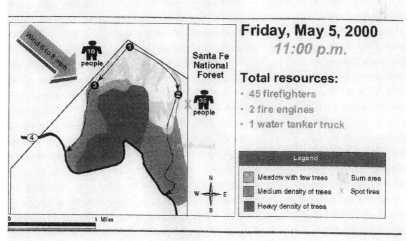

19

Tom Ribe

More Firefighters Ordered;
Crews Improve Line on East Side

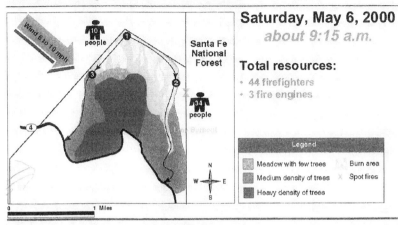

Saturday, May 6, 2000
about 9:15 a.m.

Total resources:
- 44 firefighters
- 3 fire engines

21

New Crew Black Lines West Side

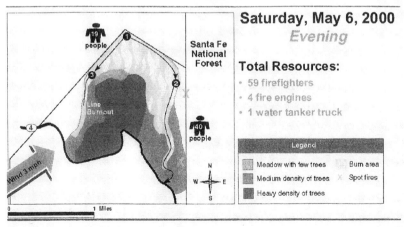

Saturday, May 6, 2000
Evening

Total Resources:
- 59 firefighters
- 4 fire engines
- 1 water tanker truck

22

Surface Fire Observed in Southwest Corner

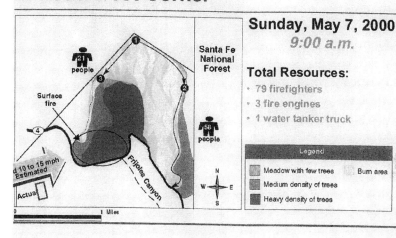

Sunday, May 7, 2000
9:00 a.m.

Santa Fe National Forest

Total Resources:
- 79 firefighters
- 3 fire engines
- 1 water tanker truck

Legend: Meadow with few trees · Burn area · Medium density of trees · Heavy density of trees

23

Trees Observed Torching in Southwest Corner

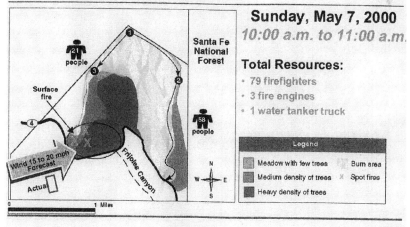

Sunday, May 7, 2000
10:00 a.m. to 11:00 a.m.

Santa Fe National Forest

Total Resources:
- 79 firefighters
- 3 fire engines
- 1 water tanker truck

Legend: Meadow with few trees · Burn area · Medium density of trees · Spot fires · Heavy density of trees

24

Aerial Ignition on West Side of Burn Area

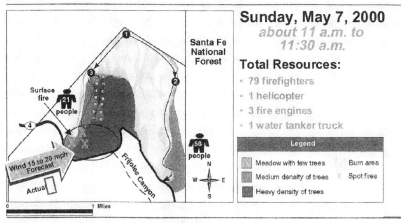

25

Fire Crosses Into Frijoles Canyon

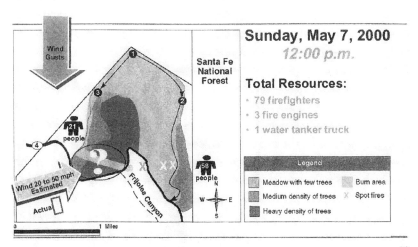

26

[1] In this case an "engine" is an oversized pick up truck with a flat bed fitted with a water tank, plenty of hose and a water pump. Otherwise known as a "brush truck" these units are designed specifically for wildland fire and are able to travel small dirt roads.

[2] Quote from the Board of Inquiry transcript.

[3] It's unclear if the crown fire that was rushing east when Kevin Joseph topped the hill died out when it hit the highway or if the crown fire continued down into the north fork of Frijoles Canyon. Today, burned trees stand on both sides of the highway where the crown fire would have come to the pavement. Whether the crown fire continued across the road or came up later from spot fires below the road is unclear.

[4] Jeremy Kruger, private interview testimony.

[5] Long-term retardants, mixed for delivery to the fire, contain about 85 percent water, 10 percent fertilizer, and 5 percent minor ingredients: colorant (iron oxide, or fugitive color that fades with exposure to sunlight), thickener (natural gum and clay), corrosion inhibitors, stabilizers, and bactericides.

[6] Kathy Allred testimony to the Cerro Grande Board of Inquiry.

[7] Kathy Allred believed that the fire was spotting off the original prescribed fire area at the top half of the mountain and that once it spotted to the east, winds from down canyon pushed it north. Her testimony to the Board of Inquiry on this point was confusing since it didn't concur with those who were watching the fire from the ground and saw the fire run from the Frijoles drainage up the east ridge of Cerro Grande.

Chapter 7

Burning Los Alamos

The ridge between Frijoles and Water Canyons divides several worlds. On its south the greater Bandelier watersheds drain an ancient, wild land once inhabited by prehistoric peoples where hidden creeks still riffle through old forests year after year. To the north of Water Canyon lies a world that has been dominated by Los Alamos and its population for more than half a century. Though beautiful wild lands exist around Los Alamos, one is never far from the hum of this odd and isolated urban area where daily life is dominated by nuclear research.

In the Los Alamos world, things are complicated human affairs driven by politics, science and technology. In the Bandelier world, the Park Service labors to protect an increasingly rarified world of human prehistory and natural process. Both worlds are capable of creating large fires – one nuclear and one forest inferno. The odd juxtaposition of these two worlds finally collided in May 2000.

Frijoles Canyon, the heart of Bandelier National Monument, is the most significant gorge in the east Jemez landscape. Fifteen miles long and 600 feet deep at its mouth, the canyon holds a perennial stream that harbors an oasis of riparian forest. In prehistoric Pueblo times the canyon marked the line between the Tewa speaking world to the North and the Keres speaking world to the South.

Bandelier's resources management staff had known for

decades of the potential for a fire originating on Bandelier land, or on Forest Service lands from south of Bandelier, escaping into Water Canyon and then burning toward Los Alamos. Prevailing winds blow from the southwest and any fire in the heavily timbered upper Frijoles Canyon or Cochiti Canyon area would tend toward Los Alamos after it crossed Water Canyon. Three large fires had already threatened Los Alamos from this area and Bandelier's staff had long considered their responsibility large in doing their part to protect the town from wildfires.

Thus the sense of defeat, in seeing the containment fires set to surround the Cerro Grande prescribed fire pushed by wind out of Bandelier and onto fuel chocked Forest Service lands, must have been crushing for everyone on the Bandelier staff. All rightly knew that this was a historic turning point for the whole region, one that would turn Bandelier's programs on their head and potentially threaten Los Alamos, a community built among extremely fire prone forests. Not only was the Bandelier fire staff losing control of the fire, they were losing control of their careers, and the programs many had worked for years to put in place.

Fire crossing the north rim of Water Canyon triggered the call for a Type 1 fire team, the highest level of response to a wildfire available. The East Jemez Resource Council, formed by Charisse Sydoriak of Bandelier and others, had agreed in 1998 that no questions asked, serious fire north of Frijoles Canyon would trigger the highest level of response from national fire fighting resources.

On May 7, just after the fire made its run down Highway 4 and leapt into upper Frijoles Canyon, Bandelier called the Boise Interagency Fire Center for a Type 1 fire incident management team. This is like going from a simple house fire, to a four-alarm fire in the world of urban fire. Type one teams involve large organizations headed up by commanders who have worked their way up through the responsibility levels in fire suppression and understand how to approach large fire incidents. They set up fire camps; small villages with everything from showers to command centers to mess halls, offices, communications centers, tool caches and subdivisions of tents for the firefighters who pour in from all over the nation.

Even with these large firefighting organizations, large fires often defy control, even with the best technology, large groups of workers and seemingly limitless funds. Fires become large because of environmental conditions such as weather and heavy, dry fuel. Until those conditions change, human control efforts often only work on the margins.

Everyone involved knew that catching Cerro Grande would require cooperation from the weather since this was a wind driven fire, assisted by drought conditions and astonishingly high fuel loading on Forest Service and, later, Los Alamos County lands. Wind, as firefighters would soon learn, was by far the most significant factor in spreading the Cerro Grande wildfire.

Once the fire jumped from Frijoles Canyon into Water Canyon it presented serious problems to fire fighters based up on Cerro Grande. Air tankers could continue to battle it, but the wind limited their efforts as spotting fire jumped swaths of retardant laid in front of the advancing fire. Ground fire fighters had to drive about 4 road miles to position themselves in front of the blaze. The fire was going too fast to make any of the dirt roads penetrating the Forest Service land directly below Cerro Grande useful. It is about two air miles to the next useful paved road to the north where fire fighters scrambled to get a new position to slow the escaped fire.

By then the fire was really moving. In Water Canyon, fire spotted on the south-facing slope, where ponderosa pine grew on steep sunny slopes opposite cooler and wetter north facing slopes of fir and aspen. The fire ran up these slopes, topped the ridge and threw embers into the turbulent air above[1]. Then fire ran over that mesa, covered with thick forests and some remnant open grasslands studded by sparse ponderosa pines and aspen groves left in the wake of a 1954 wildfire. In many places pine duff was almost a foot thick and old aspen forests lay in ruin below shoulder-to-shoulder white fir and ponderosa pine forest that had overtopped the aspen years before[2]. Juniper trees were invading from the lowlands and the old large trees left from the turn of the century stood above thickets of pole sized trees that would act as ladders to bring fire from the ground into the tops of these large trees that would have been immune from fire in a natural fire regime. This was fire-starved country where studies had shown fuel was loaded at 26 tons per acre (a forest with a natural fire cycle would have less than half that). Researchers understand that this forest had about 100 trees per acre before people stopped natural fires in 1883. By contrast, before Cerro Grande the land surrounding Los Alamos had about 21,000 trees per acre in some places[3].

Over the course of two hours, the fire raged northward. New spot fires grew on the south facing slopes of nearby Valle Canyon, (the old sheep driveway), and roared up the slopes of Pajarito Mountain, calming as it reached the relatively wet areas of mixed conifer forest. The blaze was spotting up to a half mile ahead of itself and the spots climbed into the crowns of the trees immediately sending flags of flames 100 feet tall flapping black smoke high into the air. Two hundred year old trees were dying by the hundreds. The fire was burning hot, spreading from a developing head with a convection cloud above it that was driving itself straight toward Los Alamos, preheating the forest ahead, then consuming that with a blast of fire. Meanwhile the fire spread in the dry heavy woody litter, voraciously devouring fuels like a prisoner released from starvation into a banquet of the finest foods. Years of depravation of fire that started 100 years before were rapidly made up for as fire tore through thickets of trees and drifts of down woody material.

The only way to stop a running crown fire like this is to have a substantial fuel break in front of it to force the preheating and consumption of the tree crowns to stop. The fire must run out of fuel and drop to the ground. No amount of fire retardant or water that humans are capable of delivering will affect a running crown fire such as developed on May 7. By evening the fire had burned 3 miles from Cerro Grande mountain in a swath a mile and a quarter wide.

Fires have heads and flanks. The fire pushes forward at its head that is the lead front of the fire, the most active area. A fire spreads more slowly behind the head on its flanks, like a motorboat crossing a still lake, the boat as the head and the angled line of waves behind like a flanking fire. The flank fire spreads laterally to the head fire.

Kevin Joseph, the Forest Service employee who had observed the fire escaping at the base of Cerro Grande, was the first fire fighter to head toward Camp May Road, a paved road that climbs the south rim of Los Alamos Canyon to Pajarito Mountain ski area and a historic county recreation area called Camp May up near the east rim of the Valles Caldera. Los Alamos spreads north and east from the north rim of Los Alamos Canyon, so the Camp May Road was the last chance to catch the fire before it went into town. Yet the road provided an imperfect barrier as it was right on the rim of the canyon and the fire would have to be cooled down before it reached the road. Also the road wasn't wide enough to affect a running crown fire. Thus the urgent need to burn out the fuels on the south side of the road before the main fire reached them.

The bulk of Bandelier's fire team left Cerro Grande as fast as they could and headed to Camp May Road under Paul Gleason's direction. Using information from Los Alamos Fire Department Deputy Chief Doug Tucker who was circling the running blaze in a helicopter, Paul immediately set his crew to setting a back fire along Camp May Road, establishing an all-important anchor at a point where the road veers away from the canyon. (An anchor is a strong unburnable area to which fire fighters tie fire lines.) Paul and Kevin quickly understood that the fire had developed a head that was pointed directly toward Los Alamos National Laboratory's main complex. They had to think and work fast to trip the fire, bring it down out of the trees, before it could run right into one of the nation's most sensitive and hazardous building complexes[4].

The helicopter that had been on the fire since May 5 was ferrying decision makers such as Los Alamos' fire chief up to look at the fire as well as bringing huge bucket loads of water to slow the head and knock down menacing spot fires. By evening, the helicopter was running out of time given safety limits that only allow pilots and their machines to fly for 8 hours at a time. Air tankers from Albuquerque continued to pound ahead of the fire, laying swaths of fire retardant in front of the head.

Paul's already exhausted Bandelier team, joined by some Forest Service fire fighters, backfired into the woods to the south of Camp May Road starting about a mile up from the base of the road. They rushed up and down Camp May Road, setting fire to the edge of the woods at the road and leading the fire into the woods to the south in hopes of burning off the fuel before the head of the fire reached them. This was land dominated by thickets of ponderosa pine with heavy needle duff below them, the sort of forest that develops when fire deprived ponderosa pine forests are neglected[5]. At this point the fuel loading was good for Paul's group as it allowed them to start an active fire that would consume a great deal of fuel before the running head fire came along. Meanwhile they kept a close watch on Los Alamos Canyon that yawned to their immediate north, watching for spot fires there that could negate their efforts to hold the fire.

Working into the evening, Paul Gleason and Kevin Joseph finished the backfire along Camp May Road according to where they understood from Kirk Smith's aerial observations, the head of the fire would reach the road. The fire reached Camp May Road at 5:30 pm and faltered in the area the firefighters had prepared by burning away the fuels before the fire's head. They then began burning out along State Highway 501, a larger paved road that runs from Los Alamos to Bandelier, to deprive the eastward flank of the fire fuel. On the east side of this road lay the most concealed parts of Los Alamos Lab, with hidden sites where explosive testing is done, office buildings for classified work and bunkers for explosives. This is the place where America's first three atomic bombs were built in 1945 and the historic buildings where those assemblies took place lay in near-ruin from abandonment and neglect among thick pine forests.

To the west of State Road 501 lies the Santa Fe National Forest and the fire that Paul's group was working to defeat. Joined now by numerous other Forest Service fire fighters, the crews lit backfires all along the highway, working their way back toward Bandelier's boundary and the old World War II era guard station called the "Back Gate." Cerro Grande (the mountain) was blocking wind from the west and the firefighters had favorable breezes to help their work. These backfires burned on the ground and among thickets, working as a prescribed fire might. The firefighters got almost to where the highway dips into Water Canyon and stopped where their burnout operation blended with fire burning on its own from the nearby ridge above.

Meanwhile, Paul Gleason and his crew, joined by the Santa Fe and Mormon Lake Hotshot crews worked hard at containing a spate of spot fires that popped up on the rim of Los Alamos Canyon, on the wrong side of the road and even down on the slope of Los Alamos Canyon itself. At the same time the convection of the head of the fire was dropping embers across Highway 501 onto Los Alamos Lab property where they scrambled to put out these fires before they gained any momentum. Here they confronted the Laboratory's no trespassing zones and high security closures.

Paul knew that the fire's head was running right toward the main campus of Los Alamos National Laboratory. Its path was as dangerous as could be imagined and with the wind driving the fire and seemingly limitless fuels, the fire was hopping from canyon to canyon with spot fires half a mile ahead growing to new monsters within minutes. The potential for the fire to cause serious problems for Los Alamos, and the regional population through releases of toxic materials from LANL was high. Paul had to work fast and hard and his Bandelier crew forgot their fatigue and worked with a determination to save their neighboring community.

"This was very serious fire fighting," Al King (the Fire Management Officer from Bandelier later said. That fight to contain a running crown fire before it hit Los Alamos became legendary among wild land fire fighters across the country. It was a success and a tribute not only to the strategic insights of Paul Gleason and Kevin Joseph but also to the Bandelier fire crews who worked beyond exhaustion to save their community.

By midnight on May 7, strategic air tanker drops had knocked down the crown fire at dusk and the successful backfires along two highways. The fire was contained on its most dangerous sides. As Kevin Joseph worked to evacuate the resident caretaker of the Ski Area up on Pajarito Mountain, the back fires spread to the south, toward the origin of the fire, about 300 feet.

As the wind died down with nightfall on May 7, a critical transition took place. Paul Gleason and his team briefed the newly arrived Type One Incident Command team under Paul Humphrey, and helped them take over command of the fire at six in the morning on May 8. Mr. Humphrey is one of many Type one commanders with the US Forest Service's Interagency Fire Center in Boise Idaho, based in the southwest. He had been in charge of the Dome Fire in 1996 that nearly burned into Los Alamos and the Oso Fire in 1998 that had come close to town on the north. Mr. Humphrey had agreed to take over the fire faster than normally was done due to Paul Gleason's team's exhaustion and the seriousness of the threat facing Los Alamos.

In Los Alamos Sunday night, May 7th, the alarms had spread. Police lines closed Highway 501, blocking the road to all but emergency traffic. The New Mexico State Police drove the streets of the Western Area neighborhood on the evening of May 7, urging everyone to evacuate. A dark smoke pall spread over the town cutting off the light even as summer sunset came on. People moved about loading their cars in disbelief as slurry bombers dipped close to the town on the upswings from their slurry drops on the other side of Los Alamos Canyon.

The police, and the fire fighters did not know if the fire lines along the south side of Los Alamos Canyon would hold. The Western Area was directly across the canyon from the fire and it seemed the prudent thing to evacuate that portion of Los Alamos closest to the fire.

The efforts of Paul Gleason until May 9 were heroic. His years of intensive training and experience on some of the worst fires in the West benefited Los Alamos in ways the community may not fully appreciate given what would happen with wind and spot fire the next day. Paul Gleason's fight against the Cerro Grande head fire on Camp May Road and the intersection with Camp May Road and Highway 501 would be his last battle with big fire, the culmination of the career of a true fire warrior. Mr. Gleason died of cancer in 2003.

As dawn came on May 8, Charisse Sydoriak noted the fire's behavior. "This was a wind driven fire, not a drought driven fire. When the wind died down, fire behavior was not extreme, despite heavy fuel loading."

The back burns held the fire. For now, Los Alamos seemed safe. With much less wind, crews worked to extend the black line to the south, to insure that no new crown fire would develop and that the forest could begin to cool down before any new wind in the days to come. The fire continued burning through dense fuels but its running head had been defeated and with little wind on May 8, the fire burned as a low fire between Water Canyon and Los Alamos Canyons. Paul Gleason's strategy had worked, and if anything, a desperately needed fire to reduce acute fuel loading on lands close to Los Alamos had now been inadvertently accomplished – a burn the Forest Service had been unwilling to risk due to proximity to the town.

If anything, complacency seemed to spread over the Type One team that had taken over what looked to be a contained wildfire. Blacklines had been largely completed around the two sides where spread was likely and the high mountains to the west were wet enough to slow growth there. Danger of fire growing to the south toward Bandelier seemed minimal and the cold front that had produced winds to 35 miles per hour on the 7th had moved out of the area.

Charisse Sydoriak later recalled her strong suggestion to Incident Commander Humphrey to begin serious protection measures for Los Alamos at once, such as bulldozing a wide swath of trees near the Western Area, the neighborhood of houses built in the 1950s nearest the blaze6. There a wide swath of land owned by Los Alamos County was thick with pines right to the very fences of yards. She also suggested laying heavy fire retardant near this neighborhood. These suggestions went unheeded for unknown reasons and through May 9, this vulnerable section of Los Alamos, less than a half mile from the north edge of the fire stood unprotected even though bulldozers for this purpose were standing by, ready to roll. If the fire came back to life with a new running head from inside its containment lines – a highly likely scenario given the large patches of unburned heavy fuels there – Los Alamos still lay in its path.

Given what we know now, even a fire line made with hand tools around Los Alamos would have saved many homes. Perhaps because of the inexperience of the Los Alamos Fire Department with wildland fire, a fuel break of this kind was not built before the fire, even days before, or even when the fire threatened from across Los Alamos Canyon. For whatever reason, no fire line was constructed next to the edge of Los Alamos before the fire roared toward the town on May 10.

Meanwhile back at the prescribed fire on May 9, Matt Snyder and a few firefighters continued to work on the fire to insure that it didn't spread to the west or the south, or that it didn't develop a new head and run to the north through abundant unburned fuels toward Los Alamos. The winds were cooperating and they

Progression of Fire

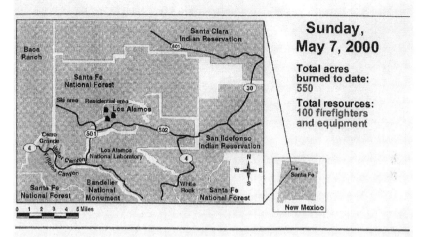

**Sunday,
May 7, 2000**

**Total acres
burned to date:**
550

Total resources:
100 firefighters
and equipment

28

Progression of Fire

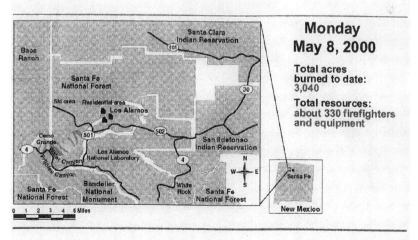

**Monday
May 8, 2000**

**Total acres
burned to date:**
3,040

Total resources:
about 330 firefighters
and equipment

29

Progression of Fire

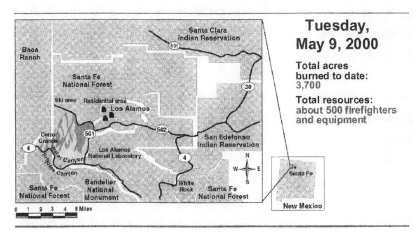

Tuesday,
May 9, 2000

Total acres
burned to date:
3,700

Total resources:
about 500 firefighters
and equipment

30

Progression of Fire

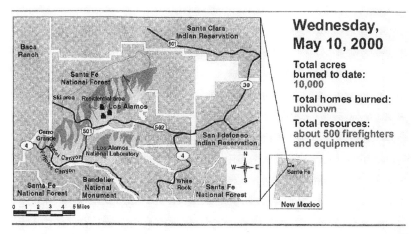

Wednesday,
May 10, 2000

Total acres
burned to date:
10,000

Total homes burned:
unknown

Total resources:
about 500 firefighters
and equipment

31

Progression of Fire

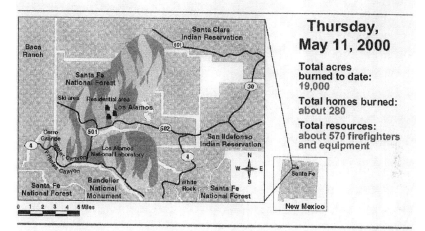

**Thursday,
May 11, 2000**

Total acres
burned to date:
19,000

Total homes burned:
about 280

Total resources:
about 570 firefighters
and equipment

32

Progression of Fire

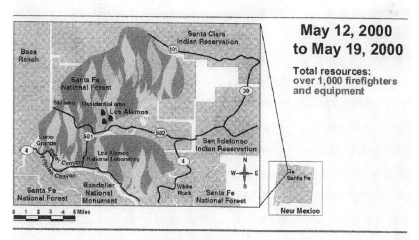

**May 12, 2000
to May 19, 2000**

Total resources:
over 1,000 firefighters
and equipment

33

secured firelines that were holding. In essence, fire in the prescribed fire area per se was now contained and finished. Had the front with wind not come through on May 7, this would have been the end of the Cerro Grande prescribed fire and its control efforts on Cerro Grande.

For the next two days the Cerro Grande fire smoldered around in the area of upper Water, Pajarito and Valles Canyons and on the lower slopes of Pajarito Mountain while Mr. Humphrey's rapidly growing fire fighting force focused on containing the fire on all sides. With highways on three sides that could act as containment lines, he worried about the west side where there was no line built and wild land extended far up into the Valles Calderas.

By May 8, fire fighters and their gear were pouring into a new fire camp set up at the Bandelier Fire Cache on State Road 4. Tents were sprouting up in little subdivisions among large trucks that served as shower rooms, kitchens, command offices, communications and a supply center. (Directly below-ground this camp was the remains of a plutonium weapon that had been detonated underground at that site in 1964.) By Monday, 137 people, seven engines, two helicopters were working the fire with airtankers from Albuquerque.

Any complacence that may have developed on May 8 and 9 was replaced by urgency when weather reports indicated that a new low pressure ridge was coming through the Southwest on May 10. It was a weak low-pressure ridge that had passed over northern New Mexico on May 7, bringing the high winds that blew the fire off of Cerro Grande (mountain). The May 10 ridge was due to be stronger and forecasts for winds more than 35 miles per hour struck fear into those involved in the fire. With lines incomplete up Camp May Road, the only real barrier between whatever fire might grow from inside the three sided containment of the blaze, the possibility of an escape across Los Alamos Canyon was very high.

Having a fire come back to life and make a new run would have been a routine event with a large fire in a remote setting. With Los Alamos less than a mile from the fireline, a normally routine escape event was unthinkable. The fire was holding at about 550 acres on Monday night, May 8, though nobody really knew how much of the fire area was burned and how far up into the high country the fire had burned.

On Monday night and Tuesday ten more 20-person crews arrived to help with the fire. The fire continued to burn in the upper reaches of Valle and Pajarito Canyons south of Los Alamos but held to the south of Los Alamos Canyon. By Tuesday, the ninth of May, the fire was being reported at 3,045 acres.

On both Monday and Tuesday, the fire was sending spot fires onto Los Alamos Laboratory land on the east side of Highway 501 near the Back Gate (intersection of Highway 501 and Highway 4). These spot fires caused serious concern at the Laboratory since this was a highly sensitive area where only people with security clearances were allowed to go and millions of dollars worth of weapons research facilities had been built among the pines. Now, wildland fire fighters were needed within the Lab perimeter to catch these spot fires and the Laboratory's own fire fighters had limited wildland fire fighting experience. (Fighting forest fires is far different from fighting structural fires where different tools, clothing and techniques are used.) These spot fires showed how dangerous the fire still was in a dry environment with a turbulent atmosphere.

For its part, Los Alamos National Laboratory had thinned a band of forest on both sides of Highway 501 from Los Alamos to Water Canyon. That fuel-break had been a source of controversy within the Laboratory, with some employees reporting upper management's reluctance to allocate funds for the project in the 1990s. The Laboratory hired Forest Service fire crews to thin in their off-season. Even so, the thinning project was never completed beyond the north edge of Water Canyon, a problem that would have serious consequences on May 10 when Cerro Grande came back to life. As it turned out, the thinning along the road had stopped right where fire fighters stopped their burnout operation on Tuesday night due to a wind shift.

May 8 and 9 were critical days for the Cerro Grande fire. The cold front that had pushed winds up to 35 miles per hour through the area on May 7 was gone and without wind, the fire settled in to calmly burning through drifts of pine needles, down logs and sticks on Forest Service land. Relative humidity was up, and the temperature dropped 6 degrees (F), helping calm the fire under cloud cover.

On Tuesday, bulldozers pushed a fire line from Pajarito Mountain Ski Area, down toward Camp May Road, hoping to make a firm line on the north edge of the fire area. Firefighters always work to build a containment line all the way around a wildfire and then work to cool down the fire within that line. Here, they also worked on burning a black-line similar to those used on Cerro Grande (mountain) to hold the fire in the high country on the west edge, on the rim of the Valles Caldera. At the same time they continued to burn along Camp May Road to the west, trying to tie in to the new bulldozer line. The night shift found the relative humidity dropping and winds increasing making firing conditions dangerous. Burn out was halted as the new weather front began to move in over northern New Mexico. Time was running out for the firefighters. At many places along Camp May Road the black line was only a quarter mile wide or less, not enough to contain a fire like the one that had roared on May 7. While Paul Gleason and Kevin Joseph and the two hotshot crews had burned enough of the roadside vegetation to stop the advancing head on Sunday afternoon, the burnout was incomplete up Camp May Road immediately to the west.

Meanwhile the south end of the fire came to life on Tuesday night as the sunset and wind began to swirl around the ridges and canyons of this complex terrain. Firefighters started to burn out along the Jemez Mountain highway (State Road 4) westward toward Cerro Grande while the fire made new runs through the treetops on Water Canyon's side. The fire was coming back to life after two days of laying low.

Fire fighting resources poured into the Cerro Grande fire camp from all over the western US. With an experienced Type 1 command team in charge, people in Los Alamos felt some reassurance that the fire would likely be held and their town spared. After all, the fire had stayed to the south of town for two days.

Tuesday night fell on Los Alamos with plenty of smoke blowing into town from the north side of Los Alamos Canyon and sparkling fires gleaming through the forest to the south of town.

The Last Domino; Failure on the Frontline

By Tuesday night, Los Alamos' Western Area remained evacuated and Los Alamos National Laboratory had been closed for two days, the longest it had been closed because of an emergency. People in the Western Area of Los Alamos had been allowed back to their homes to get things they may have left in the hasty evacuation on Sunday May 7. The northern part of Los Alamos remained inhabited, though it was only a mile from the evacuated portion and near fuel choked forests. Six helicopters were working on the fire along with 327 fire fighters. During the night on Tuesday another 175 fire fighters arrived from all over the United States.

Even with a large staff of firefighters including many highly experienced ones, major threats to Los Alamos remained by Tuesday night. Tuesday, with its low wind was a key time to safeguard Los Alamos. The fire was sitting still and the fire team had a chance to get ready for a worst-case scenario. For unknown reasons, important work was never done to prevent the fire from reaching Los Alamos if it crossed Los Alamos Canyon.

As it turned out, the calm weather on Monday and Tuesday was an interlude between two dry fronts that were passing over northern New Mexico. The front that passed on May 7 had produced the high winds that blew the fire off Cerro Grande mountain, out of control and toward Los Alamos. On Wednesday, May 10, the National Weather Service warned of another front that would bring winds similar to those experienced on May 7. The two-day calm quickly gave way to a sense of emergency. Fire fighters had to be ready for more wind and Los Alamos had to be ready for a worst-case scenario where wild fire might rush at the town with very little warning.

Fire fighters use computer models to supplement experience in predicting what a fire might do when conditions change. The Cerro Grande Fire had presented serious control problems on May 7 with spot fires springing up a half mile ahead of the blaze. This sort of fire behavior is very difficult if not impossible to combat. Experience and computer models argued for a blackened fire line at least a half-mile wide along Camp May Road if new strong winds were to come up. By Tuesday night much of the black line along Camp May Road was only a quarter mile wide or less and the fire line did not extend up into the mountains high enough to cut off a new run from the south should it bear to the west.

At this point, the fire was messy, ranging around inside a roughly 20 square mile area within incomplete containment lines.

It had plenty of large patches of unburned forest available to it and fire tends to seek new fuels. If wind increased on Wednesday as expected, the fire would heat up over its entire area as it had on Sunday. Fire running into a large pocket of unburned forest could create a new convection column that would throw embers into the wind and carry to the north with prevailing winds. That could rain hot embers in and around Los Alamos.

On Tuesday evening, state and local police again ordered residents of the Western Area, the neighborhood closest to the blaze, to evacuate. The remainder of the community would not be evacuated for another 19 hours, until the afternoon of Wednesday, May 10 when the fire was nearly upon them.

On Tuesday night, the Incident Command team held a meeting to discuss the expected winds the next day. At that meeting several people urged the team commanders to send heavy bulldozers to clear trees directly behind the homes on Los Alamos' west and north sides. Since the fire line along Camp May Road was inadequate, a wide dirt swath directly next to town would be critical if the fire blew into Los Alamos Canyon and made a run to the north. Bulldozed land would prevent forest fire from preheating homes on the town perimeter and setting them ablaze. With such a fire line, structural fire fighters from Los Alamos Fire Department would be able to watch for embers falling on homes and fight those sorts of random fires. It would greatly reduce the risk to a majority of houses in the town. Yet when two fire professionals who had been involved with the fire for some days expressed concern that the weak fire line along Camp May Road argued for bulldozing near town, they got an ambiguous response from the Type One team's Section Operations Chief.

Tuesday night's strategy meeting was also marked by sharp disagreements on how effective the fire line along Los Alamos Canyon would be. Some people present argued that it could not hold with a strong low pressure system moving through the area the next day bringing with it high winds. If the wind caused spot fires the lack of a fuel break next to Los Alamos would endanger the town. Officials from the Type 1 command assured people that air tankers and helicopters would be able to put out any spot fires that might start north of the fire's containment lines. Five hundred and three people were now fighting the fire.

Yet if winds exceed 30 miles per hour, air tankers and helicopters can't fly for safety reasons. Their drops become less effective in high wind as well. Thus the incident commanders were planning to use a tool as a last line of defense for Los Alamos that weather forecasters were saying would probably not be available. Forecasts for Wednesday's winds were for 25 to 30 mile per hour. The reality would prove to be far worse.

After the late-night strategy meeting, some fire personnel who were at the meeting went to telephones to tell their families to evacuate their homes in Los Alamos. "I was alarmed by the Type 1 teams cavalier attitude," said one. Presumably Larry Humphrey, the Incident Commander, had the authority to order the evacuation of Los Alamos at this point, or to strongly suggest to Los Alamos or state police that the town be evacuated.

By Wednesday morning no fire line had been bulldozed next to Los Alamos though bulldozers had been moved into position to work. Officials later said the bulldozer operators from a local construction firm were not "fire qualified[7]" and so had been denied the job. The two days of calm before expected wind on Wednesday had been squandered with no direct defense of Los Alamos put in place. In essence, the fire fighters were working on the existing fire as if it were nowhere near a town or nuclear laboratory, like it was a routine wildland fire of the type that spring up in remote areas of the west hundreds of times a year. The failure to line Los Alamos or at least "paint" the forest directly near homes with retardant on Tuesday would prove to be a failure of judgment to rival any made by prescribed fire crews on Cerro Grande. This failure was never investigated as official inquiries largely focused on the initial escape of the prescribed fire and its planning efforts.

Hell

Wednesday, May 10 broke as the day that hell would visit Los Alamos. Only a thin fireline and one that few professionals believed would hold a wind driven assault by fire defended the town. By late morning, it was clear winds were exceeding forecasts and pushing the fire that had been brooding around in Pajarito and Valles Canyons into a new large blaze. The relative humidity dropped through the floor (to the low teens) and the atmosphere turned turbulent and inviting to convection from fire. Sometime in the late morning, fire that had been burning in the upper ends of Valle and Pajarito Canyon came to life with a vengeance. It started as some torching trees above heavy beds of fuel and these flames, pushed by winds from the southwest coalesced into a new head. The fire blew up, roaring out of the canyons and across a swath of ridges above where the May 7 run had been. It gathered its strength, roaring into the trees with sterilizing heat that laid all life to ruin in its path.

By 11:30 an urgent radio call went out from the division commander on the Camp May Road. A spot fire had started on the north side of the Camp May Road right where the burnout operation had ceased days before. A fire engine and hand tool crews pounced on the fire, slashing desperately. It grew fast and climbed into the crowns of trees and dove into Los Alamos Canyon. There it feasted on the thick Douglas and white fir forests on the north facing slopes radiating tremendous heat across the canyon and sending up a new plume. The fire had a new head that reached the north rim of Los Alamos Canyon, a half mile from the edge of Los Alamos around one in the afternoon.

The winds could not have been worse for Los Alamos. Not only was the prevailing wind blowing from the southwest, it was strong and persistent. By one in the afternoon it was blowing with gusts to 75 miles per hour. The fire was only tripped by Los Alamos Canyon that is 500 feet deep where the fire crossed. There the northward advance of the fire was slowed by eddies of wind that swirled down from the rim in barrel shaped circulation. Those eddies served to heat the north facing slope while circulating heat to the south facing slopes on the canyon. Soon enough the fire was across, into the area called Quemazon, a Spanish word for "burned."

Far from being able to attack the fire with airplanes as the incident commanders had planned, all air tankers and helicopters were grounded due to the extreme winds and the fire command ordered all wildland fire fighters to retreat to safety zones at 11:30; places where they would be safe from the running fire. At 1:30 in the afternoon the fire was on its own. Pushed by 40 mile per hour winds it ate through more national forest land cloaked with ponderosa pine thickets.

Just a half hour before, at one in the afternoon, with little official warning, the residents of the neighborhoods north of the "Western Area" of Los Alamos were ordered to evacuate. Why the order took so long may have to do with strong pressure from Los Alamos National Laboratory officials who were hoping up to that point to reopen the laboratory and return work to normal on May 10.

Meanwhile, three miles to the south at the historic Back Gate, during the time firefighters were pulled off the fire for safety reasons, a thread of fire slipped eastward through a band of unthinned land between Water Canyon and the boundary of Bandelier National Monument. This fire spotted across the highway and onto Los Alamos Laboratory land and began a major 8-day run across the most heavily secure lands of the laboratory (see Chapter 6).

Whenever fire in timber and brush has wind exceeding 20 miles per hour behind it, its rate of forward spread (the head) will far surpass any spread to the sides (the flanks). As wind driven fires get a hot head, they race forward in a narrow advance. The convection of the heat from the head draws air in from the sides, creating drafts or surface winds toward the fire. In the case of Cerro Grande, it raced through the Quemazon forests above western Los Alamos with its main head a full half mile above the edge of the town. It got to Pueblo Canyon while still gaining momentum.

The head was moving fast, running north at just under one mile per hour, quite fast for a forest fire in timber. The fire's head was missing Los Alamos! Thanks to the work done by Kevin Joseph, Paul Gleason and the two Hotshot crews on May 7, the fire had been forced up into the mountains, running with northward winds away from Los Alamos. By killing the fire's run directly toward Los Alamos on May 7, these firefighters forced the fire up higher on the mountain when it came back to life on May 10. Ironically, given the position of the head fire running north midday on May 10, if dozer lines and slurry had been put near Los Alamos on May 9 as Ms. Sydoriak had urged, it's likely that a majority of the homes burned in Los Alamos on May 10 and 11 would have been spared.

The head is the focal point of advancing heat on a forest fire. Very large fires can develop multiple heads as the Clover Mist Fire at Yellowstone had in 1988. Depending on conditions, the head of a fire can be narrow or wide. Often head fires will crown through treetops while the following flanking fire will stay on the ground or pop into the trees sporadically. In the case of Cerro Grande on May 10, the wind was pushing the flame front nearly horizontally so it was preheating fuels ahead of itself much faster than it would have if winds had been light. High velocity winds blow embers far ahead of the main flame front, starting spot fires that can grow quickly. As the Cerro Grande fire advanced on May 10, it was throwing spot fires a mile and a quarter ahead of itself, an extraordinary distance even by the standards of some of the worst western firestorms in history. The fire was also leaning down with winds between 30 and 70 miles per hour at its back.

As the fire roared north, it hit a fuel break that had been cut in the forest above Los Alamos by Bill Armstrong and his US Forest Service crews in 1996. This band of thinned trees ran along the boundary between Forest Service and Los Alamos County lands from Los Alamos Canyon to Rendija Canyon on the north edge of Los Alamos. Bill Armstrong, the US Forest Service forester in charge of forest management on the national forest land near Los Alamos had designed the fuel break to stop a fire coming toward Los Alamos from anywhere west of town. Though he knew the most likely scenario, given prevailing winds, was for a fire to come from the south or southwest, he did all he could with the orientation of national forest boundary relative to Los Alamos and a limited budget.

The fuel break was designed to stop a crown fire by depriving it of continuous canopy fuels, by putting a big gap in the canopy that would force a fire to the ground where it would be easier to control. Unfortunately for all involved, Los Alamos County owned the land between the Forest Service fuel break and the city and the city had done little thinning or fuel reduction close to town where it would matter in an extreme firestorm such as was occurring on May 10[8]. Thus when the hot flanking fire hit the fuel break above the west side of town the fuel break knocked the fire out of the tree tops and stopped its advance toward town. Amazingly, the head of the fire, running in the treetops ran along the west edge of the fuel break. By Los Alamos Canyon and the Western Area the fire did cross the fuel break as a spot fire, climb into the tree tops again and slam into a section of residential area. Even so, the Forest Service fuel break made a tremendous difference for the Western Area, even taking into account the neglected county lands between the fuel break and the homes.

Unfortunately, as the fuel break runs north, beyond the Western Area, it converges with the upper streets of Los Alamos north community and meets the edge of town at the edge of 48th Street. Thus the head of the fire, pressing against the fuel break brushed North Community before continuing north.

The eastward burning flank burned in ponderosa pine thickets as a ground fire, working its way toward Los Alamos, mostly on Los Alamos County land. The fire dropped to the ground because it was a backing fire, going downhill. Fire burns more slowly down hill than it does on a flat or up a hill. It torched in some trees, but it burned hot on the forest floor leaving the larger trees above it green (the heat was intense enough that most of those trees would later die from damage to their cambium, the thin living layer of a tree just below the bark). The ground fire crept into the yards of Los Alamos homes along Pueblo Canyon and Los Alamos Canyon setting many homes ablaze on Fairway, Ridgeway and Sycamore Streets – streets that all run along the edges of canyons. Fire found dry grass and heavy pine needle beds in many yards and in some cases piles of firewood stacked against walls. Creeping ground fire touched fifty year-old wooden houses, dry with age and some of these started to burn. As one house began to burn, fanned by strong wind, it heated the house next to it and in many cases the next house began to burn from the radiant heat of the first.

Kevin Joseph of the Forest Service found himself working to save homes on Ridgeway Street, using people's garden hoses and hand tools to stop spot fires burning in dry grass and pine needles (that residents had been urged by officials to clean up for years before). Mr. Joseph reported that he found firewood stacked against the walls of homes burning[9]. Years of education efforts by federal land agencies and the Los Alamos Fire Department had apparently not been convincing to many residents.

Another fire behavior dynamic took its toll on the residential areas. Fire brands (bits of burning material like burning oak leaves or small sticks), flung into the sky by convection and wind from the head fire fell on homes at random in Los Alamos, igniting the flat tar roofs and then the whole house. In spite of fire fighter's heroic efforts, soon too many houses were aflame to save most. An urban firestorm swept the north and west fringes of the town.

A second unfortunate event happened as the fire passed along the fuel break above Western Area. Just after coming up out of Los Alamos Canyon and beginning its run to the north, the fire threw a spot fire across the fuel break above the Western Area. This ember found thickets of pine and heavy pine debris on Los Alamos County lands and began a patchy crown fire running straight toward the Western Area and Trinity Drive's upper most extension. There this little head of fire slammed into six houses directly and started a succession of house fires from houses that were oriented exactly with the heat of the blaze where the street curves to the north. Like dominos the houses began to burn with each heating its neighboring house in succession even though the little head that had hit Sandia Drive was by now down on the ground. City firefighters escaped as flames roared up in the houses. Already handicapped by the failure of the power and water systems in Los Alamos, they relied on water in their trucks alone as the heat and number of burning homes overwhelmed them. It was about 4:30 in the afternoon.

As the main head fire moved beyond the western edge of Los Alamos, its head stayed up a quarter to a half-mile above the residential areas next to the fuel break. It blew northward, pushed by winds from 25 to 60 miles per hour with higher gusts. The fire's head stayed narrow, running along a shelf of land interrupted by east-west canyons as it traveled. It came to a ridge of two hundred foot tall mountains that stand directly next to and perpendicular to North Community. At this point, the fire's head met with its first formidable obstacles, a rocky ridge with sparse vegetation on its south side. According to fire behavior specialists, the fire likely began a horizontally oriented barrel shaped circulation next to the ridge. Then the fire edged past the east end of the ridge (known locally as LA Mountain) and spilled as a crown fire directly into 48th Street where a line of fifty year-old, two story wooden quadruplex dwellings rapidly succumbed to the crown fire. The Forest Service's fuel break created no obstacle to the fire as it erupted around the face of LA Mountain driven by the gale force winds.

The fire ran directly into the residential area where yards and streets broke up the near-continuous canopy of trees the fire had fed on since it emerged from Los Alamos Canyon at about noon. (The town's residents had been evacuated to nearby communities the day before.) The fire dropped out of the trees as it hit 48th Street but by now winds estimated by fire fighters were as high as 70 miles per hour. These winds pressed the flames along the ground, spreading the fire in a wide tongue three streets deep eastward. Tens of multi family houses began to burn at once, their half-century-old lumber tinder dry, their flat tar roofs underlain by brittle plywood eager to explode into flames. The fire burned east to 45th street and north to Alabama Avenue before it collapsed. The houses it fed on here had been built in 1949 and 1950 with wood and some asbestos shingle siding[10]. These "Group 11" houses burned rapidly and produced intense heat and the ultimate count of "homes" lost would skyrocket as they burned, since most were multi-family (quadraplex) structures.

The fire roared up the side of LA Mountain even as it burned into the North Community. The east face of LA Mountain was burned by fire in the 1940s and was a rocky expanse that may have had the effect of cooling the fire even as it burned into the neighborhood. If the east face of LA Mountain, above the community had been covered with dense pine forest rather than rock and gamble oak, it is likely fire damage in the North Community would have been more severe.

Yet the worst for Los Alamos was not over. Arizona Avenue, which runs along the edge of the forest north of the area just described, was beginning to burn. This street curves to a thirty-degree angle away from the path of the fire's head. A shallow branch of Pueblo Canyon where forests come right into town from the east separates it from the North Community neighborhood. A large swath of trees burned only by ground fire along Arizona Avenue's south end reveal that the fire on Arizona Avenue started not from running crown fire coming from the south, but by ground fire.

Cerro Grande Fire
Destroyed Structures as of May 12, 7 pm.
Los Alamos townsite.

Black dots indicate locations of destroyed homes on this map
of Los Alamos.

Houses started to burn on both sides of Arizona Avenue at about five in the afternoon. An intense wind was running down the street and one house started the next in a rage of fire that left grey craters where homes had been.

Dr. Jack Cohen of the Rocky Mountain Research Station in

Missoula, Montana investigated the loss of homes in Los Alamos and concluded that crown fire touched Los Alamos in two places only (Sandia Drive and 48th Street). The majority of homes in Los Alamos burned when fire ran though pine needle beds in the yards and ignited wood siding, or houses were ignited by the radiant heat of the house next-door burning. Unburned tree canopies among homes in most of Los Alamos proved that ground fire burned a majority of homes and cleaning up yards and roofs could have saved most of these[11].

Forty-three buildings were burned on Arizona Avenue and another 23 on intersecting streets in north community alone. More houses were burned elsewhere in the community. These fires continued into May 11.

Meanwhile the main head of the Cerro Grande forest fire had moved away from Los Alamos but not before it brushed the edge of a new neighborhood that had been built on land recently exchanged from the Forest Service near Guaje Pines Cemetery by a local land developer. The fire had run on a direct course for the aptly named "Ponderosa Estates" where new houses had been built among crowded pine stands.

Amazingly, only one house in this new subdivision burned, thanks largely to the efforts of the land developer himself (Paul Parker) who brought in his construction crew of ten men who fought ground fire with water tenders and garden hoses and saved the homes they had helped build. Also most of the owners had worked with Forest Service representatives to prepare their properties for the inevitable wildfire.

By the evening of May 10, the forest fire had moved off into open forestland that had few human developments. Concern that the fire might burn Barranca Mesa, a large subdivision of privately built homes north of Arizona Avenue proved unfounded. By then the fire, "confused" by the complicated terrain of Rendija Canyon and its sub drainages, had flung itself into more continuous fuels to the west and was running toward a large tract of remote land between Los Alamos and the Santa Clara Indian reservation. There, the fire ran over the place where the Forest Service had been fighting the Guaje Fire on May 3 and burned clear to Chupaderos Canyon before exhausting itself in sparse fuels after a 12 hour, 8 mile wind-driven run.

The foundation of a burned home in North Community
looking west toward LA Mountain.

Destroyed cars and foundations of burned
homes in North Community.

National Guard troops guide a long-time Los Alamos family to see
the wreckage of their home for the first time.

New Mexico State Police roadblock closing Los Alamos at Totavi.

The evacuation center for Los Alamos residents in Pojoaque.

A crew of wildland firefighters moves north in evacuated Los Alamos.

The death of the north-running head was not the death of the fire. Flanking fire spread east and west away from the passing head and the west flank roared up the faces of the steep mountains above Los Alamos, crowning as it went, reducing green mountains to bristles of blackened logs. Fire moves fast up hill, especially up hills that have heavy fuels on them as they did above Los Alamos. The fire burned off the whole east face of the Sierra de los Valles from Pajarito Mountain to Caballo Mountain.

Meanwhile in Los Alamos, on May 11 and 12, fire continued to creep down the heavily forested canyons that intersect the town. Fire moved down Pueblo Canyon and its sub drainages, burning many homes built in the pines along these drainages. In Los Alamos Canyon windborn fire completely devastated the fir and spruce forest on the north-facing slope. By some miracle, that fire dynamic stopped just west of the Los Alamos Canyon bridge and the fire died sparing the trailer-house village called Royal Crest, downtown Los Alamos, laboratory buildings and a large tunnel that runs under downtown Los Alamos from within a secure area of Los Alamos Canyon.

Homes far from the main firestorms in North Community and the limited direct crown fire hits on Trinity Drive began to burn on May 11. Though eventually 58 city fire companies would be on hand to help with the residential fires, the Los Alamos Fire Department was spread thin, protecting both the Laboratory (see Chapter 9) and dealing with hundreds of residential fires in Los Alamos, when even one such fire would have required care and focus in a normal shift.

On May 11 fire fighters braved the wind and began a burnout operation along Rendija Canyon to protect Barranca Mesa homes on the ridges above. With helicopters helping, they burned out fuels all day and all night.

By May 11 the fire fighting organization had ballooned to 611 firefighters, 28 engines and 9 helicopters. Another fire (the Cree Fire) was burning in and near Ruidoso, NM (200 miles southeast of Los Alamos) at the same time and it had an even larger fire fighting organization. The fire organization for Cerro Grande ramped up to the highest level, with a second Type-One incident commander sent to set up a new command center in Espanola, twenty miles north of Los Alamos, to handle the north end of the fire, leaving Mr. Humphrey (the Incident Commander) to oversee the wildland fire forces from the edge of Bandelier to the north edge of Los Alamos. Van Bateman was the new commander for the north zone of the fire. Bob Meuchel was the Area Commander for both zones.

North zone incident commander Mr. Bateman was brought in from the Coon Creek fire on the Tonto National Forest near Globe, Arizona, a wilderness area fire that had gotten to be almost 9,000 acres. Mr. Bateman was moved to the Cerro Grande as the Coon Creek began to go out. His team's fire camp was set up on the terrace west of Espanola, a hot and dusty place but one where they could access some of the only roads into the north end of the fire. Yet their efforts and those of the south team turned out to be largely futile as the fire ran its course with little noticeable influence from human efforts.

Homes in Los Alamos would continue to burn until May 15 with the last four burning in "Sleepy Hollow" on the rim of Pueblo Canyon.

The wildfire itself had finished its major run on May 10 but large acreages continued to burn on successive days. The fire ran clear to Santa Clara Canyon on May 12, burning close to the internationally known Puye Cliff Dwellings archaeological site near Santa Clara Pueblo. The fire moved up into upper Guaje and Santa Clara Canyons on May 14 until it hit wet fuels and wound down. On May 14, the fire made a major crown fire run on the north-facing slope of Santa Clara Canyon. That area was one of the wildest and most pristine areas in the southwest, with beaver dams, large trees and deep wilderness. Much of the area on tribal land would later be salvage logged.

By May 15, despite predictions of extreme fire behavior that could push the fire into the 1998 Oso Fire burn north of Santa Clara Canyon and cause new problems near Los Alamos, a mass of clouds moved over the fire and raised humidity, shading the fire and caused all to calm down. After May 11, a majority of areas burned by the fire were burned by low intensity fire that actually increased forest health in those areas in much the same way the prescribed fire at Bandelier had intended to do.

For days, the fire continued to burn in the wilderness of upper Guaje Canyon and Santa Clara Canyons but water dropping helicopters kept it from making new runs, even as it entered the fire dependent montane grasslands of Caballo Mountain. On May 20 rain came to the fire area and by May 24 hundreds of fire fighters from the two fire camps, along with Mr. Bateman and Mr. Humphrey were on their way to the many new fires springing up in states north of New Mexico. The worst fire season in history was rapidly unfolding across the central and northern Rockies and soon fires in Idaho would make Cerro Grande's acreage look small, though the loss of homes in Los Alamos stood as the greatest tragedy of the 2000 fire season.

When all was said and done, 235 homes burned to the ground in Los Alamos leaving 405 people without houses. Many of these were apartments in multiple unit housing buildings. Eighty-five fire fighters were treated for injuries, no deaths occurred because of the Cerro Grande Fire.

[1] The author observed this phase of the fire from the catwalk of the Bandelier fire lookout.

[2] I observed the build up of fuels in these specific forests over 30 years of personal observations. I had visited the forests last in January 2000 when a low-snow year allowed me to see the fuel build up.

[3] Marlin Johnson, From a paper presented at the Forest Ecology Working Group session at the Society of American Foresters National Convention held in Albuquerque, New Mexico, November. 9-13, 1996. Pg. 1

[4] The main campus of the Los Alamos National Laboratory has large office buildings, libraries, old chemical laboratories and, significantly, the CMR building which houses plutonium, uranium and other hazardous alloys and metals. This building is fortified concrete and is scheduled to be replaced and torn down around 2011.

[5] The forest close to Camp May Road where Gleason's team was working is frequently used for recreation including "parties" where younger folks often have campfires on weekend nights. Many Los Alamos residents were astonished that the Forest Service would allow fuel loads to accumulate so close to town where so many illegal camp fires were set by people with impaired judgment.

[6] Personal interview with Charisse Sydoriak.

[7] "Fire qualified" means that a person has taken basic fire fighting training which has critical safety training related to escaping from a fast forest fire.

[8] Many residents of Los Alamos with homes on the edge of town had resisted thinning the thickets of trees for aesthetic reasons. These residents believed that the thick forests were natural and relished the privacy the forest cover gave them.

[9] Interview with then Espanola Ranger District Fire Management Officer Kevin Joseph March 20, 2001.

[10] Craig Martin, Quads, Shoeboxes and Sunken Living Rooms, A History of Los Alamos Housing, (Los Alamos Historical Society Monograph 2000) pg 44.

[11] Jack Cohen, Examination of the home destruction in Los Alamos associated with the Cerro Grande Fire - July 10, 2000. (USDA Forest Service, Rocky Mountain Research Station, Missoula, Montana 2000)

Chapter 8

Burning the Lab

In June 1954, the Los Alamos fire chief and the city manager were burning brush piles with some boy scouts at the Sawyer's Hill scout camp and community ski area in the mountains just below Cerro Grande. The pile burning went all night but in the morning, wind came up and blew sparks into the forest to the north. An active forest fire (dubbed the Water Canyon Fire) grew from those sparks and burned across Water Canyon, Valle Canyon, and Pajarito Canyon toward Los Alamos. Burning during one of the worst droughts in the last century, the fire was visible from Santa Fe and was the first forest fire of any consequence near Los Alamos since the town had been established as a secret military research facility nine years earlier.

Heinie Merker, a US Forest Service ranger recalled strange events surrounding the fire, ones that would foreshadow the Cerro Grande Fire 46 years later:

"Norris Bradbury, the director of Los Alamos Scientific Laboratory stayed up the whole night. About every half hour he would come up to our headquarters wanting to know for sure that the fire wasn't going to get across the highway that runs north and south. He didn't explain what was on the other side of the highway, but every time a spark would go over there, everything was turned loose to get on that spot fire. I found out later it was some sort of explosive stuff down there. What it was I still don't know. He was sure concerned that the fire was going to get across the highway and get into the technical area I guess all hell would have broken loose if it had.[1]"

Los Alamos National Laboratory owns 27,500 acres of land on the Pajarito Plateau between Bandelier National Monument and the town site of Los Alamos to the north. A dense cluster of buildings in Los Alamos contains the bulk of the laboratory's operations, but the large tract of land sprawling toward Bandelier has scattered facilities used for secret nuclear weapons related research. This area is a nearly flat ponderosa pine forest, bisected by various canyons. Among the trees are the remains of several old Spanish American homesteads that were occupied in the 1800s. The laboratory's land has been sealed off from the general public since 1943 and has had a mixture of environmentally disturbing activities such as explosive testing and the construction of large technical buildings and, on the other hand, large areas where little if any human activity take place at all. These wild tracts have been locked in time, with historic and prehistoric artifacts left in tact and wildlife finding a preserve of sorts.

In 1954, the laboratory's land between Ancho and Los Alamos Canyons on the east side of State Highway 501 was sparsely developed but closely secured. An old Harry Buckman saw mill dating from 1897 had been cleared away and in its place a complex of buildings had been built to engineer the implosion device needed to set off a critical nuclear reaction in the first atomic bombs. This research area was and is called "S-Site," named for the sawdust piles that lab workers found from the old saw mill. S-site included buildings erected for the fabrication of the first three atomic bombs – one that was tested at Trinity Site in southern New Mexico, and the next two which were dropped on Hiroshima and Nagasaki Japan in 1945.

With its focus on technology and the military, Los Alamos National Laboratory seemed little interested in the mundane aspect of its estate like the forests that pressed up against the edges of the buildings. The laboratory had done little forestry work before 1978 when the La Mesa Fire roared away, from a spark left from an off-road-vehicle driven on US Forest Service land, on Obsidian Ridge and into the southern reaches of the Lab's land including areas where high explosive bunkers dot the landscape. That fire seared across Bandelier National Monument and into thickets of pine that had developed on the south edge of laboratory land. According to foresters from the two major land management agencies involved with the Los Alamos area, the laboratory was briefly interested in forestry work to reduce fire danger after the La Mesa blaze. The lab's interest died out as their weapons budget swelled and the Reagan administration gave its agencies permission to downplay natural resource issues in the 1980s. That was true until the Dome fire sent a column of smoke into the air within 10 miles of Los Alamos in 1996.

The Dome Fire started with an abandoned campfire near Cochiti Canyon on US Forest Service land and grew into a major wind driven blaze that burned through parts of Bandelier National Monument's upper reaches and toward Los Alamos. The fire got to the rim of Frijoles Canyon and was ready to burn into the dense timber of upper Frijoles Canyon on National Park Service land (the area known to Bandelier managers as "Unit 9") when the wind shifted to the south and blew the fire back into itself. Meanwhile, the fear of fire spreading to Los Alamos had been so great that tens of large air-tanker runs had been made, "painting" the south rim of Frijoles Canyon with fire retardant to slow the crowning spread of the fire. The wind shift rather than the chemical bath was likely responsible for the fire's defeat.[2]

The Dome Fire inspired the first real wild fire prevention activity at Los Alamos National Laboratory. Prompted by foresters and scientists from Bandelier and by Bill Armstrong and Robert Rumilard, longtime Los Alamos area US Forest Service foresters, the laboratory began to take action. In 1996 the Interagency Wildfire Management Team was formed, consisting of the two federal land management agencies (NPS and USFS) and Los Alamos County and the laboratory. With tutoring from Bandelier scientists and Bill Armstrong of the Forest Service, the laboratory began to recognize the reality of inevitable wildfire and began to plan for a fire that would come from outside the laboratory's property, abandoning its long held view that they need only worry about fires that started on laboratory land by high explosives.

In 1996, the Laboratory re-cleared a firebreak along Highway 501 from Los Alamos to Water Canyon that had been cut in 1978.

By 1998 the laboratory was looking at the many buildings it had in dense ponderosa pine forest for fire safety, cutting trees away from those buildings and thinning trees on their many wild acres to disarm any wildfire. By the time the Cerro Grande Fire exploded, the laboratory had thinned the most vulnerable 800 of its 10,000-forested acres. Even so, it's difficult to understand why any real action on wildfire prevention took 18 years after the La Mesa fire, which made national news and burned over explosives bunkers on LANL land.

"They (LANL staff) looked at the La Mesa fire as a fluke" Bill Armstrong of the local Forest Service office said. Since it was the first major fire that had happened near the laboratory in 23 years, and with a period of unusual wetness prevailing until 1996, it's easy to understand the lab manager's view that fire was someone else's problem as they focused on their mission, which was largely detached from the natural environment. Yet, even as late as 1999, Forest Service and National Park Service fire specialists found many in the Laboratory's upper management surprised by warnings of an imminent wildfire and the severe flooding it could produce.[3]

By 2000, the same area where the La Mesa Fire had burned on LANL land was still an active laboratory work area, surrounded by a fence and patrolled by guards. This remote area of LANL, abutting Bandelier National Monument's boundary, has a variety of weapons-oriented research projects including new facilities used for photographing simulated nuclear explosions, outdoor explosives testing ranges, the "Weapons Engineering Tritium Facility," numerous highly secured office buildings where classified work goes on and old waste landfills with unknown contents dating back to the 1940s.

New Fire

On May 7, 2000, when the Cerro Grande prescribed fire escaped from Bandelier National Monument, the fire front running northward through US Forest Service land passed within one mile of LANL's western boundary. The fire ran through the burn area of the 1954 Water Canyon Fire that included big hillsides of oak scrub and shelf-lands of young aspen groves, before slowing as the wind died down in heavy fuels as described in Chapter 7. For the next three days, fire fighters chased spot fires that were igniting on the laboratory's property with the largest reaching about two acres.

May 9 found the fire still ruminating in the contained area between the Bandelier boundary, Highway 501 and Camp May Road. On its south edge, the fire was in complex terrain where Water Canyon runs up to Cerro Grande and the large shelf created by the Pajarito Fault makes a steep rise in the landscape.

Here, steep south-facing slopes and dry ponderosa pine forest fostered hot fire, which then made runs across Water Canyon into the dense north-facing fir forests which burned with successive head runs toward the east. As the fire worked its way down the canyon, toward an old homestead site near the Back Gate, fire fighters say it "hooked around," burning up against Highway 4 while being encouraged by erratic winds coming out of the huge Frijoles Canyon to the south, eddying against the cliff faces and causing fire brands to take to the sky. These embers landed on the Laboratory side of Highway 501 causing fire crews to rush in to stop the resulting spot fires. The fire crews held the fire at the Back Gate highway intersections and continued to back-burn up the highway into the Jemez Mountains into the night.

While we might imagine that fire fighters would be guarding the lab boundary to prevent the fire from crossing in, Wednesday, May 10, was a hellish day, the day the fire escaped into Los Alamos and into the Lab lands as well. The night before the relative humidity had stayed low, keeping the fire active at a time when fire fighters hoped to make some headway against it. By eleven in the morning, winds rose to 15 miles per hour and with drying of fuels and dropping relative humidity the fire began to run in the trees, spotting into Los Alamos Canyon. On the south edge of the fire winds were gusting to 35 miles per hour. Just short of noon, fire behavior was so extreme and winds were high enough that the incident commander called fire fighters off the fire lines and the air tankers were grounded at their Albuquerque base.

At this point the fire lines were vulnerable and the fire reared up in the hottest part of the day. Despite the efforts of the night before which had involved burning out lands on the north side of the Jemez Mountain Highway (SR 4) west of the back gate, the fire made a crown run on Bandelier lands, sending crown fire through an area that had experienced prescribed burning in the late 1980s. The crown fire crossed State Road 4 into Forest Service lands in the American Springs area, essentially burning in unburned fuels east of and below Cerro Grande where the fire had escaped five days earlier. This crown run coincided with the fire burning into Los Alamos miles to the north. With the crown fire came winds to 45 miles per hour, extreme winds by the standards of fire fighters. The convection from the crown fire on the ridge above the laboratory sent firebrands skyward and a spot fire started on the laboratory lands 1.25 miles from the crown fire itself. This sort of long distance spotting is characteristic of the most extreme sort of fire behavior. The fire on laboratory land ran north and east for 4.5 miles, by midnight, through grass and ponderosa pine.

While fire fighters assigned to State Road 503 and State Road 4 described spot fires and fire crossing the highway near the back gate on May 10, it is difficult to know exactly what happened at the Back Gate that day because nobody was there to witness it. Incident commanders pulled all fire fighters off the east and south lines of the fire on May 10. Dr. Craig Allen of the US Geologic Survey and patrol law enforcement rangers from Bandelier reported that there were no firefighters on the highways, which formed the fire lines, between the Camp May Road on the east and Las Conchas Recreation Area on the west edge of what is now the Valles Caldera National Preserve.

Thus the fire line between the main fire and Los Alamos National Laboratory sat abandoned on May 10 when the fire crossed near the intersection of the two state highways known as the Back Gate. Why the incident commanders had pulled all the fire fighters from this area is a mystery. Most likely they felt that the safety of fire fighters was best insured by removing them from these lines in the high-wind situation. Yet there were adequate safety zones for fire fighters to escape the blaze had it blown up in this area. Even so, with air tankers grounded due to wind, it is doubtful that ground forces would have been able to stop the flame front when it crossed onto Laboratory land on May 10.

The Cerro Grande Fire's smoke plume from the Rio Grande Valley, May 11, 2000.

By May 10, a spot fire had ignited in Water Canyon on laboratory land. Firefighters attacked this blaze but 50 miles per hour winds drove it out of control to the north and east, crossing Valle Canyon and on to Pajarito Canyon. At that point the fire was close to the central campus of the laboratory, where pine forests came to the walls of buildings from the 1950s, including buildings housing plutonium and other radioactive elements and compounds. These materials are stored in heavily fortified buildings and containers that would not be affected by fire. Even so, the fire did not damage these buildings.

The fire on Laboratory land burned as a ground-fire with some torching of trees. It cleared out almost a hundred years worth of brush and debris, sparing most of the larger pines and working its way to the north and east as a separate fire from the one that was by then raging well past Los Alamos to the west and north. The Laboratory fire behaved differently because of the relatively flat land and the lack of nearby mountains that cause turbulence and high wind. Fires on slopes tend to be far more active than those on flat land. The high tree mortality on the canyon walls around Los Alamos and the low tree mortality on the flat Laboratory lands demonstrate this reality. The forests in the Laboratory land had not become chocked with fuels the way Forest Service lands had and the ladders of heavy tree thickets that would lead flames into the tree tops apparently were not well established here.

The Los Alamos Fire Department was overwhelmed with burning houses in town but made protection of various high-security buildings in the Laboratory land a priority with some fire crews rushing between the town and the laboratory. In particular, the Weapons Engineering Tritium Facility drew constant attention from structural fire fighters, though the building is concrete with a flat roof. Other facilities such as office buildings, explosives bunkers and the new DAHRT facility (facility for studying nuclear weapons pits), with its wide area of cleared land around it, drew less attention.

The Cero Grande Fire presented a special problem for Los Alamos National Laboratory. Used to keeping everyone out of its land and facilities except people with the right security clearances, the lab had to let wildland fire fighters in to help its own fire department deal with the spot fires from May 7 until May 10. While the laboratory's own fire department was one of the best-funded and best equipped in the nation, due to its nuclear weapons spin-off funding, its staff was trained for structural fires and dealing with toxic and radioactive emergencies. Despite some training from Bandelier in wildland fire techniques in the mid 1990s, the laboratory found itself unsure how to deal with forest fires springing up in its midst.

Los Alamos's Fire Department is one of the only fire departments in the United States where its upper echelon officials have security clearances for entering nuclear facilities. The department has a dual role of being a municipal fire department for Los Alamos, and being a disaster protection force for the laboratory. With large nuclear and chemical waste dumps, a plutonium research and weapons fabrication plant (TA-55) and untold other buildings with radioactive and chemical hazards to protect from accident or attack, the laboratory's force placed its priority on the Laboratory buildings but under normal circumstances had a large enough staff to deal with house fires, burning school buildings or routine injuries in the town.

The Cerro Grande fire would push the fire department far beyond its limits.

Historic buildings in the S-Site area were quick to fall to flames and the flooding that followed in mid summer after the fire had run its course. The oldest were decaying homestead buildings left from the time of Hispano settlement on the Pajarito Plateau before the arrival of the Manhattan Project. The flat pine country that the US Military condemned in 1943 and converted to Laboratory land had been attractive to sheep herding families from the Rio Grande Valley who summered there or did some farming through the 1930s. Being behind security fences and away from the general public, several of these old homestead sites had been in a highly protected state on the Laboratory land. Old and decaying cabin and ranch buildings left from the Montoya y Gomez cabins site, the Gomez Homestead, the Grant Homestead, the David Romero Homestead and the last buildings of the Anchor Ranch were lost to the fire or flooding.

As the fire worked its way onto Laboratory land on May 10 and then persisted there for days, firefighters saw many facilities that normally only security cleared Lab staff see, such as explosive testing sites, strange office buildings where staff works in jail-like security cages inside layers of outer security perimeters, super- secure research sites and abandoned buildings frozen in time from the 1950s.

Likewise the fire destroyed very significant historic buildings from the Manhattan Project on May 11 including "V Site" which was a set of old wooden buildings where the fabrication of the explosive "lenses" for the Trinity atomic bomb was built on July 12, 1945. The device was detonated at Trinity Site in southern New Mexico on July 16, 1945.

Spreading grass fire reached V Site's walls and two of the three buildings were reduced to rubble, while a third survived. These buildings are on the National Register of Historic Places due to their historic importance in national and world history. Los Alamos native Ellen Bradbury (daughter of former Laboratory Directory Norris Bradbury) had been raising money to preserve V Site and had found support in the administration of then-president Bill Clinton and his representative Kathy Kelly, who was working on developing V Site as a museum and historic site with public access.

Though the Laboratory had allowed non-Laboratory fire fighters access to the closed S-Site and other secure area lands, no fire fighters were near V Site when it caught fire on May 11. Such structures were a low priority for the Los Alamos Fire Department that had multiple home fires and various highly sensitive weapons facilities to protect from the advancing flames.

Other historic facilities burned as well. On May 11, an old waste dump in the S-Site area called in Laboratory parlance "Material Disposal Area R, (MDA R)" began to burn. This was a waste pit from the 1940s and like many of the oldest waste disposal sites from the Manhattan Project days; the laboratory was not entirely sure what had been buried there as no records had been kept. When fire crept into the buried waste, fire fighters sprayed water on it for more than a week to no avail. It kept burning. Several wildland firefighters who were worried about the burning dump would not approach the area after the Laboratory sent in a robotic device to dig around for samples and to help extinguish the fire. This was well beyond the experience of fire fighters used to normal forest fires. Many of them expressed alarm to their supervisors and refused to go near MDA R.

The Laboratory fire moved quickly. From its birth as a spot fire in the late evening of May 10, it burned about 6000 acres of LANL land in the next day. Most of this was moderate intensity fire that didn't kill most of the pine trees it burned below, but the fire burned hotter in the Valle, Pajarito, Twomile, Threemile and Mortendad Canyons. In the larger of these canyons, the fire scorched the north facing slopes badly, burning out Douglas fir forests and creating conditions ripe for flooding and soil loss.

By May 13 the fire had burned over into the most sensitive area of the Laboratory, crossing many firing sites where high explosives have been tested in the open for decades. It burned over the building where the emergency dispatch center was operating and began working its way down all the major canyons on laboratory land to the east. The fire erupted from Pajarito Canyon at the Plutonium Processing Facility where the canyon lies immediately next to the road. The Plutonium Processing Facility (TA 55) is a building behind multiple fences with guard towers, cameras and sensors, resembling a prison. There work with Plutonium is done, weapon parts are manufactured and plutonium is stored along with plutonium-contaminated waste. Plutonium is a human-made transuranic element used in nuclear weapons. It is highly radioactive and extremely toxic in its airborne form.

The fire burned onto the Plutonium facility grounds, burning grass and some oak brush but spent itself in the sparse fuels and the bare dirt that surrounds the buildings. The fire continued down the mesa to the east, burning some vehicles and build-ings at Technical Area 46, an isotope research laboratory, before burning itself out in the sparse ground fuels of the pinon and juniper forests that stand between TA-46 and the large nuclear waste disposal area known as TA 54. As the fire approached the nuclear waste dump, White Rock (a suburb of Los Alamos east of the town) was ordered evacuated. Though all involved knew a flame front would not reach White Rock, the major concern was toxic smoke that could result from any spot fires starting in TA-54. Since large amounts of waste are stored in barrels under fabric domes there, a fire could create a serious public safety emergency, or at least panic, especially in Santa Fe where suspicion of the Laboratory runs high.

On May 13, fire burned up from Water Canyon onto TA-49 where the south fire camp was established. Fighting fire in fuel-chocked canyons proved to be difficult. The fire on public land and laboratory lands would smolder in canyons, then burst out when winds and fuels encouraged it.

The Laboratory fire burned itself out in lower Sandia and Mortendad Canyons around May 18, in pinon and juniper woodlands. Having been defeated in its northward advance by buildings and roads, on its eastward advance by sparse fuels, the fire burned in the canyon below the Meson linear accelera-tor at TA-53 and died. Over the ridge to the south, it burned into Mortandad Canyon, past some of the most significant ar-chaeological sites on the Pajarito Plateau and onto San Ildefonso Pueblo land where relic stands of old canyon-bottom ponderosa pine were killed.

The fire fighting effort on Laboratory land during Cerro Grande was markedly different from the fire fighting that happened dur-ing the 1977 La Mesa Fire. During La Mesa, the Laboratory tried to limit non Laboratory firefighters entering Laboratory land, where secret weapons research work is done and where explosives are also stored in bunkers and lie scattered on the landscape from decades of explosive testing. These facilities posed a security and safety issue. Guards were sent in with La Mesa fire fighters who were too busy digging fire line to garner weapons design secrets in any case. During Cerro Grande, fire spread fast on Laboratory land and the Los Alamos Fire department was pushed beyond its capabilities fighting multiple house fires in town and protecting buildings with dangerous materials inside. The Laboratory had no choice but to open the security gates to volunteer fire departments and wildland fire fighters who worked with minimal security interference.

As a result, fire fighters from all over the country found themselves working inside the Laboratory lands where the general public never can go. Many fire fighters told reporters that they were sent in to areas such as Mortendad Canyon where no laboratory personnel were willing to accompany them. Santa Fe Hotshots, who had been working on the fire since May 5, told of being directed to fight fire in places where it was obvious Laboratory personnel were unwilling to go. Many of these outside firefighters were concerned about their health, and for good reason. In many parts of the Lab land, high explosive fragments are scattered on the landscape and embedded in trees. In places like Mortendad Canyon, radioactive elements like Plutonium and Uranium are in the stream bed sediments and could have been absorbed into the tissues of trees and plants that were burning.

The Laboratory got an earful of firefighter worries about fighting fire and later doing rehabilitation work on the grounds of a nuclear weapons facility. The south fire camp for Cerro Grande was situated at "Technical Area 49" a tract of land that directly borders Bandelier National Monument on the south end of the Lab's reservation. Here, the Lab had agreed to build an interagency fire cache in 1998, the one from which Bandelier's Fire Use Module staged its prescribed fire activities and fire fighting activities until May 9. The site also had a Cold War history, as did much of the land the fire was burning through within the Department of Energy lands.

TA-49 seemed to be a good place for a fire camp since it was open and flat and close to the roads that would lead firefighters to the south end of the blaze. Further, it has the interagency fire station and it is right on a public highway. Yet it was also an old nuclear testing site for the Lab and word of this got out to the firefighters who were sleeping on the ground in camping tents. The site was used for under ground testing of an explosive device that included radioactive elements in 1959 and 1960. Two deep boreholes where these explosions took place have been sealed and monitored for radiation releases. The whole area around them has been subject to detailed environmental study and radiation monitoring by the lab since at least 1970[4].

Even so, the laboratory found itself dealing with frightened fire fighters who worried that camping at TA-49 would compromise their health. The lab sent people to explain to the fire fighters that only minor amounts of tritium were ever found on the surface at TA-49 and that these probably came from elsewhere at the lab and were below any level that should cause concern. The lab found itself in the same position it often finds itself in with members of the public who are suspicious of the lab's veracity and who have trouble understanding the physics and chemistry of the environmental problems the lab's activities create. It had to find a way to explain the hazards or lack of hazards clearly while not seeming condescending or dishonest. In part the lab handled this by bringing in environmental experts from the state of New Mexico Environment Department who, they hoped, would be seen as objective, since they worked for the state and not the lab. Unfortunately many fire fighters failed to see this distinction and felt distrust of all the radiation hazard information they were given.

It's difficult to know how much hazard existed for the fire fighters at the fire camp. The laboratory's long-running cleanup program had monitored the site and catalogued all the radiation hazard areas on all the laboratory's property. Yet this information was not available to fire fighters. While it seems unlikely the camp at TA-49 presented a hazard to the fire fighters, their work on the rest of the laboratory land was likely hazardous at times, especially when fire was burning contaminated organic matter or trash.

When the fire operation moved into the rehabilitation effort after the fire was contained, concerns by fire fighters working on the Burned Area Recovery Effort (BARE Team) continued. The lab offered fire fighters radiation monitoring badges such as most laboratory workers wear to monitor their exposure to radiation day to day[5]. Further, an air quality monitoring station was set up at the TA-49 fire camp. Even so, by mid June, 100 fire fighters left the rehabilitation project and asked to be reassigned to other emergencies. Given that the summer of 2000 was the worst fire year on record and major fires were burning in Colorado, Idaho and Montana, those fire fighters were easily reassigned to large project fires farther north.

Speaking about the fire fighters concerns, Lee McAtee, deputy director for environmental, health and safety at LANL, said: "many of these people come in from Timbuktu or somewhere, and they've never had any kind of experience with nuclear materials or radiation and so they don't have the experience or knowledge or familiarity with the issues to make a decision."[6]

Meanwhile, smoke from the Cerro Grande Fire drifted east and north from the Pajarito Plateau, rising high above the Sangre de Cristo Mountains at times but also blanketing the Rio Grande Valley especially at night and particularly over Taos near the Colorado border. Many people from the Taos area left the state to escape the smoke and many others expressed alarm about possible health implications from the burning of LANL property and the smoke it produced.

Some people in nearby communities tend to distrust Los Alamos Laboratory and this skepticism came to the fore as the Laboratory sought to assure people that the fire on the lab's land was not burning explosives, toxins or radioactive materials that could be carried to the public in the huge cloud of smoke rising from the fire. Because of the nature of the work done at Los Alamos, the secrecy there, and the sense that people don't get the whole story on a variety of issues relating to nuclear weapons and the waste produced in their research and development, a great deal of distrust has built up between many residents of New Mexico and the laboratory. This was most evidenced by those who chose to flee the state or the region to escape the smoke coming from the Cerro Grande Fire despite assurances, from both the state of New Mexico and LANL officials, that dangerous materials were not present in the smoke.

Los Alamos Laboratory, the state of New Mexico Environment Department, and the US Environmental Protection Agency all cooperated to sample the smoke resulting from the Cerro Grande Fire. Air sampling equipment detected some increased radio-activity due to the blaze. The laboratory and the state of New Mexico concurred that these radioactive elements were from the re-suspension of particles of naturally occurring Uranium, lead bismuth and polonium by the fire[7].

However, a leading critic of Los Alamos Laboratory, a group then-called Concerned Citizens for Nuclear Safety, disputed the lab and the state's conclusion that only naturally occurring radiation was released by the fire. The group charged that the data used to draw those conclusions was flawed and underestimated the man-made radioactive material encountered by the fire. They worried that the studies that followed the fire were rushed and their results were either difficult to interpret or were garbled when they were made available to the New Mexico Attorney General's office[8].

Russian nuclear and atmospheric scientist Sergei Pashchenko, a consultant to a non-governmental group which works to ban weapons containing depleted uranium, said he analyzed the limited data available on the lab's Internet site and determined fire-related radiation releases could not be discounted as being sourced by naturally occurring elements[9]. Sampling stations were set up in nearby communities where the plume from the fire was traveling, yet these revealed similar result as the air samples taken at Los Alamos [10]. Nothing beyond particles of uranium and decay products of radon stirred up by the blaze were present according to the three agencies doing the sampling[11].

In the end, the Cerro Grande Fire's east branch burned 7349 acres of Laboratory land, destroyed 45 structures, mostly prefabri-cated buildings, and damaged 67 other buildings. The laboratory was closed for 14 days, the longest interruption in work since the Manhattan Project. Damage to the laboratory was estimated at $135 million in 2001.

[1] From <u>Men Who Matched the Mountains, the Forest Service in the Southwest</u>. (USDA Forest Service Southwest Region, 1972, US Government Printing Office) pg. 66.

[2] This information comes from personal conversations with Charisse Sydoriak who was Chief of Resources Management at Bandelier National Monument at the time of the Dome Fire.

[3] Personal conversation with Bill Armstrong May, 2004.

[4] <u>TA-49 Operable Unit RFI Work Plan</u>, (Los Alamos National Laboratory Environmental Restoration Program 1992)

[5] I was unable to learn what radiation, if any, the badges detected.

[6] Santa Fe New Mexican (newspaper) June 11, 2000.

[7] From the LANL web site: AIRNET Data Evaluation during the Cerro Grande Fire – air quality monitoring data from the Cerro Grande fire by LANL Air Quality Group. August 2000.

[8] "Why are we Relying on Flawed Data?" CCNS, Santa Fe, New Mexico July 2000. See also Robert Alvarez and Joni Arends, <u>Fire, Earth and Water: An Assessment of the Environmental, Safety and Health Impacts of the Cerro Grande Fire on Los Alamos National Laboratory, a Department of Energy Facility</u> by (Concerned Citizens for Nuclear Safety and the Nuclear Policy Project, December 2000)

[9] "Why are we Relying on Flawed Data?" CCNS, Santa Fe, New Mexico July 2000. See also Robert Alvarez and Joni Arends, <u>Fire, Earth and Water: An Assessment of the Environmental, Safety and Health Impacts of the Cerro Grande Fire on Los Alamos National Laboratory, a Department of Energy Facility</u> by (Concerned Citizens for Nuclear Safety and the Nuclear Policy Project, December 2000)

[10] Monitoring of Los Alamos Lab Sought, Associated Press, May 26, 2000

[11] <u>Site Wide Environmental Assessment Yearbook, Wildfire 2000</u>, (Los Alamos National Laboratory LA-UR-00-3471) pg. 21.

Chapter 9

Land, Agencies and Fire

(Though some of the material here has been touched on before in this book, these chapters put the events in a more detailed perspective that may appeal to fire professionals among others.)

Bandelier is an island in a fragmented political and physical landscape. Though only 34,000 acres, Bandelier shares boundary with US Department of Energy, the US Forest Service, the University of New Mexico, San Ildefonso Pueblo, Los Alamos County, and the Valles Caldera National Preserve. All of these agencies have widely different goals and agendas and two of them had almost no interest in land management at all before the Cerro Grande fire.

Grazing, logging and fire fighting are antithetical to the sort of land restoration Bandelier has been involved in for the last 40 years. As mentioned in Chapter 2, the entire Pajarito Plateau and Jemez Mountain region had been heavily altered by livestock grazing and predator control by the early 20th century, greatly increasing fire danger and potential for high intensity wildfire. Yet the Park Service and the Forest Service took very different approaches in dealing with the effects of those early environmental insults, with the Forest Service leaving the area north of Bandelier's high country wild, but without the custodial effects of natural fire.

For its part, Los Alamos National Laboratory, which bounds

Bandelier's lower north boundary, has had only marginal interest in forest management although the lab's 24 square mile area is heavily forested and was partly burned by the 1978 La Mesa Fire. Beginning in 1992, Los Alamos Fire Department, which is highly capable for structural fires and hazardous situations, began to take an interest in wildland fire fighting and joined Bandelier's fire crews for training on at least two prescribed fires. Meanwhile, the lab's forests were largely unmanaged and given the large number of scattered, sensitive buildings and high explosive waste on their lands, prescribed fire was a risk the lab was unwilling to take. Given a general lack of interest in forest ecology, it was outside the scope of their thinking. Despite repeated warnings to the lab from Park Service and Forest Service foresters that there was high potential for disastrous wildfire on lab land, the lab resisted thinning activities to reduce fire danger. Staff members from the lab's environmental management group had to divert funds from the snow removal budget to fund the thinning along State Road 501 that kept the Cerro Grande fire from reaching the lab on May 7.

Given the general low level of interest in thinning or restoration of natural fire on both US Forest Service and Los Alamos National Laboratory lands, Bandelier has born a large responsibility in reintroducing fire in its island of parkland. Unlike parks with vast areas of wild land surrounding them like Sequoia and Kings Canyon or Glacier National Parks, Bandelier staff had been mindful of the flammability of neighboring forest and the sensitivity of all things having to do with Los Alamos. Bandelier staff wanted to do landscape level burns to restore the ecology and to largely eliminate the risk of catastrophic wildfire. With boundaries that follow political rather than geographic lines Bandelier ecologists had to bind their burns with fire lines, instead of using natural boundaries or barriers that fire managers with larger landscapes to manage often use.

Recognizing the need to deal with the extreme wildfire hazard in the eastern Jemez Mountains, Charisse Sydoriak, then Chief of Bandelier Resources Management division, helped form the Los Alamos Wildfire Cooperators that included all the federal agencies of the Pajarito Plateau, Los Alamos County, the Agricultural Extension Service and the Red Cross. They coordinated communications among wildland fire professionals, decided what would trigger evacuations, planned equipment use for large fires and held public meetings in Los Alamos to warn citizens to clear flammable debris from their homes, and to prepare Los Alamos residents for what many considered an inevitability – a firestorm like the Cerro Grande Fire. Ms. Sydoriak notified all the neighboring agencies of the planned burn at an East Jemez Resource Council meeting on May 4, 2000. Nobody from other agencies warned against lighting the prescribed burn that night.

With a staff trained at places like Yosemite National Park and other big fire parks, Bandelier's consciousness about fire sprung from in-depth studies, most done by the US Geologic Survey's Dr. Craig Allen, aimed at restoring the parks badly damaged ecosystem. Craig Allen had come to New Mexico from UC Berkeley and had done a seminal dissertation on fire ecology in the Jemez Mountains in 1980. He carefully reconstructed the range's fire history by reading fire rings on old grandparent trees, looked for ash layers in high country bogs, and studied accounts and photos of the mountains in the past. He also tied his work into extensive work by scientists such as Tom Swetnam at the University of Arizona Tree Ring Laboratory who had done work with tree ring data to establish climate and fire patterns going back at least a thousand years.

Often the scientific community's studies are not implemented in land management decisions, as academics and land agency people work in different professional worlds. When Charisse Sydoriak arrived at Bandelier in October 1991, she brought with her a desire to transform this small park into a center of scientifically based land management work. She had graduated with honors from one of California's best field biology programs at UC Santa Cruz, went on to work with Steve Botti, Jan W. Van Wagtendonk and Dick Regalhuth in one of the Park Service's most respected science-based fire programs at Yosemite National Park where she rose through the ranks from volunteer to supervisor rapidly. Going on, she headed resources management at Lava Beds National Monument, then became Chief of Natural Resources for the North Atlantic Region of the National Park Service. She then landed at Bandelier with her Los Alamos native spouse (whom she met years before at the University of California) to head the natural resources division of the park.

Charisse had a reputation as a demanding supervisor who wanted rigorous people dedicated to restoring natural landscapes and wildlife. She attracted a staff of 17 people who, together, were recognized within the Park Service as among the best natural resources management organizations in the system. She diversified Bandelier's archaeology and land management programs, tying their efforts to Craig Allen and other ecologist's work and brought money and momentum to the natural resources program. Charisse hired Al King as Fire Management Officer and inspired him to pursue the park's already well established prescribed fire program aggressively. Al had been working on the multi-park fire program at El Malpais National Monument (near Grants, New Mexico) before being elevated to Fire Management Officer at Bandelier.

Charisse and Al wanted to deal with the large unburned portion of upper Bandelier, the so-called "New Acquisition," most of which had been acquired from the Dunnigan family, former owners of the vast Baca Ranch, in 1978. This was one of the large tracts of Bandelier land that had not been ravaged by the three major wildfires that charred much of the park since 1977.

Al and Charisse wanted to correct some of the ecological problems in the "New Acquisition," problems caused by high-grade logging by the Dunnigans in the 1960s and long term problems related to livestock grazing and fire suppression. Prescribed burning of this area offered an opportunity to restore the park's highlands while also helping to shield Los Alamos from future fires coming from the large area of fire prone wildland to the south. The area south of Cerro Grande and the New Acquisition had been the source of both the La Mesa fire and the Dome fires and included a vast area of Forest Service land that had received little fire restoration work. (The Forest Service had done commercial timber sales in the area south and west of Bandelier, worsening fire danger in that area.)

While Charisse Sydoriak built up the management program in Bandelier, her style did not always sit well with neighboring land managers, many of whom were old-school Forest Service and unused to an assertive woman joining their network. Her academic approach focused on the value of ecosystems and their elements including all varieties of plants and animals, while many traditional land managers came from land-grant schools where land management meant commodity management. Sydoriak represented a deepening of the local NPS's commitment to ecologically based resource management, one familiar to the big parks of the far west but not as well established in the interior Southwest where the NPS emphasis had long been archaeology and interpretation for the public.

The military paradigm that fire fighting (including prescribed fire management) follows to some extent, is imbued with male culture, though fire camps are full of women in various positions, their presence in command positions is less common. On the 1993 Cerro Grande prescribed fire, Ms. Sydoriak took over as fire boss one day for training purposes. At least 20 Forest Service personnel were present that day to help with the fire. Some of the Forest Service fire staff present reacted badly, sometimes ignoring her commands and openly objecting to her presence to other upper level NPS staff. This sort of reaction to women is common in the old land management agencies, but Ms. Sydoriak and her colleagues at Bandelier may have been surprised by how sharply it was expressed on that day in 1993. This experience may have been a harbinger of things to come, as Bandelier's resources management program diverged from the neighboring Forest Service management program which is fraught with malaise and budget woes.

Even before Ms. Sydoriak's tenure, Bandelier had a long, somewhat tense relationship with the Forest Service, going back to the park's birth in 1916. Tension between the Park Service and the Forest Service is a national phenomenon but the two agencies work together when it comes to fire control efforts. How well they work together is defined not only by local personality and friendliness, but also by differing rules and procedures between the two agencies.

Before 1995 Bandelier often received help from various agencies for their prescribed fires. In fall 1995 when the burn unit just east and down slope of Cerro Grande was ignited, fire fighters and their engines from the Forest Service from as far away as Grants, New Mexico helped along with fire fighters training from Los Alamos National Laboratory. Forest Service crews often helped Bandelier before 1995, either as paid staff or on an even-trade basis. They would help Bandelier and in return Bandelier staff would spend an equivalent amount of time on Forest Service prescribed fires. This trading of resources was done off the books and outside of any complicating procedures. Each agency would chalk up their time with the other as "training" and indeed they would learn from each other.

Former Chief of Resources Management at Bandelier, John Lissoway also maintained a relationship with key people at the Santa Fe National Forest that allowed him to get crews when he needed them without going into the formal fire personnel dispatch system with all of its paperwork and accounting. He recounted how the Corral Hill prescribed fire in the backcountry of Bandelier in 1986 needed additional people[1]. His friendship with a supervisor at the Santa Fe Dispatch allowed him to use a fire crew that was busy thinning trees to make up for a personnel shortfall on that blaze. Corral Hill was the only prescribed fire in Bandelier history before Cerro Grande to have control problems and the Forest Service crew helped calm it down.

In this historical context the Cerro Grande prescribed fire was lit, with no Forest Service personnel on scene and little communication with the Forest Service immediately before the ignition, beyond the required notifications.

In the case of the Cerro Grande prescribed fire, perhaps because of a troubled relationship with the neighboring US Forest Service, Bandelier did not call on the Forest Service to help with the prescribed fire. Though Forest Service crews had often helped with prescribed fires at Bandelier as recently as 1995, no trading of crews took place for this burn. This was a marked departure from how fires had been staffed in the 1980s and 1990s. Though tensions between the park and the local Forest Service existed during this time, personal relationships between key players made fire resource exchanges possible.

As recently as late April 2000, the Forest Service had provided people and engines to help with the Unit 40 burn just before a spate of arson fires began to engage the Santa Fe National Forest fire fighters.

For reasons that people in both agencies were reluctant to

discuss, that sort of trade and cooperation all but broke down between Bandelier and the Forest Service by May 2000. Not only were there no Forest Service people working on the north side of the Cerro Grande prescribed fire where it abutted Forest Service land, no Forest Service people were involved at all, even though the burn plan specified that a Forest Service representative would be present on the burn, precisely to help bring in help if the fire entered Forest Service land. Bandelier requested a representative from the Forest Service but everyone was busy with the Guaje Fire, a small wildfire that had busied the Santa Fe Hotshots and others a few miles north of Los Alamos in the first days of May.

No mention was ever made in the testimony of Bandelier personnel to the Board of Inquiry about calling on the Forest Service for trade crews or even for paid crews before Cerro Grande. For whatever reason, the Cerro Grande prescribed fire was treated largely as an in-house operation despite a memorandum of understanding between Bandelier and the Santa Fe National Forest signed in 1995 to facilitate sharing of fire personnel on prescribed fires.

In fairness to both agencies, by early May, wildfires were already popping up in the Southwest, including the Outlet Fire (another escaped prescribed burn) on the North Rim of the Grand Canyon that were drawing crews into action. Most crews were standing by for large suppression fires or for initial attack assignments and were reluctant to work on a prescribed fire as the pay is far less than it is on a wildfire.

Issues of agency cooperation go to the heart of the Cerro Grande disaster. As we will see, problems getting more fire fighters from the Forest Service dispatch center and confusion between the two agency's funding mechanisms for fire caused critical delays at key times. At the same time, reluctance to involve the Forest Service and other agency personnel in the ignition of the Cerro Grande prescribed fire, for whatever reason, led to understaffing which may have been one of two key elements in the fire's ultimate escape.

---

[1] Personal interview, fall 2000.

Part Two

Chapter 10

Planning the Burn

The next four chapters offer an in-depth historical look at the Cerro Grande Prescribed Fire, from its planning to its escape.

The analysis here resulted from interviews and from hundreds of pages of the Board of Inquiry Report, the definitive investigation of the Cerro Grande disaster. The Board of Inquiry was an official investigation body appointed by the Secretary of Interior to conduct a court-like inquiry of the fire and its participants. The Board had the power to subpoena and to take testimony under oath. However the inquiry was not a criminal investigation[1].

For months after the Cerro Grande fire had burned through parts of Los Alamos and branded itself on the national consciousness, people offered their opinions of what went wrong up on Cerro Grande. Understandably, emotions ran very high in Los Alamos as many people lost their homes and possessions. New Mexicans and others shook their heads and asked, "who was that guy who started the fire and what did they do to him?[2]"

The New York Times opined: "It is also an irony that the fire was not started by some irresponsible tourist from the city tossing away a cigarette butt or kids playing with matches. No, it was started by those experts who should know better.[3]"

Naturally, these common views and others fail to tell the story in a satisfactory way. Even press accounts at the time of the blaze misunderstood the errors and bad luck that drove the fire escape. The official federal investigation of the blaze, released primarily as an exercise in political cover for the Clinton administration while the fire was still burning, was also off the mark (see Chapter 14)[4]. As the nation's attention moved on to the blazes that followed Cerro Grande, in one of the most destructive fire years on record, false impressions about Cerro Grande lingered as more houses began to burn in Montana forest fires.

What really happened up on the mountain those fateful three days? If we get inside the agencies, where professionals under oath are telling the truth about events, and in professional terms, what did they say?

The first three days of the Cerro Grande Fire can be divided clearly into two phases. First, the prescribed burn as conducted by Bandelier fire staff and second, a larger team fighting the fire as a wildfire before the fire escaped from the upper reaches of Bandelier National Monument. The disaster that led to the large wildfire and the burning of parts of Los Alamos was a result of actions taken fighting the wildfire in the first days it was declared wild.

The staff involved in the Cerro Grande prescribed fire came from a variety of other agencies and fire positions and all had worked in the fire profession for years, if not decades, all over the western United States, from the big forests of the Sierra Nevada to the desert mountains of west Texas. These were not foolish or inexperienced people.

Yet the result of their involvement in this project opened them up to the worst sort of criticism - attacks on their competence and good sense. In disaster circumstances, human nature seems to seek a person or a group to blame for misfortune. Yet the National Park Service crew on Cerro Grande was neither innocent of all charges of ineptitude nor fully guilty of most. Bandelier's fire crew found itself at a collision point of history where the effects of decades of regional land mismanagement, aided by weather, magnified questionable judgments by a variety of people into a disaster.

By looking closely at the prescribed fire and the immediate effort to suppress the subsequent wildfire, we can begin to understand how a few errors could be exaggerated into a tragedy. What could professional wildland fire managers anticipate as they went into the prescribed burn on May 4? Was it just bad luck that caused them to lose their burn? What responsibility lies outside the fire crew? Clearly the Bandelier team misread the environment or the potential of the environment to thwart their best efforts at controlling their management fire. We might try to understand exactly what human judgments were in error and what events led to the fire escape that were entirely outside the realm of the foreseeable.

Successful fire management requires practitioners to be in tune with many aspects of the environment, as well as to know how fire behaves in changing conditions and what tools work to control it under those circumstances. Fire managers go through years of working on fires and training to advance themselves to the point where they can plan or supervise prescribed or wild-fire operations. They also work within bureaucratic and legal structures which give them forms and procedures to work with to insure that every step of igniting a burn (firing) follows rules agreed to by a national system of wildfire managers.

Yet the most important aspects of effective fire management are intuitive and require knowledge of the natural world. Our understanding of fire and the natural world is incomplete. While science and regulation have sought to turn fire management into a portable package of practices, there is no substitute for a fire manager who knows the land, the region and the moods of the seasons. This knowledge takes time to acquire.

Unfortunately, today's federal land management agencies often discourage a close relationship with the land. In the National Park Service, career staff often transfer from park to park fairly frequently and staff workers in the US Forest Service or the National Park Service live under crushing loads of paperwork that keep them indoors, except when a specific task brings them outdoors. Budget cuts over the last two decades have increased the workload for a smaller staff, especially for the National Park Service, which, despite its popularity with the public, struggles with inadequate budgets year to year[5].

The Cerro Grande prescribed fire was carried out by the Bandelier Prescribed Fire Module which operates like a fire fighting crew, but is trained in managing intentionally set fires rather than fighting wildfire. Six other "modules" like theirs exist at other national park units throughout the west where they light prescribed fires under strict guidelines, monitor the ecological aspects of fire and manage its behavior. They rotate among the parks where they are assigned, working on one burn then moving on to another burn.

The Bandelier Prescribed Fire Module works directly with Bandelier's fire suppression team that in turn is part of the Resources Management section of Bandelier's three-pronged administration. All people who work in fire at a small park like Bandelier work in both fire suppression and prescribed fire, including personnel dedicated to operating wildland fire engines, fire crew members, and the Fire Management Officer who is in charge of the fire program at the park under supervision of the Chief of Resources Management. The Chief of Resources Management answers directly to the Park Superintendent, the top official at the park who in turn has supervisors at the regional level.

Mike Powell and many of the others on the Bandelier fire use module were relatively new to Bandelier. Al King had worked at both Bandelier and El Malpais, a federal conservation area near Grants, New Mexico for more than a decade and had worked on the fire crews (initial attack crews) that were sent out to put out small fires on the land surrounding Cerro Grande, including the former Baca Ranch west of Cerro Grande. Paul Gleason had little, if any direct knowledge of the immediate region but he was well experienced with fire in the Southwest more generally and he was an expert in fire behavior and fire fighting. Thus the crew largely lacked the sort of experience that comes from years of walking and working on the eastern Jemez Mountains landscape, the sort of experience that leads a naturalist to be able to read the land, its weather patterns, its moods, and its specific qualities like dryness and the lay of the land over large areas. Most important, a long-time manager may know the way past fires have behaved at different times of the year.

Since Bandelier is a small park, it has limited staff and generally calls on other agency people to help with wildfires.

Bandelier's relationship to its neighbors and its sister agencies was a critical aspect of its plans to successfully ignite prescribed fires. As in all human relations, generous and friendly relations with sister agencies pay off in the firefighting world as favors given are returned in kind. On the other hand, uncooperative spirit by agency managers can have detrimental affects when cooperation is needed. The cultural differences between many National Park Service managers and their cohorts in the Forest Service can be problematic as well, since the two agencies have divergent histories and sometimes-contrary mandates (see chapter 4). As well, the fire suppression organizations that dominate fire divisions in some land management agencies have until recently often held a dim view of prescribed fire.

The Best Laid Plans

Plans to burn the Cerro Grande burn unit began years before May 2000. A team under the direction of John Lissoway, the former Chief of Resources Management at Bandelier, had attempted to run a low intensity fire through the Cerro Grande area in 1985, 1987 and in 1992 to kill trees encroaching on the grasslands and reduce the fuel loads in the forests. All of these fires burned with such low intensity that few of the park's ecological goals were achieved. Reintroducing natural fire to Cerro Grande became more of a priority for Bandelier after the Dome Fire of 1996 which had barely been held from burning into Frijoles Canyon, Cerro Grande and on to Los Alamos by fortunate wind shifts that occurred just as it reached the south rim of upper Frijoles Canyon[6]. (A tremendous volume of fire retardant was dropped on the south rim of Frijoles Canyon to stop the northward advance of the Dome Fire.)

Relying on research by two prominent Southwest fire researchers, Dr. Craig Allen of the US Geologic Survey[7], and Dr. Tom Swetnam[8] of Arizona State University, and others in the Southwest, Bandelier had established a plan (Fire Management Plan) to restore fire to its native place in the natural world through wildland fire use (allowing lightning fires started in the right conditions to burn within limits) and prescribed burning over most of the park, with the idea that fire would return to each middle and high elevation acre of the park in fifteen year intervals. Research showed fire had burned most acres in the upper elevation Southwest at roughly that interval before people interfered[9]. The Bandelier Fire Management Plan had been through public review[10] and scrutiny by regional park officials before its publication.

Bandelier specialists finally decided to attempt the burn in the spring as research from tree ring data shows that most large spreading surface fires occurring before 1883 happened in the spring when lightning storms brought ignitions to dry fuels waiting for spring green-up. Bandelier's scientific staff wanted to emulate this natural pattern. Furthermore, past efforts to burn in the fall had not been successful because high fuel moistures (wet sticks, leaves, needles , etc.) left from the summer rains, heavy shade, and short days had prevented fires from spreading through the whole intended burn area or had kept the fires so cool that they failed to consume accumulated fuels or kill tree thickets.

Spring burning had considerable risks. New Mexico springs tend to be dry and windy so the Bandelier team would have to find a time when the winter moisture still lingered at just the right level. Further, they would have to watch weather forecasts closely to find a window of opportunity when wind would not be excessive.

Bandelier also had several human constraints in lighting the prescribed fire. First, they had to have their Prescribed Fire Module at the park and not at one of the other National Park areas that shared this "resource." Second, the Fire Management Officer (FMO) Al King had to be present at Bandelier and not traveling to help with fire in one of the other Southwest parks where he also functioned as an FMO[11]. Third, Bandelier had to prepare for the burn with permits and notification of neighbors and of state and federal agencies. Permits depended on the staffing and project schedules of these other agencies and a permit unfortunately doesn't always coincide with favorable weather for burning.

In particular, under the federal Clean Air Act which the New Mexico Environment Department enforces in New Mexico, agencies conducting prescribed fires have to obtain a smoke permit from the Air Quality Bureau (similar rules are in place for many states). There, a specialist who knows who else is burning, and issues permits to limit cumulative effects of prescribed fire, wildfire smoke, coal fired power plant emissions, and smoke from agricultural burning. He or she may also review the prescribed fire plan to make sure techniques for minimizing smoke output and smoke transmission to nearby towns are included.

Bandelier set their sites for lighting Cerro Grande on April 12, 2000. Al King was in town, the Prescribed Fire Module was at the park and ready to go and fuel moistures up on the mountain were high due to recent snowfall and cold nights. April was out of the burn season (between late May and October) when crews and equipment start to be tied up with wild fires. By burning in April, Bandelier would have an easier time calling up support from other agencies since fire staff at the US Forest Service or Bureau of Indian Affairs would only be busy with prescribed fires of their own.

Yet the April burn plan was abandoned when the smoke specialist with the New Mexico Air Quality Bureau turned out to be out of town and the required smoke permit could not be obtained. Bandelier had to wait until all the necessary elements lined up again and the permit could be obtained. As it turned out, this would not happen until the first week of May. By then the mountain and its fuels had dried out to a considerable degree, despite a dusting of new snow on Cerro Grande on May 1. Bandelier's Fire Management Officer, and its prescribed fire module had been out of Bandelier for a few days, distracted from careful monitoring of conditions on Cerro Grande. Further, the fire season had begun by the first of May, early by recent standards, and the Forest Service was busy fighting arson forest fires around Los Alamos by the time Bandelier's own prescribed fire specialists were ready to go.

Bandelier gets its funding for conducting prescribed fire from the Boise (Idaho) Interagency Fire Center (NIFC), which allocates funds for prescribed fire for all federal agencies, as well as resources for large wildfires for the whole nation. Boise directs funds to parks according to specific prescribed fire plans. For their part, Bandelier, and other parks, develop natural resource management plans including fire management plans that lay out goals for prescribed fire, both to protect nearby communities from wildfire feeding on excessive fuels, and to adjust the ecology of parks to a more natural condition.

While the money allocated to parks by NIFC can be carried from year to year if conditions amenable to burning do not develop, park managers have an incentive to finish burns within a reasonable timeframe to be in good standing when they request funds for burns in the future. Sources within Bandelier have said there was pressure from upper management to get on with burning the Cerro Grande and upper Frijoles Canyon burn units for a variety of reasons. Federal agencies were under pressure to increase the number of acres burned by prescription. The burns had already been delayed a number of years.

In Bandelier's case, the two most critical burn units in the park (see map) for the safety of Los Alamos were the Cerro Grande burn unit (number one) and the upper Frijoles Canyon burn unit (unit nine) below it. Both of these were areas of heavy fuel accumulation that had narrowly missed burning in the 1996 Dome Wildfire[12]. Bandelier managers knew another fire was likely to come from Forest Service land across Frijoles Canyon and they wanted to reduce fuels on these two areas to buffer Los Alamos from a near-inevitable disaster[13]. (Meanwhile Forest Service managers in Los Alamos had long predicted a fire start near Bandelier land that would threaten Los Alamos because of prevailing winds, and they were struggling to prepare the land near Los Alamos for such a possibility.)

Already, funding for these two Bandelier burn units had been carried year to year since 1997. Charisse Sydoriak, as the Chief of Resources Management at Bandelier was hopeful that these units could be burned. While not pushing, she made it clear to the staff that it would be good to accomplish those prescribed fires sooner rather than later for funding reasons and for community safety reasons. Bandelier's large plan to cycle prescribed fire through all the fire prone areas of the park at near-natural intervals was incomplete only on this highest elevation corner of the park. In any case, Ms. Sydoriak was absent from Bandelier during the days before the ignition of Cerro Grande. She told the Board of Inquiry that she delegated the decision of when to ignite the Cerro Grande burn unit to the Fire Management Officer (Al King) and his staff.

Finally, in early May, Bandelier's needed staff was on hand and the burn could go forward. Many of those who would conduct the burn were fairly new to Bandelier. Two staffers with long experience had recently left the park, John Lissoway who began Bandelier's prescribed fire program in 1980 had retired in 1997 and Dwayne Archuleta the park's former Fire Management Officer had moved to the Forest Service soon after. According to many inside the park, these two had been a sort of brake on prescribed fire plans that might have been overly ambitious, as both had worked on many large suppression wildfires and knew big fire and the control problems they create.

This left Mike Powell to be the burn boss, and while qualified as a division supervisor and burn boss, he was the leader of the Bandelier Prescribed Fire Module and was often traveling and may not have developed an intimacy with Bandelier that would have served him well in anticipating a possible fire escape[14].

All prescribed fires in federal land management agencies have a burn plan which details what conditions will be needed for a successful outcome, who will be on site, what equipment will be used and how exactly the burn will be ignited. The plan also discusses the goals (objectives) of the burn and any constraints such as boundaries or personnel needs.

The burn plan for the Cerro Grande prescribed burn became a big issue for the numerous investigations that followed the disaster with some people charging that the burn plan was improperly written, was not reviewed by the Superintendent, or that its authors lacked experience and used the wrong forms. At Bandelier, writing burn plans was done with various levels of review[15]. The Cerro Grande burn plan was the responsibility of Mike Powell, the burn boss, who in turn was supervised by the fire management officer (FMO) and the Chief of Resources Management. Finally, the park superintendent reviewed and signed off on the document before the burn could begin. The burn plan went under numerous reviews within the park and Superintendent Roy Weaver was involved with writing it in its final stages, as well as granting his final approval[16].

All the environmental and fire related documents at a park are written by teams of specialists, then put out for public review under the National Environmental Policy Act (NEPA) which is required for all major federal actions. NEPA requires the agency to disclose the likely environmental affects of a proposed activity and alternatives to the proposed activity.

NEPA does not require public review of burn plans or other

component actions of larger already documented plans that received public review and are subject to public appeal. (The law allows agencies to "categorically exclude" component actions of a large agency plan from further NEPA review. If this were not the case, the park would spend large amounts of time and money on environmental impact documents for myriad actions.) The Bandelier Fire Management Plan was reviewed and commented on by the public in 1997, but the National Park Service categorically excluded the burn plans for the various prescribed fires conducted under that Fire Management Plan from public review. This tiering of management activities and public review allows the public to be involved in large scale planning in a park, but keeps the park autonomous for day to day planning of activities. The public was notified about the pending Cerro Grande prescribed fire at public meetings in Los Alamos and through press releases.

The Forest Service Espanola District staff was absent from this Cerro Grande prescribed fire-planning process even though land in their jurisdiction bordered the burn area. However it is normal for agencies to plan their activities without consulting neighbors. While they were aware of the park's fire program and even specific units that were planned to be burned, the relationship between the two agencies did not include specific involvement with one another's land management activities, unless it was to provide help with wildfires or consult on regional planning issues. Although the two agencies manage a landscape jointly, their fire management planning is not cooperative. The Cerro Grande burn would have benefited from expanded boundaries that encompassed a large area of Forest Service lands so the fire could be planned to be contained by larger landscape features rather than within artificial political boundaries drawn by Congress between the Park Service and Forest Service lands. Those boundaries have repeatedly proven to be untenable for fire management.

In the early 1990s, then Bandelier Resource Manager John Lissoway discussed doing the Cerro Grande prescribed fire as a joint venture with Bill Armstrong of the Forest Service. Mr. Armstrong and the Forest Service informally discussed helping Bandelier by putting in a fuel break down on the American Springs plateau area near Water Canyon north of Cerro Grande.

The Forest Service would have cut a wide swath in the trees that could have been used as an "anchor[17]" and "safety zone[18]" for a fire that would then have been lit to run up the north face of Water Canyon and into Bandelier's three Cerro Grande area burn units. Such a joint prescribed fire would have created a large area with greatly reduced fuels that would have shielded Los Alamos from fire running north from Frijoles Canyon and the area to the south.

Had this informal idea been implemented it would have been a locally precedent-setting joint prescribed fire. The idea made sense from a landscape perspective, as the area to be burned would encompass the top and both sides of a ridge and would have made for a more manageable fire. Yet the idea was never seriously pursued. John Lissoway of Bandelier abandoned the idea because he knew it would take the Forest Service too long to get the fuel break cut down below Cerro Grande[19]. Bill Armstrong of the Forest Service agreed that a lack of Forest Service funding for such a project in the area south of Los Alamos prevented him from moving forward with the idea[20].

Oddly, the Forest Service did acquire funding for reducing fuels in a wide area north of Los Alamos in the mid 1990s although all the supervising foresters knew that almost any fire threatening Los Alamos would come from the south, due to prevailing winds, as the La Mesa and the Dome fires had.

A great deal of controversy arose from the Cerro Grande burn plan after the wildfire and in the investigations that followed the fire, though it was a near replica of the burn plan used when the same prescribed burn was attempted in 1992. That plan was for a burn attempted in October 1992. The 2000 burn had a similar prescription to the 1992 burn, which admittedly failed to achieve objectives because the site was too wet for fuels to be consumed by the low intensity fire that happened. That failure led the staff to attempt the burn in the spring, when conditions would lend themselves to a hotter burn that would clear dead fuel and kill excessive tree regeneration.

The burn planning process requires the planner to consider how complicated the burn will be and then determine how many and the experience level of people needed to complete the burn safely. Though it may seem arcane, a great deal of controversy and squirming by the Bandelier staff happened when investigators discovered that Bandelier had used the wrong "complexity analysis" in doing its plan. The complexity analysis is a process where burn planners anticipate what level of staffing will be needed for a fire, what equipment will be needed based on environmental and risk factors such as nearby communities, facilities or endangered species habitat. The complexity analysis process also anticipates what problems a landscape around a burn unit or within the burn unit could cause if the fire were to get more active than planned[21]. These sorts of questions are fed into a complexity analysis and the computer calculates numbers that then tells the burn planners what sort of resources the burn will require.

At Cerro Grande it turned out that the complexity analysis for the burn was done incorrectly because the National Park Service's fire manager's website had an erroneous formula posted on it[22]. As a result, too few people were placed as holding forces on the burn and neighboring agencies were not engaged, as they would have been with a correct and higher level of complexity. Using the wrong formula resulted in the Bandelier team coming up with a "moderately" complex burn. If they had used the up-to-date form, they would have come up with a "complex" burn rating which would have required greatly increasing the number of people on hand or to postpone the burn until conditions were more amenable to a smaller staff size. The complexity rating system used by fire planners has a nearly logarithmic scale so if the numbers arrived at are wrong, they are wrong by a wide margin.

The Board of Inquiry found that the error with the complexity rating was the only policy violation that happened with planning the prescribed burn. The error was not at Bandelier but rather with people putting policy matters on the National Park Service website in Washington. This turned out to be a major mistake by the larger NPS fire planning system.

At the same time, the complexity rating was a formalized process for deciding how complex a burn would be, and thus, how risky. People can figure out many of the same things from experience and from thinking about the situation on their own from a perspective of caution. There were obvious risk factors that the burn team knew about such as dry forests between the burn site and Los Alamos, nuclear materials and high explosives within three miles at Los Alamos National Laboratory, high fuel loading just outside the boundaries of the burn unit and the potential for high wind.

The prescription is a set of environmental, personnel and equipment conditions the fire planners believe will allow a prescribed fire to achieve ecological and safety objectives. For example, if burn planners want to keep a fire low to the ground and out of the trees, they set the fire when humidity is high and the fuels on the forest floor are relatively wet. They may choose to back the fire down the hills in narrow bands to keep it cool and low rather than starting it where it can gain a head and run hot up a hill. Conversely, if fire planners want a hot fire that may climb into some tree tops and thin out the forest by killing many younger trees, they set the fire when fuels on the ground are dry, the humidity is low and there is moderate wind.

In the case of the Cerro Grande burn, the prescription chosen was fairly aggressive. Planners and scientists wanted the fire to kill many trees that had invaded once-open forests and grasslands. To do this, they needed fairly dry conditions since much of the burn unit was grass growing among mature trees. In order for excess trees to be killed, the fire would need to have flame lengths between six and nine feet. This meant burning when fuel moistures were somewhat low with moderate wind to carry the fire in grass.

However, the prescription chosen was applied to a relatively large, complex landscape (large only relative to the size of Bandelier National Monument itself). The park fire planners applied one set of temperature, fuel moisture, relative humidity and wind condition "prescriptions" to the whole burn unit, despite the variety of vegetation types there. The prescription was broad enough to accommodate all the vegetation types caused by widely varied conditions on the site such as moisture and sunlight. Fire behavior varies in different vegetation types, from the grassy ponderosa pine stands, to the pine-mixed conifer stands, to the cool and wet aspen-mixed conifer stands or the open grasslands.

Burn Boss Mike Powell testified to the Board of Inquiry on May 14, 2000, that nobody had taken fuel moisture readings in the burn unit after April 28, a full six days before the burn was begun. Yet he also told the Board of Inquiry that fuel moisture had been read the day of the burn. In decades past, fuel moisture levels used to be measured on site with specific tools. (Today fuel moisture is often calculated from weather information.) Fuel moistures can change significantly in a week given wind and sun exposure (the burn unit faces south where sun exposure is significant) and when the burn was begun workers on the scene testified that they were concerned by how much more active the fire was in the grass than they had expected. It's not clear from the testimony when the fuel moistures were last read before the burn.

The fire team was confident that fuel moisture readings showed minimal drought conditions in the burn unit and moisture levels were within the prescription set in the burn plan. Cerro Grande had received sixteen inches of snow, or one and a half inches of moisture between March 17 and April 28. Some of that moisture would have evaporated but the down fuels would absorb much of it. As the weather warms in the spring, the evaporation rate increases and in New Mexico, the probability of new precipitation is low until the mid-summer monsoon pattern is established.

Park planners divided the burn unit into three "phases," each of which would be approached slightly differently. These corresponded roughly to the different elevation and aspect defined vegetation types and degrees of slope in the unit, but the prescription, in terms of how and when fire would be applied to those phases, was the same throughout the unit. The flat bottom of the burn unit near the highway was not to be burned until it was "extremely dry" to insure consumption of down fuels. This burning may not have happened until weeks later according to the burn plan, implying that the fire could be controlled as it moved from one phase to another. Naturally the fire got hotter on the south facing ridge lines where dry, sunny conditions existed and where prevailing winds could push the fire harder than down in the bowl or in dense forests of the lower flats of the west side where sunlight was indirect in the winter. There the forest floor was shaded and therefore wetter, and the shape of the mountain largely protected the interior cool forests from the winds that regularly tormented the peak and the north and east ridges.

Yet the three phase idea in the burn plan immediately proved unrealistic as the fire backed into phase two in the first 12 hours. Bandelier's team had planned to bring in more people and to do a "test burn" in phase two before proceeding there. Yet it was not clear how Bandelier's staff planned to keep the fire from leaving one phase and entering the next in their optimistic planning given that no fire control lines had been put in between the different phases. If they planned to put in control lines to hold the fire out of the lower phases this was not evident for personnel present or likely to be present in a realistic time frame, and putting line across the bottom of phase one would have presented firefighter safety problems given that this area included a deep draw which can cause dangerous fire behavior which can trap fire fighters.

As it was, the fire burn plan called for 21 people to staff a burn of 900 acres in three phases. This seems a small number of people for such a large area given that there were no "hose lays," (advance placement of fire hoses along the perimeters) and no dedicated additional forces that were standing by if needed. Granted they expected to be able to call up additional "contingency" fire fighters as needed to manage the prescribed fire (an expectation that proved unfounded for reasons beyond the control of the Bandelier staff). The planners expected the fire to be more aggressive down in the bottom of the burn unit, an area they didn't plan to get to for at least 24 to 48 hours after the fire control lines were established on the ridges. They seemed to anticipate that the fire would be highly manageable in the timber interior of the burn unit (an expectation that proved correct) and that a limited staff would be able to construct fire line and hold the fire on the dry grassy ridges. In this scenario, when the fire burned hottest, in the flats at the bottom of the unit (phase 3) it would have a large burned area above it to contain the hot fire and the already blackened fuels there would block escape. This plan assumed winds would blow generally upslope, as they usually do during the day in most mountain areas. What if winds instead came out of the huge Valle Grande caldera to the west as they often do?

The planner's expectations were not unreasonable if the weather had cooperated. The fire would be in prescription unless winds got above 25 miles per hour, something that the National Weather Service did not anticipate[23]. Grassy fuels burn quickly and cool. Heavier fuels of standing live trees require more persistent, higher temperatures to ignite. Grass fires are relatively easy to extinguish except in strong wind. The team had a difficult time igniting the mixed conifer trees on the west side of the burn unit when they sought to create a black line there the night of May 4. However, somewhat similar fuel types on the east side of the burn unit burned vigorously since they had more drying exposure to sun and wind[24]. In retrospect, measuring fuel moistures in many different places in the burn unit would have helped the team to understand varying conditions that ultimately led to fire control problems[25].

This was a major factor in the Cerro Grande prescribed fire gone wildfire. Somehow park planners failed to read the mountain and the weather correctly as evidenced by the short staffing of the burn, the lack of water tender equipment on the most vulnerable ridge lines[26], and the rapid application of fire to the burn unit after minimal testing of fire behavior on the late evening of May 4. Even so, their prescription and anticipated fire behavior only proved to be skewed on the east and north ridgelines where the fire slopped over the fire lines into neighboring woods because of stronger winds than forecast. Elsewhere in the burn unit, the fire burned as expected, even failing to burn at all in places on the west side because of moisture.

Burn planners can look beyond the unit they are targeting and think about what effect a fire escape would have on land nearby. What would a worst-case scenario be, if the weather changed and the fire became extreme? What would happen if embers were thrown a half-mile away and started spot fires? Is it possible that a fire could do that within the prescription chosen by the planners if the weather became drier with winds or if the temperature rose? What would the fire crews do if weather did turn on them? Would they have enough people?

The team on Cerro Grande apparently never did this critical analysis of nearby conditions adequately though Mike Powell testified that he had visited nearby lands to assess conditions. However it appears that the team mostly focused on the Cerro Grande burn unit (Unit 1) and the upper Frijoles burn unit (Unit 9). They did take into account weather data from an automatic weather station west of the burn unit, in ponderosa pine forest like those that stretched between Cerro Grande and Los Alamos. They used their experience burning Unit 40, down on the lower elevations of the park to predict what fire behavior would be in those drier forests. Neither of these prediction methods seemed to adequately take into account the conditions outside the burn unit, where prevailing winds likely would push an escaped fire.

Bandelier's staff was boxed in by politics and history. Remember, Bandelier is a small island of land in a larger landscape[27]. The National Park Service had acknowledged after the Yellowstone fires of 1988[28] that containing a prescribed fire in a limited geographic area may not be possible if wind and fuel conditions would naturally drive a fire to exceed human set boundaries and find its natural limits on a landscape level. Natural fires in pre-twentieth century times, started by either lightning or people tended to spread to the limits of fuel and weather conditions. Yet the idea of prescribed fire assumes that a team can apply fire at a desired intensity to a limited area and control it within that area with technology and personnel.

The Yellowstone experience of 1988[29] proved that idea wrong and the Cerro Grande experience of 2000 reaffirmed that drought and wind could negate control efforts[30]. The natural world invites fire to spread in dry or windy conditions on a landscape level in places like the Pajarito Plateau and the Yellowstone Plateau and it may not be realistic to expect fire to be managed within small boundaries except in the most cautious, cool prescriptions. The spread of the Cerro Grande fire was "natural" for the Pajarito Plateau and Jemez Mountains landscape according to how historic fires had spread under similar weather, though the fuel loading in the area had been greatly increased by human activities. Fires in the past had also spread over large areas though the Cerro Grande fire spread in the tree tops, something that was rare in the past[31].

The landscape of Cerro Grande and the forested lands to the north and east proved unforgiving of the team's apparent failure to plan for an escape into the country between Cerro Grande and Los Alamos. A worst case scenario, that winds pick up and relative humidity drops both at ground level and in the atmosphere above the mountain would lead the fire to start throwing embers ahead of itself, lighting spot fires, especially if the fire developed a column of heat and smoke above it which would carry embers skyward. Since the landscape dropped off rapidly north of Cerro

Grande, embers from a fire would land in a forest with much drier condition than those in the burn unit. The forests a few hundred feet lower were drier because of greater sun exposure, less precipitation and less shading than the higher forests and would burn much more actively.

Bandelier's staff desired a fairly intense fire within the limits of the burn unit, but to hold the fire within the burn unit they assumed that personnel and technology would be available and suited to counter the natural tendency of fire in this environment to spread to the limits of fire-conducive fuel and weather conditions. Technology, personnel and planning proved inadequate to counter the natural tendency of fire to spread on a fire-adapted landscape on May 7. Embers thrown a quarter to half a mile from the burn unit boundaries fell in dry, south facing ponderosa pine forests hundreds of feet lower than the burn unit. Even so, the burn planners seemed to have been optimistic that the fire would stay within their planning area. Their testimony to the Board of Inquiry never revealed a clear answer why they had not planned for the possibility of spot fires to the north or east of the burn unit.

In nature, "everything connects to everything else," as John Muir exclaimed and landscapes are divided into discrete units only in the imaginations of human beings. In the case of Cerro Grande, the forests surrounding Unit 1 to the north are steep lands with complex topography and more than 60 tons per acre of fuel loading, extreme by any measure. The Forest Service had done some thinning between Valle and Water Canyons near highway 501, thinning that would help calm the wildfire in days to come. The Forest Service had also done some commercial logging just below Cerro Grande in the 1980s, but this may have increased fire danger in the area by opening the understory to sunlight, promoting brushy growth, leaving slash piles, damaged trees, and a proliferation of pine seedlings. The majority of the land between Cerro Grande and Los Alamos had not been managed since the huge sheep and cow herds left the area in ecological ruin sixty years earlier.

As it would turn out the best-laid plans for the burn would be sabotaged by weather, outside human factors and unforeseeable circumstances.

[1] The Board of Inquiry included Bill Schenk, Regional Director Midwest Region of the National Park Service, Len Dems, Fire Management Officer, Grand Teton National Park, Pete Hart, Superintendent, New River Gorge National River (NPS), Wally Hibbard, Associate regional Director Southeast Region NPS, Mary Martin, superintendent, Mojave National Preserve (NPS), Jerry Williams, Director Fire and Aviation Management for the US Forest Service Northern Region.

[2] Since Bandelier Superintendent Roy Weaver was in the national news at the time of the fire's escape, many people assumed he was directly and perhaps solely involved in igniting the prescribed fire. It was very common after the fire to have people ask "who was that guy who started that fire?" This perception showed how poorly the media had presented the fire escape and how poorly much of the public understands land agencies and fire management.

[3] "Park Service is criticized as Fire Rages in Los Alamos," New York Times, May 12, 2000.

[4] Investigation Report, Cerro Grande Prescribed Fire, Fire Investigation Team, National Interagency Fire Center, Boise, Idaho, May 18, 2000.

[5] The National Parks and Conservation Association estimates that the 2006 National Park Service budget falls short of a basic level needed to manage the parks at a sustainable level by $600 million. The shortfall in 2000 was the same. From Restoring America's National Parks, (NPCA April 13, 2006).

[6] Personal interview with Charisse Sydoriak, June 2000.

[7] Craig Allen began studying the Jemez Mountains and fire ecology in the 1970s while a graduate student at UC Berkeley. He wrote his PhD thesis on this topic and began working as an ecologist for Bandelier before moving to the US Geologic Survey during the Clinton administration. He is one of the top national experts on fire ecology in the Southwest.

[8] Dr. Tom Swetnam is Director & Professor of Dendrochronology, Laboratory of Tree-Ring Research; joint appointments in Watershed Management, School of Natural Resources, Ecology & Evolutionary Biology, and Geography & Regional Development at the University of Arizona. His work has pieced together the fire history of the Southwest going back more than 1000 years.

[9] Wildland Fire Management Plan, (Bandelier National Monument, January 1997).

[10] The public was allowed to review an Environmental Impact Statement for the Fire Plan as required by the National Environmental Policy Act (NEPA).

[11] Al King was relatively new to the FMO job at Bandelier, having been there for only 3 months. He had no assistant as most fire management

officers do. His predecessor, Dwayne Archuleta had been cautious about fire, coming from the Forest Service fire suppression world. These personnel changes signaled a loss of institutional memory at Bandelier, and a loss of intimacy with the park's environment that recently departed fire staff had.

[12] The Dome Fire burned the area south of Cerro Grande on the flats beyond Frijoles Canyon. It was a Type II fire with a full suppression effort coordinated among crews and specialists from all over the western states. The fire was crowning in timber on the south rim of Frijoles Canyon (above Unit 9) when a wind shift blew the fire back to the south. Had this wind shift not occurred, it is highly likely that the Dome Fire would have spread to Los Alamos in the same fashion that Cerro Grande did four years later.

[13] The area west of Bandelier is crossed by many roads, is popular with people seeking a secluded area to "party" and has become more popular with off road vehicles which can start wildfires as one did in the 1987 La Mesa Fire. This is high country where lightning strikes are common and natural ignitions can start large wildfires.

[14] Mike Powell was in his twenty-first season in fire, was Division Supervisor qualified and Burn Boss II qualified. He did 5 years of prescribed burning with the Forest Service then went to the Alpine Hot Shots for 4 seasons. He was a Squad Boss for 2 seasons then went to North Star Fire crew as a squad boss. He then went to the Chena Hot Shot crew with the Bureau of Land Management in Alaska where he was Foreman for 4 seasons and Superintendent of the Chena Hot Shot crew in his last season there. Then he went to Sequoia National Park as a type III Engine Boss before moving to the Bandelier fire use module. He had been at Bandelier for two years. Had done two burn plans total including Cerro Grande. These qualifications are impressive in the fire world.

[15] Cerro Grande Prescribed Fire Investigation Report (Interagency) May 18, 2000, pg. 9.

[16] Roy Weaver's involvement with the burn plan was a huge point of contention between Mr. Weaver and the investigators involved in the May 18 report (ibid). See chapter 8.

[17] An anchor in fire terms is a point from which fire fighting can begin on a fire. An anchor is an advantageous location with a barrier of some kind to fire spread from which fire fighters can begin constructing fire lines. An anchor can be a burned out area or a cliff, a wet meadow or other similar place. Anchors are often chosen at the rear of a fire or near the point of origin.

[18] A safety zone is a place where fire fighters can retreat to if a fire gains intensity rapidly or changes direction. Line fire fighters always know of a place like a wet meadow, a road, or a burned out area where they can retreat to and escape a firestorm.

[19] Author interview with John Lissoway, August 4, 2000.

[20] See chapter 4.

[21] At the time, the National Park Service fire policy stated: "A prescribed fire complexity rating shall be completed as part of each prescribed fire plan following the process in RM-18 Chapter 10. This process determines the level of organizational structure and support needed to implement the project based on operational, logistical, safety and management needs. The complexity value breakpoints for requiring a Prescribed Fire Burn Boss Type 1 shall be 4 or more Complexity Values rated "High" OR 2 or more of the Primary Factor Complexity Values rated "High" OR when deemed appropriate by the Superintendent or unit Fire Management Officer.

[22] Cerro Grande Board of Inquiry Final Report pg. 14.

[23] The burn team was receiving regular weather updates from the fire weather forecasters at the National Weather Service in Albuquerque. They also were taking weather data from various points in the burn unit to check for key changes in weather such as drops in relative humidity and changes in wind speed and direction. This weather monitoring is standard procedure for fire fighters on all fires. On complex burns, a fire weather forecaster will be present at the fire to provide detailed site-specific forecasts.

[24] The forest on the west side of the burn was cooler and wetter due to shading from a large forest to the west. The east side of the burn unit at the same elevation has ponderosa pine with grass understory and was experiencing more sun exposure because of the open meadow to its west and a southern aspect.

[25] In his testimony to the Board of Inquiry, Mike Powell asserted that he had done adequate fuel moisture measurements to anticipate fire behavior variations throughout the burn unit. Given time constraints created by personnel travel and other responsibilities in the park, some of these fuel moisture readings may have been obsolete by the time the burn was attempted.

[26] Bandelier's staff did not want to bring vehicles to the edge of the Cerro Grande burn unit because of the fragility of the grasslands where vehicles would have been driven. Bringing an "engine" or two to the east fire line would have allowed long hose-lays down the ridge so that fire lines could have been held with some water spraying to supplement line construction with hand tools. However, driving a large vehicle to the east fire line would have been difficult at best.

[27] Bandelier was conceived as a park to preserve archaeological sites and its upper reaches where Cerro Grande stands were added later to prevent watershed damage to Bandelier from logging that was likely to occur if Bandelier did not obtain the land that contained the Cerro Grande burn unit.

[28] The 1988 Yellowstone fires were not escaped prescribed fires but were started by lightning, an abandoned campfire and a tree falling on a power line. There were 15 fires in Yellowstone in 1988.

[29] The Yellowstone fires of 1988 were a complex of several fires burning at the same time. Wildland "fire use" fires in Yellowstone, where the National Park Service sought to allow lightning fires to burn within bounds, started some of these. This fire management scheme is a variation on the idea of prescribed burning as was being practiced at Bandelier.

[30] Norman L. Christensen Fire in the Parks: A Case Study for Change Management, (George Wright Society Forum, vol, 22 no 4 2005) pg. 24.

[31] See Craig Allen studies referred to in Chapter 3.

Chapter 11

The Dominos Fall

The high country of Bandelier is cloaked with mixed conifer forests that wrap around Cerro Grande and down an eastward jutting ridge that flanks the 1200-foot deep upper Frijoles Canyon where old growth forests grow undisturbed. The uppermost end of Frijoles Canyon, which forms the heart and soul of Bandelier National Monument tops out in a bowl on Cerro Grande. Highway 4 crosses the upper end of Frijoles Canyon and forms a boundary between two burn units important to our story, burn unit one above and unit nine below and to the south.

Burn unit one was the area from which fire escaped in May 2000. Below it, Unit nine loomed large in everyone's mind. This complex and heavily fuel loaded area was possibly to be ignited within days or weeks of the ignition of the Cerro Grande unit one. Unit nine is an area of upper Frijoles Canyon, which is cloaked in mostly virgin stands of ponderosa pine, white fir, Douglas fir, white pine and aspen. It is some of the wildest country in the Jemez Mountains, steep and cool and mysterious. The bottom of the canyon harbors many of the springs from which the perennial Frijoles Creek flows and it has some old burn scars from long ago on the south slopes where oak scrub stands below scattered douglas fir.

Paul Gleason was on scene at the Cerro Grande burn specifically to observe, but most importantly to supervise, the possible ignition of upper Frijoles Canyon (Unit 9) after the Cerro Grande burn was completed. He was a veteran of 36 years of wildland fire work with both the US Forest Service and the National Park Service. The upper Frijoles unit 9 burn was expected to be hot and difficult and burning unit 1 first was essential to have a partial black-line buffer between the tricky unit 9 and the untended Forest Service lands to the north. The potential for spot fire generating crown fire in unit 9 was very high, depending on how dry the area was when it was ignited.

Almost a century had passed since fire had burned naturally through Cerro Grande's forests, and those forests had long ago grown to a height and density that made treating them with fire difficult. The forests on Cerro Grande had been logged before they were transferred to the National Park Service in 1978. At elevations above 9000 feet, forests are relatively wet and getting fire to correct the heavy intrusion of trees into meadows and once-open forests is difficult, given the shading and sparseness of ground fuels in these upper elevation forests.

All forests are in flux. When a Southwestern forest is altered by fire suppression that leads to large increases in the number of young trees present, a forest may compensate for this overpopulation either with insect outbreaks that thin the forest or with intense fire that culls or clears the forest. On Cerro Grande, the forests had been altered both by logging and fire suppression.

Whether reintroducing fire to a limited area of a high elevation ecosystem is a realistic tool for correcting forests long distorted by grazing and fire suppression is an open question, one into which the Cerro Grande experience offers great insight. Given that the Cerro Grande prescribed burn turned into a landscape scale fire, clearly the park staff's effort to burn the area hot enough to "achieve objectives" meant pushing the limit of what was safe to do with fire, even at 9000 feet. Even so, as we will see, the burn could have succeeded but for a series of bad luck and bad planning events, not the least of which was one of the worst wind storms the Jemez Mountains have ever experienced, coinciding with somewhat routine control problems on the fire itself.

View from test burn area along the north fire-line, looking east.

View from test burn area looking north toward the national forest boundary which lies beyond the treeline.

View at the north-east corner of the Cerro Grande burn unit. The
slop-over occurred in the forest in the background.
Notice tree invasion in grassland.

View of the forest type along the east fire-line.

Forest burned in the large slop-over.

View looking north along the upper west fire-line toward the peak of Cerro Grande. Note aspen stands on east facing slope where ignition was difficult. Valles Caldera National Preserve lies immediately to the west.

View of the dogleg on Highway 4 in Frijoles Canyon. The base of the east fire-line lies on the slope in the background.

Looking east along Highway 4, just east of the highway dogleg. Burned forest on right side of the highway was burned as the fire ran from the large spot-fire in upper Frijoles Canyon toward the north.

Looking north along the east fire-line which is in the green woods at the left side of the photo. The burned trees in the center of the photo mark the fire escaping from the spot-fire in Frijoles Canyon on its northward run out of Bandelier and toward Los Alamos on May 7th.

The Bandelier team chose to put a modest staff on the Cerro Grande fire and to keep personnel from other agencies off the fire until later in the burn. The burn team chose to light the fire at night, beginning at 6:30 PM, a time when few other agency people would be available for working on a trading work for future work basis. Bandelier's team chose to light the fire at night to achieve subdued fire behavior, since most nights the relative humidity increases and winds decrease, allowing for cooler burning of the flash fuels like grasses that they wanted to burn out to black-line the burn.

Mike Powell, as burn boss had been in touch with the Forest Service dispatch office in Santa Fe and was under the impression that fire crews were available if he called for them. In fact the arson-started Guaje Fire just north of Los Alamos was keeping the local Forest Service suppression organization busy as the fire had been more active and challenging to control than they antici-pated. Bandelier's Engine 91 was on that fire as well. The existence of the Guaje fire, absorbing key Bandelier resources, should have been more interesting to the Bandelier prescribed fire team. A fire like that using a considerable portion of local fire resources so early in the year, before many seasonal personnel were avail-able, was a red flag of sorts. The Guaje fire's behavior could have been instructive to the Bandelier team if they had tuned in to the problems the Forest Service was having there, though Bandelier's staff apparently was focused solely on high altitude burning con-ditions. The Guaje fire at about 7000 feet in elevation was about 7 acres and burning very actively down a slope of ponderosa pine. The Forest Service worked the fire with the Santa Fe Hotshots, 4 engines, a crew from Santo Domingo Pueblo and a load of aerial retardant[1]. This is a large list of resources for a seven-acre fire.

According to his testimony to the Board of Inquiry, Mike Powell chose to use a minimal crew on the fire, but to call for additional resources as needed. There were no official guidelines for staffing levels for prescribed fires. Using only those resources needed at a given time could contain cost of the prescribed fire. Staffing, or not staffing a fire this way was a huge gamble since the crews the Forest Service dispatcher told him would be avail-able could be called out to other fires at any time.

Burning in the middle of the night required plenty of daytime preparation, including hauling heavy water packs up the mountain. By the time the crew of Northern Pueblo Agency people reached the peak with the Bandelier team, they were exhausted from hauling water and climbing the steep slope of the mountain. Others, including 53-year-old Paul Gleason would do the hike several times over the next few hours, often with loads. Each crewmember had carried a backpack pump holding 5 gallons of water (40 pounds) up the hill and the fire use module had made two trips each with more backpack pumps. They had staged drip torches, and drip torch fuel along the planned black line. So there were 30 backpack pumps up on the mountain along with various hand tools.

Fire fighting is challenging work. Not only do hand crews labor with specialized hand tools for hours on end, they often have to hike long distances, carrying chain saws, fuel and personal supplies. Helitack (crews that do initial attack on fires from helicopters) are often dropped miles from the fire they will work on, having to hike over wilderness lands with no trails. Smoke jumpers work the same way, dropping into fires on parachutes, then hiking out, sometimes for days when the fire is over. All hand crews experience long hours of labor and walking and there can be little doubt that by the end of the summer, the Northern Pueblo Crew would be in much better physical shape than they were at the beginning of the summer, in May, when they were up on Cerro Grande.

Some of that fatigue could have been limited by allowing some use of trucks for hauling gear on the lower half of the mountain where an overgrown road (a "two-track" in land manager lingo) winds up to the shelf below the Cerro Grande summit. Top Bandelier administrators had forbidden the use of trucks or ATVs on the mountain in preparation for the burn to prevent damage to the fragile soils and vegetation.

Yet this judgment, to prioritize vegetation preservation over the inherent risk of fire escaping to the north into dense forests could have been questioned, especially since the area is not a designated wilderness area where vehicle use is forbidden. The National Park Service is perhaps the only agency that would exercise such a subtle, valid and important interest in protecting plant life from vehicle damage. In this case, having some pumper trucks (engines) on the north and east edges of the fire may well have been worth the damage they may have caused, especially since the risk of fire escape in those directions was high.

This vehicle free approach cost the crews energy since so much gear had to be hefted up the mountain on people's backs. Coupled with the low staffing level: 12 NPS people and 17 Northern Pueblo crew members, the fatigue factor was intense, especially given that on May 4, the relative humidity did not drop as much as the fire planners had hoped, making for a more active fire than they had anticipated. While the fire conditions were still in prescription the 29 people on the burn were scrambling to keep ahead of their black lining operation right away after they decided to change the fire from a "test burn" to an actual prescribed fire at eleven o'clock at night on May 4.

Initially, the fire planners had expected to create a swath of blackened grass surrounding the burn unit by swatting out the edges of the burn with tree branches as they worked their way down the shoulder of the mountain. This is standard fire fighting method in grasses. Swatting out fire is exhausting work and with a small team, this idea was abandoned around one in the morning and the lower edge of the fire was allowed to creep down the mountain and into the darkness below. Stopping swatting out the grass fire would have major repercussions. No longer were they creating a cold black line to contain future fire. Now they had downward creeping fire over a considerable length of line. That fire was backing into a shallow canyon, a place where it could create siphoning winds and back down unevenly and make fast upslope runs in unburned fuels, creating serious fire risk for firefighters. The whole federal fire service had learned its lesson about fire in this sort of topography from lethal experiences on the South Canyon and Mann Gulch fires where fire fighters were trapped in canyons with fire rushing up at them from below with no escape.

Had the lower edge of this black line been extinguished with the help of the Pueblo crew as planned, the prescribed fire could have been lit within that black line in a much smaller area. Ultimately the change from a cold black line operation to a long ignition on the top of the mountain would preclude attacking the fire directly when it was declared a wildfire the next day.

This was a key decision for the fire crew. By letting the lower edge of the fire go on without control, they no longer were just creating a black line to surround the fire unit, they were *burning* the interior of the unit. Deciding to allow the lower edge to burn down was not a strategic decision for fire management so much as an effort to preserve the energy of an already tired crew. As the fire crept down hill, it encountered steeper slopes and generally fire grows slowly downhill. The burn supervisors may have expected slow downhill growth, especially at night. Instead, the fire crept around itself to the east and made some hot uphill runs, two of which resulted in spot fires over the control line. Spot fires at night are a warning of dry fuels.

The fire's downhill growth forced the fire crews to keep burning the fire line down the ridge, ahead of any hot runs that could come uphill from below. With heavy smoke coming from below them, the fire workers couldn't see what the fire was doing on its southern edge. At night, they could only see flare-ups, by their bright light.

By allowing the fire to burn down the slope untended, the burn boss made the decision to trade one form of hard work for another. The shorthanded crews could either exhaust themselves swatting out the lower edge of a limited black line, or they could continue to light more black line to the east to stay ahead of any runs the fire made against their fire line. Mike Powell and Al King may well have been counting on the fire going out in dense woods below as it did in the 1993 burn attempt. There were plenty of dense woods below them to the south. Thus they may have expected the fire to cool down after it crept through several hundred feet of grasses and sparse trees. In any case, the fire did not cool down except perhaps in some places like the aspen groves in the center of the unit. The fire kept looping around on itself and making vigorous runs up hill, often crowning in trees as it went and the fire fighters were forced to keep building line to stay ahead of it.

By midnight, the Northern Pueblo Black Mesa crew was exhausted and unfit to continue working. The Bandelier fire supervisors sent them down the mountain, not just for rest, but also for good. It is normal for fire crews to work on fires for long shifts, sometimes more than 18 hours at a time. This crew turned out not to be fit for an 8 hour shift and the fact that the fire boss sent them down permanently, rather than just for rest, showed his intense displeasure in their performance. Al King reported to investigators that the Pueblo crew showed a complete lack of experience. Al had been pairing up the more experienced crew members with the rookies to train them before they collapsed. This approach was stopgap at best, and with the Bandelier team stretched to its limit, there was no time for supervising the Black Mesa crew on what should have been basic and routine fire control work.

It's not clear why the Black Mesa crew was not able to do the work assigned them. While it is true that they had worked hard before they lost their energy, the demands of federal fire work would argue that the crew needed to be in better shape. It was early in the fire season and it may have been their first fire assignment but even so, to be issued their "red card" certification as fire ready, they would have had to have passed rigorous physical fitness testing and gone through annual classroom and field training. Whether this crew had passed its physical fitness tests was never investigated.

The night of May 4 was not working out well for the Bandelier team. Relative humidity had stayed low enough all night that the grass was burning more actively than they seemed to have hoped. Normally grass and pine needle debris are highly sensitive to shifts in relative humidity, absorbing moisture from the air quickly and burning more slowly as a result. The grass burned with vigor all night. Worse perhaps was the dashed expectation that the fire would go out in the trees as it had on the 1993 burn. This time it was burning in the forest just fine, except when they wanted it to. The fire slopped over into the forest briefly to the north soon after the test burn was completed. Yet Mike Powell later testified that the fire behavior was "in prescription" or within safe limits except when wind gusts came up.

Perhaps Mike Powell and Al King had planned for easy black lining on the east and north lines of the fire during the night. If the grass had burned as it did during the 1993 burn, the small crew of people they had on hand would have been more than adequate for putting in the control lines before the real burning to be done during the daylight hours. The 1993 burn had been in the fall of a normal precipitation year while the 2000 burn was being done in the spring, after an unusually dry winter. Subtle shifts in the details of the weather portended much worse fire conditions over the next two weeks. Difficultly in controlling the line-burning was just the beginning of their troubles.

The Cerro Grande burn unit is a large area. Its perimeter fire line is at least 3 miles long and the burn supervisors were covering much of that distance on foot repeatedly as the night went on. Though the team broke the line up into sections with Al King supervising the line burning on the west side and Matt Snyder supervising on much of the east side, there was still plenty of distance for so few people to hike and work on. By 2 in the morning the crew was still working hard at keeping the east fire line ahead of any runs from below. They could rest some but then they would be back at work. Fatigue was an increasing problem.

At about 2:30 in the morning Mike Powell went down to the command post at the cross-country ski area parking lot at the bottom of the burn unit. He used the phone there to call for more firefighters after he and Paul Gleason had agreed that they would be shorthanded the next day if new crews were not brought on by at least ten in the morning when the fire would really wake up and get active. The burn supervisors had planned to work a mix of the Pueblo crew and the Bandelier Fire Use Module members through the night, resting people so that a good team, with some additions from Bandelier would be ready to do the main work of burning the inside of the upper part of the unit (Phase 1) when the morning work shift began. With the loss of the Pueblo crew, the personnel situation was messy and Mike knew he needed new people to help hold the lines first thing in the morning.

Mike assumed that by calling the Santa Fe Zone dispatch office at the Santa Fe National Forest, he would easily get a crew or two to come up. After all, he had checked with them a day earlier to see what "contingency" personnel were available and they had told him that one crew was available in one and a half hours and another was available in three hours. That fit the burn plan guidelines. Now it was time to call for some of those people. The need was urgent.

Little did he know he was opening a can of worms and beginning the fall of one of the major dominos in the Cerro Grande disaster.

There are two ways to get personnel for a prescribed burn. One is to call the crews up directly and ask them to come help with your burn in advance or at the time of need. This is done commonly with the many semi-independent fire crews associated with Indian reservations (managed by the Bureau of Indian Affairs) or other crews with loose affiliation with public land agencies. Bandelier's mistake may have been in not arranging directly for additional Indian crews to be on site from the beginning of the burn, just in case. The expense would have been minimal.

The second way to get crews and other equipment is to call the local zone dispatcher and ask for them. In the past, Bandelier had not had any problem doing this. John Lissoway recalls that he needed help with a prescribed fire in the 1980s when he was Chief of Resources Management at Bandelier and John Romero, the senior dispatcher at Santa Fe pulled a crew that was busy thinning trees on the Santa Fe National Forest and sent them over quickly. During the 1970s through the early 1990s, Bandelier would get crews and equipment for prescribed burns on a trade basis with neighboring national forest districts.

In any case, Bandelier had not arranged for more people to be present at the beginning of the burn. All the investigations that followed the Cerro Grande disaster faulted the NPS for short-staffing the fire. Why they chose to have relatively few people on the fire is a matter of speculation. Some people with intimate knowledge of the Bandelier budget process have suggested that Bandelier's Resources staff may have been trying to do Unit 1 (the Cerro Grande burn unit) "on the cheap" to save funds for the more complex and demanding upper Frijoles Canyon burn unit (Unit 9) which they hoped to burn immediately after they finished Cerro Grande (weather permitting). This is informed speculation.

Mike's call went to Joseph Leon at Santa Fe Dispatch, a BLM employee who was sitting in for the regular night dispatcher. It's likely that Mike woke Joseph up with his call at 3 in the morning since there is probably very little radio or phone traffic that time of night, even when a large fire is burning in the district. The Guaje Fire north of Los Alamos was winding down and two other small fires were all but out.

Joseph told Mike to call back at seven in the morning when

a supervisor would be on hand. Mike called again at 6:30 in the morning and got no answer at all. Joseph Leon may not have had enough confidence to call up crews for a fire, or if it was even appropriate for him to call crews for a fire at that hour, for another agency. The "other agency" matter was the real kicker. Yet Mr. Leon's failure to act on Mike's urgent request ended up having major ramifications for the control of the fire on Cerro Grande.

Joseph Leon later testified that once he knew Mike Powell was asking for personnel for a prescribed fire, he assumed that a prescribed fire had all personnel resources pre arranged and that a call for additional resources may not be urgent. He said the call from Mike Powell was calm and did not give the impression of urgency.

Mike said to the Board of Inquiry: "I don't think I said NOW. It's like I need a crew for a prescribed fire. To me... I'm calling at 3:00 in the morning. You know. I didn't just wake up in the middle of the night and think, hey I need a crew."

Mr. Leon was unaware that Bandelier was conducting a large prescribed fire even though Bandelier had notified zone dispatch twice the day before that they were going ahead with the fire and to confirm that "contingency resources" (in this case a type one hotshot crew, helicopter, and type two crew) were available if needed according to the burn plan. The dispatcher confirmed that the contingency crews were available at 2 o'clock in the afternoon on May 4.

The dispatcher sits at a large control board for a radio system that is able to communicate with two-way FM radios over a significant portion of northern New Mexico, as well as with other agency people on their two-way radios and phones. They have a phone list and a computerized list of what fire crews are available to go out on fires and which ones are already out on fires, which fires and where. In a sense, the dispatcher is the center of all activity on a national forest, dealing with communications between Forest Service workers of all types far out in the backcountry. Before the time of cell phones, the two-way radios on the belt's of most federal agency workers were their only communication with the world except when they could get to a phone or meet face to face with someone. (As time has gone by, those two-way radios have gotten increasingly advanced, with many able to tie into the phone system as well as to receive automated weather information from remote computerized weather stations out in the forest called RAWS systems.)

Santa Fe's dispatch center had been in frequent communication with the Bandelier staff over the preceding week while the Unit 40 burn by the park entrance was being done. On May 4 when the Bandelier team shifted its attention to Cerro Grande at least two calls had been made to the dispatcher to let them know the fire would begin. Normally such information is posted on the dispatcher's board so when shifts end, the new dispatcher can see what has been happening. Also logs are kept of all important radio traffic and the relief dispatcher reviews the past shift's logs as they come on their shift. Finally, dispatchers brief each other on what has been happening before they clock out at the end of each shift.

For whatever reason, the Cerro Grande prescribed fire was not posted on the dispatcher's radio log and Joseph Leon was not informed of the pending prescribed fire when he began his shift the evening of May 4. Also the dispatcher's log lacked entries of Mike Powell's 2 pm notification about the burn the previous afternoon. The Bandelier burn had failed to register at the Santa Fe dispatch office.

Mike Powell called the dispatcher to get a new crew (20 people) and a helicopter up to the burn right away at three in the morning on May 5. Since he had lost the Northern Pueblo Agency crew, he needed additional personnel first thing in the morning. If he had wanted a crew at noon the next day, he would have called at the beginning of the work day, knowing that the dispatchers had told him the previous afternoon that crews were available in one to three hours travel time.

Mike's request was delayed five hours, until 8:00 in the morning when dispatch center supervisor John Romero came in and got the note about Mike Powell's 3 a.m. request. At that point he called Mike Powell directly and asked him if he was having trouble with the prescribed fire and if Bandelier had declared it a wildfire. Mike said the fire was not a wildfire but that he needed additional personnel quickly.

Mr. Romero, long experienced in New Mexico wildfire understood the location and its potential problems and called the Santa

Fe Hotshots and Sandia Helicopter to get up to Cerro Grande. In doing this, John created a problem. He believed he had no way to legally pay for emergency fire fighting resources to be sent to a "vegetation management burn." All resources dispatched from the Zone dispatch had to be charged to an account and he had no official way to charge relatively expensive hotshots to a National Park Service management project, unless it was declared a wildfire. If it was a wildfire, funding was routine regardless of what jurisdiction the fire was burning on.

The problem was a bureaucratic one, where the National Park Service, as a Department of Interior agency had an accounting system for paying for people and supplies used on prescribed (management) fires, while a whole different system was used to pay for wildfire, no matter where they were burning. Congress appropriates money for wildfire separately from budgets for prescribed fire.

If Bandelier had hired crews to come and work on the fire from the beginning, or had put in a "standing order" for crews through dispatch, which would have committed those crews to the fire with an accounting system to pay for them, whether they were physically present on the fire or not, then all those personnel would have been charged directly to the account Bandelier and the National Park Service maintain for prescribed fire and for the Cerro Grande prescribed fire in particular. Since this had not been done, Bandelier had inadvertently created bureaucratic hurdles for fulfilling its resource orders. Already the park was taking its chances that crews would be available on short order.

Bandelier had never had this problem with Santa Fe Zone dispatch before. Al King testified that they had obtained crews for the Unit 40 burn the week before from Zone Dispatch without any accounting questions. Perhaps John Romero and the dispatchers were now hesitant to send people and equipment to a prescribed fire since the whole Southwest Region was now on a high alert for fire, with unusually dry conditions and the potential for high winds. In Arizona, fires were burning in similar country to the Santa Fe National Forest and already several wildfires had happened, and one in Bandelier where the seven acre Escarpment Fire had been started by lightning on April 28[2]. Perhaps Santa Fe Dispatch was keeping its crews on the ready since its primary mission is initial attack on new fires, and putting out fires.

Cerro Grande was not a wildfire…yet. John Romero knew the potential for control problems was high so he got creative. He charged the Santa Fe Hotshots and the Sandia Helicopter to the account that was open for the Guaje Fire and sent them instead to Cerro Grande. This was a risky move for John since it would raise the cost of the Guaje Fire and could cause problems if scrutinized. John Romero knew that Bandelier was burning in dry conditions, at a time when the surrounding Santa Fe National Forest had banned campfires and prescribed fires. John understood the potential for real problems and called Rich Tingle, supervisor of the Santa Fe Hotshots and asked him to get his crew up to Cerro Grande.

While it may seem logical that Mr. Romero at dispatch was reluctant to send suppression fire crews to a prescribed fire, his hesitation may have been contrary to federal policy established in the 1995 National Fire Plan that said that all requests for resources for any kind of fire were to be treated equally. The 95 NFP sought to encourage prescribed burning to restore ecology of public lands and to lessen fire danger to communities surrounded by forest like Los Alamos. As well, the National Wildfire Coordinating Group, an organization of national land management agency officials, had written a letter to dispatch centers and their supervisors in 1997 directing that resources were to be made available to prescribed fire on an equal basis with wildfire.

At the same time, the Southwest Mobilization Guide (a handbook for fire fighting resources), updated in 2000, told land managers to call all type 2 crews directly, outside of the dispatch system. Yet Bandelier was not calling for a Type 2 crew, they wanted the Hotshots specifically because they knew they were nearby and capable. The confusion from conflicting directives created chaos in the dispatching of personnel to the Cerro Grande prescribed fire at the Santa Fe dispatch center. In retrospect, the Bandelier staff's assumptions about how dispatching could be done to a prescribed fire were in line with national policy at the time.

Indeed the dispatch problem for Bandelier on May 5 exemplified a big problem that Congressional investigators under the General Accounting Office pointed out in their investigation of the Cerro Grande disaster; that agencies were not following the National Fire Plan that Congress had mandated in 1995. Among other things, the plan mandated that agencies cooperate on prescribed fire and that barriers between agencies be broken down to facilitate prescribed burning on inter agency, landscape levels.

Yet when all was said and done, perhaps the dispatch problem with Santa Fe and Bandelier was another example of long-standing sour relations between the two agencies. The Santa Fe National Forest and Bandelier National Monument have had tense relations for years and Bandelier's ignorance of the Santa Fe National Forest's ban on prescribed fire, begun on May 3 (though not applicable or binding on Bandelier anyway), could have incited bad feelings at the Santa Fe National Forest, feelings that Bandelier was not being a team player, or even, that Bandelier's staff was careless, or worse, to start a prescribed fire against the implied warning of the national forest's prescribed fire and campfire ban.

John Romero succeeded in getting the Santa Fe Hotshots mobilized toward Bandelier. Hotshots are the most highly trained of firefighting crews and are specifically funded out of national budgets for large fire situations and initial attack. The idea of "hotshots" arose from the Civilian Conservation Corps camps of 1942. Many CCC workers fought fire, but the best of them were formed into "hotshot" crews. The idea persisted, gaining particular strength in the setting of large brush fires in southern California. Today hotshot crews based at many national forests and national parks specialize in initial attack – the first crew to attack a new wildfire. They can be seen driving toward fires far from their home bases in the height of fire season. Their work is demanding, but their pay is good. Being seasonal employees, they are laid off in the fall.

In the off season they may be used for management burns or vegetation clearing, but during fire season, hotshot crews exist to help with new fires. Early May 2000 was definitely fire season and the Hotshots were already tired from the Guaje Fire.

John Romero sent the Santa Fe Hotshots to Cerro Grande because they were the closest crew at hand. He also knew they were good and since he suspected problems on Cerro Grande, they would be most effective at helping with any control problems.

It would have been easier, budget-wise, to send a type two crew, perhaps from one of the nearby Indian Pueblos, but that would have taken longer and John sensed the urgency growing on Cerro Grande.

The Santa Fe Hotshots had the day off and though they got the call to assemble at the point where their bus and tools were stored as soon as possible, members of the crew later testified that they had not been given a sense of great urgency. They were told to be to their base in two hours, having been called at around 7 in the morning. It therefore took until 11:30 to get to the parking area at the base of Cerro Grande.

From Bandelier's perspective, the Hotshots were 9 hours late, starting from the time the call was made for them at 3 a.m. So much for the assurance Santa Fe Dispatch had given repeatedly in the days before the prescribed fire, that a crew would be available within 2.5 hours if called.

It then took the Hotshots another hour from the highway to hike up to the point where the fire had escaped its east line (a major slop-over) and was burning down toward Water Canyon. This slop-over was consuming the energy of several Bandelier crew-members and pulling them away from patrolling the fire line. The delay in reaching the point where help was needed, counting the delay caused by the confusion at dispatch and the time involved in mobilizing the crew, caused the slop-over to become quite large and the hotshots worked hard for hours to put in a hand line and get it under control. The hotshots were struggling to catch up to the fire as soon as they got there.

If a larger team had been on the fire to begin with, this catch-up would not have been necessary, since the slop-over would have been attacked while it was still small. Or, if the hotshots had arrived at the fire at 8 in the morning as Mike Powell and Paul Gleason had intended when the 3 a.m. call was made to dispatch, the slop-over would have stayed small or never happened to start with and all the people on the fire could have returned to the original burn plan which called for the fire to be kept inside the upper burn unit (phase one) and not expand the burned area beyond that until much later that day.

Until the large slop-over began at ten in the morning on the 5th. The Bandelier team, including the Bandelier Engine 91 crew, (fresh off the Guaje Fire) was handling the other small slop-overs that happened on both the north and west sides with relative ease. The fire was staying within its boundaries until ten in the morning. When the large slop-over happened at ten, Bandelier's team had four very capable fire fighters working hard on it, but four was not enough. When the Sandia Helicopter showed up, it dropped two fire fighters off who joined the battle sometime between 10:30 and 11:00. Still, the fire continued to spread.

The slop-over defied control. With no large water sources like a water tender truck or an engine up on the ridge, the team had to depend on hand tool work to stop a fire running in grass and quickly getting into timber. The strategy of holding the fire in bounds within areas of blackened grass had failed in one key spot and without large equipment or large crews of people to catch the escape, the fire was rapidly going out of control.

The helicopter began to bring buckets of water from the large pond on the Baca Ranch, in the Valle Toledo, but the travel time between the pond and the slop-over was at least twenty minutes and none of the fire fighters expressed that the bucket water drops were making much of an impact on the slop-over. Then, someone from Santa Fe Dispatch called to say they didn't have a written agreement with the Baca Ranch owners allowing them to use water from their cattle ponds. This diverted the helicopter to either Los Alamos reservoir or Cochiti Reservoir, lengthening the time between water drops on the fire.

When the Santa Fe Hotshots did arrive on the slop-over, they began to work furiously on building a fire line around it. Fire behavior was extreme at times and it was catch up work. Rich Tingle, supervisor of the Santa Fe Hotshots, called for an air tanker to deliver a load of fire retardant on the slop-over at around noon. Everyone present knew he was right to do this and everyone in charge knew the retardant was the end of the prescribed fire and the beginning of the Cerro Grande Wildfire.

Thus the slop-over was the key event in losing the burn since it required so much human energy to control it. It became the focus of the whole burn team though many of them had to stay spread out on other parts of the burn perimeter to watch for other escapes. If the Northern Pueblo crew had not failed and had been on the fire line ready to work the next morning as planned, the slop over probably would not have happened. Likewise if resources had come from Santa Fe Dispatch beginning with the 3 a.m. call, the slop-over would not have grown to the point where it stressed the whole organization. The dominos had fallen, one into the next and now the Bandelier team was exhausted, and scrambling to keep their prescribed fire from becoming a larger mess than they had ever intended.

Once the fire was declared a wildfire by Paul Gleason at 11:30 he became the Incident Commander. Now critical strategy had to be devised for putting the fire out as quickly and safely as possible. As it turned out, the suppression effort turned out to be a risky, dangerous undertaking, and one ultimately that would be sabotaged by the weather.

[1] Interview with then Espanola Ranger District Fire Management Officer Kevin Joseph March 20, 2001.

[2] The Escarpment Fire turned out to be a sore point between the Forest Service and the Park Service. On April 28, Phill Neff of the Jemez Ranger District talked to Al King of Bandelier about the Escarpment lightning fire that was burning in Bandelier's wilderness near the Forest Service boundary between Frijoles and Alamo Canyons. Al King indicated to Mr. Neff that Bandelier wanted to designate the Escarpment Fire as a "fire use" fire, meaning allow it to burn for the benefit of the local environment. The area where the fire was burning had been burned by the 1977 La Mesa Fire. Mr. Neff told Mr. King that the Forest Service in no way would support such a decision given that fire danger rating was very high and Energy Release Component (ERC) ratings were indicating dangerous conditions. Also the Escarpment Fire was close to a plantation of pine on Forest Service land that needed protection for commercial reasons. Mr. King said that he agreed and would convey a recommendation to suppress the fire to his supervisors. Yet the fact that Bandelier staff was considering fire-use for the Escarpment Fire relayed a feeling of recklessness to the local Forest Service staff. Only days later the Cerro Grande prescribed fire began.

Chapter 12

Tool Turned Monster, Fighting Fire

Once declared a wildfire, the Cerro Grande Fire had an open budget from general fire suppression funds and few barriers to any level of staffing that the incident commander, Paul Gleason, felt he needed. Moreover, some highly qualified fire people were by now arriving at the mountain, as were more crews to take on the fire, which by noon on May 6 was putting up a large plume of smoke worrying many people in Los Alamos.

Yet, declaring the fire a wildfire did little to change the overall strategic problems that the prescribed fire planners had faced. After all, fighting the fire meant keeping it within bounds just as doing the prescribed fire had meant keeping it within bounds. The prescribed fire area had been chosen based on somewhat natural limits to the fire such as ridge tops and the highway. Fighting the fire would have to be done under similar strategies. Under the prescribed fire plan, the whole of the burn unit would be burned slowly from top to bottom, with the edges held always to keep it within set bounds.

Wildland fire fighting is done by containing fires and then choking off their fuel supplies. With structural fires, a building is doused with water or some other chemical to extinguish flames. In wildland fire, areas aflame are often too vast to be doused with water or retardant from airplanes. Thus retardant and water from hoses or helicopters is used to strengthen containment lines or to try to knock down the head of a fire as it moves across a landscape, not to directly extinguish the whole fire.

Prescribed fire managers had hesitated to send any personnel into the interior of the burn unit since fire burning the bases of the many dead trees there could fell those trees onto fire fighters. This was considered a significant hazard. Also as mentioned, fire fighters don't like to build "under-slung" fire lines across steep slopes, since rolling burning debris or falling burning trees can easily breach fire line below significant fire. Already the Santa Fe Hotshots had reluctantly been building under-slung line around the slop over on the northeast side of the blaze.

Incident planners had to take into account a wide range of problems and possibilities on the fire, not the least of which was the weather. The National Weather Service was predicting increasing winds for Sunday night and Monday. Increased winds move fires by increasing their flame lengths which in turn cause the fire to preheat, then burn new fuels, often fuels that were out of reach of the fire when it was burning coolly without additional wind. Specifically wind can push fire from the ground into mid level fuels then into treetops making uncontrollable crown fires. This is the worst-case scenario for any wildfire in Ponderosa pine forest.

Yet at that point, Cerro Grande was not a crown fire. Fire fighters often deal with blazes like Cerro Grande as it was on May 6. The trick is anticipating what could go wrong then having a plan and resources available if it does go wrong. Even so, fire is highly unpredictable and planning for escapes is difficult given weather changes and the way fire behaves on complex landscapes. Fire fighters had been educated by the slop-over how active the fire would be if it got into the woods to the east, something the pre-scribed fire planners had not anticipated.

Just as in the prescribed fire, the fire fighters decided to "put a line" around the burn unit and then keep the fire from crossing it. A critical decision faced by both Paul Gleason, his Bandelier team, and the wider group of local fire officials who met at about three o'clock in the afternoon on May 6 was to decide how to attack the fire. John Miera and Paul Orosco from the Espanola and Jemez Districts of the Santa Fe National Forest flew over the fire in the Sandia helicopter just before this meeting. How to attack the fire was a difficult and critical decision and one that drew much suspicion and criticism in the weeks that followed.

Officials at the strategy meeting had two options for fighting the fire. One was the "direct" method that would mean putting a line around the fire close to the existing edges of the fire as possible. Two variations on this approach were considered. The second option was to do an "indirect" attack that would involve putting a line around the fire according to the geography of the area and containing the fire within the wider area. The people at the meeting that included the fire management officer from the Forest Service Jemez Ranger District, the fire management officer from Los Alamos National Laboratory, the Los Alamos County Fire Chief, the Espanola District Ranger, and the Bandelier Superintendent talked over the options and decided on the indirect method of attack.

"Going indirect" in this case meant using the fire lines that had been planned for the prescribed fire such as the highway that made a good fireline on the south. The north and much of the east sides were already lined with the work of the Bandelier crew and the Santa Fe Hotshots. Of course this method also involved putting much more fire on the ground and that fire would be exposed to unpredictable winds.

A great deal of controversy arose from the decision to contain the fire with the original boundaries chosen for the prescribed fire. Some suspected that the indirect approach was chosen to finish the prescribed fire, a view reinforced by a statement overheard from a Bandelier staffer who said that the indirect approach would help meet objectives. Yet people from other agencies arrived at this decision, people who had no interest in Bandelier's objectives at that moment. Objectives are goals in a prescribed fire, not in a suppression operation. Paul Gleason who was the Incident Commander for the initial wildfire suppression operation and a deeply experienced wildland fire fighter was known as a person who believed in containing fire with fire and thus the indirect approach was attractive to him. Whether the Bandelier staff was motivated by "resource objectives" in choosing the indirect attack method can never be known yet for years afterwards the impression that the Park Service chose this method for resource objective reasons persisted[1].

Once the indirect approach was chosen, it could be pursued quickly since a much larger team was on hand than was there before the fire was declared a wildfire. Thus the fire lines could be burned out down the two ridges quickly and then more decisions could be made about how to deal with the interior of the burn unit. The interior was largely unburned except for the top third. Fire fighters don't like to leave "islands of unburned fuel" in burn units as they can ignite when nobody's watching and fire can run toward edges and out of the control area or they can produce embers that fly beyond control lines[2].

Thus it's not enough to put a fire line around a burn unit or around an area you expect a fire might cross. One has to burn out all the fuels that are likely to burn soon. Perhaps the cost of keeping fire personnel out on the lines ($5000 per day for a 20 person crew) makes fire bosses more inclined to burn out the interior of burn units quickly so everyone can be done and the fire closed out.

In the case of the Cerro Grande wildfire on May 6, 2000, the fire fighting strategy was looking similar to the prescribed fire strategy but at an accelerated pace. The same fire lines were used, and the firing of the interior planned. The only difference was the wildfire had plenty of people and money, while the prescribed fire was short of people and had a limited budget.

Whenever a wildfire happens, the incident commander in charge prepares a Wildfire Situation Analysis, (WFSA) which is a written plan for how the fire will be attacked. Paul Gleason, Al King and Roy Weaver worked on the first WFSA for Cerro Grande at about 2:30 in the afternoon on May 6. WFSAs tell where the fire will be contained, what major environmental concerns must be addressed such as endangered species habitat or human developments that could be threatened and it lays out the risks such as firefighter safety. Cerro Grande's WFSA emphasized the threat the fire posed to Los Alamos and the nuclear weapons lab there.

Signing the WFSA at 4:30 Sunday afternoon, Roy Weaver noted that a Type 1 team had been ordered and they would prepare a new WFSA. The group meeting of agency people had decided to go right to a Type 1 team, the highest level of fire fighting organization available on the federal level. Often wildfires first are assigned to Type 2 teams, an organization dispatched by the regional fire organization as opposed to a Type 1 team that draws directly from the federal Interagency Fire Center in Boise, Idaho.

Back up on Cerro Grande, the fire fighters went to work with the indirect approach, working with the Mormon Lake Hotshots, the Santa Fe Hotshots and a crew from Jemez Pueblo and some Bandelier people to burn out the fire lines down the east and west ridges. The plan was to put in those black lines quickly, then burn out the land inside the fire lines, mop up, pack up and go home.

Since the winds were blowing from the southwest, the most difficult area to work was the east line that was being burned down through a grassy pine forest. The wind driven fire was burning against this fire line. The Santa Fe Hotshots, under Rich Tingle, headed up this work, trying to create a swath of black with a highly flammable forest at their back, with no natural barrier to the fire to work with. They worked almost all night on Saturday night, finally reaching the road at two o'clock in the morning on Sunday where it makes a sharp dogleg through the north fork of Frijoles Canyon.

This area was a problem area for the fire fighters. Using the road as a fire line made sense except that the road dipped down into a low spot and moved across two slopes, moving from a south facing slope to an east facing slope with the attendant changes in forest type. The division chief, Kirk Smith of the Mormon Lake Hotshots, had to worry about fire's tendency to chimney up drainages and make a run up inside the burn unit. More troubling was the possibility that the fire would throw embers down into the canyon below the road and create a large fire in the thick timber there. Preventing this possibility became the main focus of the fire fighters as they worked.

For this reason, at two in the morning, when the fire fighters brought the black line down to the highway at the dogleg, they started to work along the highway, burning out next to the road. They had planned to burn all the way to the bottom of the west fire line, about three quarters of a mile to the west. However, things went wrong before they had a chance to complete the line burning so it would surround the designated area.

As mentioned, fire fighting teams break up the line surrounding a fire into divisions and each division has a commander who focuses efforts on that section of land. It was clear that Kirk Smith was in charge of the east fire line and the division it represented. Russ Copp was in charge of the west fire line. Yet neither of these men was sure where their division ended on the highway and each assumed someone else was in charge of the section of highway along the south side of the fire. This confusion was more than academic as events of the next few hours would prove.

In the late morning of May 7, Paul Gleason turned his attention to the unburned fuels inside the fire lines. Since fuels within a fire line can create major fire runs, it was necessary to get the fuels inside the burn unit to burn, so the whole area would be blackened and could be mopped up. Thus the Sandia helicopter was fitted with an aerial ignition device under the command of Kirk Smith. They dropped balls of potassium permanganate over an area on the northwest part of the burn unit, hoping it would light fire to creep across and finish consuming the interior fuels. The ping-pong balls were not starting fire in the area intended. That operation was quickly abandoned when the helicopter crew noticed fire running from the bottom of the west fire line along and across the highway to the east, climbing into the trees. This was a major change, a radical escalation of fire behavior. No longer were the crews working on containing the fire area, they were now fighting a firestorm that was breaching the fire lines.

Since the bottom of the west fire line had been neglected, fire had crept across a grassy area where plenty of old dead aspen logs lay and had made its way to a patch of woods next to the highway. The fact that nobody had clearly identified that area as part of their "division" and that no crews were clearly assigned to patrol the forest next to the highway turned out to be a major oversight by the command team. Though there were two or three engines at the fire, none was patrolling the road carefully, watching for spot fires. Everyone was focused on burning out at the dogleg on the east side. Now fire was racing toward that dogleg, in the treetops, totally out of control.

Russ Copp, a senior firefighter from the Coconino National

Forest in Arizona had plenty of experience with wildfire in dry ponderosa pine forests. He had been called to Cerro Grande to be the west division chief. He arrived at the burn unit around dinnertime on Saturday night and supervised a crew from Jemez Pueblo as they burned and dug fire line from the knoll half way up the west fire boundary to the highway. He also had an engine with its three person crew assigned to him but since that truck couldn't' drive off the highway, it stood by on the highway and worked along the road keeping an eye out for spot fires.

Though he had two fire monitors whose job was to take weather readings every half hour and watch the fire, he released them with the Pueblo crew and the engine crew at eight in the morning. Thus, at eight in the morning Russ Copp found himself largely alone on the west line, feeling it was secure and safe.

His sense of satisfaction followed a grueling 12-hour shift of lighting fire in strips extending into the burn unit perpendicular to the fire line they were creating along the edge of the unit. This technique was tiring but had the advantage of creating a wide black line that would hold the fire if the winds shifted. In contrast, the fire line on the east side of the unit was narrow and vulnerable, because the wind was against the workers on the east and in favor of Russ Copp's crew. If his black lining fire burned away from him to the east, that was according to plan since a fire line existed to the east and burning the interior of the unit was needed as well. The helicopter firing operation worked along the inner edge of the hand burning he and the Jemez crew had initiated all of Saturday night.

Russ had gotten to know that part of the mountain well and was watching the way the fire was behaving; its low creeping behavior, with occasional trees torching and runs in the grass creating no problems. Yet at the bottom of his line, the low-key fire behavior would turn violent when it snuck from light fuels into thick forest, pushed by rising winds.

The fire commanders timed the convergence of fire lines poorly. Paul Gleason had planned to burn along the highway from the dogleg westward over to the base of Russ Copp's west fire line. Firing along the highway would be done into the wind so the fire would blow back onto itself and the blackened area. Russ finished his fire line long before the crews working the east fire line were ready to begin burning along the highway beyond the dogleg in the canyon.

This timing error happened partly because the original prescribed fire planners had assumed that the fire would not burn well in the flats down by the highway. So no plans to deal aggressively with the south fire line (the highway) had been made. Perhaps this was because the team was so focused on the volatile and dangerous east line. Perhaps they were short a crew needed to burn the south line, along the highway and rightly wanted the east line finished before any fire on the south was lit. In any case, having Russ Copp burn to the highway well before the fire line had been burned along the highway created a major problem that apparently nobody anticipated.

In a sense, those dealing with the fire may have become complacent about the west boundary of the fire. With Russ Copp's expert leadership there, and a perceived low risk of an escape from that side given the highway fuel break and the accessibility of fire equipment to that side, all eyes were keenly focused on the east line. By releasing his tired crew, Mr. Copp himself may have become more sure of the danger posed by the fire on the west side than the situation would prove to warrant. He also knew that the presence of the highway meant that engines with water and high-pressure pumps could arrive swiftly if any problem developed. Even so, the crew as a whole seemed to have turned their attention away from the west side, especially after the aerial ignition failed to put significant fire into that area.

Midday Sunday, wind became the driving force of the Cerro Grande fire. Though later nobody could agree on the wind speeds at 11:00 in the morning near the highway, they were significantly higher than what the crew had experienced since the first match was lit on May 4. Though some say the wind was around 50 miles per hour at the base of the fire line at 11:00 on Sunday morning, it seems most likely that the wind speeds peaked at 20-35 miles per hour and that the steady drying of the fuels that had been occurring on Cerro Grande since the last snow, almost a month before, accounted for the extreme fire behavior that suddenly erupted. Wind, combined with low relative humidity, dries leaves, branches, logs and standing trees faster than still air does.

The most reliable wind measurements near Cerro Grande

come from a Department of Energy operated weather station on the top of adjacent Pajarito Mountain. That station measured top wind speeds of just over 27 miles per hour after 11:00 on Sunday. By two in the afternoon, the Pajarito station was clocking winds at 34 miles per hour. That weather station measures free flowing wind more than a thousand feet above where the highway passes along Cerro Grande and could register higher winds than one would expect at a lower elevation among trees – such as where the fire escaped from the base of the west fire line. It's also possible that the topography of Cerro Grande channeled and increased winds leaving the vast Valle Grande and pouring into the Rio Grande Valley to the east.

Chuck Maxwell of the National Weather Service in Albuquerque, who was in charge of providing the weather information to the National Park Service during the Cerro Grande prescribed fire (spot weather forecasts), agreed that there is no record of very high wind (above 30 miles per hour) on Cerro Grande on Sunday. Rather, he suspects that the extreme fire behavior of midday probably occurred because of wind and very dry fuels[3]. The fact that moderate wind caused the fire to crown and that spot fires grew rapidly indicate extremely dry fuels. The spot fires in Frijoles Canyon were somewhat sheltered from the wind yet they grew rapidly.

Kirk Smith saw the fire kindle strongly in the forest near the highway from the helicopter as he finished the aerial ignition effort. He also saw that nobody was there to tend that fire, that no engine on highway patrol was nearby, despite the billowing smoke.

The fact that this fire climbed into the trees in a dominantly mature Douglas fir forest meant that flames at ground level were being fanned by strong enough winds to extend their heat into the crown of the forest with only moderate amounts of ladder fuels to help the process along. The fire rushed into the forest canopy where it drove eastward along the highway and began to throw embers onto the south side of the highway. Kevin Joseph, the Forest Service staffer from the local ranger district, drove up in his truck from the east right at this point and jumped out with his fire tool into the woods on the south side of the highway, attacking new spot fires even as the fire blasted east, and split into two fire fronts.

The fire quickly developed two heads. One rushed to the southeast and roared to the edge of the north fork of Frijoles Canyon, throwing embers down into the canyon where they rapidly started spot fires that observers in aircraft said grew to 3 to 5 acres in a matter of minutes.

The second head of the fire rushed right to the dogleg and to the crews waiting there at the base of the east fire line. What happened at this point is the major point of speculation and mystery in the whole Cerro Grande disaster. Within a half hour, the fire would escape from Cerro Grande and Frijoles Canyon altogether. Opinions vary on precisely what occurred but the tracks the fire left on the ground and the stories of witnesses, particularly Kathy Allred, above in her lead plane with the fire retardant tankers, lead to two possible scenarios.

The head of the fire that rushed from the bottom of the west fire line running to the east, threw embers down into Frijoles Canyon and these quickly started a spot fire of almost 20 acres. The firefighters on the ground and in the air tankers focused on containing that fire and managed to keep it from crossing the highway to the north. Even so, this canyon fire threw embers into winds channeling up Frijoles Canyon toward the north and these embers then started new spot fires well across the highway on the east side of the east fire line. These spot fires spawned others, with the wind that ran up the slope to the north, like skipping stones. Today, a line of burned patches of trees on the east flank of Cerro Grande, beyond the east fire line, supports this scenario for the path of escape for the fire.

The second scenario, advocated by Kathy Allred who viewed the escape from her airplane, was that those persistent winds from the west blew embers across the east fire line above the highway and these embers started spot fires that spread to the north in winds channeling northward out of Frijoles Canyon. Clearly the surface winds were being heavily influenced by topography. Up-canyon winds out of Frijoles Canyon were dominating easterly winds out of the Valle Grande. Fire running in those east running winds cut northward once it dropped behind the low ridge on the east fire line.

The differences between these two scenarios are minor and have little bearing on the lessons learned from the Cerro Grande escape. If the fire escaped across the east fire line, it means that the best efforts at holding that line failed. On the other hand if the east fire line held, and no spot fires of consequence spread from there, the escape from the untended south fire line, along the highway becomes the source of the larger escape toward Los Alamos. In either scenario, it was backfires, lit to contain the original prescribed fire, that escaped.

Back down at the highway where the crews were gathered, the northern head of the crown fire from the west side (separated by a narrow island of trees from the southern head) rushed along the highway toward the dogleg and slammed into the dogleg and the east fire line. At this point all fire activity on the mountain was increasing as winds buffeted the mountain.

Strong winds blowing to the north pushed the spot fires like skipping stones, up the flank of Cerro Grande and over into Water Canyon on Forest Service land, well outside of the designated burn unit. Once in Water Canyon, the next canyon to the north of Cerro Grande, erratic winds and dry fuels caused new spot fires to grow rapidly. Having dropped in elevation, these new fires were in much drier fuels than those up on Cerro Grande and they found unlimited fuels to burn as the winds, now strongly northward, picked up embers, blew them ahead of the new fire in Water Canyon and started more fires yet a quarter to a half mile ahead of the main flame front. Fire started on the mesa between Water and Valle Canyon and then on the south facing, very dry slopes of Valle Canyon where pine needle drifts were a foot thick in many places among pine stands. Then the fire flashed on over into Pajarito Canyon, gaining strength as it went, flaring tall flags of flame into the afternoon sky as two hundred year old ponderosa pines torched.

This rapid advance of the fire took about an hour to cover less than 5 miles between Cerro Grande and Pajarito Canyon to the north where Paul Gleason and Kevin Joseph, along with the Bandelier fire team, were now preparing for it on the Camp May Road up Pajarito Mountain. Over the next two days, as winds greatly calmed, they and others would work hard to hold the fire there. The fire's pause at the edge of Los Alamos Canyon represented a line in time between the failure of the prescribed fire and its suppression and the inevitable burning of the forests around Los Alamos and some of the homes in the community.

By looking closely at what happened up on Cerro Grande between May 4 and May 7, we see a domino effect of errors by a variety of people from different agencies, compounded by wind. While it's possible to dissect the events on the mountain and see the mistakes and understand why the fire escaped, it's clear that, overall, the Bandelier team was taking a big chance in conducting a controlled burn of this size in spring.

Even so, the National Weather Service did not forecast the winds that hit the fire on May 7 and then escalated over the next week. These winds were extraordinary by historical standards and it's safe to say that, had the winds been within normal spring ranges, the fire could have been contained on Cerro Grande. As aviator Kathy Allred later testified, "It looked pretty good, and if the winds hadn't come up, it looked like a good burn[4]."

Many of the staff of the National Park Service at Bandelier argued strongly that if reinforcements had arrived without the unnecessary delay from the Forest Service dispatch center, the slopover never would have grown beyond a small area, the fire would have been limited to the upper part of Cerro Grande, and probably would have been put to bed up there. Whether the Bandelier team would have continued their prescribed burn down the mountain if the Santa Fe Hotshots had arrived early on May 5 rather than midday is a matter of pure speculation.

It's clear that once the fire was declared a wildfire, more fire was lit on the mountain in an aggressive effort to contain the burn unit. The fire that escaped from Cerro Grande came from the fire that was introduced to the mountain after the fire was declared a wildfire, when rapid burning of the east and west fire lines was occurring to create containment lines around the interior of the burn unit. In a prescribed fire setting, such burning would have taken place more slowly, if at all. Ironically the wildfire declaration and the increased staffing it brought led to a rapid increase in the amount of fire on the mountain and ultimately fires in places where wind was able to carry it quickly out of control.

In a personal conversation with then-Interior Secretary Bruce Babbitt in October 2005, Secretary Babbitt remarked, "They never should have lit that back fire![5]" This comment showed a grasp of the true nature of the Cerro Grande event, five years later by a person whose career was significantly affected by it, and the political fallout that followed[6].

A second line of thought holds that the Cerro Grande fire would have escaped control on May 7 whether it was still a relatively small prescribed fire or whether it was being addressed aggressively as a wildfire. The high winds on the east and south fire lines at eleven in the morning on May 7 caused the fire to heat up in many places inside the burn unit.

On May 5 and 6, firefighters complained that the fire was not burning well or evenly inside containment lines on the upper and middle part of Cerro Grande to allow the unit to finish burning. This meant that large islands of unburned fuels existed inside the burn unit, close to the east fire line. At least one firefighter observing from the west fire line watched as the fire made a significant run from inside the burn unit toward the east fire line, growing into the crowns of the trees midday on May 7, at the same time the fire was rushing eastward along the highway at the bottom of the burn unit. The unburned fuels within the fire lines were capable of burning rapidly with head fires once wind pushed nearby fire toward them. This was exactly what Paul Gleason was trying to prevent with the helicopter ignition late morning on May 7.

Much unburned fuel existed in the interior of the burn unit, even up high on the mountain where efforts to burn that fuel had been ongoing for three and a half days. Yet the inability of the firefighters to send people inside the unit (for safety reasons) to ignite those fuels prevented an even ignition of the area in a safe sequence that may have prevented the fire from building up a head.

It's impossible to know what would have happened if things had turned out differently at key points in the prescribed fire and the subsequent wildfire containment effort up to midday on May 7. What's certain is that the Cerro Grande fire went from being a routine local fire control effort within a 900-acre area, to a major wildfire that ultimately spanned 42,400 acres because of *winds* and dry, abundant fuels. The fire was wind driven from May 7 until 10 and while northern New Mexico was in a pronounced drought in May 2000, that drought was but one factor, along with heavy fuels that the fire fed on once it was running on US Forest Service and Los Alamos County owned lands.

---

[1] See <u>Interagency Strategy for the Implementation of Federal Fire Management Policy</u>, June 2003.

[2] Ultimately the Cerro Grande wildfire crossed the Camp May Road when an unburned island of fuel heated up and threw a spot fire into Los Alamos Canyon on May 10.

[3] Personal interview with Chuck Maxwell.

[4] Kathy Allred, lead plane pilot in testimony to the Cerro Grande Board of Inquiry.

[5] Personal conversation with Bruce Babbitt, October 12, Santa Fe, NM.

[6] Secretary Babbitt was criticized for not standing up more strongly for the National Park Service's prescribed burning program that was key to reducing fire danger and restoring the parks. His sharp criticism of the Bandelier staff and his willingness to allow that staff to be eviscerated by a cycle of blame angered many. Yet the Cerro Grande fire happened in the run-up to the 2000 presidential election when Democrats such as Mr. Babbitt were hoping for a transition from the Clinton administration to an Al Gore administration. Sensitive to the appearance of mismanagement, such as had dogged the Department of Energy, Mr. Babbitt perhaps sought to shift blame for the Cerro Grande fire down the ranks.

Chapter 13

Wind and Drought

The conventional wisdom from the person on the street through-out New Mexico following the fire was that starting a prescribed fire in a windy spring was a foolish thing to do.

Perhaps so, but the winds that struck the Cerro Grande fire on May 7 were the beginning of an extraordinary wind event, well outside of the norms of spring weather in New Mexico. On May 10 winds in Los Alamos were clocked at more than 35 miles per hour, well above the norms for spring in New Mexico. The Bandelier crew was prepared for and anticipated normal spring winds but once those winds exceeded 30 miles per hour as may have happened on Cerro Grande on May 7 when some observers reported gusts to 50 miles per hour, even the best fire fighters could only run ahead of the fire and try to catch its head, miles to the north.

Winds were key to the fire's escape from control and many officials and members of the public wondered how wind was taken into account in the burn planning. The answer to this came in testimony before the Board of Inquiry, which investigated the fire in August 2000.

During that inquiry, the park staff stated that the fire weather forecasts provided by the National Weather Service, which are updated several times a day, provided no forecast of winds above 25 miles per hour during the time when the park staff planned to burn. Forecasters from the National Weather Service testified that they are incapable of accurately predicting winds in the mountains in the spring and that their wind forecasts are only good for 3 days at the most. In many larger burns, including the 2007 Upper Frijoles Canyon prescribed fire at Bandelier, a NWS weather forecaster is part of the burn team and is able to give accurate forecasts on the local landscape level. In 2000, Bandelier was receiving its forecasts from the Albuquerque NWs office.

Did the park staff understand how much uncertainty the National Weather Service had about wind speeds in the fire weather forecasts? It was never clear that the park staff knew how uncertain wind predictions were or if they had ever asked about certainty levels or if the NWS staff had emphasized how uncertain their forecasts were. Given that prevailing winds in the spring often blow northeast on the Pajarito Plateau, this was a central question for holding the fire from reaching the fuel thickets near Los Alamos. The National Weather Service testified that Bandelier fire staff maintained an active communication with them regarding the weather. Both agencies performed without error their professional and legal requirements for weather forecasts and communication about those forecasts.

In any case, the winds that hit the Jemez Mountains on May 5 and again on May 10 through 21 were unusually strong, even by windy New Mexico spring standards. The weather station on the peak of Pajarito Mountain recorded winds more than 50 miles per hour, especially after May 10.

The Bandelier team also watched weather forecasts, both long and short term, to project how weather would change fuel conditions and thus fire behavior. Fire crews can ask for "spot weather forecasts" from the National Weather Service that give an update of weather conditions for a particular location. Yet weather forecasting is an imperfect art, as the crews would soon learn the hard way. They planned the burn in a window of weather that seemed to be stable and provided the conditions needed to meet their prescription.

Wind and weather forecasts become one of the most important issues in the Cerro Grande Fire, both from the point of view of an angry public and investigators. Was it reasonable for the Bandelier crew to expect forecasts of low wind speeds to be reliable? Should the National Weather Service have warned

Bandelier's staff that the probability of winds exceeding forecasts was relatively high?

The National Weather Service provides both short and long term forecasts to firefighters during any prescribed or suppression fire. The weather forecasts given to the Bandelier team predicted no unusual winds on Cerro Grande during the prescribed fire. Yet the National Weather Service admitted that forecasting wind in the spring in New Mexico is nearly impossible, especially in the mountains where local topography can funnel winds and where upper level winds can mix down toward the surface unpredictably.

In early May 2000, a low-pressure area was stalled north and east of New Mexico, separated from a high pressure over the four-corners region by a twisting stationary cold front. The high pressure that had built over the four-corners region signaled the end of winter weather patterns when fronts off the Pacific Ocean move onshore, sometimes bringing snow and always bringing windy conditions. Such high-pressure systems often bring wind as air shifts between a high and a low-pressure system. Northern New Mexico was between these two pressure extremes.

Spring brings with it an unstable atmosphere as high cold air mixes with lower layers of air warmed by intensifying sun hitting the land. Strong airflows higher in the atmosphere can blow down toward the earth. These upper level winds, upon reaching the land, can be strong and such strong winds blew across the eastern Jemez Mountains intermittently beginning on May 7. This weather pattern happens to some extent every spring in New Mexico, yet winds were unusually strong in 2000, possibly because flows from as high as 20,000 feet above the surface were mixing down to the ground.

Meteorologists are able to measure atmospheric instability and report it using a numeric tool called the "Haines Index" which describes the movement and moisture content of the atmosphere above a region. Scientists calculate the Haines Index for a region daily and fire fighters use that information, combined with the moisture of fuels in an area to predict how likely a fire is to grow and become difficult to control. The Haines Index runs from 2 to 6, with two being stable, moist atmosphere and six being a dry, unstable atmosphere that could cause extreme fire behavior.

Beginning on May 3, the day before the Cerro Grande prescribed fire was begun, the Haines Index was at its maximum of six for the afternoon burn periods and remained at this maximum reading until May 8 when a weak cold front with some precipitation moved into the area.

As the Bandelier team learned on the night of May 4 when the fire was begun, the night was dry with little increase in relative humidity. They had planned to burn out the north and part of the east fire lines in the night when they would take advantage of the low relative humidity to keep the fire low and cool. Instead, relative humidity remained below 10%, which meant that the fire burned actively in the grass, and while this was within expectations, it caused the fire to burn down to the west of the test burn area, diverting people and effort to an area they expected to work on later. The fire also crept down to the south faster than they might have expected, causing them to abandon control efforts on that edge and fully commit themselves to the burn, sooner than they had said they would in their written burn plan. Further, the low relative humidity was part of a drying trend that affected all the fuels on the mountain and led to the blowup on May 7 and the fire's escape from the control area.

The high Haines Index foretold a rapid closing of the window of time when conditions on the mountain would be "in prescription" for the prescribed fire. In reality, the Haines Index numbers (available from forecasters as early as the last week of April) meant that the Bandelier team would never have had time to finish their prescribed fire before conditions became dangerously dry and windy as they did on May 7.

Haines Index numbers are part of the information that the National Weather Service uses to give fire managers overall warnings of high fire danger. Watching trends in Haines Index numbers gives fire managers a sense of where fuel and wind conditions are going and how fast those conditions are changing. It's valuable as a composite figure that summarized complex data for fire managers.

In the case of the Cerro Grande Prescribed Fire the Haines Index was very high on May 4, the day the fire was lit. That meant that the atmosphere had a high potential for drying the fuels on the ground, that the atmosphere close to the Jemez Mountains was "volatile." Other measurements of fire potential such as the "Energy Release Component" (ERC), which measures how much heat energy a fire has the potential to release, based on fuel moisture and other factors were also high, but not extremely high when the fire was lit. Even so, the ERC measurements on May 4 were like those normally measured in June, the peak fire season in the Southwest.

When asked if they considered the high Haines Index in their fire planning, Al King told the Board of Inquiry that they didn't feel the Haines Index was relevant to prescribed burning since "the crew is able to control the amount of fire reaching the fuels." Mike Powell agreed saying "I don't think there was discussion of what the Haines Index of 6 might mean. In my mind, we were burning grass. We were not going to get a plume-dominated event. To me it's kind of irrelevant to put it that way. One of my hopes was it may mean the smoke goes up a little higher. Like I say, we're burning grass and you know, to get a plume-dominated event out there would be weird."

Mike was referring to a "plume dominated event" meaning a forest fire that has created such strong heat convection above itself that the smoke convection plume is drawing increased winds toward the fire. Yet to achieve a plume, a fire needs to reach a certain size and have high heat producing fuels like forests to create enough heat. Mike's comment showed he assumed that grass burning for the fire line would be predictable and trouble free.

Though the Haines index was an important measure of how volatile weather conditions were on Cerro Grande, it was not the only measure. The fire weather forecasts provided to Bandelier by the National Weather Service were not reassuring. On May 3, the forecast called for "continued very dry and unseasonable warm through the remainder of the week with low relative humidity at night in the mountains." May 4 called for more of the same: "very dry with near record warmth and high Haines index..." By the afternoon of May 5, the forecast warned of increasing afternoon winds "of 25 miles per hour *or greater.*"

In order for the prescribed fire to succeed, it needed to stay in prescription. Conditions needed to remain within a range that science and experience indicated would allow the fire to remain controllable. The most critical element of that prescription was fuel moisture levels high enough to keep fire behavior modest. Forecasts for unseasonably high temperatures and low relative humidity meant that fuels would be drying fast, especially grass and pine needles.

Forests were drying out earlier than they did in many years. Though ERC measurements were still on the low end of high fire danger, they were trending upward fast and other events in the region pointed to drought presenting a problem for any fire managers in New Mexico.

Live fuels started to dry out in northern New Mexico early in 1998 when a series of drier than usual winters left the Jemez Mountains with lower than average snowfall from October until May. Though an inch and a half of moisture fell on the plateau below Cerro Grande in March and April, that moisture was the first moisture beyond a trace since September 1999. Winter moisture is extremely important to these forests, since the snow pack soaks the ground and large fuels and it waters trees in a way that light snow or short rainstorms don't.

Even if weather information statistics and composite statistics like the ERC and the Haines Index were not convincing to the prescribed fire planners, recent events in New Mexico showed that fires were more active than usual for spring. The difficulty the Forest Service had controlling the nearby Guaje Fire on May 2 and the fact that a 400 acre fire had occurred in January in the Pecos Wilderness (less than 20 miles east of Cerro Grande at high altitude), a time when fires usually don't happen at all, indicated that the rising ERC and Haines Index numbers were measuring real fire danger.

At the same time, the Park Service was depending on fire weather forecasts and spot weather forecasts as the basis for igniting the fire when they did. Yet the Weather Service testified to the Board of Inquiry that the accuracy of wind forecasts in the mountains is questionable since local conditions vary and can change quickly, something weather forecasters are unable to always stay ahead of.

For their part, the Park Service did not plan for a worst-case scenario with winds, though they could have known that weather forecasting is an inexact science. Since the prescribed fire was being conducted at the limit of its prescription due to delays in getting the Bandelier staff ready for the burn, the risk from winds and dry fuels was greater than it would have been two weeks earlier when the staff had originally intended to burn. They failed to prepare, in concrete terms, for winds exceeding prescription especially given that the fire area was large and the fire would be burning for many days even in the best conditions. With more time with fire on the ground, there was more time for wind conditions to change. The odds of winds remaining within prescription over the expected life of the prescribed fire were low, at best.

Chapter 14

The Aftermath

As May matured and the days lengthened toward full summer, the Cerro Grande Fire, calmed by rain, burned away to the north and west, leaving behind the cooling rubble of 250 homes in Los Alamos and 39 buildings at the Los Alamos National Laboratory. The huge plume of smoke that had dominated the northern New Mexico sky for two weeks dissipated, and evacuated residents returned to their homes or sought new housing to replace houses left in ruin.

The backdrop to Los Alamos, once a rolling mountain-scape thickly forested with pine and mixed conifer, inviting and offering solitude and complexity to many hikers, now lay open and bare, the forest floor exposed like a new desert with millions of trees burned to black skeletal form above the ashen ground. It was as though the town had been moved to the base of a Mojave Desert mountain range. Los Alamos and its environment had been utterly transformed in a centurylong crescendo of events that laid waste not only to the physical environment, but to ideas and careers as well.

For weeks a surreal atmosphere settled in a town surrounded by smoking, blackened mountains above two neighborhoods where many houses lay in complete ruin. Understandably the Los Alamos public was extremely disturbed by the events of early May. A mix of anger, grief, confusion and frustration was moderated only by the generosity of Santa Fe and other New Mexico

View from south rim of Los Alamos Canyon looking over burned
land above Los Alamos. Photo by Bruce Bannerman.

communities who opened their homes and their wallets to the people of Los Alamos, despite a usual sense of cultural separation that exists between Los Alamos and the rest of northern New Mexico. At the same time, as a precaution, top Bandelier staff members fell under the protection of special agents from the National Park Service[1] who kept a close eye on their homes and their persons from marked and unmarked ranger patrol vehicles that came from as far away as Yosemite National Park.[2]

The fire also brought in the Red Cross and the Federal Emergency Management Agency. Homeowners received federal compensation for losses, often along with private insurance payments. All told, the fire cost more than a billion dollars both in suppression and compensation costs and losses to LANL. The suppression costs were $33.5 million and repairs to Los Alamos National Laboratory came in at $203 million. Of the $1 billion spent on the fire and its aftermath, only 3% of that cost was for fire suppression[3].

Whatever the reality of the Bandelier staff working to reduce fire danger on their lands over 20 years, of the neglected national forest landscape, the history of abuse of the land through grazing and fire suppression, the failure of most Forest Service managers to address developing problems until they were catastrophes laying in wait, the extraordinary windstorm that coincided with human error...whatever the reality of a community that had largely ignored warnings of an inevitable fire storm, Los Alamos was now a disaster area, a community changed forever by the power of forest fire.

If the fire had been started by an abandoned campfire, like the Dome Fire, or by an off-road motorcycle, like the La Mesa Fire, or by lightning like the Lummis Fire, the search for culprits would have been less important and the land management agencies could have played a hero role, catching and prosecuting the civilians responsible or wringing their hands at the high incidence of lightning in the Jemez Mountains. With Cerro Grande's complex origin story involving a poorly understood fire management program at a national park, the media and startled politicians were all too eager to simplify the situation and cast the tragedy in a narrative that would sell to an angry and sometimes confused public.

News organizations turned their cameras not only to the burned out neighborhoods and the anguished faces of those who had lost their homes, but to state and federal officials who quickly fell into two perceptual camps; the victims of and the perpetrators of disaster. Politicians scrambled (in the developing court of public opinion that the media shepherded with its reflexive interpretation of events as one party against another) to put themselves in the victim camp and blame was doled out to anyone associated with the National Park Service at Bandelier. With little analysis of the history or reality of events at the prescribed fire or the broader historical and ecological context of the fire, Bandelier and its staff were quickly assumed by many to be a team of incompetents, or worse.[4]

As the fire's ashes cooled, officials in the state and federal governments scrambled to protect themselves from whatever consequences the disaster would have for them. The US Forest Service set out to distinguish itself from the National Park Service and join the camp of victims of disaster. New Mexico's then-governor Gary Johnson wrung his hands in anguish while the national media turned to the National Park Service and by extension the US Department of Interior and the Clinton administration for answers to what much of the media portrayed as an obvious display of ineptitude. Long strained relationships between agencies frayed and a great test of character began as a power struggle unfolded in the context of repercussion and blame in what would turn out to be a pivotal presidential election year.

The philosophy of the National Park Service, to prioritize protection and restoration of its land, coincided with a genuine concern for Los Alamos and an effort by Bandelier to actually safeguard the community by reducing fuel loading on its land and preventing extreme fire from passing through or from Bandelier toward Los Alamos. This work was not matched by the Forest Service, which controlled a majority of forestland near Los Alamos. The political boundaries between the two agencies that fire managers were forced to use as prescribed fire boundary units were untenable from the perspective of fire behavior. Bandelier's staff was trapped in this tragic irony that would haunt the agency and its people for years to come.

When one looks closely at the events following the declaration of wildfire on May 5, the prescribed fire area lit by the Bandelier crews did not pose control problems. The escaped fire that burned away toward Los Alamos was fire lit as a containment fire (black line) by a joint Park Service and Forest Service team that was working to quickly encircle a safe area nearly a mile from where ignition stopped on the prescribed fire itself.

While this may seem like splitting hairs since the suppression action would not have been needed had the prescribed fire not been posing control problems, from a fire management perspective it is important. Not until the Board of Inquiry did any official review look at the methods of suppression when the prescribed fire transitioned into a wild fire. The argument about whether to contain the prescribed fire at the top of the mountain "directly" or "indirectly" turned out to be fateful for Los Alamos because it was untended fire set to black line far from the prescribed burn that ultimately escaped.

Even so, the media and investigations that followed paid little attention to the history of fire danger reduction by Bandelier and the efforts the park staff had made in Los Alamos to educate people about fire danger. The errors real or perceived, on the Cerro Grande prescribed fire were the focus of the public and the investigations that would follow.

Yet everyone involved in fire professionally in the Los Alamos area knew a Cerro Grande type fire was an inevitability. Fire professionals from various agencies knew the woods around Los Alamos would eventually burn with ferocity given the forest structure and fuel loading. The only question was when and what would start the fire that few expected to be controllable. Unfortunately for the National Park Service, their prescribed fire, rather than a natural event or a public error, started the fire. A sense of inescapability was then lost in the blame-game that consumed public perspective of the disaster. As such, no investigation was done of the failure of the Forest Service and Los Alamos County to effectively reduce fuels and fire danger on their land near town and no investigation was done of the failure of Congress to fund fuel reduction near Los Alamos or of the disinterest by the Laboratory's administration regarding something as pedestrian as forest fires.

Hand Wringing, Investigations and More Investigations

Fortunately for Americans, disasters provoke investigations, which seek to find any culprits, identify any failures of whatever systems were in place to prevent a disaster, and hopefully satisfy a grieving or angry public that the same thing won't happen again. Unfortunately many investigations obscure the truth by asking the wrong questions or narrowing their focus because of bias or ignorance by those who launch them.

The Cerro Grande Fire spawned a school of investigations that swam into the charged atmosphere of a nationally known disaster. With much of the press reporting implicating the National Park Service's prescribed fire crews as the source and cause of the disaster, the investigations began in an atmosphere of recrimination and blame rather than looking at all the elements of the disaster for a full understanding. Of four official investigations conducted of the burn, only one was exhaustive enough to be fair to those involved with the prescribed fire and even it failed to address the regional fuel management problem.

The investigations that followed the Cerro Grande Fire all asked the basic question: did the Bandelier staff comply with all the rules and regulations that govern the conduct of prescribed burning? These were not criminal investigations but efforts to find where breakdowns in planning or implementation took place.

Three federal investigations of the prescribed fire operation on Cerro Grande occurred. The first was ordered by Secretary of Interior Bruce Babbitt and became officially know as "The Investigation Team Report." The General Accounting Office (GAO), ordered by New Mexico Senator Pete Domenici, conducted the second. The last was a Board of Inquiry, which was set up by National Park Service Director Robert Stanton. The last, the Board of Inquiry, was the only exhaustive investigation with a broad mandate and with a wide spectrum of inter agency experience on its panel. (Even so, this investigation focused on the conduct of the prescribed burn and the suppression efforts that followed before the fire reached Los Alamos and did not address the historic failure to manage fuels closer to Los Alamos, in essence the core issue in the ignition of structures in the town.)

The Investigation Team Report

The first investigation of the prescribed fire escape was ordered by Interior Secretary Bruce Babbitt who oversaw the National Park Service as a Cabinet officer to President Bill Clinton. It became popularly known as the "May 18 Report" because its findings were released on May 18. On May 11, when houses were still burning in Los Alamos and when all of the Park Service team involved in the prescribed fire were evacuated from their homes and suspended from their jobs, Secretary Babbitt ordered a regional level official from the US Forest Service, the Bureau of Land Management, the National Park Service, the Department of Energy and a Bureau Chief from the State of New Mexico to interview all the parties involved.

On May 18, 2000, a crowd gathered at the Sweeny Convention Center in downtown Santa Fe, thirty-five miles by road from Bandelier, to hear from a panel of experts and from Secretary of Interior Bruce Babbitt about the fire. Secretary Babbitt stood before the national press and an agitated crowd to announce the results of the first and hastily drawn together investigation of the Cerro Grande disaster. His panel followed him with graphics projected on a screen and hand outs for the public.[5] With the fire still burning just to the west, the national news media was eager for this report's results. Its conclusions would form the opinions of a majority of the public on the causes of the fire and the guilt of the people involved.

Babbitt's findings at first satisfied the public that there were specific people to blame for the disaster and they were federal employees, something national and local press reports had concluded for some weeks.[6] In the months that followed, however, the May 18 Report findings became so controversial that the report itself became the focus, in part, of the later Board of Inquiry[7] because of the lack of depth of its analysis or fact finding and because the report was full of errors down to mislabeled maps. Apparently the investigation's purpose was to make the Clinton administration look concerned and serious about the fire while it structured its response to minimize political damage to itself.

Secretary Babbitt stated that he alone was in charge of handling the Cerro Grande disaster for the Administration and that "the White House was not very involved - I had no discussion with Clinton or Gore" about the Cerro Grande situation.[8]

The May 18 Report concluded, "federal personnel failed to properly plan and implement the Upper Frijoles Prescribed Fire[9] which became known as the Cerro Grande Prescribed Fire. Throughout the planning and implementation critical mistakes were made." The report went on to accuse the Bandelier staff of failing to consider firefighter and public safety, failing to have substantive review of the burn plan, failing to use the right burn complexity analysis, failing to evaluate conditions on nearby land before lighting the prescribed fire and failing to "provide adequate contingency resources[10]" to successfully suppress the fire.[11]

These charges, taken together, showed that the investigative team (who were high level land management agency officials) was concerned that Bandelier staff had underestimated the potential for escape and the potential for high fire intensity in the burn unit, given the prescription and the actual conditions. Overall their instincts were correct, but their efforts to pin their feelings on specific policy violations were problematic given the speed with which the investigation was conducted.

Secretary Babbitt's team interviewed various people including the relevant Bandelier National Monument staff and others in the Forest Service and Weather Service to find out if the Bandelier team had adhered to the requirements they live under as fire managers. The investigative team later told the Board of Inquiry that they were under intense pressure to finish their report quickly to satisfy a waiting press and, by implication, the Secretary of Interior, who wished to settle the sore matter of the Cerro Grande Fire quickly in what was turning out to be a difficult political environment. The investigative team's work was hasty, their interviews (conducted by "special agents") were cursory at best, according to some of those they contacted.[12]

Secretary Babbitt's team worked from the premise that national fire policy was sound when the fire occurred, thus absolving official Washington of responsibility for the fire or the development of conditions where a town and its residents could have been placed in harm's way by federal conduct.[13]

Superintendent Roy Weaver was the highest-level manager at Bandelier and the Investigation sought him out in what former NPS Director Roger Kennedy would later call a "witch hunt."[14] A veteran Park Service senior manager, Mr. Weaver later told the Board of Inquiry that he "disputed the findings of Secretary Babbitt's investigation 100% because the investigation was effectively completed in three days."[15] The investigation accused Superintendent Weaver of rubber-stamping the burn plan for the prescribed fire without reviewing its contents.

In a private interview conducted in his home in August 2000, Weaver described part of his interview with the investigation team on that key point which would cost him his job: "They quite arrogantly thumped down the prescribed burn plan onto the table which had my signature on it and asked me; is that your signature? I said yes. He asked if I had signed and approved the plan, but I should have been thinking proactively and I wasn't. I said I had kind of skimmed through it and looked at a few things here and there and I looked at the assignments of personnel but I didn't go into detail. I indicated that I hadn't. I should have been thinking where this question was leading but I think a good investigator should also have asked "were you unfamiliar with the plan?" or "what has been your participation in the plan." I had no idea where this was leading until I saw the accusations on network TV. I should have followed up by saying that I didn't review it then because I didn't need to because I had been participating in the planning process since the very beginning. I had been briefed on the planning through the whole process. They didn't. It's that kind of interview that led them to conclude that the superintendent had played very little role in reviewing or approving the plan or as they said, rubber stamping the plan which I didn't, but I can see how they concluded that based on the interviewing technique. I'm convinced they had an agenda and they were looking for a smoking gun and when they found what they perceived was a smoking gun, why pursue the matter further? Subconsciously, they didn't want to know anything different."[16]

Weaver and the other members of Bandelier's team felt victimized by the Babbitt investigation team and its politically driven rush to come up with what they saw were pre-drawn conclusions at the height of the fire emergency that personally affected the team as Los Alamos residents. "The whole investigation should have been put off for some time," said Weaver. "We were all being evacuated, we were all in shock. Charisse's home was threatened, we didn't have any time to go through a briefing, we didn't have access to our computers, our files or our notes."

In their own defense the Bandelier team later refuted many of the charges pressed against them by the May 18 Report in a roughly fifty page rebuttal distributed to anyone who would read it. Two professional fire managers reviewed the burn plan before Superintendent Weaver approved it and Mr. Weaver was involved in writing the burn plan. The charge that they had not used the right "complexity analysis," in their view, was a bureaucratic argument involving which form was the correct one to use at the time, with fault ultimately falling on the Park Service staff elsewhere who posted the wrong form on an internal web page. On the point that Bandelier staff had failed to consider conditions on nearby lands, Mike Powell, the Burn Boss, claimed he had visited but had not measured fuel moisture levels on National Forest land to the north or east of the burn unit. This final charge implied a larger problem, that Bandelier had not enlisted the help of Forest Service personnel to help them hold the prescribed fire off the agency boundary that crosses the top of Cerro Grande mountain in an ecologically arbitrary fashion.[17] Indeed, the understaffing problem on the Cerro Grande burn was serious.

The investigation team interviewed Mike Powell on May 14. From the transcript it is easy to see that he made a poor impression, perhaps because he was in shock and numb from the huge events that were still unfolding on that date and because he didn't have his notes or time to collect his thoughts. Even so, his responses to their questions were vague, confused, and at times alarming.

His failure to staff the burn beyond a minimal number or to have serious fire fighting gear (such as water pumping "engines") standing by or even to have people standing by to change shifts, and his apparent lack of planning for any escapes or problems, was apparent. He indicated that he had expected the fire to burn down into the timber and cool off due to wet conditions overnight. Yet when the fire proved more active and fast-burning in the upper end of the unit at night, even torching trees (an indication of low *live* fuel moisture and dry air), he seemed calm about leaving only 4 people on the fire[18] when he left to go back to his office with no apparent plans to return until later in the morning. Powell's answers before the investigation board could easily have given the impression of inattention by the whole Bandelier staff, since his supervisors allowed a burn to be conducted without a guarantee of adequate personnel for the critical day shift of the first day.

Yet Mr. Powell was not an inexperienced fire fighter and his reputation in the national fire community was strong. Charisse Sydoriak, who hired him at Bandelier, was known to scrutinize her hires closely and demanded much of them. Powell was in his twenty-first season in fire, was Division Supervisor qualified and Burn Boss II qualified for prescribed fire. He had done five years of prescribed burning with the Forest Service and then went to the Alpine Hot Shots for four seasons as a squad boss for two of those seasons. He then joined North Star Fire crew as a squad boss, then went to the Chena Hot Shot crew where he was foreman for three seasons then Superintendent in his last season. FInally, he moved to Sequoia National Park as a type III Engine Boss before coming to head the Bandelier Fire Use Module, where he had been for two years. So this was a man with a great deal of experience with fire suppression on big fire events as well as with containing prescribed fires. He had experience with extreme fire behavior. It is unclear why he and the others of good experience on the fire took few precautions with staffing and equipment unless they were assuming fuel moisture levels were higher in the forest (not in the meadows) than they turned out to be.

The May 18 Report went straight into the hands of a waiting national media who had already concurred with Secretary Babbitt's conclusion that the source of the Los Alamos disaster was the Bandelier crew. Babbitt's team failed to address the broader fuel problems in the Los Alamos area or problems with the initial or secondary suppression effort as contributing sources of the escape toward Los Alamos.[19] When Secretary Babbitt then put a stop to prescribed burning throughout the national park system on May 12 he succeeded in casting doubt on the systemwide burn program which had had very few problems and continued to be the lead prescribed fire program for all agencies nationwide.

For their part, the Bandelier staff issued a 41-page rebuttal to specific points they found in error in the May 18 report.[20] The

Bandelier staff would be able to expand on these corrections in their lengthy individual testimonies before the Board of Inquiry beginning in late June.

In the fall, when the Board of Inquiry had completed its exhaustive interviewing of a broad range of witnesses, it released its report that dismissed the Board of Investigation report in diplomatic terms. "...it became readily apparent to our members that the May 18 report served as a good beginning point for our review. However, Board members acknowledge the fact was developed under an extremely compressed timeframe. This limitation precluded its authors from having the time required and ability to fully investigate all facts and circumstances surrounding the fire and its outcome. Board members further recognize that this timeframe made it impossible for the investigative team to interview all key personnel having first hand knowledge of prescribed fire planning and implementation, dispatch coordination procedures, and firefighting strategies and tactics and to consider these areas in relation to compliance with all applicable legal and policy requirements."

They went on: "It became apparent to the Board during the course of review and dialog with key witnesses, that the Investigation Team report was not always consistent with the facts and, sometimes, inappropriately measured performance against policy requirements believed to be consistent with the 1995 Federal Fire Policy, but not yet adopted in agency manuals or handbook direction. The magnitude of loss certainly influenced the swift reaction and call to accountability as reflected in the rapid completion and release of the Investigation Report." The Board of Inquiry's final report went on to directly contradict findings in the May 18 Investigation team report.[21]

In essence Secretary Babbitt's investigation team fell into scape-goating, rather than taking a broader look at the disaster. Their focus was largely on the conduct of the prescribed fire rather than the escape of the black lining used to contain the original prescribed fire. Certainly if Bandelier had not conducted their prescribed fire the entire disaster would have been postponed. Their conclusion was that the Cerro Grande prescribed burn had been mismanaged and that that in itself led to the burning of Los Alamos homes and the closing LANL for two weeks. Yet in their haste, the Board of Investigation only partially understood what happened at the prescribed fire.

In a time of disaster and high public scrutiny, top officials at the Interior Department abandoned the Park Service and one of its most critical programs of land restoration and public safety rather than use the Cerro Grande Fire as an opportunity to call for serious national action on wildfire fuel reduction and public responsibility in the flame zone.

The Independent Review Board

Perhaps in response to the criticism of the Board of Investigation, Secretary of Interior Babbitt appointed a second investigation team to look at the outcome of the Board of Investigation (May 18). This one had no members of the National Park Service on its panel and was called the Independent Review Board.[22] The Independent Review Board validated the findings of the first investigation except to say that the National Weather Service, which had been criticized by the May 18 Report for not complying with policies, had complied with its policies for providing spot weather forecasts.

If Secretary Babbitt had hoped to calm criticism of his Board of Investigation with this second effort, its report drew little notice because of its similarity to the original May 18 report.

Meanwhile, New Mexico Senator Pete Domenici had his own investigation in mind.[23]

The GAO Report

The General Accounting Office is one of two research organizations that Congress can call upon for investigations. Senator Domenici asked the GAO to look into the Cerro Grande prescribed fire but apparently his request limited their work to the "what went wrong" with the prescribed fire. Barry T. Hill, an associate director at GAO, presented the GAO's report at a hearing of the Senate Committee on Energy and Natural Resources on July 27, 2000.

The GAO took a slightly broader view of the fire disaster than the May 18 Report had. Rather than focus solely on the Bandelier staff's actions, the GAO looked at interagency cooperation, contingency resources, and fuel loads near Los Alamos. Even so, the GAO did not consider these issues as fully as they could have, leaving many questions hanging.

The GAO brushed aside criticism of the May 18 Report that the burn plan had been faulty and did not comply with federal regulations. Rather, they suggested that the policy that guides preparation of prescribed burn plans be revised so that in risky situations, burn plans would have to be "peer reviewed" by others outside the home agency.

This idea comes from the broader scientific process where any study results are peer reviewed by other experts before the scientific community accepts them. In the case of fire planning, the GAO was suggesting that the US Forest Service should have been allowed to review the burn plan, particularly the Fire Management Officer of the local ranger district. This idea was an effort to pry open the burn plan approval process that had happened at Bandelier, where Mike Powell's burn plan was approved by Al King, the park FMO, then approved by Charisse Sydoriak the park's Chief of Resources Management and then by Roy Weaver the park Superintendent. The implicit suggestion by the GAO and later by interviewers with the Board of Inquiry was that the in-park staff was either too close to the burn idea to review it objectively or that they lacked experience to see problem areas that may have existed in the plan.

Nevertheless, in the world of fire management it was and is unheard of for one agency or jurisdiction to ask for review of its burn plan by another agency whose management goals are different.

The burn plan, the GAO said, "could have been improved." They noted that early May is the beginning of the fire season in the Southwest with typically high winds and that a three year drought in the region had contributed to the escape of four other prescribed burns in the Southwest in the prior two weeks. They also charged that the NPS's professional webpage instructions for determining the complexity of a burn were "incorrect" and that use of these instructions led to Bandelier's staff underestimating the difficulty of the burn and the amount of staff and equipment that would be needed to contain the burn.

This point was a vindication for Mike Powell who had disagreed with the Board of Investigation in its charges that he failed to give enough attention to the complexity analysis of the burn, when he wrote the burn plan, largely because of an obsolete complexity form posted on the National Park Service website.

The GAO recognized the problems that Bandelier had getting help with the fire on the first morning, when the dispatcher at the Santa Fe Dispatch Center had told them to call back hours later and even then the helicopter and hot shot crew requested did not arrive until six and a half hours after they were needed. The GAO recognized that merely identifying fire crews or equipment in the abstract before a burn is not the same as actually being able to get them to the scene to help out when the situation is urgent.[24] The problems Mike Powell had in reaching crew leaders and then the delays that occurred due to bureaucratic confusion once he turned the problem over to the Forest Service dispatch were a key factor in the fire going out of control, according to the GAO.

"The Cerro Grande fire demonstrated that there is a great deal of confusion among the federal land management agencies about the availability and the use of contingency resources. This confusion led to differing expectations among the Park Service personnel responsible for managing the burn, the Forest Service staff responsible for dispatching contingency resources to Bandelier..." the report stated. "The agencies need to work together to make sure that these policies and procedures are clarified and the implementation standardized. Then when contingency resources are identified in a prescribed burn plan, they can be provided when needed, regardless of whether the burn is a wildfire or a prescribed burn. If they cannot be provided, the burn should not proceed. If this confusion had been worked out prior to the Cerro Grande fire, it is possible that the fire never would have gotten out of control."[25]

The GAO also touched on "cooperation and coordination" among land management agencies. First the GAO refuted widely reported "warnings" that the Lab's Deputy director for Operations Richard Burick and the Forest Service's dispatcher John Romero had supposedly made to Bandelier, before the fire, not to burn.[26] For the first time, officially, investigators verified what Bandelier's staff had been saying all along; that nobody warned them not to start the Cerro Grande prescribed burn. Mr. Burick had told a hearing of the House Resources Committee on June 7, 2000, that another Lab official had warned the park not to burn, statements that amounted to perjury: " I was not at the meeting, although my wildfire specialist Mr. Gene Darling was.[27] It is my understanding it was a prefire, preburn meeting to discuss the conditions where the fire was going to be set... I understand, also personnel from the Santa Fe National Forest... and I think Mr. Gene Darling has testified to the GAO that his exact words were 'please don't set that fire.'"[28]

Mr. John Romero of the Santa Fe National Forest told the Santa Fe New Mexican (newspaper) on May 20 that he had warned Mike Powell not to start the Cerro Grande prescribed burn on the morning of May 4.[29] Powell denied that this warning was given and the GAO report agreed with Mr. Powell. Mr. Romero's statement about warning Bandelier came as part of his defense against statements that the Santa Fe Forest Dispatch office had botched the request for more help with the Cerro Grande prescribed burn early in the morning of May 5.[30]

The GAO faulted Bandelier for not working with the Forest Service to protect Los Alamos given the known risk that fire from the upper Bandelier area posed to the town. Bandelier officials had been working for years with the local Forest Service to plan a large interagency burn project but Bandelier had given up in frustration when it became clear that the Forest Service would not get funding for their side of the job for at least a decade because of a lack of commitment to the project from the regional and national Forest Service offices.[31]

The GAO missed the point that heavy fuel loads north of Bandelier meant that the Forest Service should have been helping hold the prescribed fire with plenty of their staff on hand for the prescribed burn as had been done on other Bandelier prescribed fires near the national forest boundary before 1995.[32] When Bandelier carried out a prescribed burn down the ridge from Cerro Grande (burn Unit 8) in 1993, there were thirty extra people on hand from the Forest Service, Jemez Pueblo and New Mexico State Forestry, with five engines.[33]

While much of the GAO report was accurate, the report

slipped into misunderstanding on the key point of how the prescribed burn was attacked once it was declared a wildfire. Senator Domenici and others without fire experience had faulted Bandelier for not using bulldozers and chainsaws to fight the fire on Cerro Grande because, as they misunderstood, Bandelier was trying to protect its lands from the damage bulldozers would have caused to the park rather than aggressively fighting the fire with these large tools.[34] The GAO faulted the park for not building the western fire lines with "bulldozers and chainsaws" and using black lining with fire instead. Chainsaws were used on the west and east fire lines but bulldozers were not because of the steepness of the terrain and because all involved, including Forest Service personnel, agreed that bulldozers were not useful in that situation.[35]

Many people outside the wildland fire community seem to have great faith in technology such as fire retardant aircraft and bulldozers to stop fires in ways that other tactics cannot. This faith is not necessarily shared by professional wildland fire fighters. Public faith in technology is consistent with our society's broader faith in technology as a panacea for our problems. Yet bulldozers are only useful in certain fire fighting situations, particularly when a long distance fire line can be put in with bulldozers, then backfiring accomplished from the bulldozed line toward the approaching fire front. This was not an option on Cerro Grande and the fire lines that were put in on the dangerous east side of the burn were as good as a bulldozed line would have been even if running a bulldozer on those steep slopes had been possible. The danger firefighters faced on Cerro Grande was from embers spotting across the fire line. Bulldozers would not have helped address this risk.

It would have been possible with difficulty to bring fire engines up to the upper east fire line on the prescribed fire but Bandelier staff had chosen not to because of the damage driving these heavy vehicles through un-roaded (though not designated wilderness) areas would have caused. The upper part of the Cerro Grande burn unit is too steep for vehicle access.

Bandelier had also used chainsaws extensively on Cerro Grande both in fire fighting and in preparing the area for the prescribed burning in 1992 and in 2000. The likely point of escape for the fire was a collection of aspen trees that had been cut down before the 1992 burn attempt.

The GAO also implied that Bandelier had not fought the fire aggressively with bulldozers and chainsaws because NPS policy directs field staff to "use fire suppression tactics that minimize costs and resource damage."[36] Bandelier staff did not constrain fire fighting tactics for cost reasons as evidenced by its call for a type one crew and numerous retardant drops (which cost around $5,000 each) when the fire was first declared a wildfire.[37]

Even so, the GAO recognized that the fire escape came from black lining on the lower west side of the burn unit and that the prevailing winds from the west across the burn unit made using fire as a containment tool on this side of the area risky at best. The decision to use that approach to contain the original fire from the discontinued prescribed fire had been made jointly by Paul Gleason, the National Park Service incident commander for the initial attack on the fire and the three highly qualified Forest Service fire professionals who had joined the effort by Sunday: Russ Copp, Kirk Smith and Paul Tingle. The fire did not escape because this was a bad strategy, but because personnel were not kept on hand to watch along State Road 4 at the bottom of the west containment line - a fact the GAO recognized.[38] This staffing shortfall was key to the fire's escape.

Finally the GAO faulted the larger policy guidance that burn bosses for the national park system used for developing burn plans and deciding how many resources and with what experience should be sent to a prescribed fire.[39] This guidance was changed in response to the Cerro Grande fire.

The GAO report proved to be a mixed bag, often on the mark, sometimes missing the point and sometimes in error. Though the report touched on the larger issues that had led to the incineration of many homes in Los Alamos, it failed to delve into the big questions of why a fire of that scale was possible near a community of national importance such as Los Alamos.

As former National Park Service Director Roger G. Kennedy would say in his 2006 book <u>Wildfire and Americans</u>: "Conflicts of evidence were appearing. The GAO concluded that warnings from these other agencies had not been communicated to Bandelier before they started the prescribed burn. Such a conclusion, broadening the range of responsibility and opening larger questions, was not welcome to those wanting the whole subject to settle quickly on scapegoats and get off the front pages. Nobody associated with the history of fire management within or near Los Alamos would come out well if that history were reviewed. And it was in no one's interest to tackle the role of "the Lab" in setting a precedent for locating large numbers of people at government expense in fire-prone areas, and leaving them without warning, without systems to meet fires when they came, and without adequate means to get out quickly... so scapegoats would have to play their assigned role while everyone else went back to business as usual."[40]

Congress Investigates

Congress held two sets of hearings directly related to the Cerro Grande fire in late July. The first of these was before the Senate Committee on Energy and Natural Resources then run by Republicans and called by then New Mexico Senator Pete Domenici. New Mexico's Democratic Senator Jeff Bingaman also sat on the committee.

The hearing featured some emotional statements by long-time critics of the public lands such as then-Senator Frank Murkowski of Alaska who gave Senator Domenici a chance to ask highly critical questions of then-National Park Service Director Robert Stanton. Nobody from Bandelier or from the larger fire fighting effort or from Los Alamos was called to testify. Barry Hill who had headed the General Accounting Office investigation and some of the staff from Secretary Babbitt's two investigations were witnesses, insuring that the disaster would only be viewed broadly and in the context of the GAO and Board of Investigation reports from the safe distance of Washington D.C.[41]

The House of Representatives held its own hearing before the House Resources Committee on July 7, 2000. Though then-Congressman (now US Senator) Tom Udall from northern New Mexico was on the committee, Representative Chenoweth-Hage, Republican from Idaho, who was an outspoken critic of public land agencies, chaired it and used the hearing to make broad points about the failings of federal management.

The Board of Inquiry

For the embattled staff of Bandelier National Monument who had been blamed for the fire disaster by the two past investigations, by the Secretary of the Interior, and in Congressional hearings, finally got a chance to fully tell their story with the appointment of a Board of Inquiry (BOI) in June 2000.

Bandelier Superintendent Roy Weaver had been placed on administrative leave on May 11 (he later took early retirement) and the Bandelier staff directly involved in the prescribed fire was on leave and barred from access to their offices and files.[42]

Given that past investigations and hearings had concluded that Bandelier staff violated policies and directives when they planned and executed the prescribed fire, National Park Service Director Robert Stanton brought together a group of professionals from various agencies to deal with the anger and confusion that followed the two investigations commissioned by Secretary of the Interior Babbitt. Stanton's effort would be the official "Board of Inquiry."

The idea of a Board of Inquiry has its roots in military justice. For example, British military boards of inquiry are commissioned to study troubling events up to the point at which criminal charges may be in order. The board of inquiry itself may not bring criminal charges. The basic idea of a board of inquiry is to conduct an internal investigation that does not attribute blame and thoroughly collects all relevant evidence with the purpose of preventing a recurrence. Boards of Inquiry are widely used in the United States for high-level investigations into transportation accidents and other unfortunate events where officials may have made mistakes. The Cerro Grande Board of Inquiry followed these principles and its deliberations were not public.

The Board of Inquiry was to "review the facts and circumstances surrounding the Cerro Grande prescribed fire and its escape as a wildland fire." The Board was to conduct a thorough and impartial review that could lead to personnel actions within the National Park Service.[43] Headed by National Park Service Midwest Regional Director William Schenck, a man with what Roger G. Kennedy called "pronounced conservative views,[44]" the mission for the BOI was conceived by National Park Service Deputy Director Denis Galvin who directed the Board to use the procedures for a criminal case but in the context of a personnel action. This would give the Bandelier staff due process and give the staff opportunity to answer charges made in earlier investigations.[45]

The people assigned to the Board of Inquiry, except for the Solicitor of the National Park Service, were all experts in fire management and asked questions reflective of deep involvement with fire management. The BOI consisted of: Bill Schenk, Regional Director Midwest Region NPS, Len Dems, Fire Management Officer at Grand Teton National Park, Pete Hart, Superintendent New River Gorge National River, Wally Hibbard, Associate Regional Director Southeast Region NPS, Mary Martin, Superintendent Mojave National Preserve and Jerry Williams, Director of Fire and Aviation Management for the US Forest Service Northern Region.

Mr. Galvin recalled that a prescribed fire called the Outlet Fire had escaped at the Grand Canyon at the same time the Cerro Grande prescribed fire went wild because of the same weather event. "Right away I got skeptical about blame," he said.[46] The Outlet Fire was a National Park Service prescribed fire with few management errors which became a wildfire because of strong wind that burned for days simultaneously with the Cerro Grande fire in the same forest and fuel types on the North Rim of the Grand Canyon some four hundred miles due west of Los Alamos. The Outlet Fire threatened no communities, did not get as large as Cerro Grande and, because of its remote location got little attention in a press riveted by destruction of human property at Los Alamos.

Deputy Director Galvin directed Regional Director Schenck to get past the blame game and find out what really happened so that the fire community could learn from any tactical errors and avoid future escapes. Though some may be skeptical of this investigation, since the National Park Service was in charge of an investigation of its own employees, the presence of other agency officials on the BOI and the thoroughness of its hearings allowed the Board to develop a good reputation with those who were still keenly interested in the fire, which for the most part no longer included the national press or the new administration of President George W. Bush by the time its final report was issued in February 2001.[47]

The Board of Inquiry (BOI) met in a hotel in Santa Fe from June until October 2000 and interviewed 26 witnesses in person or by phone. They carried out their inquiry in relative secrecy with a tape recorder and court reporter to produce 1600 pages of transcripts which were sequestered at the National Park Service regional office in Omaha, Nebraska and not available to the public or the press. The BOI focused on the time when the prescribed fire was planned up through its ignition and to the point where the Type 1 team took over suppression operations.

The author asked for the transcripts of the BOI when I was alerted to their existence by Park Service staff in late summer 2000. The Park Service refused my request and I filed a formal request under the Freedom of Information Act for their release. Over a three-month period, the Denver office of the National Park Service sat on my request for the information, then informed me that the Secretary of the Interior had "taken control of the... documents." From a legal perspective it didn't matter who had control of the documents since the Freedom of Information Act sets strict guidelines on what specific types of information can be withheld from the public. They did not refuse release based on FOIA criteria but made vague statements about jurisdictional issues. Clearly the government was reluctant to release the transcripts. Naturally this increased my interest.

My attorney Richard Mietz sued the National Park Service under the citizen's suit provisions of the Freedom of Information Act and in an out-of-court settlement the NPS agreed to allow me to review redacted transcripts at a Park Service library in Santa Fe. It took me fourteen months to get the material.[48]

During the time the Department of the Interior was in possession of my FOIA request, they issued the Final Report of the Board of Inquiry in the spring of 2001. Whether my FOIA precipitated a public "final report" or whether that report was planned before my request is unknown.

Upon reading the transcripts, which were exhaustive and detailed court-style examinations and cross examinations of key witnesses, it became clear that the original May 18 investigation of the Cerro Grande Fire ordered by Secretary Babbitt was substantially in error, largely because of the haste with which it was done. Yet this was the investigation which had formed the basis for most international press reports on the fire and was the basis for public and political opinion about the culpability of the National Park Service staff. The Board of Inquiry spent a great deal of time focusing on the hasty process under which that investigation happened with at-times grueling interviews of those who conducted the investigation.

The main purpose of the Board of Inquiry was to find out exactly what mistakes, if any, were made by the Bandelier staff since the two earlier investigations had concluded that they had violated policies and procedures that govern prescribed burning within the National Park Service. Specifically the Board sought to:

- Consider the facts and circumstances of the incident and those that may have contributed to it.
- Consider legal and policy requirements that apply to the facts of the incident and determine compliance with those requirements.
- Conduct an objective critique of the actions of individuals directly responsible for the incident, including a review of operational procedures.
- Make written findings to the convening official for recommending corrective action.[49]

By the end of the weeks of testimony every aspect of the Cerro Grande Fire had been examined and reexamined often to the extreme discomfort of those on the witness stand who included a range of people from all the agencies involved in the fire.

While many in the public accused the Park Service of starting a prescribed fire in the spring when "it is always windy," this issue was worked over in detail by the BOI who sought to question the Bandelier staff about the care they took in reading weather forecasts, measuring fuel moistures and in understanding how complex managing the fire could be if conditions like wind changed. The BOI questioned the National Weather Service about their fire weather forecasts provided to Bandelier and about whether they had warned Bandelier not to burn as some had alleged (they had not). Thus the Inquiry focused on specific questions of conduct that the fire professionals on the BOI could identify and their questions were focused, persistent and relentless.

The BOI focused on critical events in the prescribed fire and subsequent wild fire that contributed to the fire fighters losing control of the blaze. In the end, they were unable to resolve some disputes between various players when testimony was in conflict. Some of these disputes were important for understanding who made mistakes as well as for avoiding similar mistakes in future fire situations.

For example, the most critical breakdown in the first hours of the fire was the misunderstanding and communication failure that happened between Mike Powell, the Cerro Grande Burn Boss and the Santa Fe National Forest dispatcher in the early morning hours of May 5. The perspective of the Bandelier crew and the Santa Fe Dispatcher varied and the BOI wound its way through budget problems and definitions of prescribed fire versus wild fire and the way one agency charges another for resources as they sought to untangle this event.

The Forest Service night dispatcher, Mr. Leon, told the BOI that Mike Powell's call at three in the morning was purely an update call, not a call for specific resources. He reported that Mike promised to call in the morning with a specific order for resources. The confusion about the early morning calls between Mike Powell and the Santa Fe fire dispatcher went on from there. Mike Powell stated that he called the dispatcher again at 6:30 a.m. to again ask for resources. The dispatcher told the BOI that he received no such call. Mike Powell called again at 7:30 and reached John Romero who called Al King, Bandelier Fire Management Officer to inform him that the crew and helicopter could only be sent if the fire was changed from a prescribed fire to a wildfire in order for the Forest Service to be able to attach the order to an account. Naturally the Bandelier team would only want to change the fire status from prescribed fire to wildfire as a last resort. The BOI heard differing accounts of these conversations and their timing and recorded these critical events as "facts in dispute."

The BOI disagreed with Secretary Babbitt's May 18 and May 26 investigations on whether the Bandelier staff had violated federal policy in their conduct of the prescribed fire. These findings came after thorough questioning of both the fire crews and of those who conducted the early investigations.

Central to this discussion was the dispute over the "complexity rating" system for the fire and whether Mike Powell as Burn Boss had underestimated how complex, and thus risky the prescribed burn would be. The May 18 report had charged him with underestimating the complexity by using the wrong forms to develop his complexity analysis. The BOI found that the National Park Service had provided the wrong forms to Bandelier over their web site and thus the park staff was innocent on this point.

This issue may seem arcane yet underestimating the complexity of a burn leads to all sorts of unintended consequences. In the case of Cerro Grande, it meant that the Bandelier team had too few people on hand to hold the prescribed fire according to the investigators and the BOI.

The May 18 investigation had further charged that Bandelier staff under estimated or "under rated" the complexity of the burn regardless of what forms and instructions they were using, particularly regarding the threat to the boundary of the burn (possibility of escape), the possible fire behaviors that could be expected given the fuels on the site and the complexity of the objectives of the burn. The BOI agreed that the staff had underestimated the difficulty of the prescribed burn, which should have been guided by "intuitive judgment and experience." They said the understaffing of the burn and the skill levels of those called to assist with the burn would have been increased had park burn planners understood how difficult and complex the burn was to accomplish. The BOI focused not only on the burn boss but also on the reviewers of the burn plan on this central issue.[50]

In the process of focusing on how the burn plan was reviewed and by whom, the BOI came to disagree with the May 18 Report investigators who had charged that the burn plan "was not substantially reviewed" before it was submitted to the park superintendent for signature as required by National Park Service policy. The BOI disagreed with Interior Secretary Babbitt's investigators and concluded that the burn plan had been thoroughly vetted through a series of meetings with qualified park staff before being signed. The BOI did fault those who reviewed the burn plan for not noticing weaknesses in the plan such as the requirement for a small holding crew, which resulted from rating the burn "moderately" complex. The BOI echoed other recommendations that landscape scale prescribed burns have their burn plans reviewed by off site technical people. Such reviews could draw other agencies into helping execute a prescribed fire.

The Board went on to criticize the Cerro Grande burn plan, which called for the burn unit to be broken into three phases corresponding to different fuel types. They noted that each of the phases had a different objective, with different flame length goals for different degrees of vegetation mortality needed to restore the area's ecological vitality. The BOI pointed to the fact that the three phases required three different prescriptions to meet the planner's objectives. In essence, the BOI called the burn plan unrealistic and too complex for the expertise of the burn boss Mike Powell, who was qualified as a Type II burn boss, when a more highly trained Type I burn boss would have been needed to execute the complex multiphase burn.

It is not clear that the Bandelier staff was ever intent on doing the burn in three phases and the BOI report seemed to beg this question. Was the prescribed burn three burns with different prescriptions? The BOI pointed out that the three phases needed different prescriptions to meet objectives yet by doing the burn all at once it's not clear that all three phases could be in prescription. If the weather were drier than the prescription called for, the three phases (areas) would burn hotter than planned and create control problems.[51] The forested bowl of the center of the burn unit, phase three, burned poorly even with aggressive ignition. So the wooded bowl needed a drier prescription. Once in phase two at the bottom of the unit near the highway, the fire burned aggressively.

Charisse Sydoriak, then-Chief of Resources Management, testified to the Board of Inquiry that the park staff didn't want to break the Cerro Grande burn unit up into different pieces to be burned at different times to avoid cutting hand line throughout the unit, an expensive and destructive process.[52]

In any case, the burn team would have needed to have adequate staff and equipment on hand to cut the fire off at the vaguely defined end of phase one if they had planned to stop the burn from going into the other phase areas, since they had not dug a hand line or laid out a charged water hose between the phase units. The BOI pointed out weak "spotting and containment" calculations in the burn plan which may have contributed to understaffing. (Spotting predictions are a key measure of fire behavior since spotting occurs less in high humidity, low wind, or when fuel moistures are relatively high.) Spotting creates large fire control issues since it can force a fire crew to search for and contain small smoldering embers in large areas next to a fire and spot fires can go undetected until they pose serious control problems.

The BOI also pointed out that the Bandelier team's decision to stop extinguishing the downhill side of the phase one ignition was a key error since it decreased the options that the Bandelier crew had as the first night progressed.[53] The original plan was for the crew to ignite fire in the grasses at the top and sides of the phase one burn unit and put the fire out on both the top edge and the bottom edge to create a containment black line. Using fir branches and back pack pumps as tools, this work proved exhausting for the number of people on hand and they gave up putting out the bottom edge of the burn, letting the fire back down the mountain. The fire backed down faster than the crews were able to contain and led to the slop-over that forced the fire to be declared a wildfire. Again the shortage of staff led to unplanned events.

Secretary Babbitt's May 18 Investigation had charged that Bandelier did not have adequate "contingency" planning in case the weather changed and the fire went out of prescription. The BOI disagreed with this finding on a technical level. Again they turned their attention to the complexity rating the fire had received by the fire planners, (which was too low for the terrain and possible highly localized weather events) because of misinformation supplied to Bandelier by an NPS Fire and Aviation website. The BOI stated that Bandelier did have adequate contingency plans for a moderately complex burn, such as the website's data had advised Cerro Grade would be. However, if the correct complexity analysis had been provided to Bandelier, they would have had far more people and equipment on hand. Even so the

BOI again recognized the critical failure of the Northern Pueblos (Black Mesa) fire crew and the fact that their premature release from the fire for being unfit and untrained threw fire staffing into a crisis mode.

On the most contentious and critical error in the fire disaster, the failure of the Santa Fe Dispatch to provide a new crew urgently when contacted at three in the morning on May 5, the BOI had plenty to say. First they criticized the Santa Fe dispatch employees for inconsistent statements about what they had heard from Bandelier and when - a veiled charge that dishonesty had been conveyed by Santa Fe National Forest staff to the May 18 investigators.

Yet the BOI focused on Bandelier's end of the exchange, charging that Mike Powell had failed to convey the absolute urgency of getting a new fire crew to the burn unit first thing in the morning on May 5 to replace the failed Northern Pueblos crew and to prevent the National Park Service crew from working excessively long shifts in violation of federal policy. In essence Mike Powell had agreed to comply with the timeline of the night dispatcher in Santa Fe who misunderstood the urgency of Mike's request and suggested that the order be placed with his supervisor rather than taking action as Mike Powell said he asked him to. The BOI recognized the key role Paul Gleason played in realizing that Mr. Powell and the Santa Fe dispatchers had failed to line up a specific fire crew with a specific arrival time at the burn unit. Mr. Gleason pushed this process until the Santa Fe Hotshots were ordered though their arrival was later than had been requested by almost three hours.

Bandelier's staff testified to the BOI that the Santa Fe dispatch office knew very well about the prescribed fire and had told Bandelier in the afternoon of May 4 that the dispatchers could get a crew up to Cerro Grande within two hours and a second could respond in 3.5 hours. Thirteen hours later, when Bandelier staff called dispatch with a request for a crew they were met with a five-hour delay, during which the slopover went from a quarter acre to many acres and required converting the fire from prescribed to wildfire.[54]

The May 18 Investigation had concluded that the late arrival of the Santa Fe Hotshots to the burn unit had consequences for the control of a "spot fire" (it was a slopover, not a spot fire) but did not have consequences for the overall outcome of the early fire suppression effort. The BOI strongly disagreed with this conclusion, pointing out how the tardiness of the Santa Fe Hotshots had thrown the prescribed fire operation into disarray and led to a wildfire declaration and use of expensive aerial resources (a helicopter and a retardant dropping aircraft) in a situation where ground crews, if on site, could have controlled the slopover and allowed the prescribed fire operation to either continue carefully or be shut down after the slopover experience.

As discussed elsewhere in this book, Santa Fe dispatch was confused about how they could assign resources to a prescribed burn being done outside the Forest Service and what the "ordering protocols" were for resource orders for prescribed fire instead of wildfire. This confusion led to delay by Santa Fe Dispatch that turned out to be critical to the escape of the fire toward Los Alamos. The BOI called on all federal fire agencies to standardize ordering and payment procedures for resources for prescribed fires to prevent future delays and confusion, something that has been done in the years following Cerro Grande.

The BOI concluded that the underrating of the burn's complexity, combined with the failure of the Northern Pueblos crew led to the NPS staff being over extended when the two slopovers occurred in the first night. The NPS staff had to leave their patrols along the perimeter of the burn to deal with the slopovers, something that would not have been necessary if more staff had been present.

The BOI also disagreed with the May 18 Investigation finding that the plan for suppressing the fire was not followed once it was converted from a prescribed fire to a wildfire. The BOI concluded that the fire suppression plan, called a Wildland Fire Situation Analysis (WFSA), was followed but the BOI recognized the fire crew's failure to adequately patrol the highway portion of the fire containment line from the bottom of the west fire line to the bottom of the east fire line. This staffing oversight led to the escape of the fire from the bottom of the west fire line, driven by winds across the highway and into Frijoles Canyon.

The BOI addressed one of the most critical issues, whether doing a prescribed burn at all in the spring of 2000 was wise, when many felt the region was in drought. The BOI agreed that "moderate drought existed in northern New Mexico during the spring of 2000 as confirmed through the accepted measures of drought..." They looked at the Palmer Drought Index and the National Fire Danger Rating System Energy Release Component (ERC)" which calculate fire activity based on fuel and atmospheric conditions[55]. These measures indicated moderate drought and cause for extra caution.

The National Weather Service testified to the Board of Inquiry that their measure of drought for northern New Mexico on May 4, 2000 was either moderate or severe depending on which maps one referred to[56]. The Bandelier staff defended their choice to burn on May 4 by pointing out that they knew of no prescribed fire restrictions that were in place either for the National Park Service or the larger US Forest Service and that the regional fire preparedness level was at three, which is a moderate level of "alertness" for fire fighting forces. Bandelier's staff also pointed out that the lightning caused Escarpment Fire a few days before Cerro Grande and their own prescribed fire days before at burn unit 40 had not displayed extreme fire behavior indicative of the effects of drought.[57]

On the charge that the burn planners had failed to assess fuel conditions on lands near the burn unit for possible fire behavior and public safety, the BOI agreed with Bandelier staff that that conditions outside the burn unit had been monitored. However the BOI noted that evaluating fuels and the possible fire behavior if there is an escape is difficult to do on a landscape scale. There are no standards or guidelines for how burn planners are to consider fuels away from a burn unit. Even so the BOI stated, "judgments regarding adjacent lands should have been more thoroughly considered drought, potential magnitude and persistence of winds, and the risks of exposure due to extended operations." In other words, doing the prescribed fire would take many days and the risk of high winds over many days was high and those winds could spread fire out of the planning area.

The BOI disagreed with the May 18 Investigation's charge that Bandelier had not adequately notified other agencies of their burn plans. The investigators had charged that even if Bandelier did notify the other agencies they had failed to notify them of the scope or complexity of the burn planned. The BOI stated that Bandelier had complied with all policies and that over the course of months and weeks before the burn, Bandelier had informed other agencies of the scale of the burn.

The May 18 Investigation also charged that Bandelier did not have a burn boss with adequate qualifications for the complexity of the Cerro Grande burn. The BOI disagreed and stated that Mike Powell was qualified for the complexity of the burn that the National Park Service professional website had led him to believe he was undertaking. The BOI pointed out that policy at the time allowed Type II burn bosses such as Mike to undertake complex burns. Later policy was changed to insure that only Type I burn bosses undertook complex, landscape scale burns. Both Al King and Paul Gleason, present at the Cerro Grande burn were qualified as Burn Boss Type I but neither had that position for the burn for the critical first 12 hours of operations.

Finally on the key issue of wind, the BOI interviewed Bandelier staff and the fire weather forecasters from the National Weather Service in Albuquerque regarding who knew what and when about the devastating winds that raked the prescribed burn area on May 6 and then continued on and off for the next two weeks as the Cerro Grande fire spread into and past Los Alamos. The May 18 Report investigators had charged that the National Weather Service did not provide three to five day wind forecasts which would have precluded lighting the prescribed fire had it been known that 30 mile per hour winds were possible for May 6. The BOI discovered that the National Weather Service is unable to predict winds with any accuracy beyond a twelve hour time, especially for a professional weather forecast like those given fire managers because of constantly changing conditions, particularly in the mountains. Springtime in New Mexico is often windy, but can also have periods of calm and Bandelier staff did gamble that the timeframe that they chose for their burn would be calm.

The Bandelier staff had done all that professional fire managers ever do in terms of monitoring the weather. They consulted data from remote weather stations near the burn unit, they took detailed weather observations throughout the burn unit before and during the burn, and they maintained twice daily contact with fire weather forecasters at the National Weather Service in

Albuquerque for big picture weather changes and the all-important "spot weather forecast."

After the Board of Inquiry finished examining the charges made by the Independent Review Board (May 18 Investigation or Report), they made personnel recommendations for the key players on the burn. These would turn out to have little bearing on what actually happened to those people.

First the BOI considered Superintendent Roy Weaver who in the public mind was "the guy who started the fire.[58]" The BOI found that he fulfilled all his responsibilities to review the burn plan and discuss it with other agencies while surrounding himself with a "staff that was fully qualified to implement the fire program at Bandelier National Monument." They did express concern about Roy's role in interagency communication broadly, acknowledging the "differences of opinion and hard feelings (that) separate agencies in this sub geographic region." While not blaming Mr. Weaver for those differences they suggested he could have better explained the park's prescribed fire program to other agencies. The BOI recommended that no personnel action be taken against Roy Weaver, as he had not violated policy or procedure. By then Roy had already taken early retirement.

Next in command, the BOI looked at Charisse Sydoriak, Chief of Resources Management at the time of the fire, one of four cabinet officers to the park superintendent. Ms. Sydoriak was known as ambitious in carrying out a broad science based program and had continued the prescribed fire program at Bandelier begun by her predecessor John Lissoway, and helped institute the Prescribed Fire Module (specialized fire crew) at Bandelier.

In her testimony to the Board of Inquiry, Ms. Sydoriak had stated that she was a "big picture" person, not given to micro managing the day to day work of the fire staff as they prepared plans for prescribed fire and then carried out those burns and other matters. The BOI recognized her for taking an active role in reviewing the Cerro Grande prescribed fire plan as required by policy. The BOI was critical of her big picture thinking regarding the burn:

"Based on her extensive background, the Board feels that Ms. Sydoriak has the capability to critically evaluate those elements that affect complexity associated with landscape scale prescribed fires. In light of several exacerbating factors, including the proximity of private land, potential fire behavior, local attitudes and concerns, and objectives that influenced the complexity of this prescribed fire, the Board finds that she and her staff did not fully recognize and account for the risks surrounding this project... In addition, the Board acknowledges that Ms. Sydoriak assisted in increasing the complexity rating from low to moderate based on intuitive judgment and experience. The complexity rating was still lower than likely to have been calculated using the correct form.[59]"

The BOI recommended more fire training for Ms. Sydoriak.

What happened to Ms. Sydoriak after the prescribed fire was instructive and typical of what happened to the other Bandelier staffers involved with the burn. Once the Cerro Grande burn turned into a wildfire, Ms. Sydoriak and most of the resources management staff at Bandelier were barred from their offices and the park, which was closed, to them and the public for some days during the emergency. This was unusual since there was no immediate danger to people entering the park headquarters area and much of the staff had emergency management experience and could be trusted to operate in an emergency environment. Blocking access to staff offices probably was done to protect documents in those offices – in a crime scene atmosphere.

Ms Sydoriak and her family were evacuated from Los Alamos and she was not given a role in the large fire suppression operation that unfolded around Los Alamos after May 11, which was unusual for a person with her training when a fire was burning in her jurisdiction. In the blame and recrimination that prevailed after homes were burned in Los Alamos (including those across the street from Ms. Sydoriak's home) it became clear that her career at Bandelier was over. She was put on paid leave by the Park Service, and she remained in this limbo while she looked for another job, eventually getting hired by the Bureau of Land Management in the Denver, Colorado area where she worked for seven years until she took a job at Sequoia and Kings Canyon National Parks in California.

As mentioned, Al King was the Fire Management Officer at Bandelier at the time of the Cerro Grande prescribed fire. In this position he was in charge of the fire program at Bandelier on the technical level. As FMO, he was supervisor of all fire staff at Bandelier, including Mike Powell, burn boss for Cerro Grande.

Traditionally, during both prescribed or suppression fires, the staff from an agency or from a blend of agencies will take on roles in the staff for the specific fire that are appropriate for their fire training but which may not reflect their job status in normal life. On the Cerro Grande prescribed fire, Al King took the position of "holding specialist" which put him, for purposes of the prescribed fire, subordinate to Mike Powell who was burn boss, at the top of the fire command structure.

This reorganizing of staff for a fire is used on project fires where staff is brought in from many agencies and from distant places. A person who is normally a forest supervisor for example, in charge of a whole national forest may be assigned a job as a "division chief" on a particular fire according to his training and experience and he or she may be answering to someone with far less status than his own outside of the fire incident command situation but who has more experience with fire suppression.

In this context of the hierarchy for the prescribed fire, the Board of Inquiry was critical of Al King for not continuing to supervise Mike Powell and scrutinize the decisions he was making for staffing and holding resources. "The Board finds that although he was holding specialist on the day of the burn, as the park FMO, he was in position to exercise professional judgment over staffing levels and necessary adjustments to maintain subsequent staffing cycles. There were several key decision points where Al King could have influenced the burn boss' decisions." The Board singled out the decision to let the lower edge of the black line burn freely in the grass at the top of the burn in its first few hours, the failure to secure a replacement crew for the Northern Pueblos crew immediately and the call for only a helicopter and one fire crew for the next morning when more people should have been called.

Thus the confusion created by having Mike Powell assume the role of burn boss for the Cerro Grande prescribed fire, presumably for training purposes, created an atmosphere where others may not have been as critical of his decisions as they would have been in the day to day work environment when no fire was being worked.

After the fire, Al King left Bandelier and left New Mexico for a job at the National Interagency Fire Center in Boise, Idaho as a Safety and Prevention Specialist for the National Park Service. He has since retired.

Next the BOI moved on to Mike Powell, who was leader of the "Fire Use Module" at Bandelier. As burn boss, Mike was in charge of making sure the Burn Plan, which he wrote in collaboration with others, was implemented on the ground and that the team changed its responses as conditions of the fire changed. Most of all, he was in charge of staffing the burn.

The BOI focused its most pointed criticism toward Mike Powell. The final report said:

"In his role as burn boss, the Board finds that Mike Powell failed to provide for adequate staffing and did not make necessary adjustments to maintain subsequent staffing cycles. When staffing became a problem, he failed to communicate to others regarding the inability to secure these resources. When the Northern Pueblo Agency crew was released near midnight on May 4, Mike Powell failed to provide for adequate staffing in their absence. At approximately 0600 hours, when it was observed that the fire was backing faster than anticipated, Mike Powell failed to fully anticipate holding needs through the day operational period. Although Mike Powell had been replaced as burn boss, his actions regarding holding resources continued to affect operations throughout the operational period. Specifically when the slopover occurred on the morning of May 5, it required nearly all holding resources to contain it and left the lower edge of the fire perimeter in Phase I unattended. Later that afternoon when the fire moved into the Phase II area, holding options became greatly diminished. This sequence of events led to the Wild land Fire Situation Analysis alternative of indirect attack which required more firing over more operational periods, greatly increasing the overall risks. Ultimately, firing operations associated with the indirect strategy led to the escape of the fire out of the Cerro Grande project area."

"The Board also finds that Mike Powell in his capacity as burn boss did not adequately adjust actions when observed fire behavior became different from anticipated fire behavior. As an example, it was assumed that the fire backing in Phase I would self-extinguish. When it became apparent that this was not the case, Mike

Powell did not increase staffing to assure control of the lower perimeter in Phase I. This decision eventually allowed the fire to move into the Phase II area, which further exacerbated holding problems on the project. These series of decisions/actions set the stage for greater difficulty of containment of the burn within Phase I and increased the likelihood of exceeding work/rest guidelines, and reduced tactical options as the project progressed.

After making the 0300 telephone call to the Santa Fe Dispatch and finding that his request for additional resources could not be confirmed within the desired timeframe, Mike Powell should have contacted the Dispatch Center manager and the Bandelier FMO to expedite this process. [60]"

The Board recommended more fire training for Mr. Powell.

According to colleagues, Mr. Powell was devastated by the disaster that followed the Cerro Grande burn escape. Since January 2007, Mr. Powell has worked as District Fire Management Officer (DFMO) for the Goosenest Ranger District of the Klamath National Forest in Macdoel, California near the Oregon border.

It was never clear why Mr. Powell and the others felt they could hold a fire over hundreds of acres with so few people, even if the original intended staffing level had held through the second day. While more people cost more money, park staff testified that budget constraints did not affect their choices.[61] In most situations, prescribed fires have plenty of staff. For example, at Yosemite National Park in the fall of 2006, the National Park Service burned 65 acres in mixed conifer and giant sequoia at the Mariposa Grove with a staff of 67 people from two agencies. This level of staffing was normal for prescribed burning in most national parks even back in the 1990s, before the Cerro Grande disaster changed fire procedures in the land management agencies.

A burn boss is under a great deal of pressure because of the responsibility he or she has for making decisions to keep a prescribed fire on track, particularly in terms of assigning personnel to the right tasks at the right time in terms of what the fire is doing, and in looking ahead to predict what the fire might do and what people and tools will be needed to respond to changes. It may be tempting for those outside the wild land fire world to second guess the work of a man like Mike Powell, but the pressure he was under, even before the fire went awry is hard for outsiders to understand.

According to many in the fire profession, some professional fire managers developed a hesitation to take on the burn boss position after Cerro Grande because of the experience Mike Powell had on that fateful day in May 2000.[62]

Next the BOI turned its attention to Paul Gleason. At the time of Cerro Grande, Paul was Adjunct Professor of Fire Science at Colorado State University and Wildland Fire Management Specialist for the National Park Service with the Denver Regional Office.

Bandelier was fortunate to have Paul on hand as he was a highly respected person nationally in the wildland fire world. He had spent 36 years in fire, working his way up from a line firefighter in southern California in the 1960s through the most hard-core of fire suppression assignments, heading hotshot crews in Oregon and Washington before moving up to upper level regional fire assignments in the Forest Service and ultimately the National Park Service in Colorado.

Paul had worked on two other disastrous fires before Cerro Grande. In 1966 he was with the Dalton Hotshot crew on the Loop Fire in the Angeles National Forest in California when 12 people were killed as fire swept up a canyon and burned over their crew. Then on June 26, 1990, Paul was working on the Dude Fire, which started in an extreme drought year on the Mogollon Rim country of the Tonto National Forest in Arizona. The fire developed a convective column, which collapsed, sending a strong downburst over the fire area, causing fire to spread down and across the slopes rapidly. Six fire fighters were killed and Paul was one of the first to discover their bodies. He also saved the life of fire fighter Jeff Hatch on the fire, going into the fire to rescue Hatch who was overcome with heat and smoke. These disasters inspired him to pioneer many effective methods for advancing wild land fire fighter safety that were adopted throughout the fire service.[63]

Paul came to Bandelier at Al King's request to be burn boss for the upper Frijoles Canyon burn (Unit 9) which had a chance of being burned after the Cerro Grande unit was finished, but more likely would be done the next year. The Cerro Grande prescribed burn was an opportunity for Paul Gleason to learn the topography and the fuels of upper Bandelier and to get to know the staff.

Soon after arriving at Bandelier, Paul had surmised that because of dry fuels, Unit 9 was unlikely to be burned anytime soon. He helped move supplies up onto Cerro Grande, acted as an observer for the first day of burning, and planned to return to Colorado the next day.

Paul's plans changed when he noticed that Mike Powell was having trouble getting more people and tools from the Santa Fe Dispatch. "I was pissed because this was the first geographic region I had worked in where you call for help and you don't get it," he told the Board of Inquiry.[64] Paul volunteered to take over command of the fire at six in the morning on May 5 when it was clear Mike Powell was both exhausted and frustrated. By one in the afternoon that day, he took over as Incident Commander for what was by then a wildfire and he held this position until the Type 1 Incident Command Team took over the fire as it paused on the south side of Los Alamos Canyon.

Paul Gleason was the most experienced fire fighter on the Cerro Grande prescribed burn and his reputation as an expert in safety preceded him to his interview before the Board of Inquiry. When the BOI issued its report it acknowledged his role in the fire and said, tellingly: "The Board recognizes that at the time Paul Gleason volunteered to assume command, he was left with few options for influencing the successful outcome of this fire.[65]" The BOI did not recommend any further training or other action against Paul Gleason.

Speaking to an interviewer from the Wildland Fire Leadership Development Program the day before he died, Paul Gleason said of Cerro Grande; "We made our decisions in good faith and using our best judgment based on what we knew. I remember how difficult it was to go to talk to the people in Los Alamos and tell them who I was, what we did, why we did it. I have to live with those decisions because at that time it was my responsibility.[66]" Paul Gleason died of cancer in Colorado in February 2003.

[1] The security operation for the Bandelier staff was known within the National Park Service as "Operation APOYO" and involved 31 law enforcement agents brought in from a long list of western national parks and monuments and even from the Minnesota Forestry Division.

[2] Roy Weaver, the Superintendent of Bandelier who the media had portrayed as the main person in error regarding the escaped fire reported that the people of Los Alamos were extremely kind and sympathetic to him and that he did not feel threatened. He often expressed gratitude for the kindness of the community following the fire.

[3] The True Cost of Wildfire in the Western U.S. (Western Forestry Leadership Council, April 2003) pg. 9.

[4] Editorial, Santa Fe New Mexican [Santa Fe, NM] May 12, 2000.

[5] The Investigative Team for Secretary Babbitt's first investigation included Jim Loach National Park Service Midwest Region, Tom L. Thompson US Forest Service Rocky Mountain Region, Tony Deflin, New Mexico Department of Forestry, and Tyler Przybylek of the US Department of Energy Albuquerque Office. There were 20 supporting staff members on the effort as well.

[6] "Review Reaffirms Blame for Bandelier." Santa Fe New Mexican May 27, 2000.

[7] See Cerro Grande Prescribed Fire Board of Inquiry Final Report. February 26, 2001. Executive summary.

[8] Personal communication with Secretary Babbitt, April 22, 2007.

[9] This prescribed fire was known as the Cerro Grande Prescribed Fire, not the Upper Frijoles Prescribed Fire as the May 18 report states. Upper Frijoles Canyon though nearby is a separate burn unit, which is referred to by park staff and the public as "Upper Frijoles."

[10] As detailed in Chapter 5, contingency resources are back-up crews and equipment that could be drawn on if requested to assist with a prescribed fire. A small park like Bandelier has a limited fire staff and cache and must call on the local Forest Service dispatch for these resources when needed. So Bandelier could not "provide" contingency resources and the US Forest Service was slow to provide these resources when they were ordered by Mike Powell in the early hours of May 5 for complicated reasons that later became the cause of national policy change.

[11] Cerro Grande Prescribed Fire Investigation Report, Executive Summary pg. 1, May 18, 2000.

[12] Personal interview with Al King, Charisse Sydoriak and Roy Weaver, August 2000.

[13] Roger G. Kennedy Wildfire and Americans, (Hill and Wang, 2006) for a discussion of federal policy that placed Los Alamos in the "flame zone." See also Chapter 16.

[14] Roger G. Kennedy, <u>Wildfire and Americans</u>, (Hill and Wang, 2006) pg. 101.

[15] Quote from the transcript of vol. one Board of Inquiry hearings June 2000.

[16] Personal interview with Roy Weaver, August 12, 2000, White Rock, New Mexico.

[17] Kevin Joseph, the Fire Management Officer for the Espanola District of the Santa Fe National Forest had told Mike Powell that he wanted a representative of the Forest Service on hand when the burn was done since the burn was on the two agencies' boundary. On May 4 when the burn was started no Forest Service "representative" was available so this part of the agreement and was violated. It's not clear if the Bandelier staff made an effort to call a Forest Service representative on May 4. If they had had a Forest Service person on hand they could have helped with communications with the dispatcher on the night of May 4, when significant communication problems hampered efforts to get more people up to Cerro Grande.

[18] The four people working on the fire on the night of May 4 were tired from working more than 15 hours and were in charge of watching an active fire line that was half a mile long over hilly terrain where large clumps of grass made walking difficult.

[19] Even after the 40 mile per hour winds hit Cerro Grande mountain on May 6, causing the backfire near the highway to spot into Frijoles Canyon and then to the north into Water Canyon, the fire set by the prescribed fire crew at the top of the burn unit never did escape again. It is easy to wonder then if the wildfire suppression organization had sought to pinch off the fire directly ("going direct") around the prescribed fire itself whether the escape ever would ever have happened?

[20] "<u>Errors and Omissions in the May 18, 2000, Cerro Grande Prescribed Fire Investigation Report</u>" prepared by Al King, Mike Powell, Charisse Sydoriak, Paul Gleason, and Roy Weaver July 5, 2000. Not an official publication of the National Park Service or Bandelier National Monument.

[21] Cerro Grande <u>Board of Inquiry Final Report</u> pg. 3.

[22] The Independent Review Panel consisted of Mike Long of the Sate of Florida Division of Forestry, Paul Declay of the White Mountain Apache Tribe, Elaine Zielinsky US Bureau of Land Management from Oregon and Lyle Laverty Regional Forester for the US Forest Service, Rocky Mountain Region.

[23] Senator Domenici had been highly critical of the public land system in the United States. At the time the Cerro Grande Fire broke out, he was under pressure from the public to help buy the Baca Ranch next to and west of Bandelier and to establish it as part of the public lands of the United States. He would do so reluctantly and only with an unusual management system that placed the Valles Caldera National Preserve in neither the national forest nor the national park system but under a quasi-private

"trust." By 2009, a significant campaign to transfer the Valles Caldera National Preserve to the National Park Service was underway due to a failure of the VCNP trust. This effort, if successful will greatly expand the area which the Bandelier fire crews are responsible for managing.

[24] The Santa Fe Hotshots, a highly experienced type-one fire crew is in high demand for initial attack. The Santa Fe Hotshot had been on the Guaje Fire and had their days off when they were called to Cerro Grande to help with a prescribed fire. For Bandelier to assume that a type one crew would be available, when this crew is the main type-one hotshot crew in northern New Mexico is to presume quite a bit given that lightning and arson fires were already keeping the hotshots busy and the likelihood of them being out on a call was high given that fire season had begun by May 1.

[25] GAO Final Report pg. 7.

[26] Santa Fe New Mexican May 20, 2000.

[27] Mr. Darling testified to the Board of Inquiry on July 27, 2000 that he had never warned Bandelier regarding the prescribed fire and that he had only made a passing comment in a conversation that occurred between him and Bandelier staff member Holly Snyder about the prescribed fire in an informal exchange between two fire fighters of the two agencies who were tending to a minor flare up of the prescribed fire Bandelier was wrapping up near the Bandelier entrance road on May 4.

[28] Transcript of testimony before the National Parks and Public Lands Subcommittee and the Forest and Forest Health Subcommittee of the Resources Committee, US House of Representatives. Mr. Burick's quoted testimony appears at line 1459.

[29] Ben Neary, "Official Contradicts Report," New Mexican [Santa Fe, NM] copyright story May 20, 2000.

[30] The confusion and perjury involved with Dick Burick's statements and the context of John Romero's statement that he had "warned" Bandelier about the burn are set out in an investigative story written by John Marble of the Los Alamos Monitor (newspaper) on October 27, 2001.

[31] Interviews with Forest Service and National Park Service officials.

[32] Interview with John Lissoway August 4, 2000, White Rock, NM. The author was working on a fire crew on the Unit 8 burn which was an aggressive burn intended to kill thickets of fir trees. The burn was very active and hot in some areas while burning too cool in others.

[33] Since Bandelier is a small park it relies on the Forest Service for help with most fire suppression situations inside the park. Bandelier has a prescribed fire module (10 people) and an engine with a crew of four in the park as well as a few other staff with red cards.

[34] All public land agencies avoid the use of chainsaws in designated wilderness areas to protect these places from mechanical intrusions. The Wilderness Act of 1964 excludes mechanical devices from designated wilderness. Cerro Grande however is not in a designated wilderness area.

[35] "Dozers" were used on the La Mesa Fire in 1977 inside Bandelier National Monument. Their use was highly controversial given their marginal benefit for fire containment and the damage they did to archaeological sites.

[36] GAO Final Report pg. 10.

[37] Memo from Charisse Sydoriak, Chief of Resources Management at Bandelier to National Park Service Intermountain Director Karen Wade August 18, 2000.

[38] GAO Final Report pg. 12.

[39] This policy guidance is part of the Fire and Aviation Handbook for the NPS known as "RM-18".

[40] Roger G. Kennedy, Wildfire and Americans, (Hill and Wang 2006) pg. 98.

[41] Transcript of Hearing before the Committee on Energy and Natural Resources United States Senate 106th Congress July 27, 2000 transcript number 5311-24 US Government Printing Office.

[42] Personal interview with burn staff. The Bandelier staff was prevented from going to their own offices or reading the files in their own desks to respond to investigators from the Department of the Interior or to queries from the press.

[43] Board of Inquiry Final Report, February 26, 2001, page 2.

[44] Roger G. Kennedy, Wildfire and Americans. (Hill and Wang 2006) pg. 99.

[45] In personal interviews, the Bandelier staff had been frustrated and angry that they had not been able to fully explain themselves to the investigators from the Department of Interior who they said conducted hasty interviews.

[46] Roger G. Kennedy, Wildfire and Americans. (Hill and Wang 2006) pg. 100.

[47] Secretary of Interior Bruce Babbitt urged the new administration to pay attention to the Cerro Grande investigation because he believed there were serious issues that needed Washington's attention. Mr. Babbitt suspected perjury had been committed in the early investigations and that prescribed burning policies needed to be refined for the future. The new Interior Secretary Gale Norton who came into government from the petroleum industry would turn out to have a very different interest in public lands and one which focused very little on conservation activities like prescribed burning or management of national parks. Her interest was almost entirely on opening public lands to oil and gas drilling which she did in spades over her term.

[48] The Omaha office of the National Park Service read the transcripts before I did and blacked out certain references to individuals. For example they blacked out almost every reference to the Eight Northern Pueblos (Black Mesa) fire crew that could not perform up on the mountain on the first night of the prescribed fire. It is unclear why, under the Freedom of

Information Act, such references were omitted since the Act allows for withholding only certain types of information such as personnel information. The redactions provided me with an interesting challenge of figuring out who key people were in critical events. Had this been more difficult, a second legal challenge to the censoring of the transcripts could have been engaged.

[49] Cerro Grande Board of Inquiry Final Report ,February 26, 2001, pg. 2.

[50] ibid pg. 16.

[51] The third phase of the prescribed burn was the forested interior bowl of the burn unit. By surrounding this with black in phase one and two, the burn planners may have envisioned running a head fire through the third phase to achieve nine foot flame lengths and high tree mortality among the excessive small diameter trees in phase three. Given the wetness of the phase-three area, there could have been little need to worry if fire entered this area prematurely on the top edge of the forested bowl as a backing fire. In this fuel type such a fire would have barely burned or gone out.

[52] Cerro Grande Board of Inquiry testimony transcript, vol. 3. pg. 14.

[53] Cerro Grande Board of Inquiry testimony transcript, vol. 3, pg. 25.

[54] Summary Statement to the Cerro Grande Fire Board of Inquiry July 27, 2000, Roy Weaver, Charisse Sydoriak, Mike Powell, Al King.

[55] Board of Inquiry Final Report, (February 26, 2001) pg. 34.

[56] Board of Inquiry hearing, conference call transcript for August 11, 2000.

[57] Roy Weaver, Charisse Sydoriak, Mike Powell, Al King, Summary Statement to the Cerro Grande Fire Board of Inquiry (July 27, 2000).

[58] The author has a great deal of contact with the traveling public. I have heard from numerous people from outside New Mexico variations on the question: "whatever happened to that guy who started the fire?"

[59] Board of Inquiry Final Report, (February 26, 2001) pg. 42.

[60] ibid page 44.

[61] The Bandelier staff testified to the author in a personal interview in August 2000 that it was the practice of the National Park Service at the time to keep costs down on prescribed fires by keeping a minimal staff on hand and depending on contingency resources to supplement when needed. The staff recognized that this was a poor process after the fact and the Park Service now provides adequate staff on prescribed fires in part because of major revisions to federal fire policy in response to the Cerro Grande Fire.

[62] Conversation with Mike Beasley, then Fire Use Manager at Yosemite National Park, September 2006. (Mr. Beasley now works for the Six Rivers National Forest in California.)

[63] Paul Gleason, "LCES," Original Document, June 1991, Wildland Fire Leadership Program. Paul Gleason pioneered the core fire fighter safety concept of "LCES" or lookouts, communications, escape routes and safety zones. This is a system intended to prevent entrapment of fire fighters

by running fire such as happened on the Mann Gulch, Dude, Loop, and South Canyon fires among others. Paul advocated posting a lookout away from the work area who can watch the larger fire behavior, maintain communication with all fire fighters, and always identifying an escape route and a place wherein fire could be escaped (safety zone). This is now standard practice on federal fires.

[64] Transcript of the Cerro Grande Board of Inquiry, Volume II, pg. 460.

[65] Board of Inquiry Final Report, (February 26, 2001) pg. 44.

[66] Interview by Angela Tom and Jim Cook on the Wildland Fire Leadership Development Program website. February 26, 2003.

Chapter 15

A Changing World, Wildland Fire Management After Cerro Grande

Since the 1977 La Mesa Fire burned through 16,000 acres in and around Bandelier National Monument, the Southwest fire world has changed in ways that few could have anticipated in those earlier days. After the 1980s, researchers noticed that infrequent large wildfires of short (average one week) duration were being replaced by much more frequent and longer burning (five week) fires. These changes coincide with climate change driven shifts in seasons, with warmer springs, drier vegetation, and earlier and more rapid snowmelt which have resulted in fire seasons that are now longer than in previous decades.[1]

The Cerro Grande Fire and the intense season of fire that followed it along with the Southwest fire seasons of 2002, 2005 and 2007 showed remarkable increases in acres burned, more than six times the amount of acreage than was burning annually before 1980. For example the Rodeo-Chediski Fire in the Apache Sitgreaves National Forest in June 2002 burned 463,000 acres, ten times the acreage of the Cerro Grande fire. There is no doubt among fire professionals that unprecedented changes are happening in wildfire activity. Fires are more active, consume more live vegetation and spread more readily than in years past.

Yet the number of acres burning every year is still far below what naturally burned before modern human interference with fire beginning at the turn of the twentieth century. Before fire suppression, as much as 13,590,796 acres of land could have been burned annually by wildfire in the 11 western states whereas today, even in intense fire years like 2007, approximately 1,408,500 acres burned.[2] The difference between the number of acres burned annually and the area that would have burned annually without human interference is termed the "fire deficit."

Though area burned alone is not a complete measure of changes in fire regimes over time, apparently wildfire was much more widespread in the past though those fires were rarely crown fire conflagrations such as we see today in the Southwest. For example, studies of charcoal in bog sediments in the Alamo Bog in the Valles Caldera National Preserve show regular fire activity going back 9,000 years in the Jemez Mountains. Though 5,200 historic fires have been mapped in the Jemez Mountains between 1909 and 1996,[3] this shows a decrease in fire activity over pre-suppression fire patterns.

While the Jemez Mountains and the Pajarito Plateau were ripe for a large fire due to the land management problems, climate change, on a larger scale, may have converged with fuel conditions to enable the fire storm around Los Alamos. At the time of Cerro Grande the public and professionals were just becoming aware of a trend toward increased fire intensity and were experiencing the first major firestorms that have since become somewhat normal, especially in the northern Rocky Mountains.

Policy, Resistance and Conflagration

Federal fire policy in the United States is made on two levels. Federal land management agencies make policy and Congress can weigh in as well, passing legislation to mandate specific fire management directions.

Fire policy on a national level was in continuous flux before Cerro Grande, as agencies gradually moved away from the full suppression responses of the early 1900s toward more nuanced responses to wildfire. Policy has changed even more dramatically since 2000. Cerro Grande forced the reevaluation of federal wild-fire management more than most fires because it was a prescribed fire which escaped and because various problems were met with in responding to the blaze.

The Cerro Grande Fire sent immediate shock waves through the fire world when on May 11, 2000, Secretary of Agriculture Dan Glickman and Interior Secretary Bruce Babbitt suspended all prescribed burning west of the one-hundreth meridian (the north and south line across North America where aridity increases). The ban affected all federal land management agencies and was designed to give agencies time to ensure regulations related to prescribed fire were adequate and being followed.[4] On May 26, 2000, Secretary Babbitt lifted the prescribed fire ban for all agencies except the National Park Service, furthering a sense that the Park Service's fire program nationally was somehow deficient. This extended ban for the NPS was in response to the Independent Review Board's May 18 report on Cerro Grande which blamed Bandelier for several violations of federal policy – violations which the Board of Inquiry later largely refuted.

Before 1995, all federal land management agencies operated under a variety of fire policies. After the busy 1994 fire year in which 34 fire fighters were killed and over $1 billion was spent on fire suppression, the Secretaries of Agriculture and Interior mandated that all agencies responsible for burnable federal lands come under uniform and cohesive fire management policies called the Federal Wildland Fire Policy and Program Review[5].

The reforms recognized the essential ecological role of fire in many ecosystems and institutionalized the long-standing view that not all wildfire is bad and that it could and should be used in some cases to restore the health of the land. The 1995 Federal Wildland Fire Policy and Program Review also mandated that each agency and its subunits produce "fire management plans" (FMPs) that would guide its approach to all fire and that these plans be consistent with federal fire safety policies.

The temporary ban on prescribed fire was the first indication that policy changes would follow Cerro Grande. As the 2000 fire season became one of the most active on record with many big fires and much private property damage, a great deal of attention focused on fire management and how well the 1995 reforms of fire management policy were working. While ecologists were noticing that 2000 was a large fire year because of climatic conditions, the public focused on fire fighting and its effectiveness in preventing property damage as many new structures were being built in formerly wild areas.

By 1996, despite the mandate from cabinet level secretaries, it became clear that the 1995 policy changes were not being implemented by many agency units in the field. (Bandelier wrote its first Fire Management Plan in 1997 and revised it in 2004.) The Forest Service in particular had difficulty implementing the mandate for Fire Management Plans. Without a FMP, a national forest or park would continue to respond to all fires with full suppression.

While the Forest Service did pay increased attention to fire fighter safety following the 1995 policy, in some forests it used new fuel reduction mandates as a justification to implement remote timber sales that in some cases worsened fire danger on the national forests and did little to protect communities. The failure to write and implement FMPs caused Forest Service officials on some national forests to use full fire suppression even in wilderness areas far from human settlements where, arguably, it would be less expensive to allow fires to reduce fuels naturally if conditions allowed.

The 1995 Federal Wildland Fire Policy and Program Review encouraged agencies to diversify their approach to fire management and thus brought national policy closer to the management approaches key to National Park Service fire management, including prescribed fire. Yet the failure of many national forests to write fire management plans revealed entrenchment of fire suppression policies and how, for budget or other reasons, fire managers were hesitant to try new approaches.

The Santa Fe National Forest released its Fire Management Plan in late 2000, five years after it was mandated to do so by Washington. This was likely in response to a new order from the Forest Service Chief issued in March 2000 warning noncompliant forests to issue their plans by December 2001.[6]

   The fire management planning process met institutional inertia no matter how much Washington, including Congress, got involved in pushing the national forests to plan proactively. The Forest Service budget process rewarded national forests for taking a reactive stance toward fire by funding initial attack and fire suppression with virtually open budgets. Forest Service officials knew they could fund staff and equipment when they tapped into fire suppression accounts.[7] Adopting a more diverse approach to fire management risked reducing its budgets (in 2008, 45% of the Forest Service budget was for fire management). After a hundred years of fire suppression, the Forest Service seemed reluctant to diversify because fire suppression comes with nearly open ended accounts while prescribed fire requires more focused budgeting.

   In 2000, following the huge fire year, and following the expensive ($178 million dollar) 1999 fire season, top levels of public land management in Washington turned their attention to revising the 1995 Federal Wild land Fire Policy and Program Review. The Cerro Grande fire was a main event that forced high level attention to the shortcomings of the 1995 policy such as an inconsistent commitment to fire use and prescribed fire, uneven fire management planning and poor coordination between federal agencies.

   President Clinton asked his secretaries of Interior and Agriculture to prepare a report with recommendations in response to Cerro Grande and the other large property-destroying fires of 2000. This report became known as the "National Fire Plan" which provided a framework for an increase in funding fire programs in federal agencies and a big push to reduce fuel loads near communities in the "wildland urban interface (WUI)." The report also recommended treating fuels on a landscape scale, as the Cerro Grande prescribed fire had set out to do. With the National Fire Plan came money, $2.8 billion.[8]

   The National Fire Plan was a significant shift in public policy, recognizing as it did that small diameter fuels resulting from decades of fire suppression were a key risk factor for high intensity blazes that threatened human property. The report suggested that 89 million acres of national forest land were susceptible to moderate or high intensity fire because of these fuels. The fuel hazard lesson was well known to the National Park Service for more than a century and to many within the US Forest Service but its recognition on a national policy level would shift the focus of multiple use land management since the policy included funds for on-the-ground activity.[9] Overall, the National Fire Plan focused on the scale of the problem faced by federal fire managers, pointing to 70 million acres of land at high risk for severe wildfire.

The experience at Los Alamos and in communities in Colorado, Montana and Arizona in 2000 had an effect on federal policy. The fuel choked forests around Los Alamos were not unique and President Clinton's cabinet focused on those fuel conditions.

As a result of the National Fire Plan, Forest Service began to address fuel hazards near communities and, controversially, they often used the new funds to cut trees (large and small) far away from communities in ways that few fire scientists believed would affect large fire behavior and benefit towns or cities. A debate ensued as to what constituted hazard fuels and whether cutting large trees increased fire hazards especially in drier forests like those in the Sierra Nevada Mountains and in intermountain West. Conservationists disputed whether large, commercially valuable timber could be removed with National Fire Plan money to satisfy commercial interests.

By 2008, another major shift in federal fire policy emerged after the intensive 2007 fire-year where almost 2 million acres burned in Idaho, forcing federal fire fighters to abandon fire suppression efforts on multiple remote fires and focus on protecting communities and communication sites. This shift in tactics was an admission that old fire suppression techniques would no longer work on fire of the scale we may expect as global warming continues to intensify fire seasons. The shift toward "point protection" where communities and outposts are protected and back country fires are often allowed to burn (as they are in Alaska), may also reflect falling staffing and declining fire fighting budgets.

Agencies were shifting toward these new approaches to wildfire management called "appropriate management response" or AMR where agencies take a much more flexible approach to wild land fire as they did in Idaho in 2007[10]. A single fire could be managed for resource benefit – to enhance the ecology of an area or increase the safety of nearby communities - at the same time other parts of that fire were being suppressed as a hazard.[11] Under the AMR changes, fires would be viewed as wildfire or prescribed fire even as the agencies moved to protect "points" or human values. This change may be in response to the recognition, gained at Cerro Grande and in Idaho 2007, that many fires are not controllable with any human effort. With global warming and the changes it brings, along with decreasing fire budgets and shrinking fire fighting organizations, fires will have to be managed more realistically to reduce fuel loads over large areas at minimal expense.

The AMR policy also allowed agencies to treat human-caused fires for resource benefit rather than automatically fighting all human-caused fires as has been done in the past. This is a huge shift, allowing fire managers to assess the possible benefits of any fire regardless of its origin.

With the arrival of the Obama administration, the changes made to the 1995 Fire Policy and the 2001 revisions were clarified and new emphasis has been put on interagency cooperation (a major lesson-learned from Cerro Grande), landscape scale fire management and fire use and prescribed fire. Obama's natural resources team solidified the most progressive changes in fire policy long sought by ecologists and the changes clearly reflect lessons learned from Cerro Grande.

At Bandelier National Monument in July 2009, a lightning fire called the San Miguel Fire in the remote Bandelier Wilderness was allowed to burn for almost two weeks since the fire was burning in such a way as to benefit vegetation. Bandelier cooperated with the Santa Fe National Forest in allowing the burn to cross agency boundaries and burn both within Bandelier and the Forest Service Dome Wilderness area. This sort of interagency cooperation is exactly what the Obama administration is seeking to increase the acres treated with management fires across the West.

Cerro Grande had specific affects on federal fire policy, as agencies reviewed the tragedy to find lessons to be learned. For example, agencies have recognized that if landscape scale prescribed burns are to be attempted, they must be sequenced correctly across the landscape. Just as fire crews will "back" a fire down a particular slope to prevent a fire from rushing up that slope, prescribed fires must be laid out across a landscape to prevent fire escapes with prevailing winds into heavy fuels that might threaten communities, as happened at Los Alamos.

In short, the federal response to the Cerro Grande Fire and other big fires of 2000 was to promote prescribed fire and the use of "wildland fire use" where fires started by lightning in remote areas are allowed to burn, within limits. In a sense, the federal government, backed by teams of scientists, vindicated the fire management activities of the Bandelier National Monument staff on the philosophical level, while seeking to address the problems the Park Service staff faced in both managing fuels in an island among acres of unmanaged fuels and in working with other agencies to control the Cerro Grande Fire.

Bandelier and Prescribed Fire

In 2006 Bandelier cautiously restarted its prescribed fire program. The staff started with a reburn of the area near the Entrance Station that had been burned just before Cerro Grande in 2000. Then they took on the largest and most dangerous unit in the park, the dreaded Unit 9 in upper Frijoles Canyon.

The Upper Frijoles burn was done in early November 2007 when fuel moistures were relatively high from a moderately wet summer. The burn unit included two forks of Frijoles Canyon, with considerable oak brush and dry pine forest on the south facing slopes, and the cool and moist canyon bottom and north slopes and flats on the mesa tops which were messy mixed conifer forests left from logging that happened before the Park Service got the land.

The lessons of Cerro Grande had been learned by all involved as evidenced by the large organization of people from several agencies spread out to hold the burn. Three engine crews from the US Forest Service were joined by two others from volunteer fire departments and two from Bandelier and one from Los Alamos County. Holding crews from Zuni Pueblo and New Mexico State Forestry fanned out to monitor hard fire lines that surrounded the whole 1,500 acre unit. Three ignition crews ignited the fringes of the burn unit and the flats above the canyon by hand. Bandelier Fire Use Module was joined by Zion Fire Use Module and the Alpine Hotshots from Rocky Mountain National Park. The canyon itself was ignited by a helicopter dropping balls of potassium permanganate.

Though cautious regarding the wetness of the fuels, the Upper Frijoles Burn was a success in that agencies were again working together and bringing extra forces to bear on prescribed fire near a community. While some may say the Upper Frijoles Burn was burned too coolly to reduce a century of fuel buildup, the fire seemed to be a catharsis, a time when Bandelier and its new management could show itself and the world that it had learned the lessons of Cerro Grande.

In October 2008, Bandelier burned about 250 acres around the Headquarters complex in lower Frijoles Canyon, burning around the area visited by more than 200,000 visitors a year. This burn addressed drifts of fuel and thickets of small trees in the ponderosa pine and also burned out brush on the south facing slopes below the cliffs where Bandelier's primary archaeological resources of interest to the public lie.

Again, the Headquarters burn was conducted with extra caution with Forest Service and Los Alamos County engine crews joining the Black Mesa and Bandelier Fire crews to hold the burn. While the cost of having so many people on hand for a burn that was surrounded by mostly inflammable cliffs and slopes may have been expensive, the focus on safety and the protection of Bandelier's prescribed fire program demanded the expense.

Such caution and overstaffing of burns, though expensive, is likely to be the norm nationwide after Cerro Grande. Not only does this insure public safety, it also maintains and trains a robust fire organization nationally in the conduct and benefits of prescribed fire.

As the first decade of the new century wanes, Bandelier is planning prescribed fires in collaboration with the Santa Fe National Forest and with the Valles Caldera National Preserve. At last the biggest lesson of Cerro Grande, the need for landscape scale prescribed fire conducted through interagency collaboration, is becoming a reality.

With the likelihood that the Valles Caldera National Preserve may soon be managed by the National Park Service, the responsibilities of Bandelier's fire staff may soon be greatly expanded and opportunities for collaboration with the US Forest Service on large prescribed fire will further expand.

[1] A.L Westerling, H.G Hidalgo, D.R. Cayan, T.W. Swetnam, "Warming and Earlier Spring Increase Western U.S. Forest Wildfire Activity" in Science vol. 313 pg. 940.

[2] Michael Medler, "The Fire Deficit" presented at the 3rd International Fire Ecology and Management Congress, Tucson, AZ. November 2006.

[3] C.D. Allen, M. Savage, D.A. Falk, K.F. Suckling, T.W. Swetnam, T. Schulke, P.B. Stacey, P. Morgan, M. Hoffman, and J. Klingel. 2002. "Ecological Restoration of Southwestern Ponderosa Pine Ecosystems: A broad Perspective. (Ecological Applications vol. 12 no.5, 2002) pg. 1418-1433.

[4] The prescribed fire ban also came after the Outlet Fire on the North Rim of the Grand Canyon, a prescribed fire which escaped simultaneously with the Cerro Grande Fire and burned 14,000 acres on both National Park Service and Kaibab National Forest land.

[5] The South Canyon fire in Colorado claimed 14 wildland fire fighters lives in 1994.

[6] Forest Service Chief's directive, March 2000.

[7] Randall O'Toole, An Analysis of Fire Budgets and Incentives, (Thoreau Institute, 2001) pg. 26. O'Toole's economic analysis is first rate but his prescriptions for correcting budgetary abuse are libertarian in focus.

[8] Timothy Ingalsbee, Federal Wildland Fire Management Policy: An Introduction to the Fire Policy Reviews and Reforms of 2000 (American Lands Alliance).

[9] Study of the Implementation of the Federal Wildland Fire Policy. National (Academy of Public Administration. Phase One Report. December 2000), pg 9.

[10] The AMR policy originated with the National Fire and Aviation Executive Board.

[11] Bandelier park officials were accused of trying to both suppress the Cerro Grande fire and continue their prescribed fire goals on May 5 when the indirect suppression approach was chosen. Its important to note that both Forest Service and Park Service fire fighters jointly chose the indirect approach. This controversy carried over to the national level with affirmations from top fire officials that fire could not be managed for more than one goal. Either fire was suppressed or allowed to burn for resource benefit, not both, until the AMR proposal of 2007. This policy shifted in 2008 when federal policy allowed fires to be managed for multiple objectives.

Chapter 16

Anticipating Fire, Los Alamos and the Inevitable

It is difficult for people who have not experienced disaster to understand the trauma, grief and anguish that calamities bring to people's personal lives. For the people of Los Alamos, the trauma of being torn from their lives by evacuation, then waiting to find out if their homes were still standing, was compounded by their loss of work and ultimately having the environment of their community permanently changed.

People in the United States have come to expect that government will protect them from preventable disaster with flood control systems, weather and tsunami warning systems or military defenses. Americans expect government to anticipate danger and protect them when possible. This is perhaps one of the most important functions of national government.

Yet disaster often exceeds people's preparations, and defenses can turn out to be inadequate or neglected as in the case of hurricane Katrina and the antiquated levee system in New Orleans. People who live in areas frequented by tornados know that they must have their own shelters because nothing can be done to prevent or divert tornados or hurricanes.

There are gray areas of disaster preparedness that leave people vulnerable to known risks. When people build homes in areas vulnerable to large natural events like hurricane, fire, and flood, they must be prepared for such inevitabilities. People who build homes in flood plains know that their homes are at risk, yet local governments permit flood-zone construction and the federal government subsidizes flood insurance and has paid for reconstruction along major river systems that flood frequently.

In western states like New Mexico, forest fires pose a known, high probability risk to many communities. Forest fires have been burning towns and remote houses for more than a century in the West. Does government have an obligation to protect communities from forest fire, especially if it owns and manages the land surrounding the community? Should residents expect that the best available fire abatement methods are in place always?

As with tornados, there is only so much the government can do to protect people from large forest fires which no amount of technology can halt in many cases. Yet many in the public believe falsely that large forest fires can be stopped and in Los Alamos the presence of a good fire department developed to deal with the sprawling laboratory complex and its many hazards may have given the public a false sense of security regarding all types of fire.

The public has a responsibility to be aware of risk and to take personal action for minimizing exposure to hazards that can lead to disaster. In the case of wildfire, the public can build or modify their houses to be fire resistant, clear flammable materials from their land and participate in government so agencies are compelled to manage nearby lands to minimize the possibility of extreme fire behavior when fires happen. Given that forest fires are frequent and inevitable, fire management rather than fire prevention must be key to protecting property.

In Los Alamos' situation, there are many layers of government that have responsibility over the environment, from the county government to the Department of Energy that runs the Laboratory to the US Forest Service that manages the forest land above Los Alamos to the National Park Service that manages Bandelier to the south. The Los Alamos Fire Department is one of the best funded and most highly trained fire departments in the nation for structural fire, chemical spills, radiation hazards and medical evacuation. Yet it turned out their firefighters had little training in forest fire fighting although Los Alamos is surrounded by flammable forest.[1]

Los Alamos County owns a significant band of ponderosa pine forest around Los Alamos but the county had done little to reduce fire hazard in those woods, in part because of pressure from some residents wanting to maintain the aesthetics of the view from their homes. The forests were in an ecologically degraded condition due to fire suppression yet that condition was familiar to people and seen as wild and desirable. Los Alamos County had not thinned thickets of trees in many cases to reduce fire hazard for homes on the edge of the forest nor had the county developed a program to require residents to clear sticks, needles, firewood and trees away from homes, especially on the edges of town next to the woodlands.

Likewise, for the US Forest Service that manages tens of thousands of acres surrounding Los Alamos, thinning and prescribed fire which may have calmed the Cerro Grande Fire were only done minimally before May 2000. It seems only the National Park Service was involved in fire risk abatement in a serious way and their efforts had the opposite of the intended results in May 2000.

Should community members in a place like Los Alamos be able to assume that all agencies have employed the best available knowledge to reduce the threat of fire to private property and human life? Is it possible to insure that a community will not be touched by flames that inevitably burn in a ponderosa pine forest?

Looking back, we can wonder how Los Alamos as a community anticipated the inevitable fire. Were people warned of the risk since many residents lack knowledge of their natural environment and cannot be expected to understand forests and ecology and the dangers they pose? Was the danger successfully conveyed and if so, how did residents respond to warnings from fire professionals that people needed to take responsibility for their own safety?

Building a Town in Harm's Way

When the Los Alamos Ranch School was built on the farm fields of a homestead in 1917, the Midwestern school masters may have been aware that forest fire was frequent in the Jemez Mountains. Yet at that time, fires that did occur would have been relatively tame with forests still fairly healthy[2] from a long history of frequent ground fires that ended around the turn of the century. Thus the Los Alamos Ranch School founders had little to fear from fire, especially since they built the school in an area of grass and mature pines where fire would be fairly easy to defend against.

When J. Robert Oppenheimer came to the Pajarito Plateau on one of his many visits from New York in the 1930s, he may not have been familiar with the risk of fire from a slowly unraveling ecology of northern New Mexico's landscapes. Oppenheimer owned a cabin on Grass Mountain in the Pecos River Valley east of Santa Fe and on his hiking and horse riding trips around New Mexico he had discovered for himself the beautiful Pajarito Plateau.

In 1943, at the peak of World War II, President Harry Truman directed a team of the world's best physicists to see if an atomic bomb could be developed quickly from Albert Einstein's revolutionary physics ideas, if possible, before Adolph Hitler or the Russians could.

The US Army set about searching for an appropriate place to conduct what became known as the Manhattan Project, considering remote locations in Nevada, Utah and two in New Mexico's Jemez Mountains. At the prompting of Robert Oppenheimer, director of the project, the area north of Bandelier National Monument was chosen because it provided access to materials from Santa Fe and Albuquerque, transportation for people from eastern states and it was hidden and remote in then sparsely populated New Mexico.

Never, apparently, did Oppenheimer and his army assistants consider the wildfire-prone nature of the Pajarito Plateau and the danger forest fire could pose to the laboratory and its support community as they built the facility in a place the Spanish called Quemazon or "big burn." The Manhattan Project would be completed in two years and nobody anticipated that Los Alamos would continue as a laboratory beyond that. In a war environment, such considerations were abstract. The fact that the Jemez Mountains have one of the highest numbers of lightning strikes annually of any area in the United States and that wildfire had been occurring on the area chosen for the laboratory every five to fifteen years was both unknown and apparently not accounted for in the decision process[3]. For the laboratory's founders, landscape considerations were limited to remoteness and the ability of the army to seal and protect the Los Alamos site from spies (who were present inside the laboratory anyway) or saboteurs[4].

After 1945, Los Alamos did survive as a laboratory and became the largest single employer in northern New Mexico. Laboratory officials seemed concerned only about protecting secret information and facilities from intruders. Fences and patrols, guard stations and badges blocked out people who didn't belong. With most of Los Alamos' population coming from distant cities, Los Alamos became a small urban area culturally removed from the region in which it was set and largely detached from the natural world around it. Historian Hal Rothman referred to Los Alamos as "the white collar version of a company town."[5]

As the next four decades rolled by, Los Alamos continued to be the primary research and development facility for nuclear weapons for the United States while also engaging in a range of other science projects. Thus the people of the community were consumed with secrecy, scientific research and family life in the midst of the "baby boom."

Understandably the people of Los Alamos expected land management agencies who took care of the surrounding forests to see to their safety from any danger that might arise from the woods. The workers at Los Alamos would do their part to protect the nation from Soviet and Chinese adversaries, and they expected the US Forest Service and National Park Service to protect them from the dangers of the woods. After all, the federal government had eliminated wolves and grizzly bears from the Southwest on behalf of cattle ranchers by the 1930s. It was reasonable to expect that other threats would be dealt with as well.

It turned out that Los Alamos' expectation of safety in its assigned environment was misplaced. Beyond the concerns of a few relatively powerless individuals within the US Forest Service, that agency rarely took a particular interest in the land around Los Alamos. The US Forest Service and its political directors in Washington D.C. paid little more attention to Los Alamos' safety then they did to the thousands of other western towns scattered among national forests from the Front Range to the Pacific Ocean (see Chapter Four). If anything, the national forest around Los Alamos received less attention from the Forest Service than did forests near towns like Salmon, Idaho, Westfir, Oregon or Oakhurst, California because Los Alamos area forests were unproductive for grazing or logging. [6"]

The Cerro Grande Fire taught a core lesson that has applied many times since. People have to know how to protect their own private property from fire. They have to think about fire outdoors; a basic element of nature that people have known for thousands of years. They need to know that dry grass and pine needles burn almost explosively and must be kept cleared away from their homes and off their roofs and that pine, spruce or fir trees must be cleared away from the house for thirty feet while any stands of pine on their land must be thinned so that canopies of the trees are not dense enough to easily carry fire. This sort of information along with the sense to install a non flammable roof, are key for surviving forest fire, yet only a few people in Los Alamos had taken these precautions.

Second, a community must become involved with the health of the forest beyond the fences of their back yards. If a forest is dense and obviously prone to forest fire as the forests around Los Alamos were, the community must ask questions, apply pressure, volunteer, and insure that the forest close to town is thinned and opened up for a considerable distance from the edge of the homes in place. The people of Los Alamos for the most part failed to become involved in this matter before May 2000, leaving their safety in the hands of a few Forest Service and Park Service officials whose warnings to Congress, the Department of Energy, Los Alamos County, and the citizens of the community itself, went largely unheeded[7].

Los Alamos is a small town with a small newspaper. Every spring starting in 1998 the US Forest Service, National Park Service and Los Alamos County[8] would hold a public meeting on forest fire safety in Los Alamos that was announced in the local newspaper, among other places[9]. Those who organized the meetings said they were generally well attended by Los Alamos standards though the attendance fluctuated and did not reach many who lived on the fringes of the town. At these meetings, printed matter was handed out and almost inevitably Craig Allen, the local expert on the ecology and forest history of the Jemez Mountains, would give a presentation on the increasing fire danger and the inevitability of a large fire burning near town based on fuel loading and the lack of fire in the immediate Los Alamos area since 1886[10]. His concerns would be echoed by Bill Armstrong of the Forest Service.

These meetings and warnings were in the long tradition of Albro Rile, the late Los Alamos Fire Chief who for decades issued trademark stern warnings about the danger of home fires imprinted on generations of Los Alamos residents.

Beyond public meetings, the Forest and Park Services had difficulty coming to terms with the obvious indifference about fire among many in official and private Los Alamos. Finally Claudia Standish and Robert Rummilard of the Los Alamos Forest Service office began to contact residents on the fringe of the community house by house to inform them of the need to make their properties fire ready. They handed out printed matter and spoke with receptive people. Even so, Ms. Standish was uncomfortable with the idea of visiting private property in the capacity of a federal forester.[11] In the end, according to an investigation by fire behavior expert Dr. Jack Cohen of the rocky Mountain Research Station in Missoula, a majority of homes that burned in Los Alamos did so because of fuel loading in the yards and on the roofs of the houses.[12] Thus many of the homes that burned could have been saved had residents taken the precautions advised by fire experts. Many homes that were prepared survived.

Yet a larger issue faced the town with the overly thick forests that surrounded it with tons of dead material on the forest floor. Except for a narrow band of Los Alamos County land that surrounds the town, a majority of the land near Los Alamos is managed by the US Forest Service which had great difficulty getting funding for thinning work in the five years before the Cerro Grande blaze.[13] Of course the efforts to create fuel breaks around Los Alamos and to thin the forests near the town beg the larger question of why the Forest Service allowed their lands to deteriorate to a condition of extreme ecological decadence and flammability to start with. Given the decadent condition of the forests near Los Alamos, Forest Service officials like Bill Armstrong did what they could to mitigate an ecological disaster that had been developing for 140 years on the Pajarito Plateau.

Armstrong, a tall, bright, soft spoken forester has been working on the forests around Los Alamos since the 1980s when he says he first approached the Santa Fe National Forest Supervisor for funding to reduce fire loads around Los Alamos and the Santa Fe Watershed above nearby Santa Fe. He found the agency unresponsive to his urgent requests for action. "I don't know why they did nothing. The agency was without direction, hamstrung by regulations and without leadership from Congress," he told me.[14]

Armstrong did manage to get funding from Los Alamos County to cut fuel breaks around Los Alamos in 1998 but this only seemed to remove a sense of urgency from other thinning efforts closer to Los Alamos. In Armstrong's view, fuel breaks such as those he cut where 80% of the forest was removed and the slash burned were only useful to contain low intensity fires like prescribed burns rather than the sort of super-fire that he and others anticipated and which happened as the Cerro Grande Fire. A larger effort at fuel reduction, especially to the south of Los Alamos, was needed, yet a project to do just that was obstructed by funding problems and a lack of political interest for more than a decade, until finally it was too late.[15]

Protecting Los Alamos or any other forest-surrounded community can happen on two levels. The forest must be managed so that when fire comes to the land it burns in a calm way with good results for the plant and animal life and minimal threat to property. Second, the community itself and the houses and commercial buildings must be built and landscaped to anticipate fire and minimize risk for community members and their property. In many communities such as Santa Cruz and Idyllwild, California there are strict laws requiring vegetation clearing around private buildings with fines for those who don't comply.

Yet all of these efforts by officials to protect a town poorly located for fire safety were hamstrung by public complacency. Perhaps few members of the public visited the forests near Los

Alamos to see their fire susceptibility or understood what they were seeing once there. Perhaps those who did venture into the woods believed that action would be taken to address the danger in time, and everyone seemed to believe we had plenty of time. It's clear that a majority of the local public was unaware or unconcerned about the fire danger near Los Alamos. Had they realized it, perhaps, they would have created a community effort to restore the forest health and protect the community.

Los Alamos is a town where great faith is placed in the power of technology given that some of the most advanced technology on earth has been developed there. Yet technology has its limits when it comes to natural disaster management. For example, a Los Alamos resident who lost his home in the blaze told me that if the fire services only had more advanced technology they could have stopped the Cerro Grande Fire from reaching Los Alamos. He elaborated on a high tech scheme for fighting fire that sounded futuristic, (and detached from the real world of wildland fire) then berated the agencies for fighting fire with outdated tools out of stubbornness.

This sort of faith in technology to correct the effects of environmental mismanagement is consistent with a broader quasi-religious trust Americans place in technology to solve a variety of problems posed by nature and to shield them from the natural world (including disease). Yet those who work with wildfire know that the scale of large fires and the behavior of wind and fuel driven fires defies even the most advanced and heavily applied technology and personnel. Big, drought or wind driven fires can only be controlled on the margins and they generally burn until they run out of fuel or the weather changes.

In perhaps no other area is our detachment from our natural environment more dangerous than regarding wildfire and the danger it poses increasingly to towns built in fire's path. The public cannot depend on the poorly funded and confusingly mandated US Forest Service to protect communities like Los Alamos, Boulder, Colorado or Stanley, Idaho especially when that agency suffers from a lack of public support for its efforts to correct past mistakes. Nor can the public financially starve the National Park Service, hamstringing its efforts to restore forest health in our national parks and monuments then blame that agency when its efforts are out ahead of much public understanding and seem counterintuitive to a public that is increasingly detached from our deteriorating natural environment.

The Cerro Grande Fire was a tremendous learning experience for Americans and for professionals in fire management. It indeed was a tragedy by committee where real responsibility for the disaster was spread from sheep ranchers, loggers, and forest rangers a century ago, to those who built Los Alamos where they did, to people in both the US Forest Service and the National Park Service and Los Alamos County and to the residents of the community themselves. It was a disaster caused by people being removed and distracted from where they really are and from our culture's failure to tune in to the details of nature, to care about nature and understand our basic connection to its well being. Crude exploitation of a fragile environment has its consequences and the price is often paid by people in the future and by the innocent lives of wildlife over decades.

It was a harsh and painful lesson and one where we quickly realize blame is a poor substitute for compassion and understanding. Time has largely healed the wounds of Cerro Grande. People have rebuilt their homes and their careers and emotions have settled. Bandelier and the National Park Service have returned to their wise and timely work of restoring fire to landscapes that need it and the Forest Service is increasing its own efforts to bring fire back to a fire starved land of the Jemez Mountains and forests throughout the West.

Fall in Los Alamos has a new beauty to it. The scar of the Cerro Grande Fire is filled with large patches of orange and gold as millions of new aspen shoots turn in the fall. Ponderosa pine planted by birds and volunteers stand ten feet tall and grass invites elk and thousands of birds to the land. The earth is rebounding and we see the resilience of people and the land in this beautiful and internationally significant place.

[1] The Los Alamos Fire Department turned to Bandelier National Monument's fire program for training in fighting wildland fire in 1993 when John Lissoway offered to help train fire fighters on the County Line prescribed burn and others. According to personal conversations with Los Alamos officials, that training was not maintained and when the Cerro Grande fire occurred few on the Los Alamos Fire Department had direct experience, equipment or planning experience for wildland fire.

[2] A healthy forest is one where the forest's structure does not leave it prone to stand replacement fires if such fires are unnatural for the forest type in question such as ponderosa pine forest in the Southwest. The health of the forest extends to its ability to support a broad range of native plant and animal species in successful interdependence.

[3] With most of the founders of Los Alamos coming from vastly different environments from New Mexico and with little or no knowledge of the environment and its ecology, we can expect that most looked at the forests and mountains around Los Alamos as scenery much as people of their time viewed national parks as static places to be frozen in time as scenery for public enjoyment. The environmental movement was yet 25 years in the future and the founders of Los Alamos were decidedly urban in their outlooks.

[4] See "Making of the Atomic Bomb" by Richard Rhodes, Simon and Schuster August 1995.

[5] Hal K. Rothman, On Rims and Ridges, (University of Nebraska Press 1992) pg. 178.

[6] The Forest Service loses money on timber sales and livestock grazing on most if not all of its lands. See Randal O'toole, Reforming the Forest Service (Island Press 1988).

[7] Los Alamos Forest Service forester Bill Armstrong stated that he had warned the DOE repeatedly in the 1997, 1998 period about an inevitable forest fire. He engaged the Lab officially through the DOE's Site-Wide Environmental Impact Statement (SWEIS) process for Los Alamos. Yet through this public process the DOE came out with scenarios for fire that started on lab land. Mr. Armstrong made repeated efforts to get funding for fuel breaks and thinning near Los Alamos and only succeeded in minimal project money in 1998 for the fuel breaks that went a long way toward protecting Los Alamos. His band of heavily thinned forest ran along the Los Alamos County property boundary and caused the fire to drop out of the treetops, greatly reducing damage to neighborhoods. Bill Armstrong deserves the gratitude of the people of Los Alamos for these efforts which have been little recognized. See Chapter 7.

[8] This group of agencies referred to themselves as the Los Alamos Wildfire Cooperators. This was an information sharing organization rather than a

cooperative land management organization according to Bill Armstrong.
[9] Former Espanola District Ranger Lori Osterstock held meetings with civic groups in Los Alamos starting in 1993 regarding the big forest fire to come. Ranger Osterstock was a highly progressive fire manager who instituted some of the first "fire use" fires on the Santa Fe National Forest near Truchas the early 1990s in the face of great public resistance.

[10] Dr. Craig Allen wrote his PhD dissertation for UC Berkeley on the fire ecology of the Jemez Mountains and worked as a research scientist for the National Park Service at Bandelier then later for the US Geologic Survey at the "Jemez Mountains Field Station" which is located at Bandelier Headquarters. He is widely published on a national level and is one of the most highly respected fire ecologists in the United States.

[11] Personal interview with Claudia Standish in Santa Fe, 2001.

[12] Dr. Jack D. Cohen "Examination of the Home Destruction in Los Alamos Associated with the Cerro Grande Fire,"(Fire Sciences Laboratory, USDA Forest Service Missoula, Montana July 10, 2000).

[13] See Chapter 4.

[14] Interview with Bill Armstrong February 26, 2004.

[15] See Chapter 4. The Valles Ecosystem Management Area would have used historic stand condition models developed by Wally Covington at Northern Arizona University in Flagstaff. The planned fuel reduction would have tried to mimic historic stand conditions by thinning along all the available roads near Los Alamos, thinning small trees from the forest and burning the slash and then burning the south facing slopes in canyons with high intensity fire to reduce fuels and stimulate grasslands.

Afterword

In early November 2007 a long line of fire vehicles drove up the winding road from the lower reaches of Bandelier National Monument into the Jemez Mountains. They started at the same interagency fire center that the crews that started the Cerro Grande prescribed fire seven years earlier had started from. They drove up the same road and some of them parked in the same place where the 2000 prescribed fire team had parked.

While the prescribed fire crew of 2000 had consisted of a group of Bandelier National Monument fire specialists assisted by a Bureau of Indian Affairs crew, the November 2007 caravan looked like a fire fighter parade. There were six engines in addition to Bandelier's two, mostly from the US Forest Service and Los Alamos County Fire Department. The Alpine Hotshots from Rocky Mountain National Park joined the Fire Use Modules from both Bandelier and Zion National Park. A full crew of Type 1 firefighters from Zuni Pueblo joined two New Mexico Department of Forestry crews supported by Bandelier helitack and its contract helicopter.

For months in advance, fire lines had been dug and trees had been thinned along the fuel laden Forest Service boundaries south of Bandelier National Monument. Calls had been made and commitments of money and time were set. On the first day of the burn Dean Henry stood in a clearing made by crown fire during the first days of the Cerro Grande Fire as it raged out of the northern-most fork of Frijoles Canyon on the south side of Highway 4. Dean had 100 people standing by and as "burn boss" he was about to direct an almost 2,000 acre prescribed fire, directly at the base of Cerro Grande and in the fuel choked Frijoles Canyon area that Bandelier's staff had been trying to burn for more than twenty years.

With people in green and yellow fire clothing lining the highway above us and fire engines idling, Dean stood with those of us standing with drip torches in hand. I mentioned that it was a big responsibility we were all taking on. Mr. Henry then listed the people and equipment he had on hand and summarized the planning he had made for this moment. He smiled nervously and told us to begin ignition.

Cigarette lighters came from people's pockets and lit the grass at our feet. We tilted our drip torches until the fuel flowed out and we lit the torches in the patches of fire at our feet. We lined up and looked to our immediate supervisor Frank Gonzales who told us to move west.

Across the grass we walked in a careful line, stepping over the trees that had been killed in the Cerro Grande fire, igniting wood and grass. Smoke rose up and obscured the road. Los Alamos was just a few miles over the ridge and the some people from that town were anxious about the first large prescribed burn Bandelier had attempted since the Cerro Grande disaster seven years before.

This was the 8th prescribed fire I had helped ignite and as we walked into dense downfall and heavy brush the fire whooshed up and came up behind me. As a short-term, on-call firefighter, I was happy to be back in nomex clothes, back on the base of Cerro Grande where the fire I had studied so carefully burned years before. My torch was spent when we got to the point across the highway from where the east fire line on the Cerro Grande prescribed fire had tied in to the road. I came up to the highway and looked back, back over most of a decade when Bandelier had been paralyzed by the huge events of 2000, unable to rebuild its prescribed fire program even after the other units of the National Park system emerged from the prescribed fire ban issued by Interior Secretary Babbitt after the Cerro Grande.

The "Upper Frijoles Burn" of late fall 2007 was a triumph for the Bandelier staff. It was the first entry by fire into upper Frijoles Canyon since the 1880s and the thick fuels there burned moderately as the fire was timed after a wet summer and late enough in the year that only a few hours of vigorous fire (the "burn window") would be available. It was a cautious burn, not only by the prescription of weather, fuel moisture and time of year, but also by the way the fire was staffed and executed.

There were ample personnel and equipment on hand and the US Forest Service was fully cooperating with the National Park Service. Yet this level of organization was not unique to this prescribed fire, it was now the norm for prescribed fires on federal lands. That change was directly a result of the Cerro Grande Fire.

Here, in the upper reaches of Frijoles Canyon, the landscape of disaster and disappointment and damaged careers, fire was again creeping through a hungry landscape. Bandelier's fire staff looked on with well-deserved pride and satisfaction. A decade of pain and confusion was going up in smoke around us as experienced people joined with and unleashed the most primal of forces to restore this spectacular corner of America's National Park heritage.

For more than a century, serious foresters and ecologists have come to understand the need for restoring fire to its natural place in most western forests. The efforts of the National Park Service to lead the way in this ecological revolution have slowly met with approval by a new generation of foresters in the US Forest Service who now understand the need to restore forest health through this most basic of forces.

The Cerro Grande Fire provided the nation a chance to pause and reflect on fire policy and the condition of our public forests in the West, just as did the Yellowstone Fires of 1988. The lessons learned, though painful and costly to the people of Los Alamos, vindicated the fire policies initiated by Harold Biswell and others decades earlier.

Fire has an obvious natural place in forests from New Mexico to Alaska, and the changes in fire management policy, especially in the US Forest Service have been difficult for an agency which built its reputation on its fire fighting, not fire managing abilities. Yet in 2010, with the challenges of managing fire smoke and industrial sourced carbon dioxide in the escalating climate change crisis, it may be that we lose some ground in our efforts to restore fire to the forests that need it for their health and for their abilities to sequester carbon dioxide.

Likewise what some have termed the "fire industrial complex," those businesses dependent on public land fire suppression for income, along with the Forest Service that gets more than 40% of its budget for fire suppression, could begin to roll back the progress we've made in returning well managed fire on a large scale in western forests. The pressure to revert to the unworkable and destructive, yet emotionally and financially satisfying, full suppression policies of the past is intense in 2010.

We can only hope that wisdom prevails over expediency and greed, and the lessons of more than a century of forest fires in the West can prevail over those who would imagine fire suppression as a general policy could somehow yield something more than the ecological and fire disasters it created in the past.

Fire is a spectacular, yet subtle process on the landscape. It relates to all aspects of a forest in ways we don't fully understand. We must respect it and learn from it the same way we must continue to learn from the mysteries of all of nature, as our species struggles desperately to survive in a world where nature truly bats last, but always prevails.

Index

A

Abiquiu 18, 74
Alaska 4, 44, 72, 234, 299, 330, 349
Allen, Craig ix, 15, 41, 86, 92, 100,
194, 207, 208, 219, 233, 236, 341,
346
Allred, Kathy 141, 142, 144, 155,
269, 271, 273
Alpine Hot Shots 234, 291
American Springs 65, 194, 224
AMR policy 331, 334
Apache 20, 21, 22, 29, 56, 320, 325
Arizona 4, 10, 19, 21, 22, 53, 96,
116, 131, 179, 180, 181, 186, 207,
219, 233, 253, 266, 317, 330, 346
Armstrong, Bill ix, 60, 62, 63, 66,
97, 98, 176, 191, 192, 204, 224,
225, 341, 342, 345, 346

B

Babbitt, Bruce xvi, 16, 271, 273,
286, 287, 288, 289, 291, 292, 293,
299, 300, 303, 305, 307, 319, 322,
327, 348
Baca Ranch 51, 78, 93, 113, 118, 123,
124, 125, 129, 208, 218, 257, 320
Bandelier viii, ix, xv, xvi, xvii, xx,
xxiii, xxiv, xxv, xxvii, 3, 4, 5, 9,
12, 15, 18, 25, 32, 39, 41, 42, 43,
44, 46, 51, 54, 56, 59, 60, 62, 63,
65, 66, 67, 71, 75, 76, 77, 78, 79,
81, 84, 85, 86, 87, 88, 89, 90, 91,
92, 93, 94, 95, 96, 99, 100, 101,
102, 103, 104, 105, 107, 108, 110,
114, 115, 117, 118, 119, 120, 121,
122, 123, 124, 125, 126, 127, 128,
138, 141, 143, 145, 156, 157, 160,
161, 162, 164, 168, 175, 186, 188,
190, 191, 192, 193, 194, 196, 200,
204, 205, 206, 207, 208, 209, 210,
211, 216, 217, 218, 219, 220, 221,
222, 223, 224, 225, 226, 227, 229,
231, 232, 233, 234, 235, 236, 237,
243, 244, 245, 247, 248, 249, 250,
251, 252, 253, 254, 255, 256, 257,
258, 259, 261, 262, 264, 270, 271,
273, 274, 275, 276, 277, 278, 280,
283, 284, 285, 286, 287, 288, 289,
290, 291, 292, 294, 295, 296, 297,
298, 299, 300, 301, 303, 304, 305,
306, 307, 308, 310, 311, 312, 313,
314, 315, 316, 317, 318, 319, 320,
321, 322, 323, 325, 327, 328, 331,
332, 333, 334, 336, 338, 344, 345,
346, 347, 348, 349
Bandelier, Adolph 12, 46, 76
Bandelier Fire Use Module 218,
234, 249, 291, 332
Bandelier National Monument
viii, xvii, xx, xxiii, xxv, 3, 4, 5,
9, 12, 15, 18, 25, 39, 41, 42, 43,
44, 54, 59, 63, 75, 76, 77, 78, 87,
93, 96, 99, 101, 102, 103, 107,
128, 138, 143, 145, 156, 175, 190,
191, 192, 200, 204, 216, 227, 233,
237, 255, 288, 300, 312, 320, 322,
325, 331, 332, 338, 345, 347
Bannerman, Bruce x, xxiii, xxiv, 282
Bateman, Van 186, 187
Berkeley 70, 81, 207, 233, 346
Bishop, W.C. 26
Biswell, Harold 81, 349
Board of Inquiry 114, 119, 141, 155,
211, 215, 222, 226, 227, 232, 233,
235, 244, 251, 273, 274, 278, 279,
285, 286, 287, 288, 289, 292, 294,
300, 301, 302, 303, 304, 305, 306,
307, 308, 309, 310, 311, 312, 313,
314, 315, 317, 318, 319, 320, 321,
322, 323, 324, 327
Bond, Frank 23
Bradbury, Ellen 197
Bradbury, Norris 189, 197
Buckman, Harry 27, 28, 47, 59, 190

O

Obama Administration xx, 331
Oppenheimer, J. Robert 338
Oso Fire 162, 186
Outlet Fire 211, 301, 334

P

Pacific Northwest xxix, 28, 90, 92,
    96, 100
Pajarito Canyon xxiv, 5, 6, 27, 59,
    60, 168, 169, 173, 174, 189, 195,
    198, 270
Pajarito Plateau 4, 6, 18, 20, 23, 25,
    26, 27, 28, 41, 42, 43, 44, 45, 46,
    47, 50, 59, 74, 75, 77, 79, 86, 87,
    94, 105, 190, 197, 199, 202, 205,
    206, 231, 275, 326, 338, 342
Pashchenko, Sergei 203
Pecos Wilderness xxv, 279
Peterson, John 90, 92
Pleistocene 6, 7, 15
Powell, Mike 103, 107, 108, 112,
    113, 115, 116, 119, 120, 121, 125,
    133, 140, 144, 218, 223, 227, 230,
    234, 235, 244, 247, 248, 249, 251,
    252, 256, 278, 290, 291, 294, 295,
    296, 304, 305, 306, 308, 311, 314,
    315, 316, 317, 318, 319, 320, 323
Prairie dog 9, 14
Puebloans 4, 7, 12, 18, 19, 20, 46,
    75, 88, 99
Pueblo Indians 4, 6, 7, 12, 17, 18,
    19, 20, 74, 75, 88, 92, 107
Pyne, Stephen xxx, 96, 99

R

Ramon Vigil Land Grant 25, 45
Red Cross 206, 283
Remillard, Robert 60, 63, 65
Rendija Canyon 63, 176, 181, 185
Rile, Albro 341
Rio Arriba 24

Rio Grande xxv, 4, 5, 7, 8, 9, 10, 12,
    18, 19, 21, 22, 23, 24, 27, 43, 79,
    107, 131, 195, 197, 202, 268
Rio Grande Valley xxv, 5, 7, 9, 10,
    12, 18, 19, 23, 24, 43, 195, 197,
    202, 268
Rio Puerco 22
Rocky Mountains 3, 7, 8, 14, 73,
    180, 188, 319, 320, 326, 332, 347
Rodeo Chediski Fire 325
Romero, John 119, 120, 122, 123,
    125, 197, 250, 252, 253, 254, 255,
    295, 296, 304, 321
Rothman, Hal K. xxx, 29, 96, 99,
    339, 345

S

Sandia Pueblo 18
Sangre de Cristo Mountains 4, 5,
    9, 22, 43, 46, 202
San Ildefonso Pueblo 12, 18, 199,
    205
San Miguel Fire 331
Santa Ana Pueblo 18
Santa Clara Pueblo 45, 77, 186
Santa Fe xvii, xxv, 4, 5, 24, 25, 27,
    29, 43, 46, 58, 59, 63, 65, 74, 75,
    76, 77, 87, 90, 91, 93, 96, 97, 100,
    102, 110, 112, 115, 116, 117, 119,
    120, 121, 122, 123, 124, 125, 127,
    131, 133, 135, 136, 137, 141, 161,
    189, 199, 200, 204, 210, 211, 244,
    249, 250, 252, 253, 254, 255, 256,
    257, 258, 261, 262, 264, 271, 273,
    281, 287, 295, 296, 302, 304, 308,
    309, 316, 318, 319, 320, 321, 328,
    331, 333, 338, 342, 346
Santa Fe dispatch 115, 117, 119,
    124, 210, 250, 252, 253, 254, 256,
    257, 258, 295, 304, 308, 309, 316,
    318
Santa Fe Railroad 24
Santa Fe Zone dispatch 110, 116,
    249, 253

About the Author

TOM RIBE is an expert on public lands policy and law. He has his MS in Environmental Studies from the University of Oregon, has worked for the U.S. Forest Service and the National Park Service. He has written extensively on public lands. He lives in Santa Fe, New Mexico.

Made in the USA
San Bernardino, CA
05 November 2013